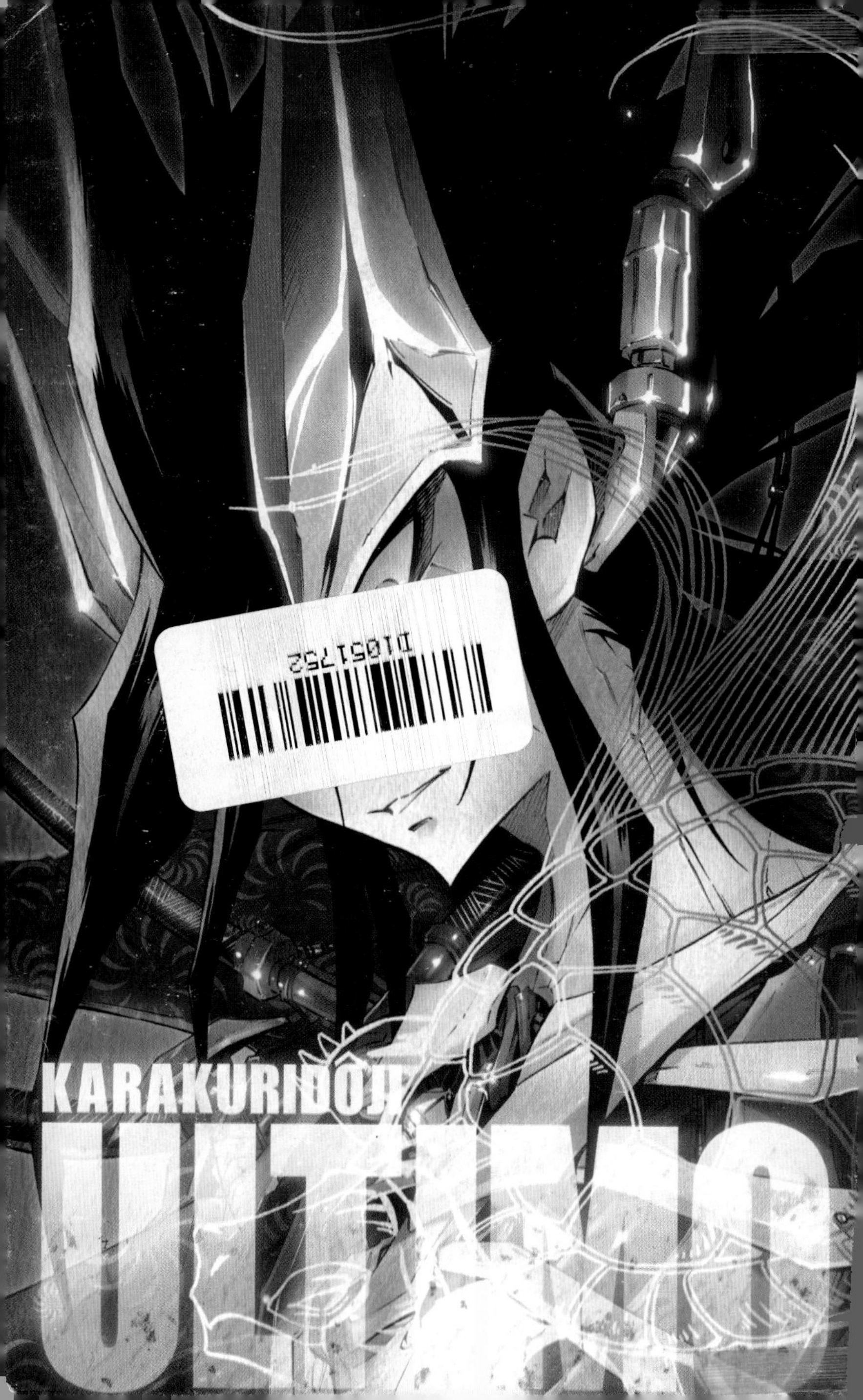
KARAKURIDOJI
ULTIMO

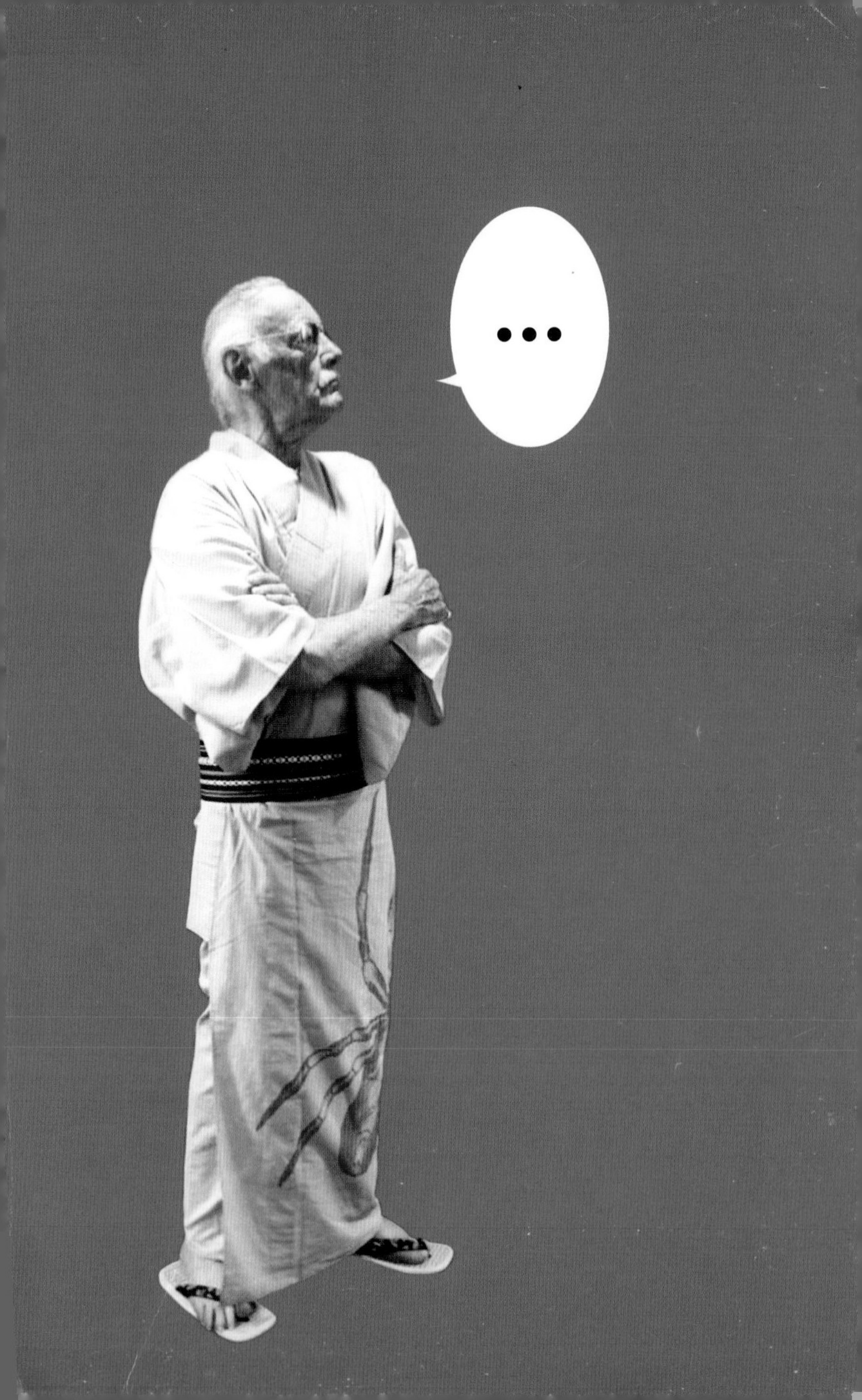
•••

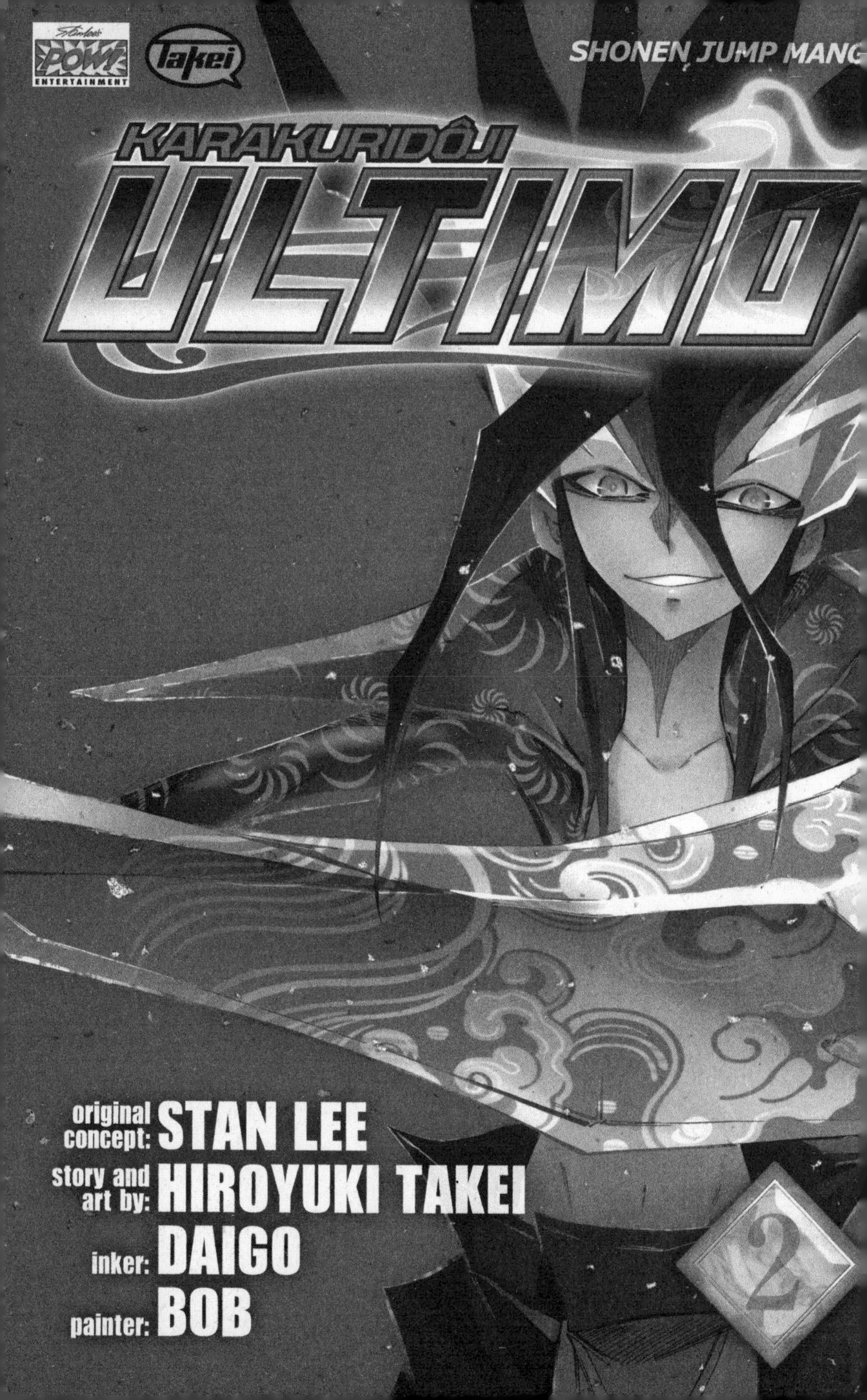
POW! ENTERTAINMENT
Takei
SHONEN JUMP MANGA
KARAKURIDÔJI
ULTIMO
original concept: STAN LEE
story and art by: HIROYUKI TAKEI
inker: DAIGO
painter: BOB
2

Karakuri Dôji Ultimo

Characters

Agari Yamato

Ultimo

The Story Thus Far

In 12th century Kyoto, a bandit named Yamato encounters a mysterious man named Dunstan and two karakuri dôji, dolls who embody ultimate good and evil. Good...evil... Which is stronger? The curtain rises on the ultimate battle!

West Tokyo in the 21st century, Yamato is reborn as Agari Yamato and reencounters the good dôji Ultimo. But evil dôji led by his old nemesis, Vice, have returned as well. A mysterious man named Iruma, accompanied by an evil dôji named Jealousy, who embodies Envy, pays Yamato a visit. Iruma urges Yamato to sell him Ultimo for one hundred million yen!! Will Yamato take the money or will good overcome greed?

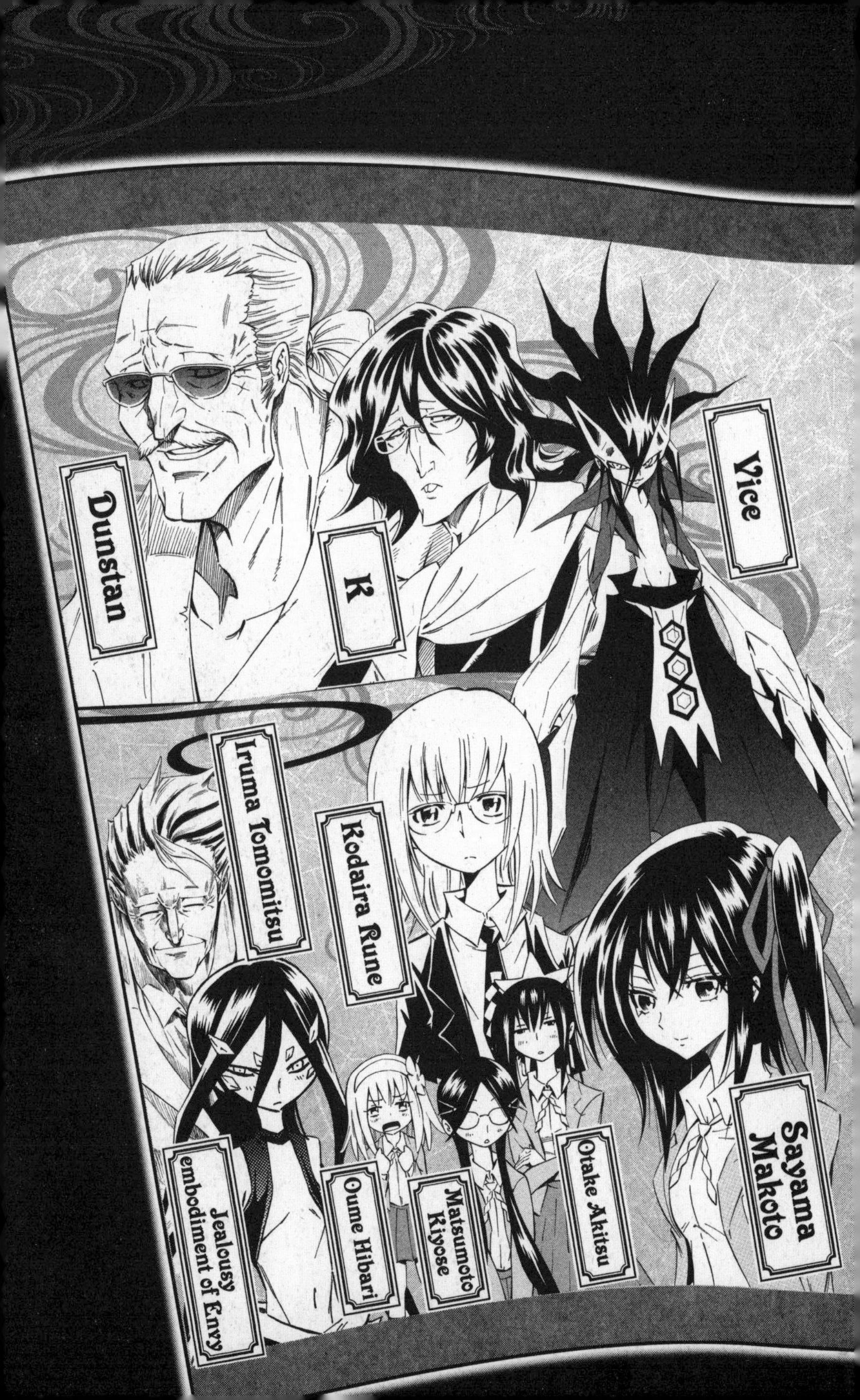
Vice
K
Dunstan
Kodaira Rune
Iruma Tomomitsu
Sayama Makoto
Otake Akitsu
Matsumoto Kiyose
Oume Hibari
Jealousy embodiment of Envy

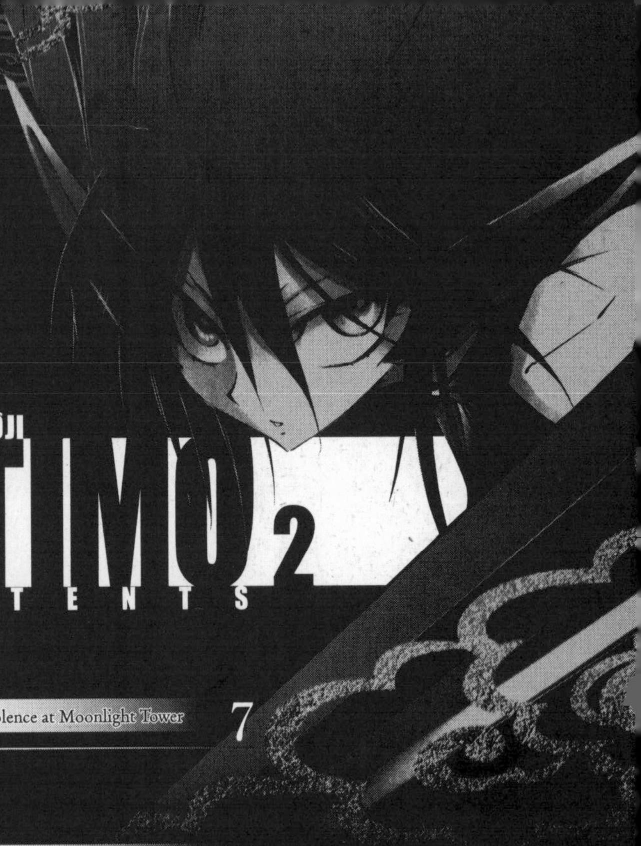

KARAKURIDÔJI ULTIMO 2

CONTENTS

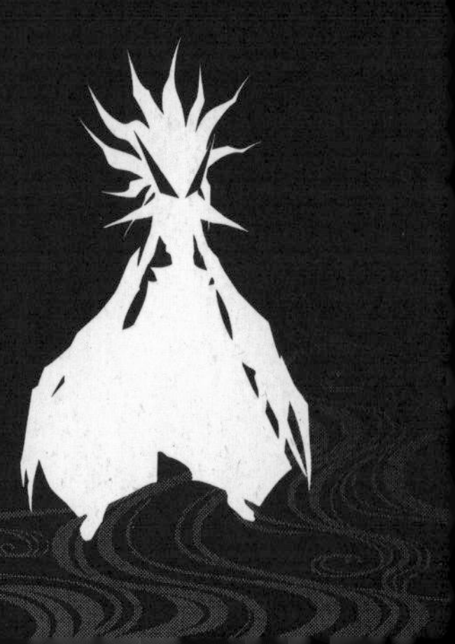

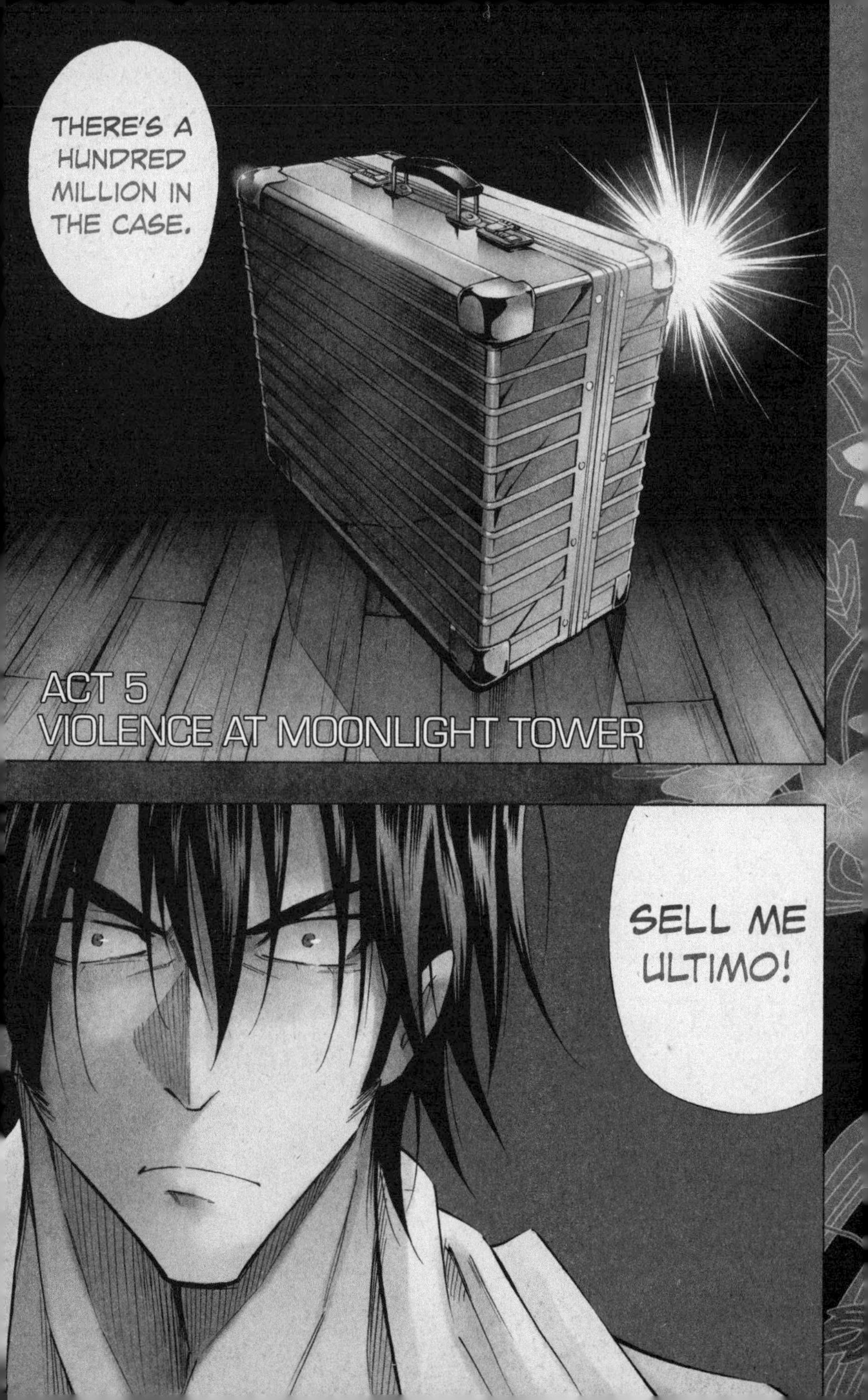
THERE'S A HUNDRED MILLION IN THE CASE.
ACT 5
VIOLENCE AT MOONLIGHT TOWER
SELL ME ULTIMO!

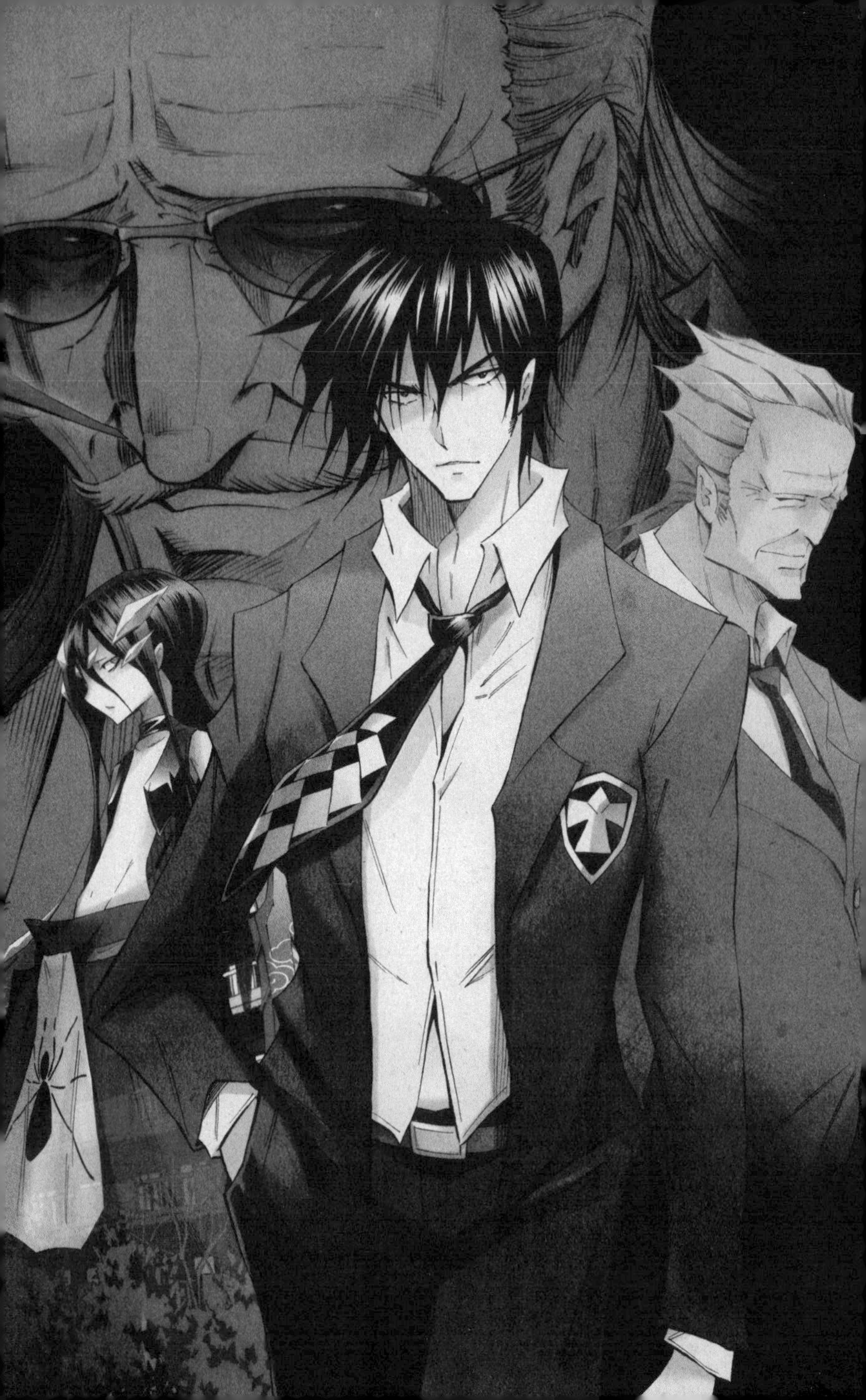

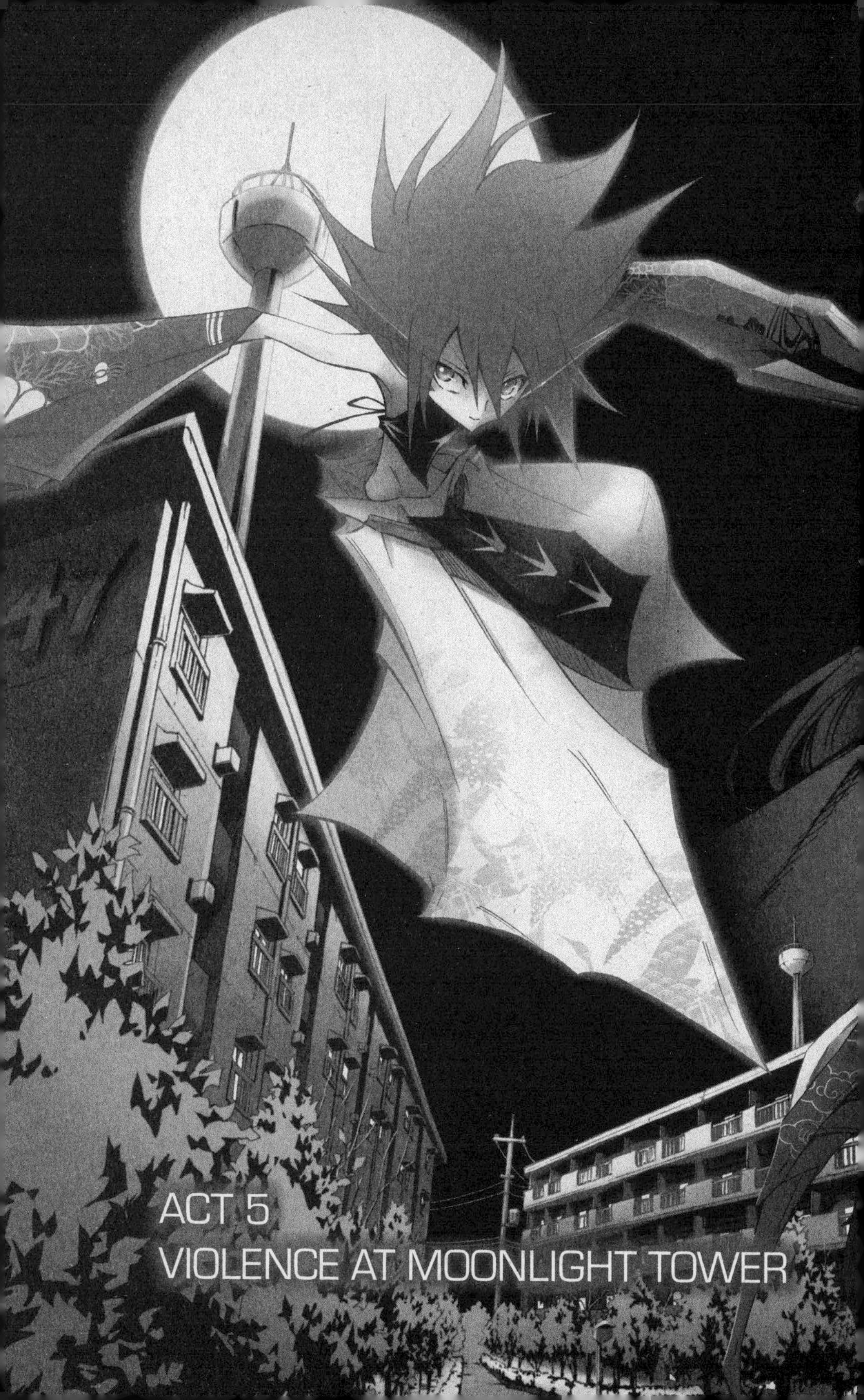
ACT 5
VIOLENCE AT MOONLIGHT TOWER

KARAKURIDÔJI
ULTIMO

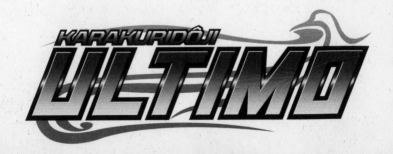

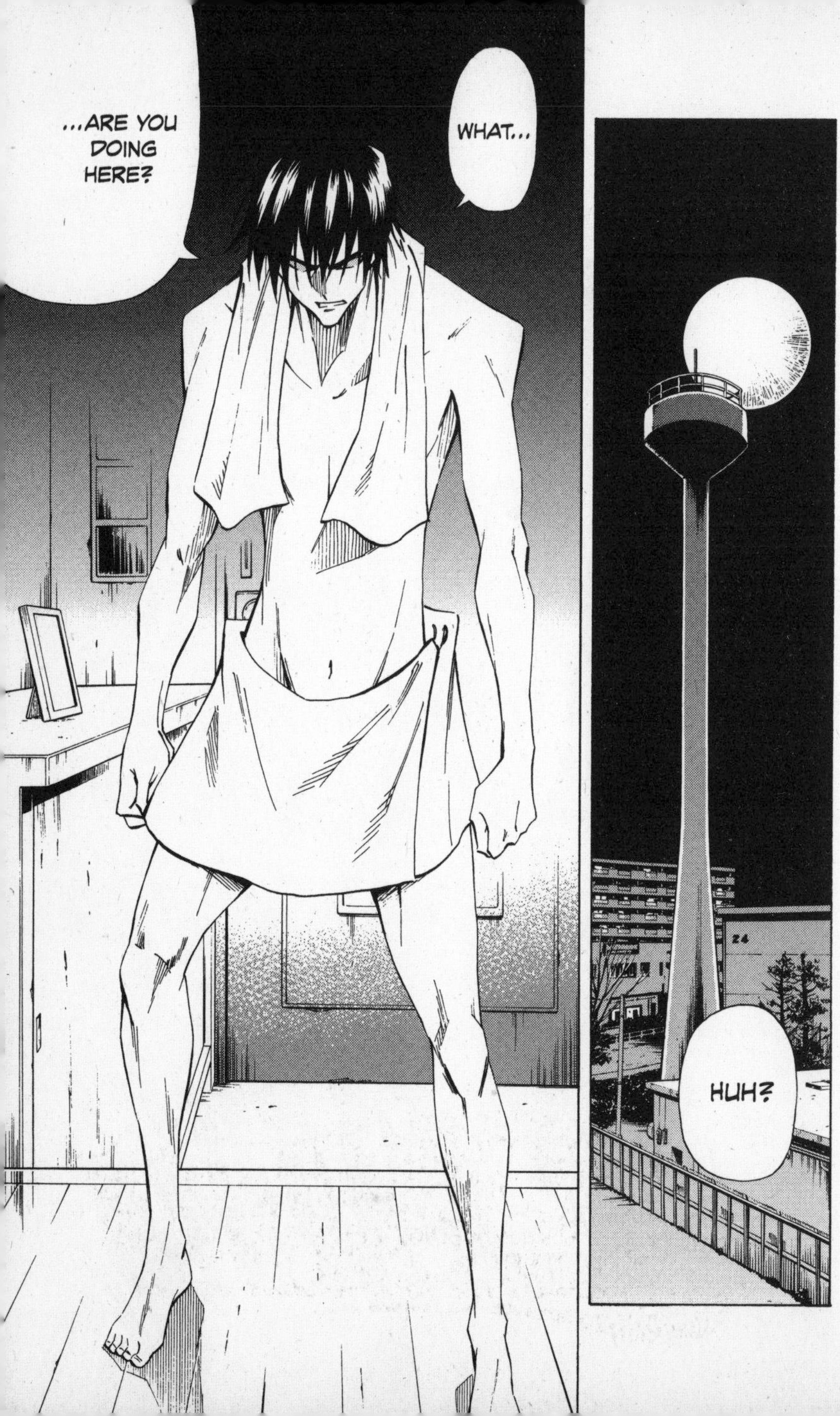
HUH?
WHAT...
...ARE YOU DOING HERE?

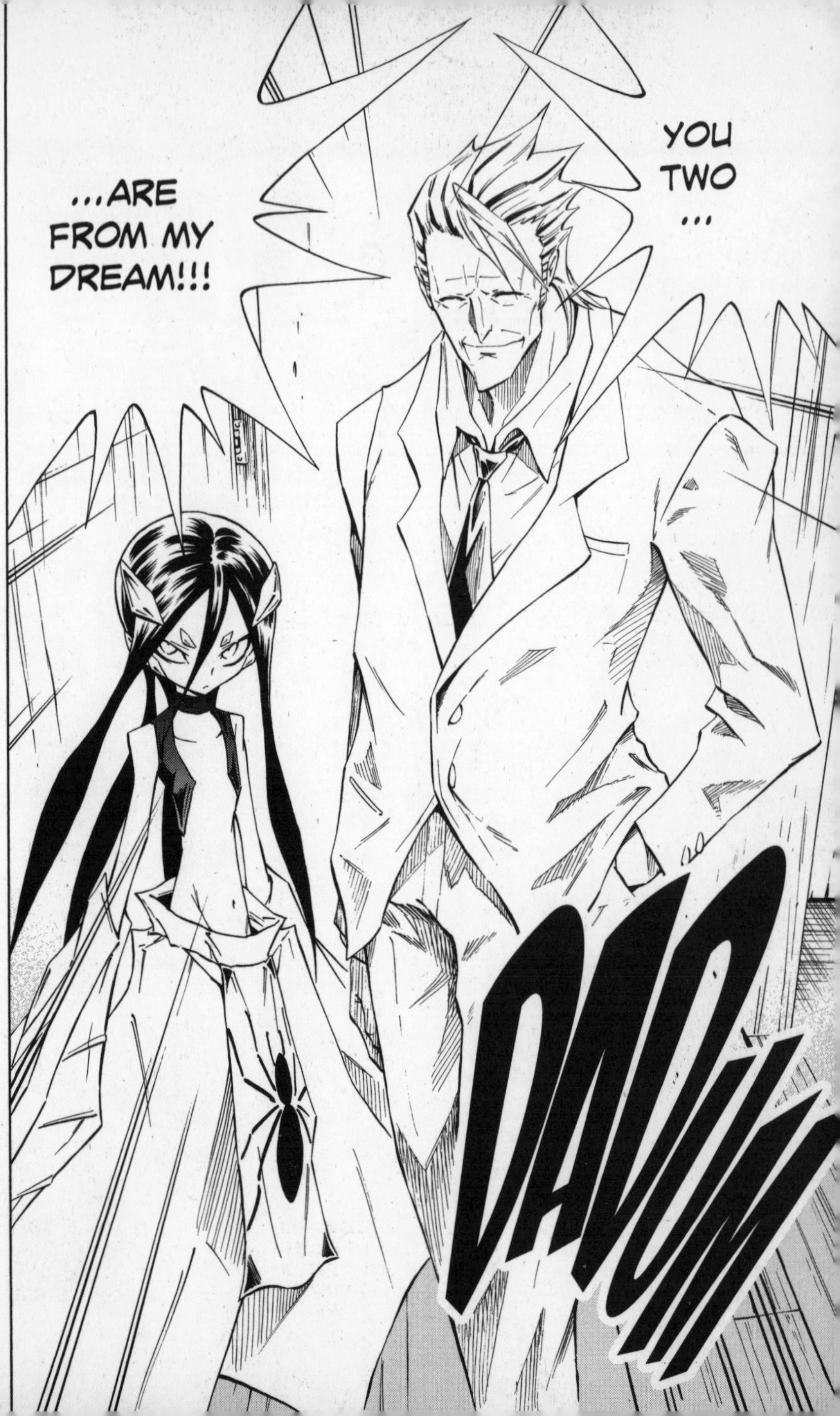
YOU TWO ...
...ARE FROM MY DREAM!!!

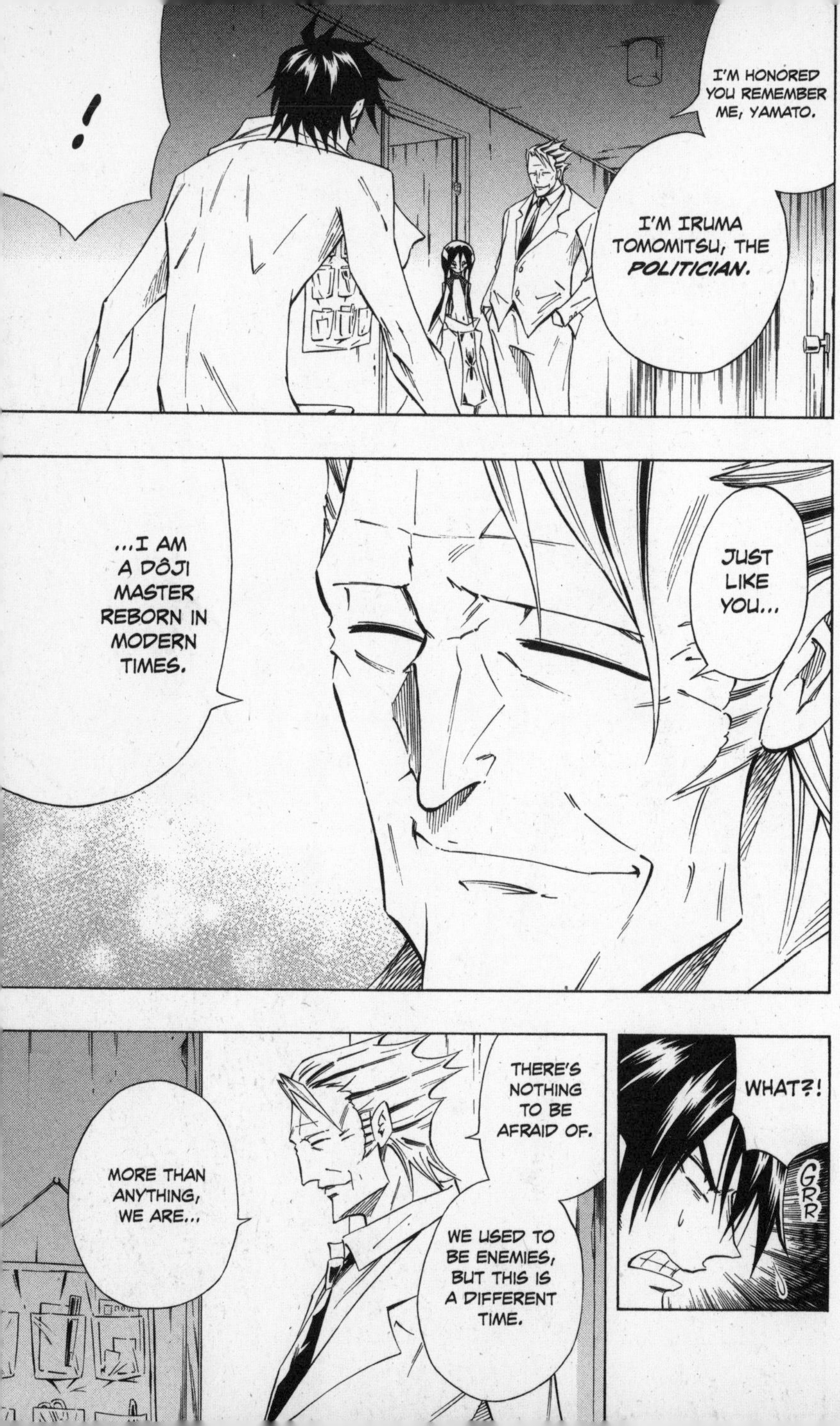
I'M HONORED YOU REMEMBER ME, YAMATO.
I'M IRUMA TOMOMITSU, THE **POLITICIAN**.
!
JUST LIKE YOU...
...I AM A DÔJI MASTER REBORN IN MODERN TIMES.
WHAT?!
GRR
THERE'S NOTHING TO BE AFRAID OF.
WE USED TO BE ENEMIES, BUT THIS IS A DIFFERENT TIME.
MORE THAN ANYTHING, WE ARE...

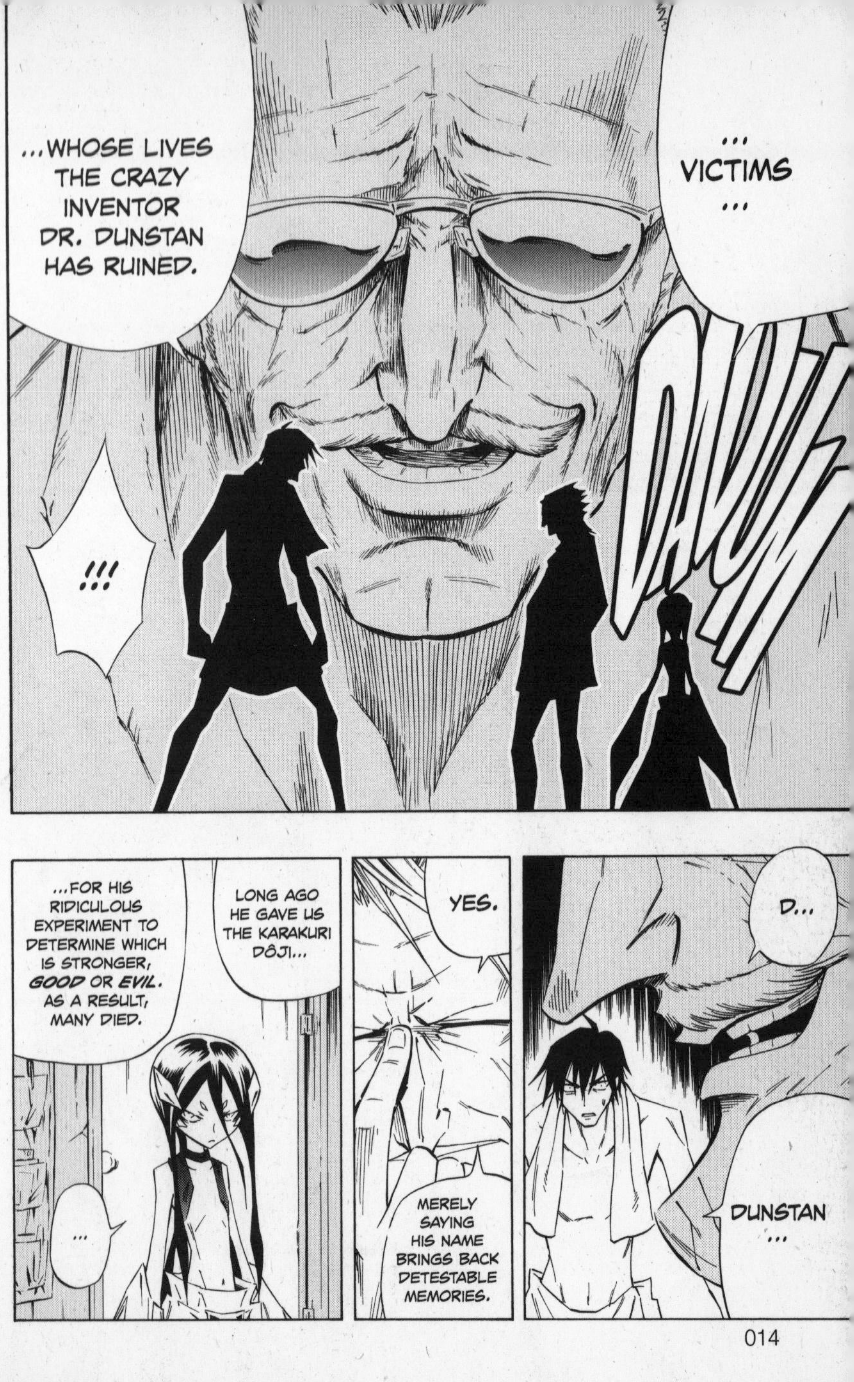
... VICTIMS ...
...WHOSE LIVES THE CRAZY INVENTOR DR. DUNSTAN HAS RUINED.
!!!
D...
DUNSTAN ...
YES.
MERELY SAYING HIS NAME BRINGS BACK DETESTABLE MEMORIES.
LONG AGO HE GAVE US THE KARAKURI DÔJI...
...FOR HIS RIDICULOUS EXPERIMENT TO DETERMINE WHICH IS STRONGER, GOOD OR EVIL. AS A RESULT, MANY DIED.
...

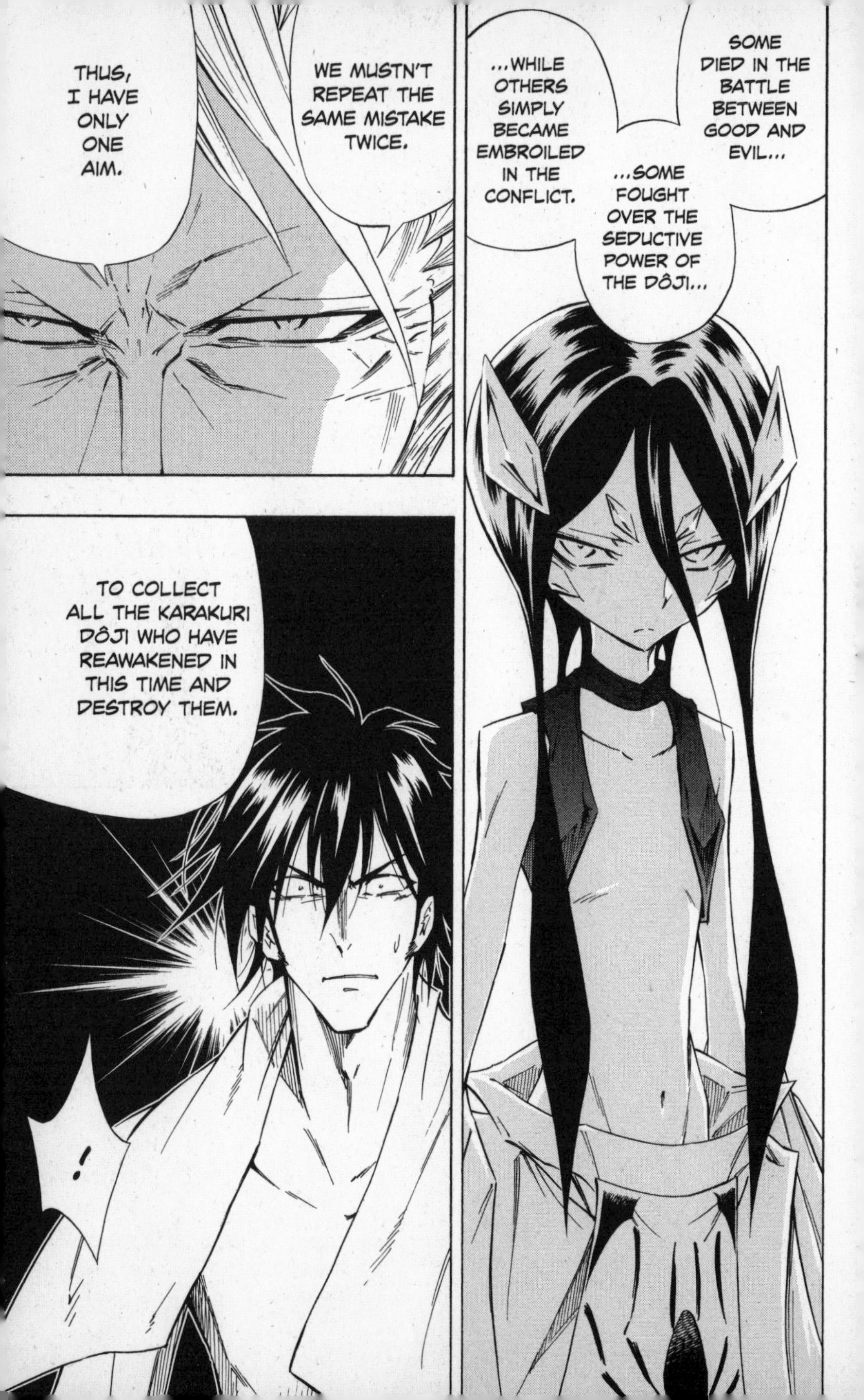
SOME DIED IN THE BATTLE BETWEEN GOOD AND EVIL...
...SOME FOUGHT OVER THE SEDUCTIVE POWER OF THE DÔJI...
...WHILE OTHERS SIMPLY BECAME EMBROILED IN THE CONFLICT.
WE MUSTN'T REPEAT THE SAME MISTAKE TWICE.
THUS, I HAVE ONLY ONE AIM.
TO COLLECT ALL THE KARAKURI DÔJI WHO HAVE REAWAKENED IN THIS TIME AND DESTROY THEM.
!

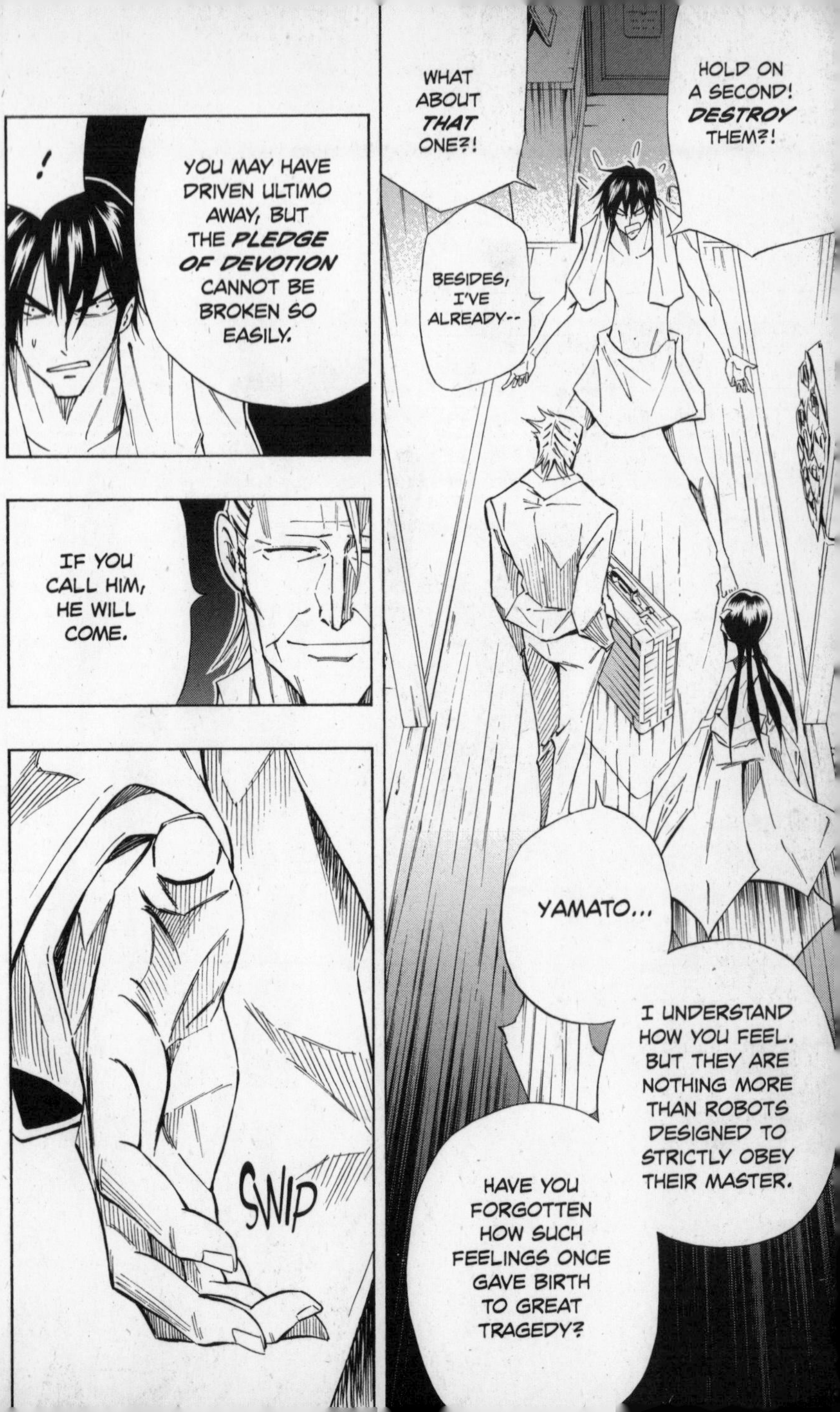
HOLD ON A SECOND! DESTROY THEM?!
WHAT ABOUT THAT ONE?!
BESIDES, I'VE ALREADY--
YAMATO...
I UNDERSTAND HOW YOU FEEL. BUT THEY ARE NOTHING MORE THAN ROBOTS DESIGNED TO STRICTLY OBEY THEIR MASTER.
HAVE YOU FORGOTTEN HOW SUCH FEELINGS ONCE GAVE BIRTH TO GREAT TRAGEDY?
!
YOU MAY HAVE DRIVEN ULTIMO AWAY, BUT THE PLEDGE OF DEVOTION CANNOT BE BROKEN SO EASILY.
IF YOU CALL HIM, HE WILL COME.
SWIP

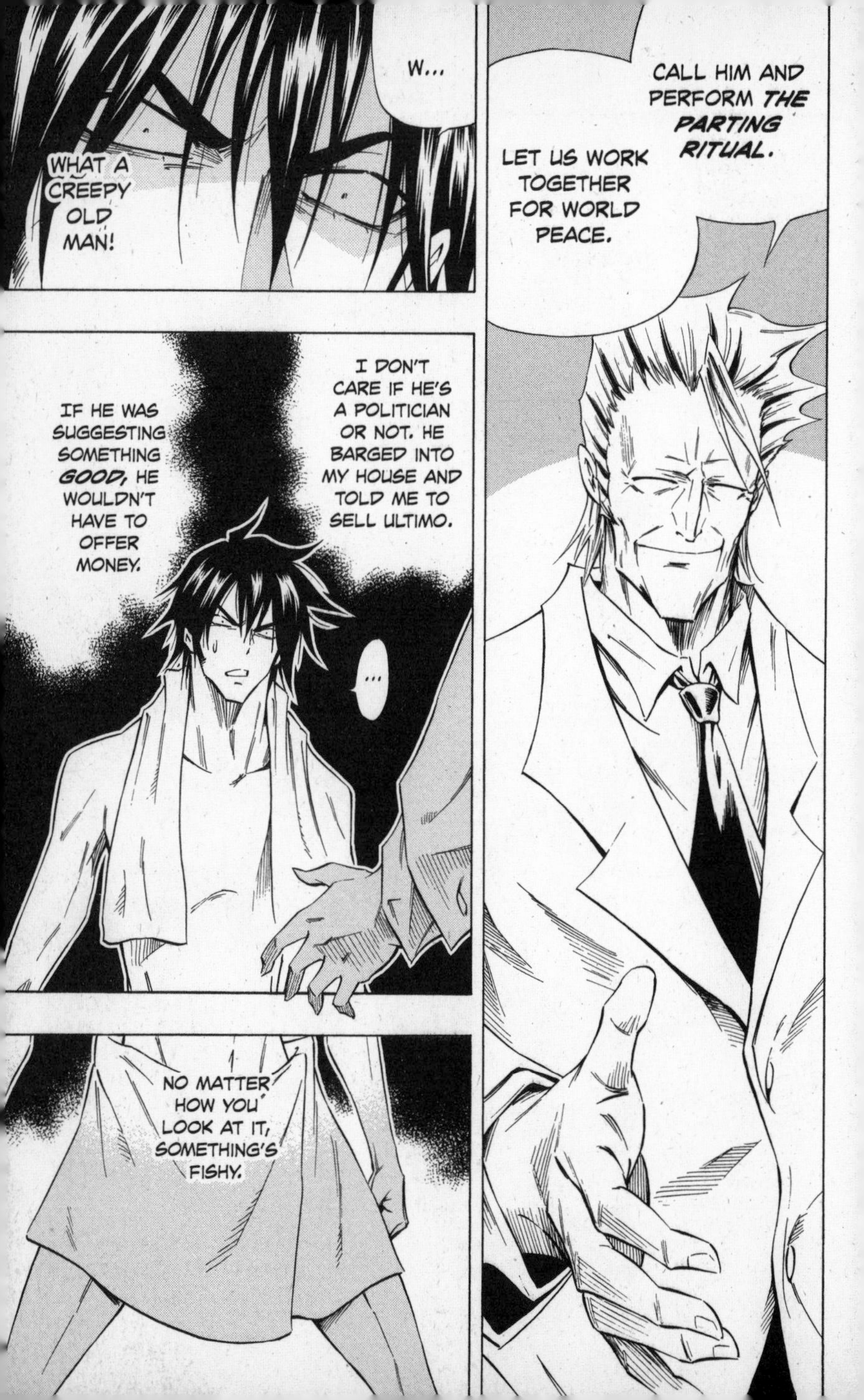
CALL HIM AND PERFORM *THE PARTING RITUAL*.
LET US WORK TOGETHER FOR WORLD PEACE.
W...
WHAT A CREEPY OLD MAN!
I DON'T CARE IF HE'S A POLITICIAN OR NOT. HE BARGED INTO MY HOUSE AND TOLD ME TO SELL ULTIMO.
IF HE WAS SUGGESTING SOMETHING *GOOD*, HE WOULDN'T HAVE TO OFFER MONEY.
...
NO MATTER HOW YOU LOOK AT IT, SOMETHING'S FISHY.

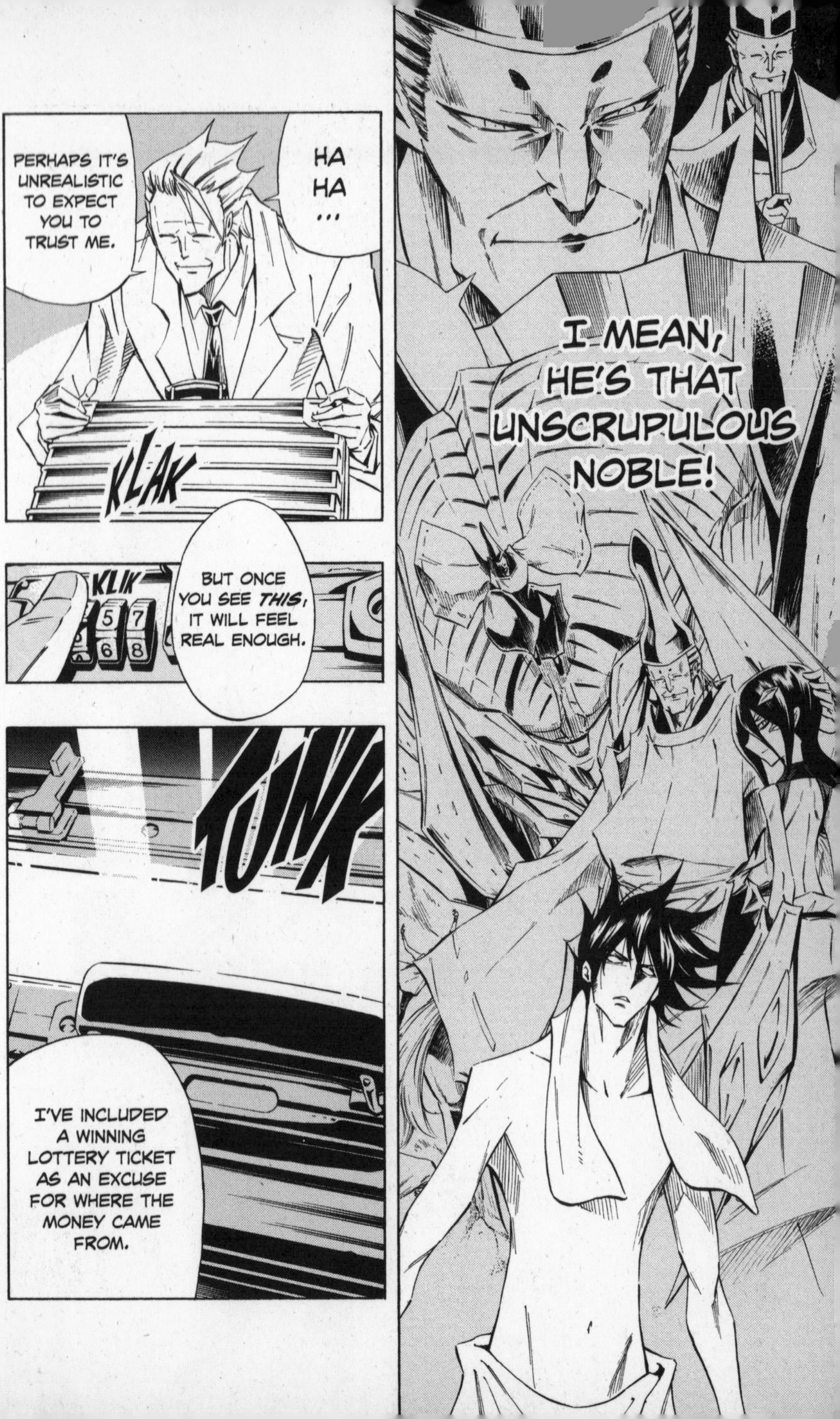
I MEAN, HE'S THAT UNSCRUPULOUS NOBLE!
HA HA ...
PERHAPS IT'S UNREALISTIC TO EXPECT YOU TO TRUST ME.
KLAK
BUT ONCE YOU SEE *THIS*, IT WILL FEEL REAL ENOUGH.
KLIK
TONK
I'VE INCLUDED A WINNING LOTTERY TICKET AS AN EXCUSE FOR WHERE THE MONEY CAME FROM.

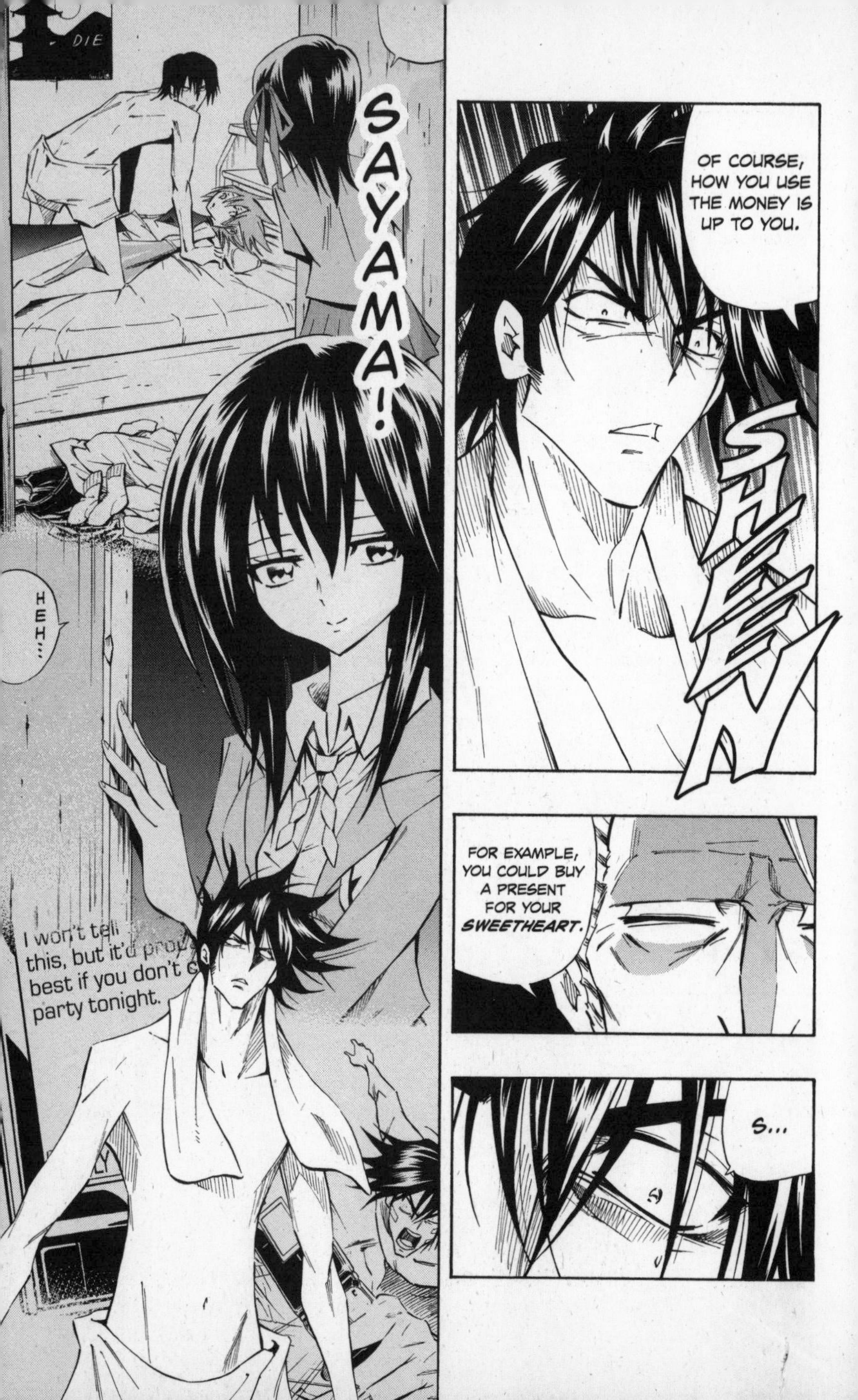
OF COURSE, HOW YOU USE THE MONEY IS UP TO YOU.
FOR EXAMPLE, YOU COULD BUY A PRESENT FOR YOUR **SWEETHEART**.
S...
DIE
SAYAMA!
HEH...
I won't tell
this, but it'd pro
best if you don't
party tonight.

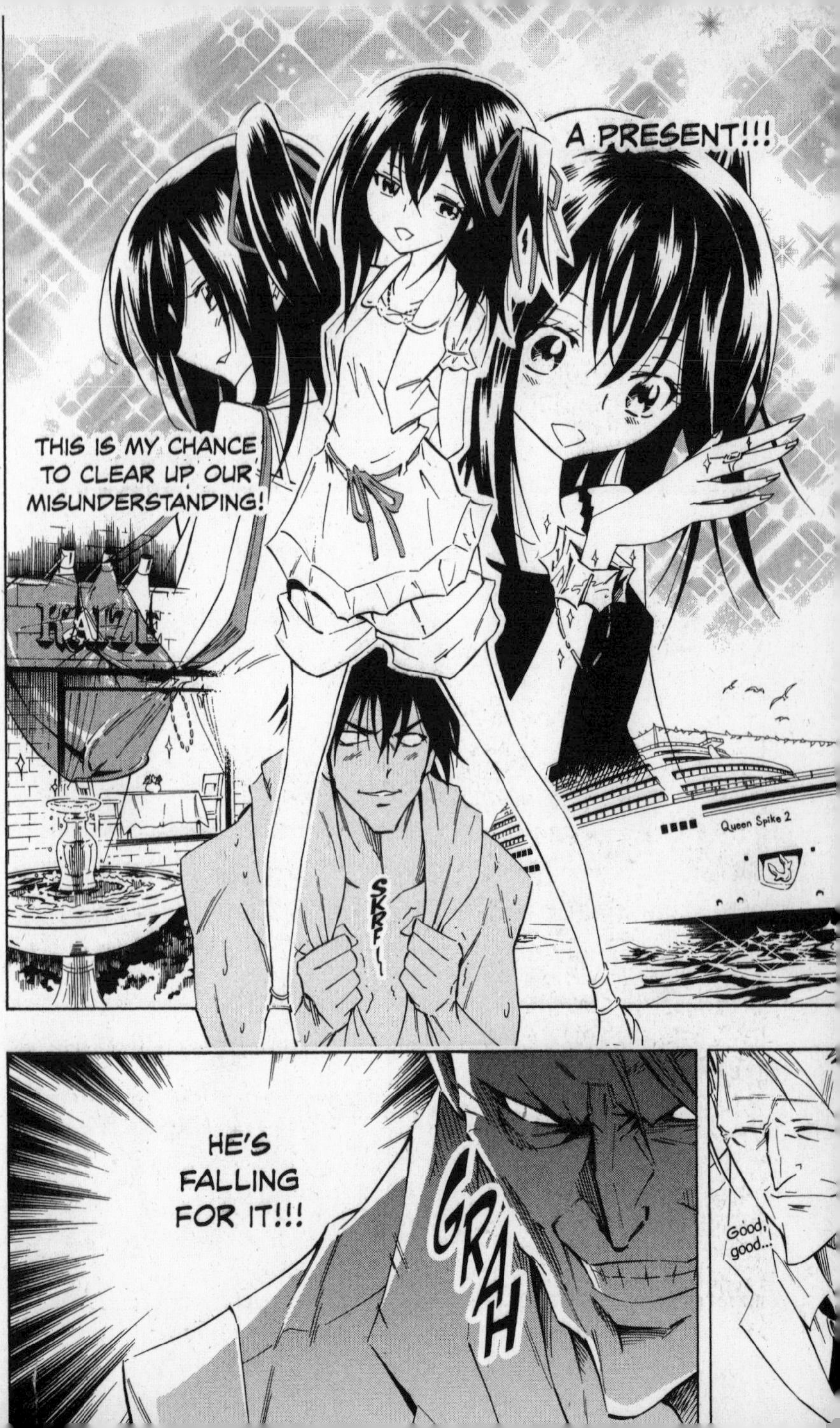
A PRESENT!!!
THIS IS MY CHANCE TO CLEAR UP OUR MISUNDERSTANDING!
SKRF
Queen Spike 2
Good, good...
HE'S FALLING FOR IT!!!
GRAH

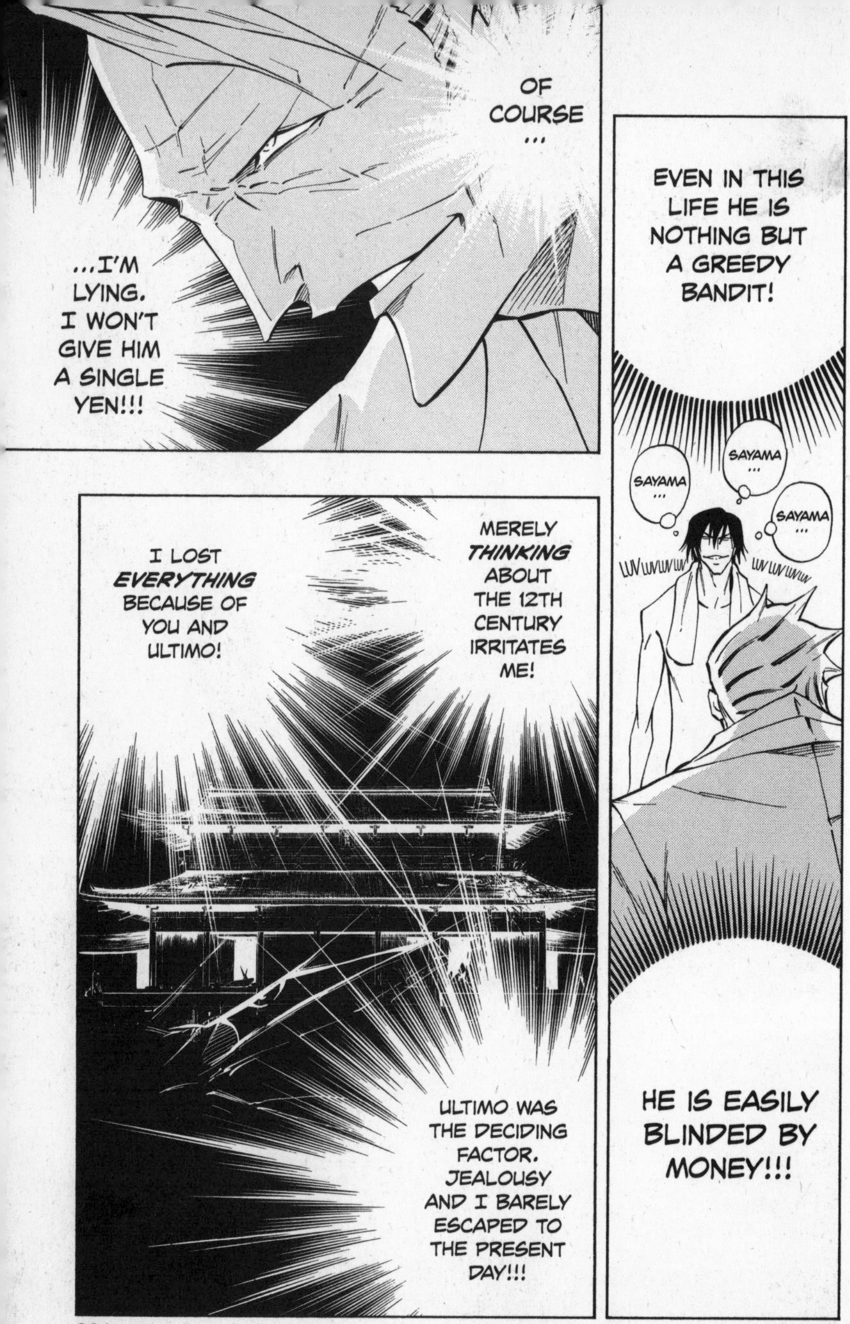
EVEN IN THIS LIFE HE IS NOTHING BUT A GREEDY BANDIT!
SAYAMA ...
SAYAMA ...
LUV LUV LUVLUV
SAYAMA ...
LUV LUV LUV LUV
HE IS EASILY BLINDED BY MONEY!!!
OF COURSE ...
...I'M LYING. I WON'T GIVE HIM A SINGLE YEN!!!
MERELY *THINKING* ABOUT THE 12TH CENTURY IRRITATES ME!
I LOST *EVERYTHING* BECAUSE OF YOU AND ULTIMO!
ULTIMO WAS THE DECIDING FACTOR. JEALOUSY AND I BARELY ESCAPED TO THE PRESENT DAY!!!

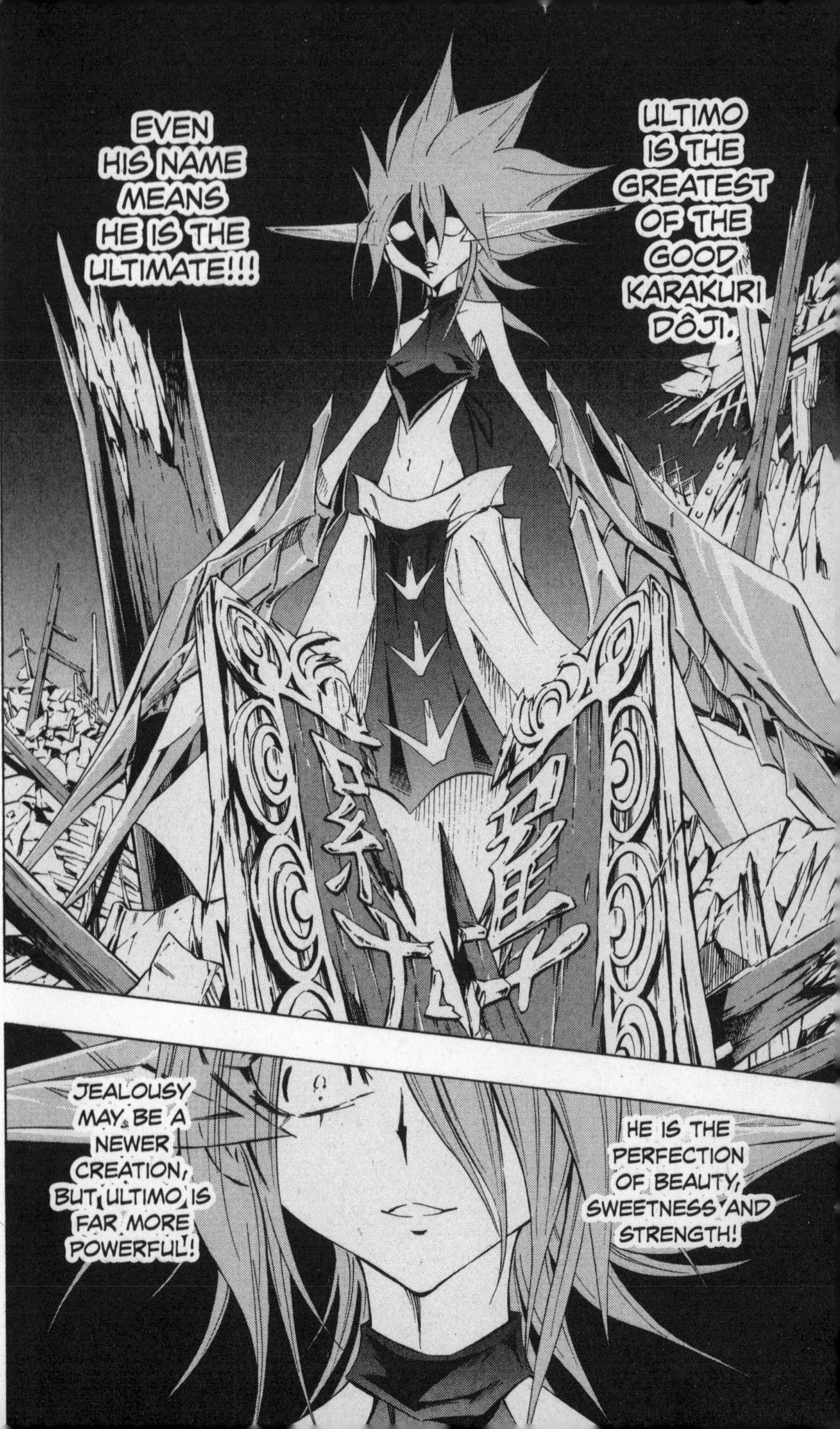
ULTIMO IS THE GREATEST OF THE GOOD KARAKURI DÔJI.
EVEN HIS NAME MEANS HE IS THE ULTIMATE!!!
HE IS THE PERFECTION OF BEAUTY, SWEETNESS AND STRENGTH!
JEALOUSY MAY BE A NEWER CREATION, BUT ULTIMO IS FAR MORE POWERFUL!

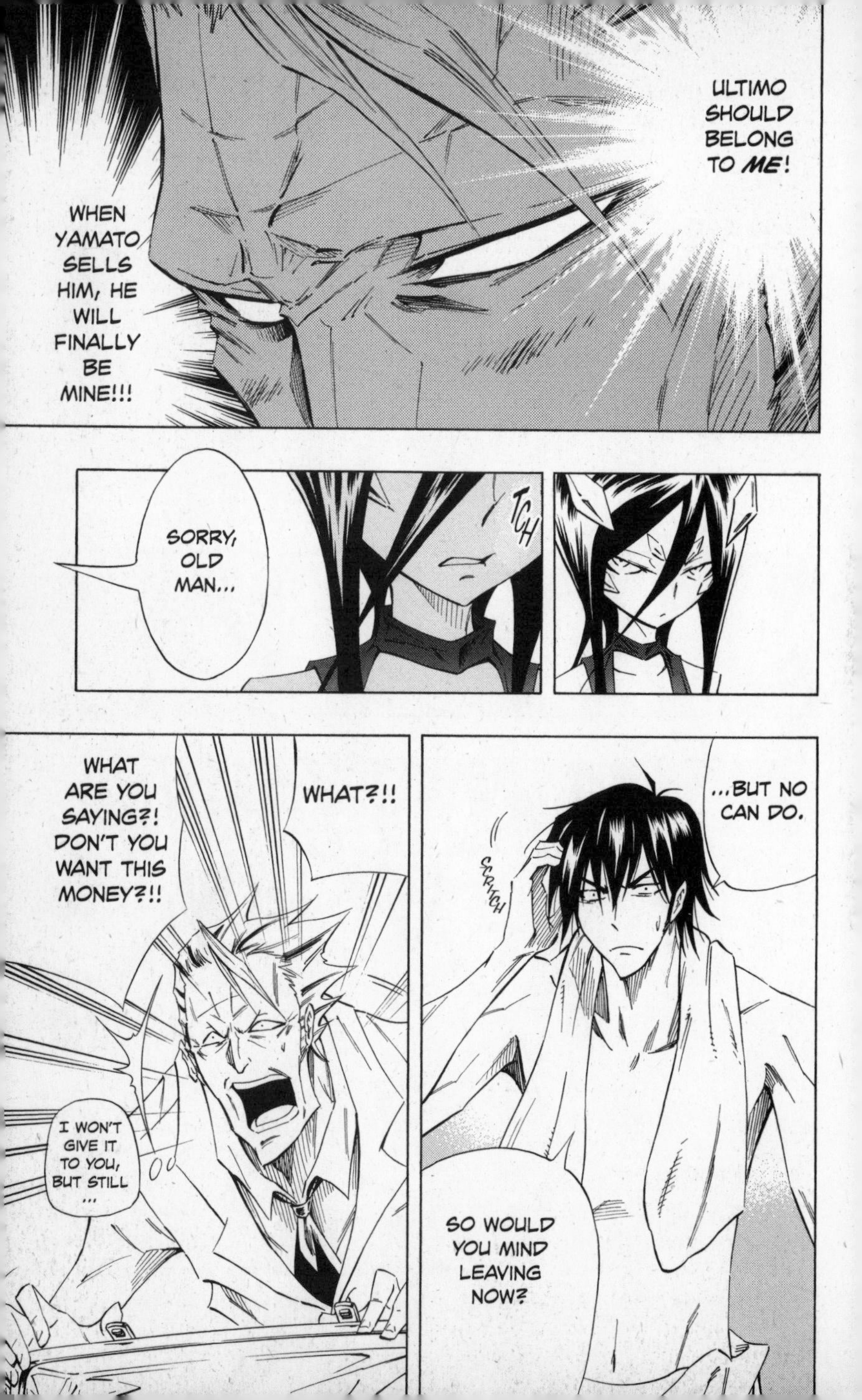
ULTIMO SHOULD BELONG TO *ME*!
WHEN YAMATO SELLS HIM, HE WILL FINALLY BE MINE!!!
TCH
SORRY, OLD MAN...
...BUT NO CAN DO.
SCRITCH
SO WOULD YOU MIND LEAVING NOW?
WHAT?!!
WHAT ARE YOU SAYING?! DON'T YOU WANT THIS MONEY?!!
I WON'T GIVE IT TO YOU, BUT STILL ...

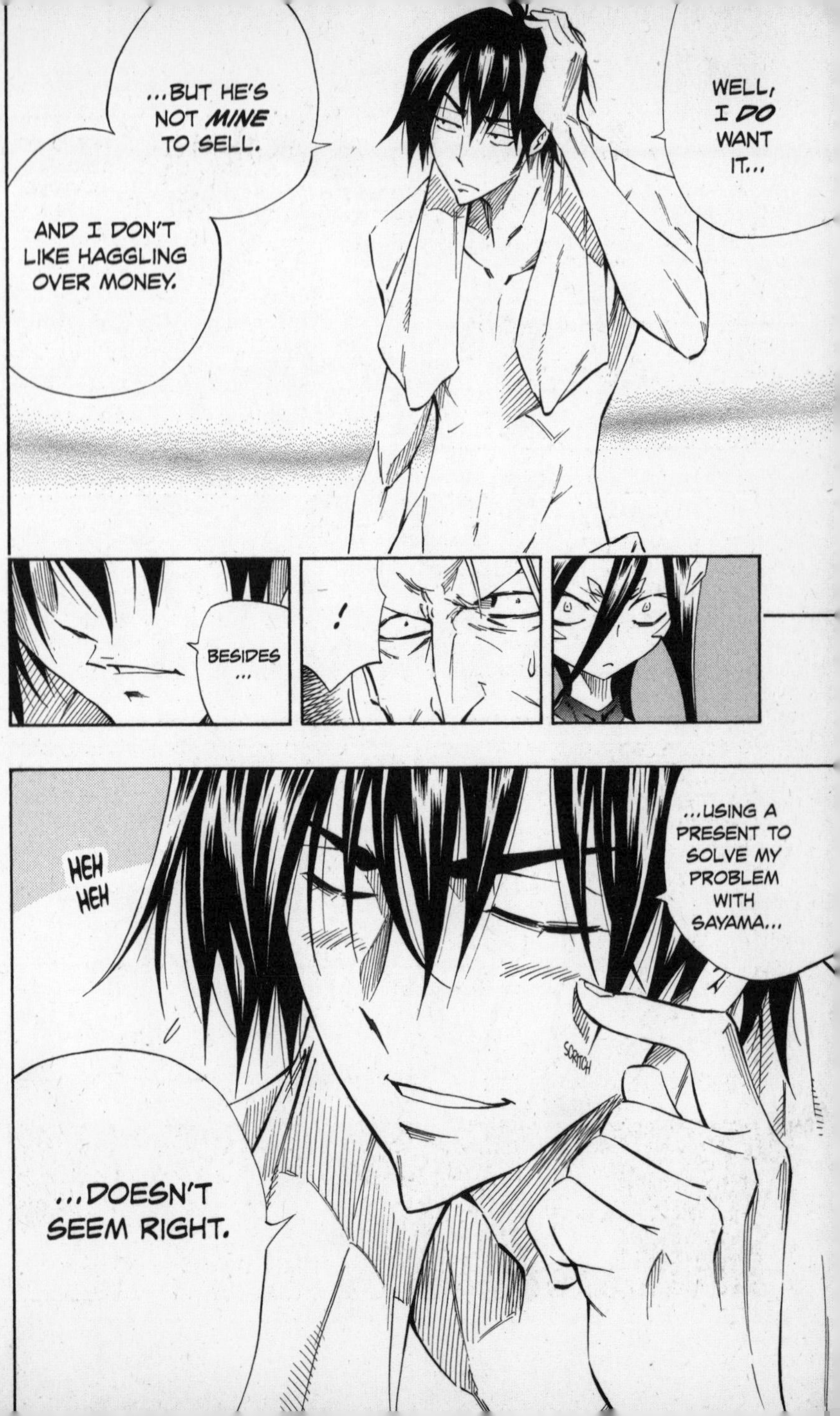
WELL, I DO WANT IT...
...BUT HE'S NOT MINE TO SELL.
AND I DON'T LIKE HAGGLING OVER MONEY.
!
BESIDES...
...USING A PRESENT TO SOLVE MY PROBLEM WITH SAYAMA...
HEH HEH
SCRITCH
...DOESN'T SEEM RIGHT.

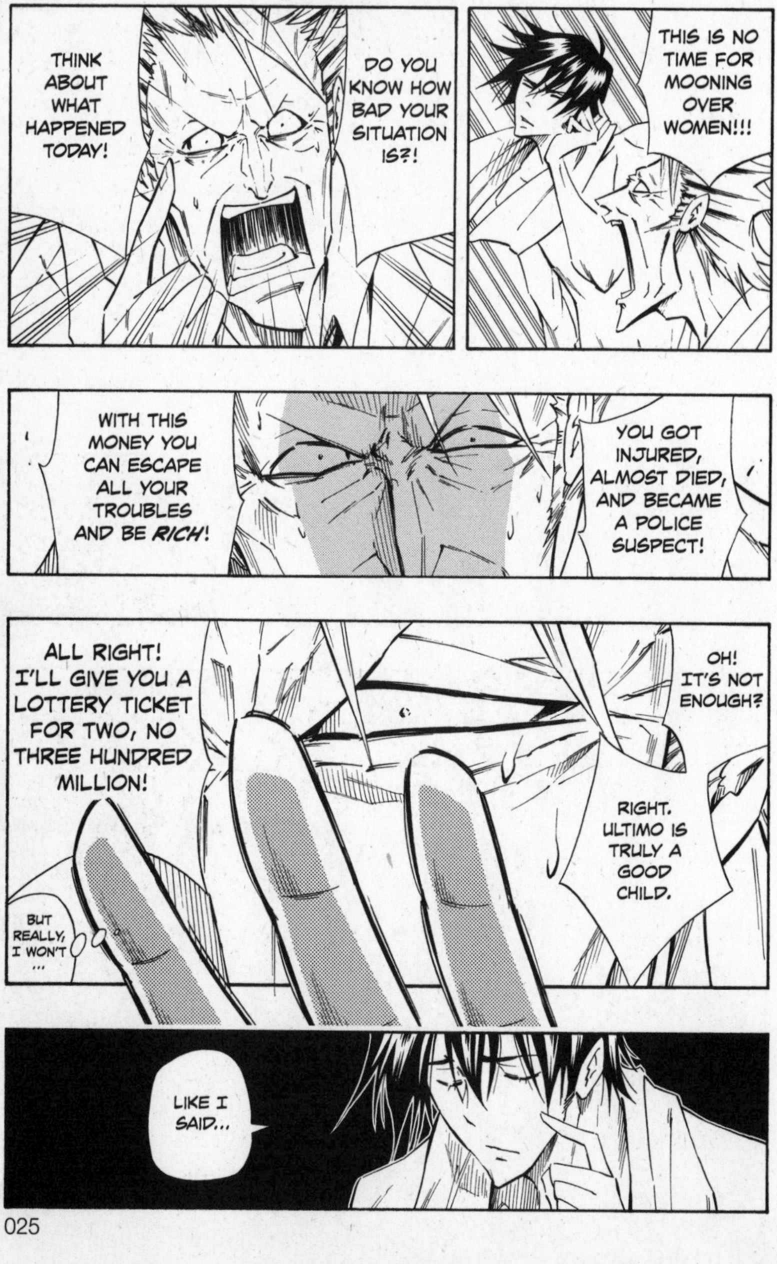
THIS IS NO TIME FOR MOONING OVER WOMEN!!!
DO YOU KNOW HOW BAD YOUR SITUATION IS?!
THINK ABOUT WHAT HAPPENED TODAY!
YOU GOT INJURED, ALMOST DIED, AND BECAME A POLICE SUSPECT!
WITH THIS MONEY YOU CAN ESCAPE ALL YOUR TROUBLES AND BE *RICH*!
OH! IT'S NOT ENOUGH?
ALL RIGHT! I'LL GIVE YOU A LOTTERY TICKET FOR TWO, NO THREE HUNDRED MILLION!
RIGHT. ULTIMO IS TRULY A GOOD CHILD.
BUT REALLY, I WON'T ...
LIKE I SAID...

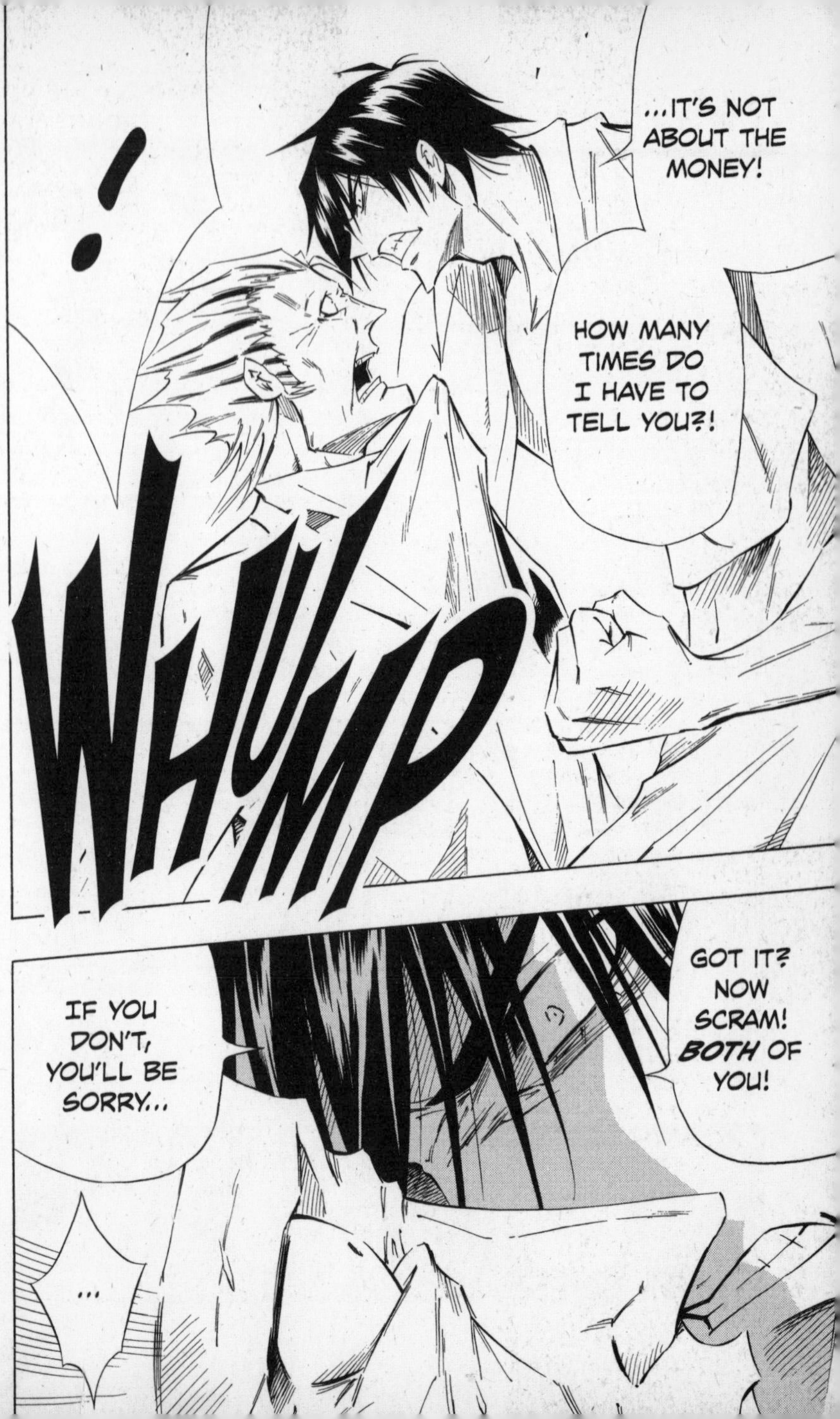
...IT'S NOT ABOUT THE MONEY!
HOW MANY TIMES DO I HAVE TO TELL YOU?!
!
WHUMP
GOT IT? NOW SCRAM! *BOTH* OF YOU!
IF YOU DON'T, YOU'LL BE SORRY...
...

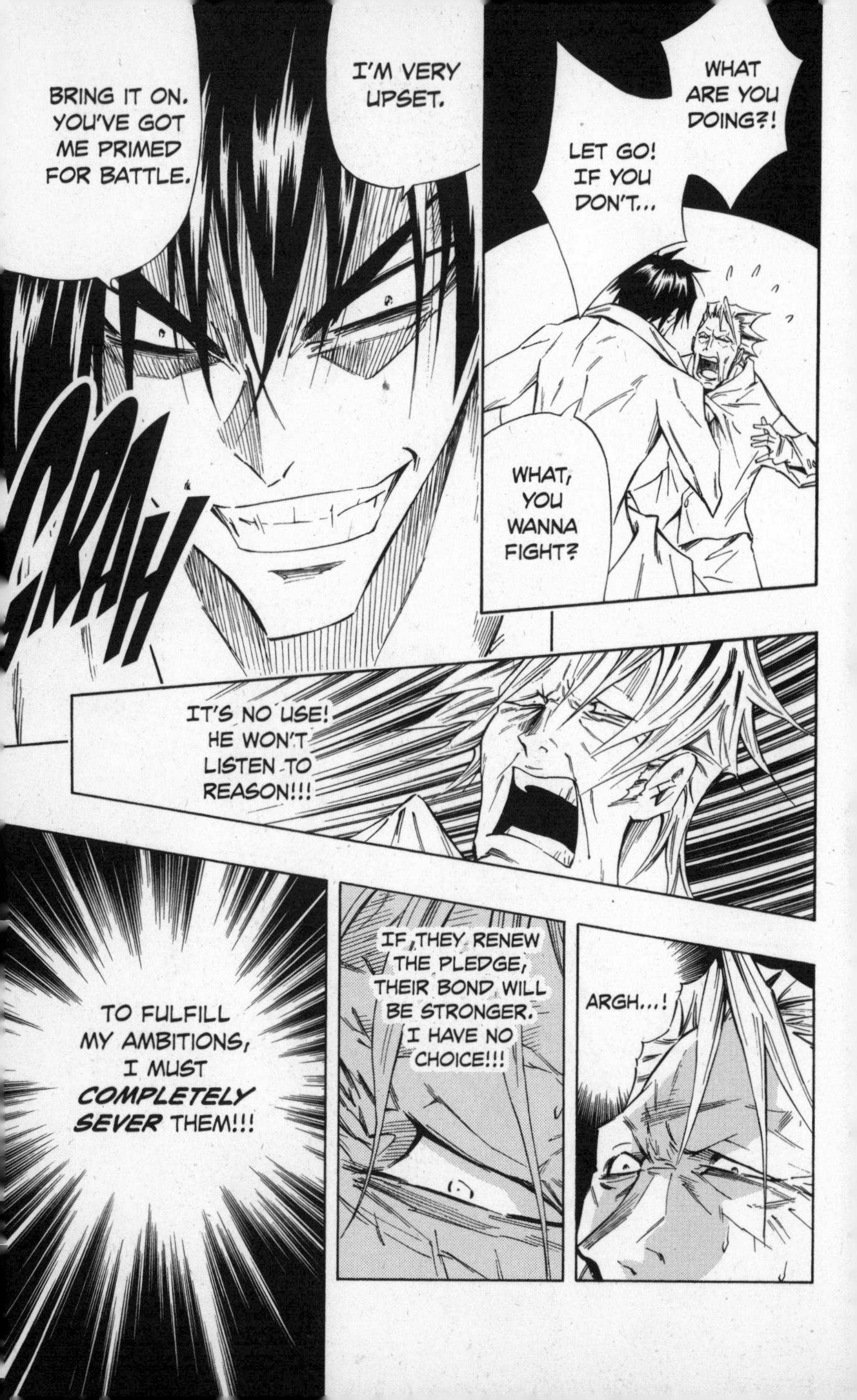
WHAT ARE YOU DOING?!
LET GO! IF YOU DON'T...
WHAT, YOU WANNA FIGHT?
I'M VERY UPSET.
BRING IT ON. YOU'VE GOT ME PRIMED FOR BATTLE.
IT'S NO USE! HE WON'T LISTEN TO REASON!!!
ARGH...!
IF THEY RENEW THE PLEDGE, THEIR BOND WILL BE STRONGER. I HAVE NO CHOICE!!!
TO FULFILL MY AMBITIONS, I MUST *COMPLETELY SEVER* THEM!!!

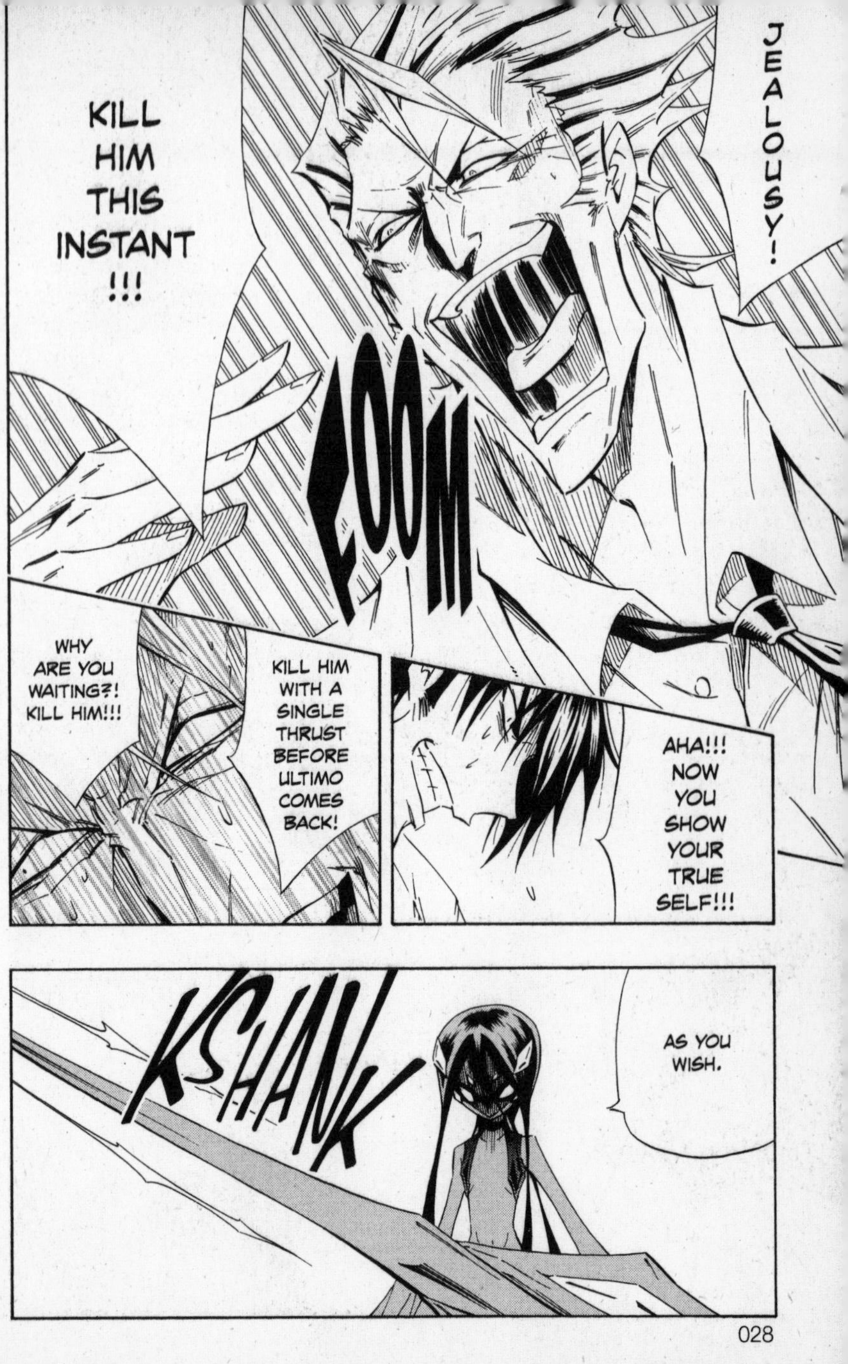
JEALOUSY!
FOOM
KILL HIM THIS INSTANT!!!
AHA!!! NOW YOU SHOW YOUR TRUE SELF!!!
KILL HIM WITH A SINGLE THRUST BEFORE ULTIMO COMES BACK!
WHY ARE YOU WAITING?! KILL HIM!!!
AS YOU WISH.
KSHANK

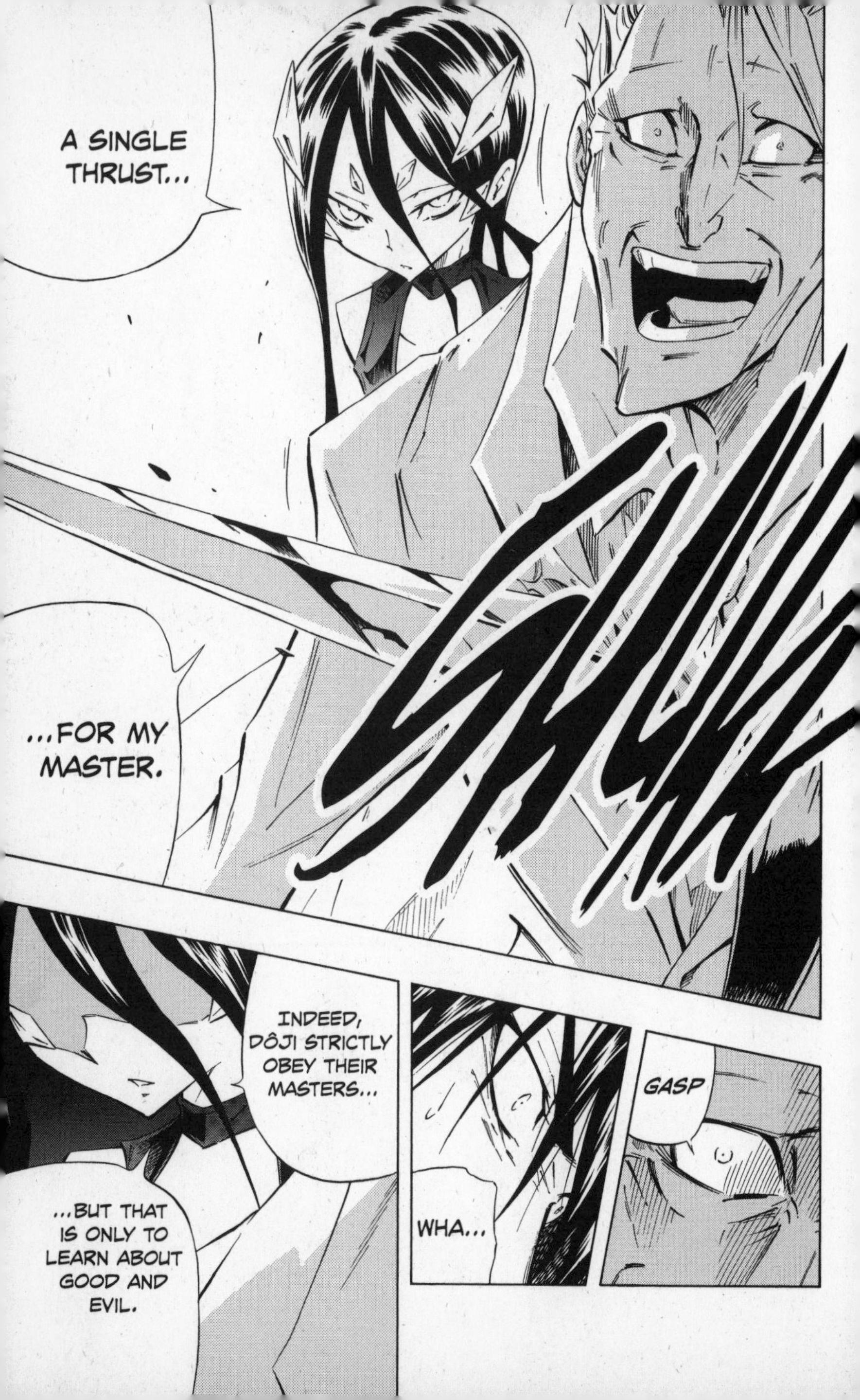
A SINGLE THRUST...
...FOR MY MASTER.
SHUK
GASP
WHA...
INDEED, DÔJI STRICTLY OBEY THEIR MASTERS...
...BUT THAT IS ONLY TO LEARN ABOUT GOOD AND EVIL.

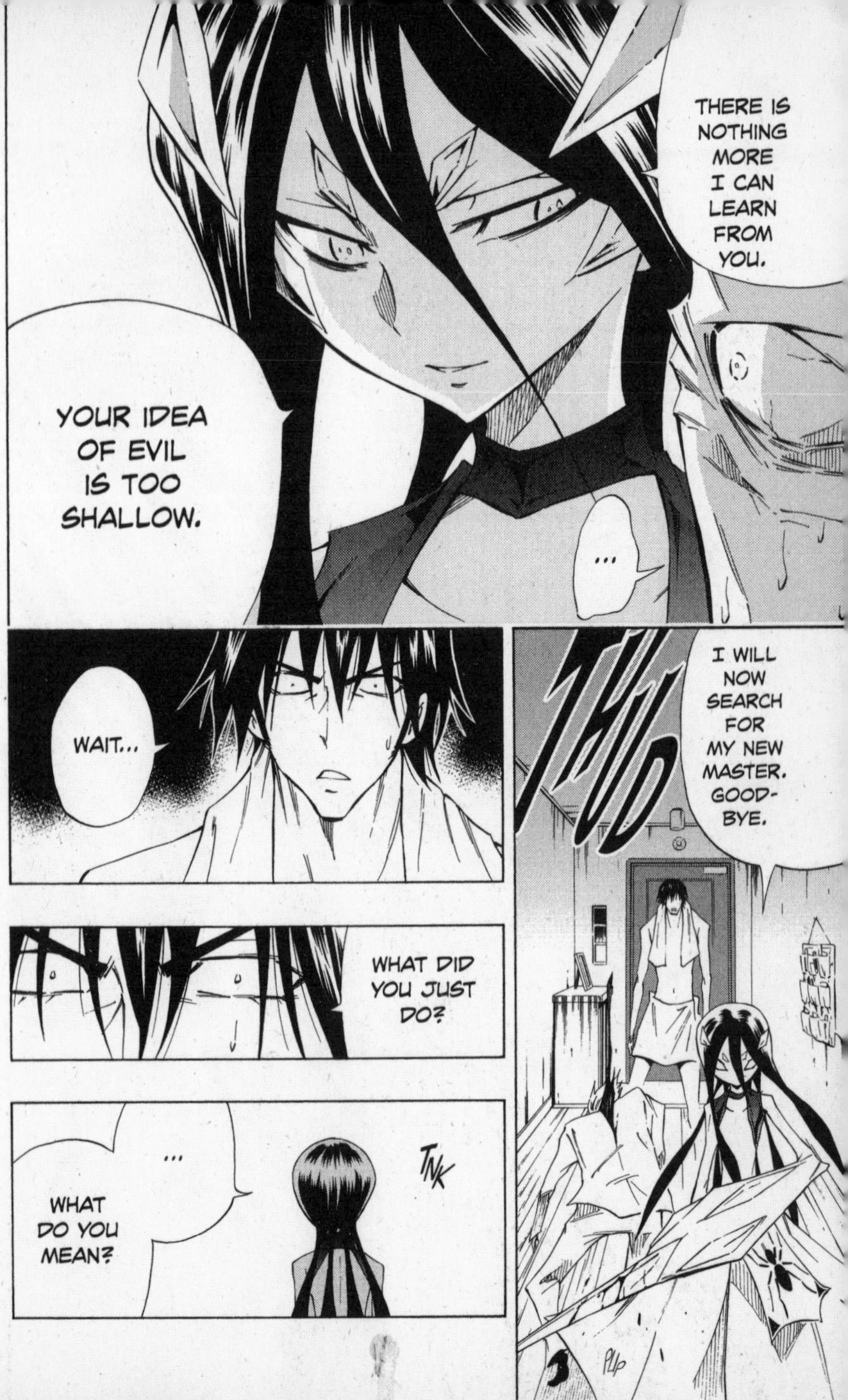
THERE IS NOTHING MORE I CAN LEARN FROM YOU.
YOUR IDEA OF EVIL IS TOO SHALLOW.
...
THUD
I WILL NOW SEARCH FOR MY NEW MASTER. GOOD-BYE.
PLIP
WAIT...
WHAT DID YOU JUST DO?
...
WHAT DO YOU MEAN?
TNK

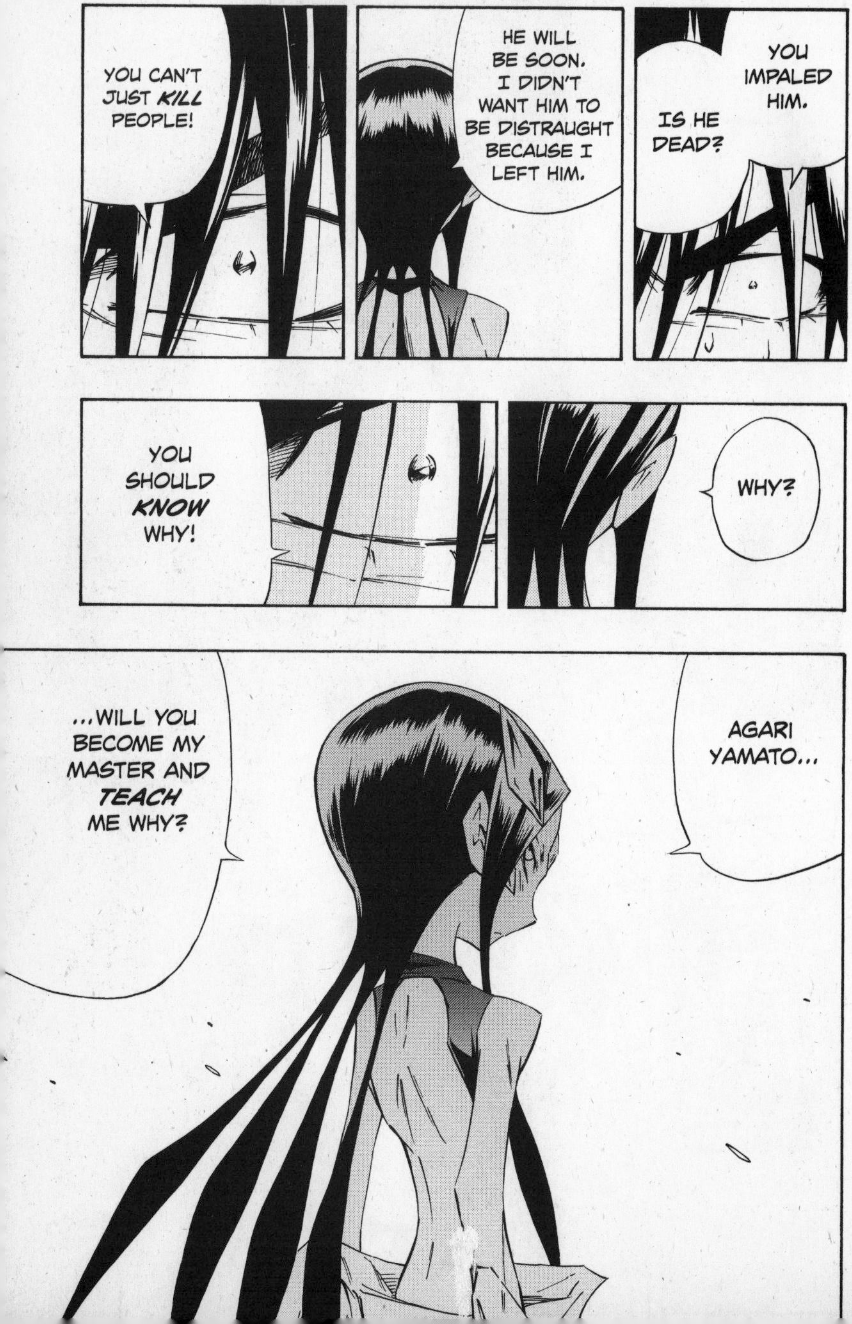
YOU IMPALED HIM.
IS HE DEAD?
HE WILL BE SOON. I DIDN'T WANT HIM TO BE DISTRAUGHT BECAUSE I LEFT HIM.
YOU CAN'T JUST KILL PEOPLE!
WHY?
YOU SHOULD KNOW WHY!
AGARI YAMATO...
...WILL YOU BECOME MY MASTER AND TEACH ME WHY?

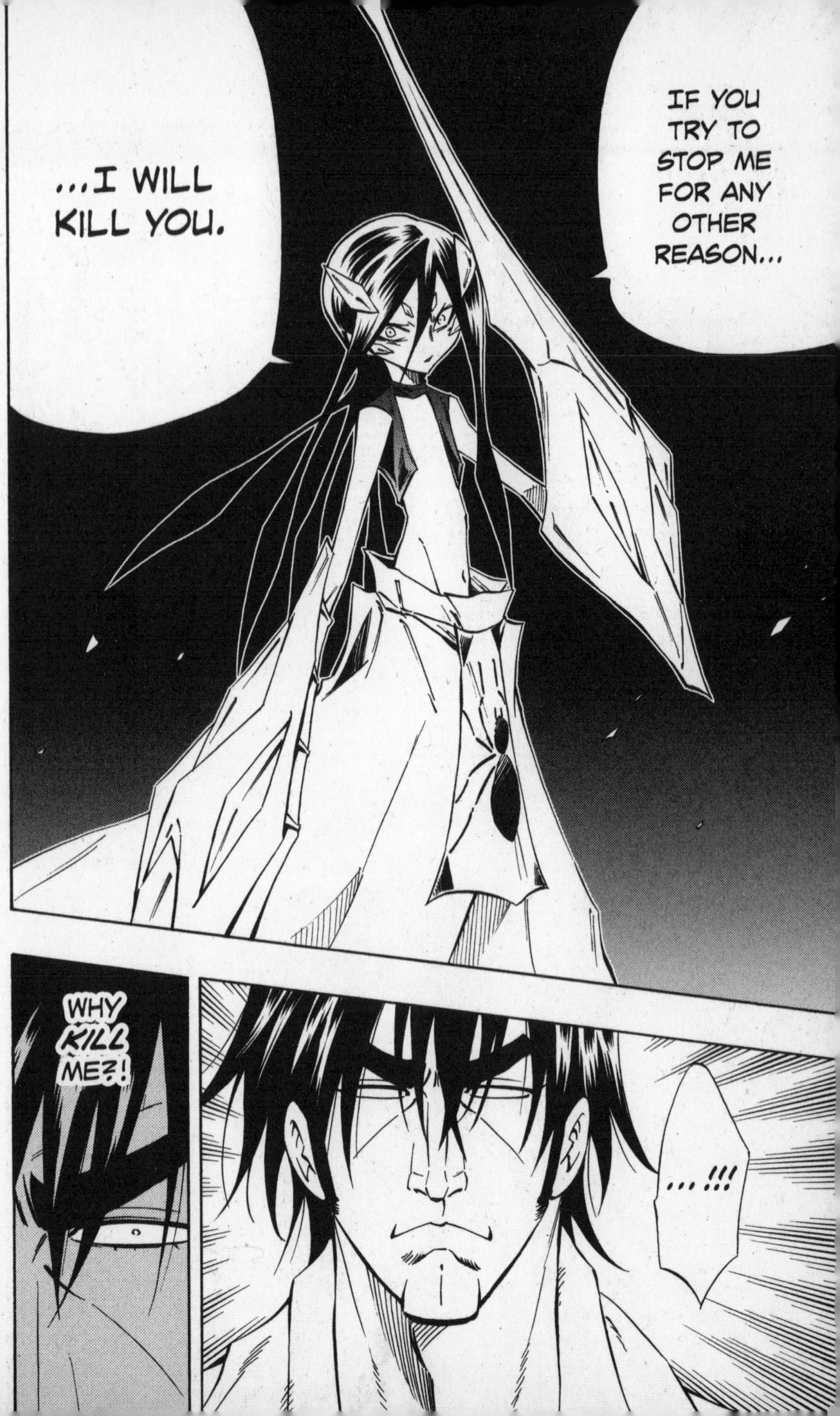
IF YOU TRY TO STOP ME FOR ANY OTHER REASON...
...I WILL KILL YOU.
...!!!
WHY KILL ME?!

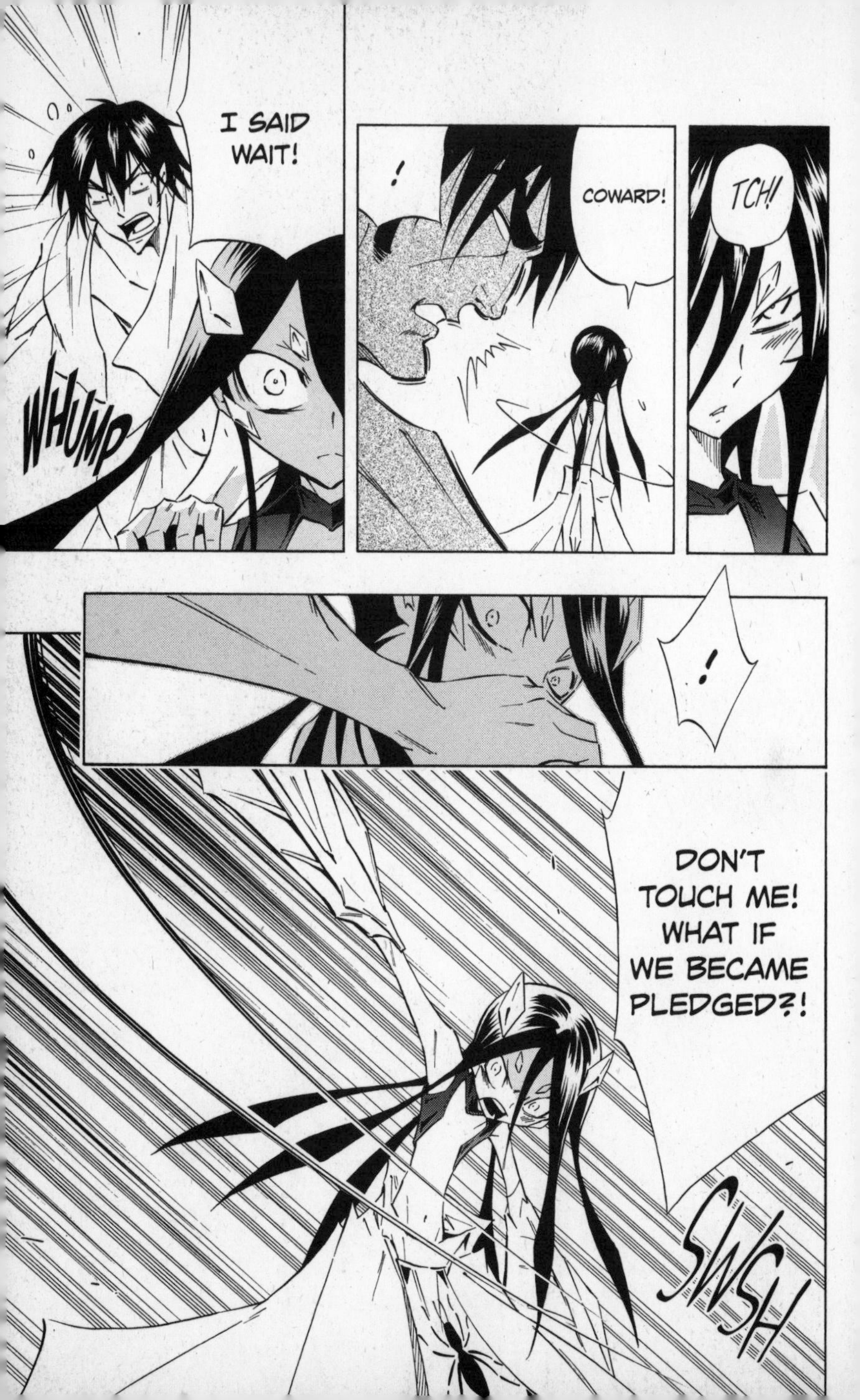
TCH!
COWARD!
!
I SAID WAIT!
WHUMP
!
DON'T TOUCH ME! WHAT IF WE BECAME PLEDGED?!
SWSH

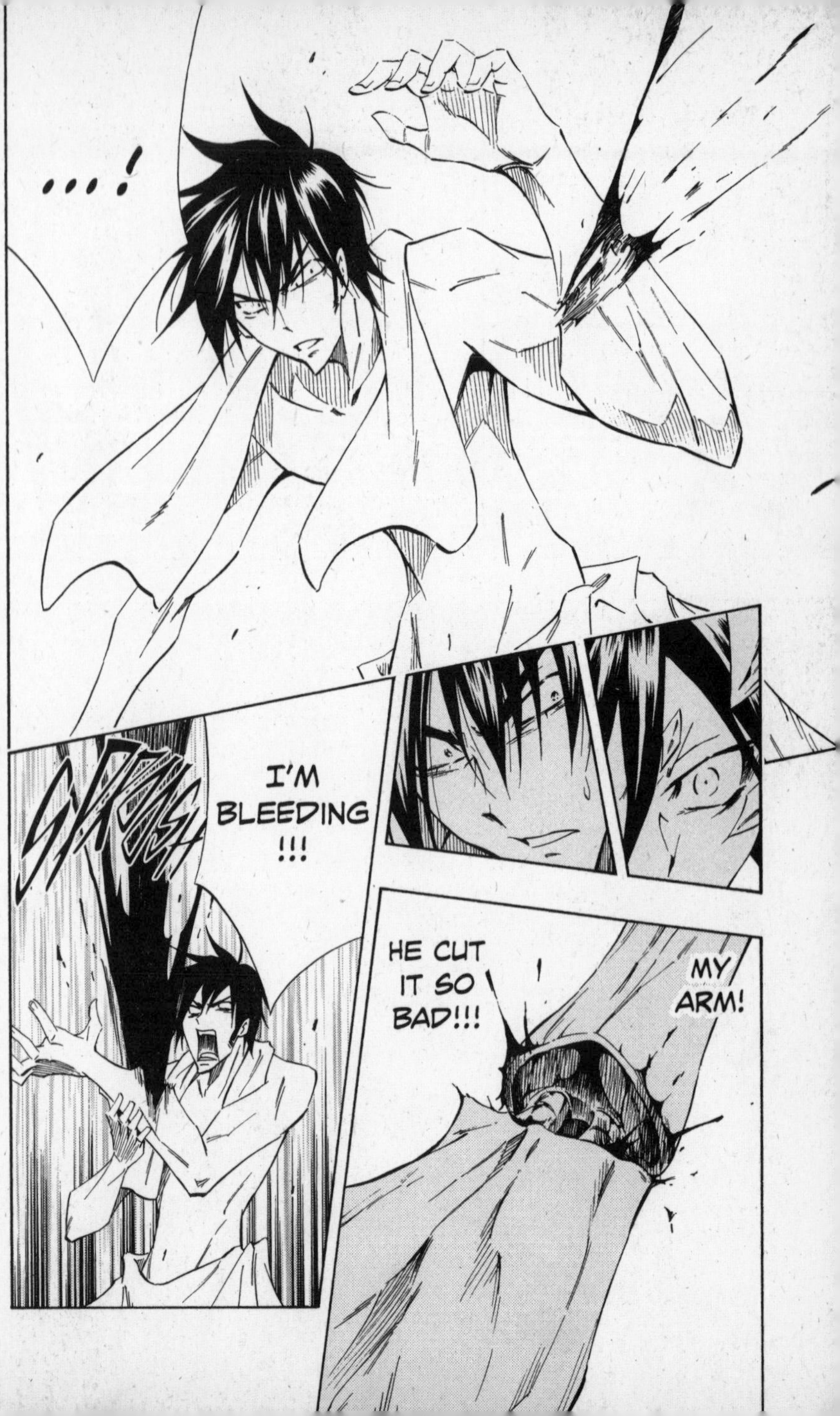
...!
MY ARM!
HE CUT IT SO BAD!!!
I'M BLEEDING !!!

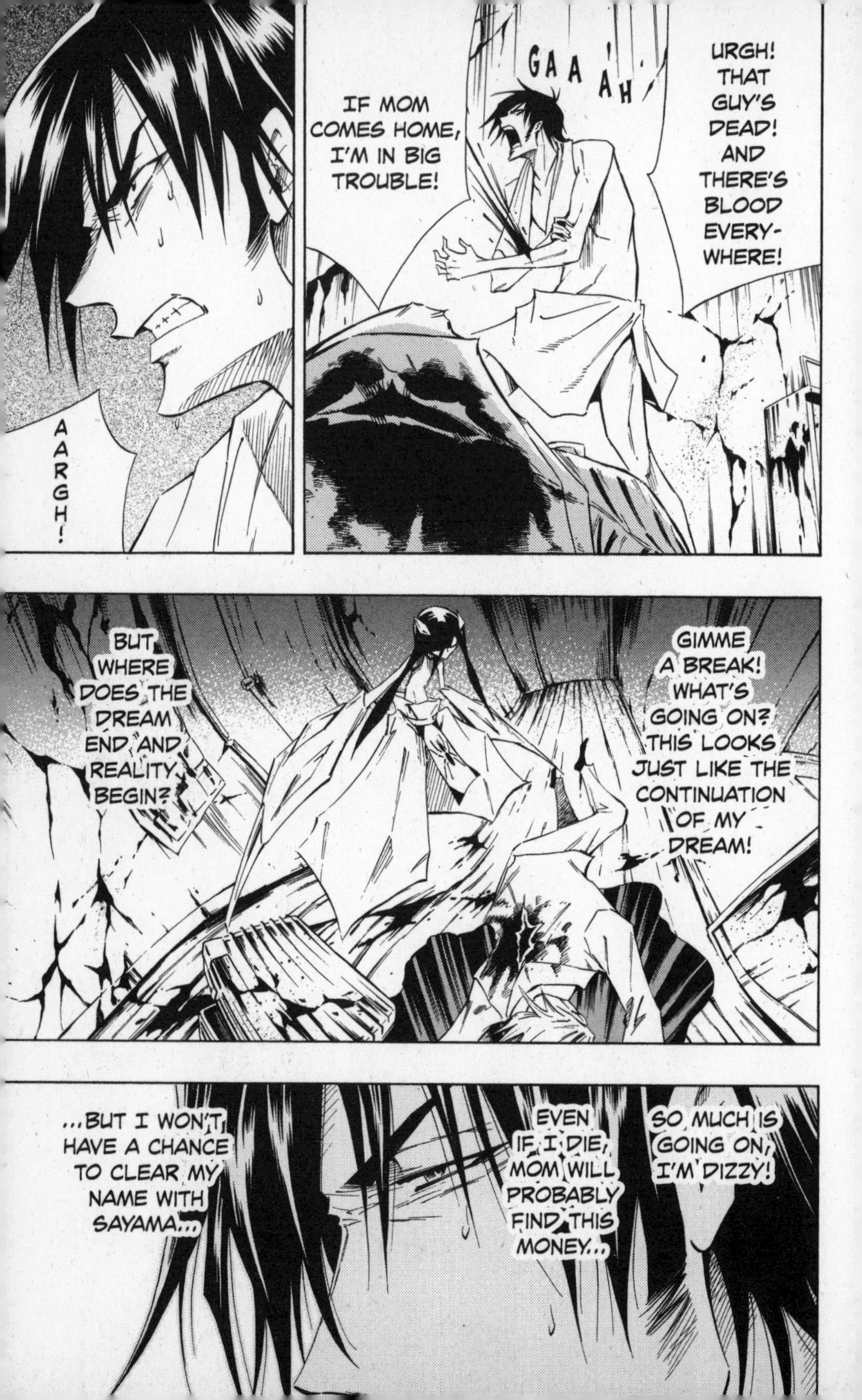
URGH! THAT GUY'S DEAD! AND THERE'S BLOOD EVERY-WHERE!
GAAAH
IF MOM COMES HOME, I'M IN BIG TROUBLE!
AARGH!
GIMME A BREAK! WHAT'S GOING ON? THIS LOOKS JUST LIKE THE CONTINUATION OF MY DREAM!
BUT WHERE DOES THE DREAM END AND REALITY BEGIN?
SO MUCH IS GOING ON, I'M DIZZY!
EVEN IF I DIE, MOM WILL PROBABLY FIND THIS MONEY...
...BUT I WON'T HAVE A CHANCE TO CLEAR MY NAME WITH SAYAMA...

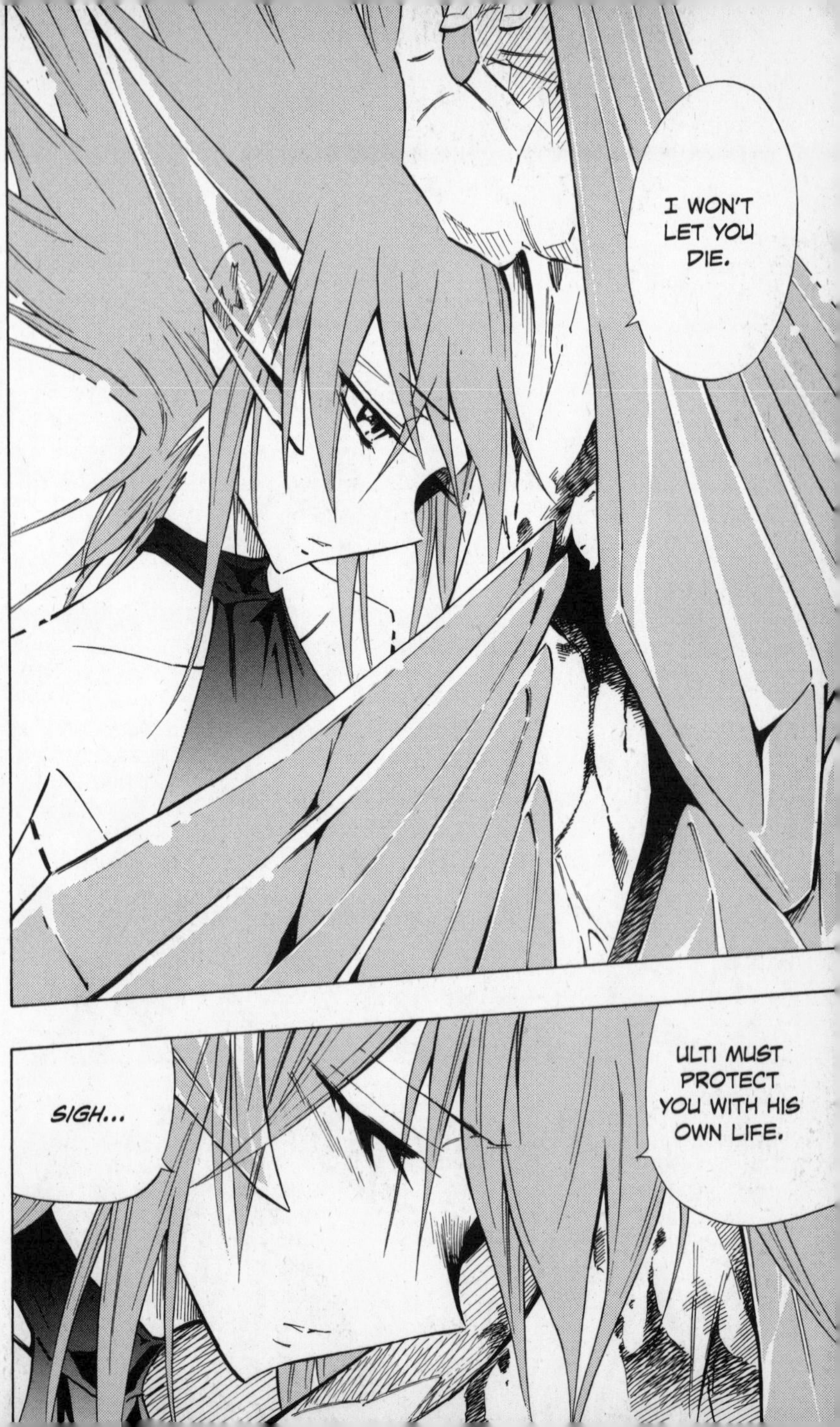
I WON'T LET YOU DIE.
ULTI MUST PROTECT YOU WITH HIS OWN LIFE.
SIGH...

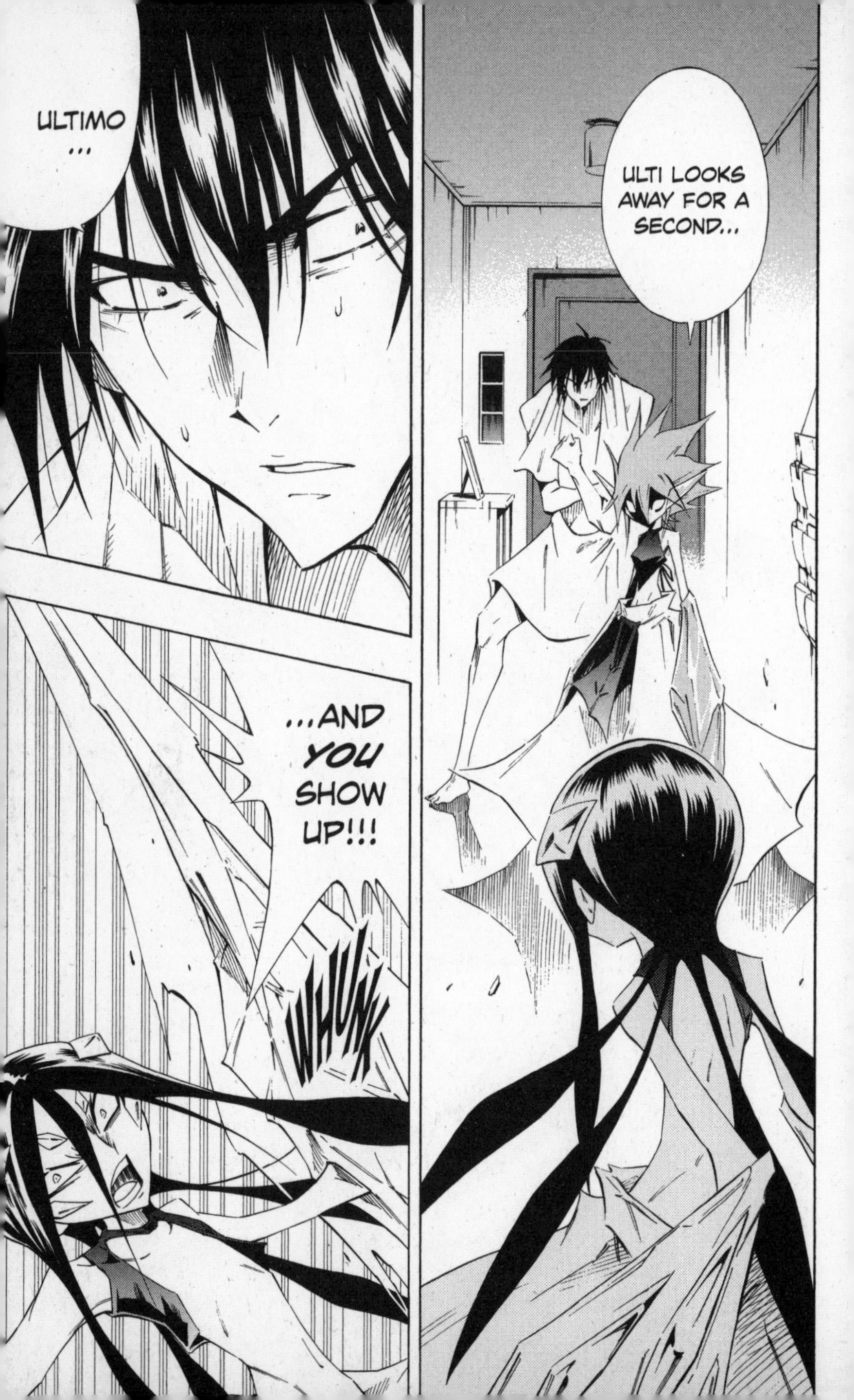
ULTI LOOKS AWAY FOR A SECOND...
ULTIMO ...
...AND YOU SHOW UP!!!
WHUNK

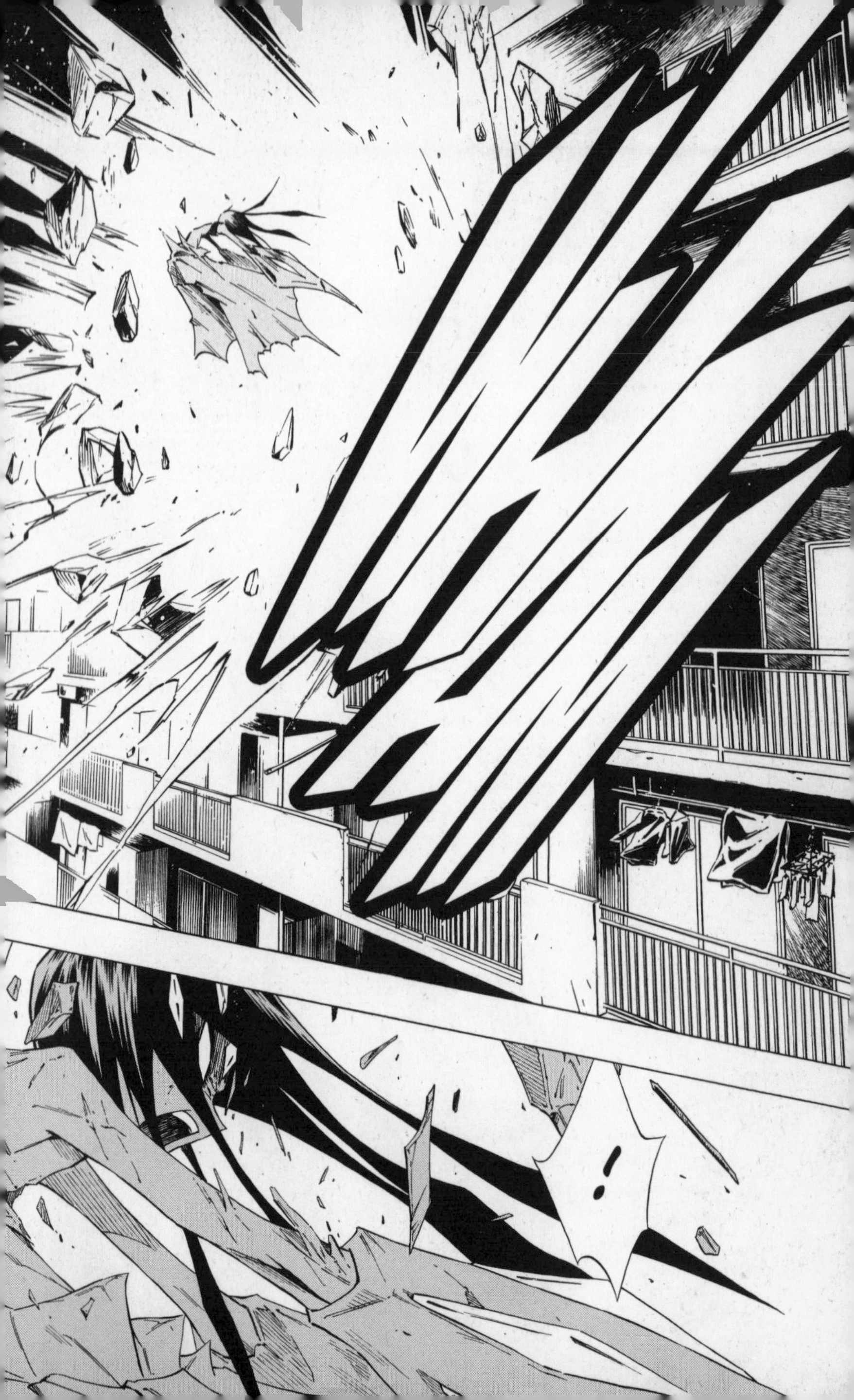
!

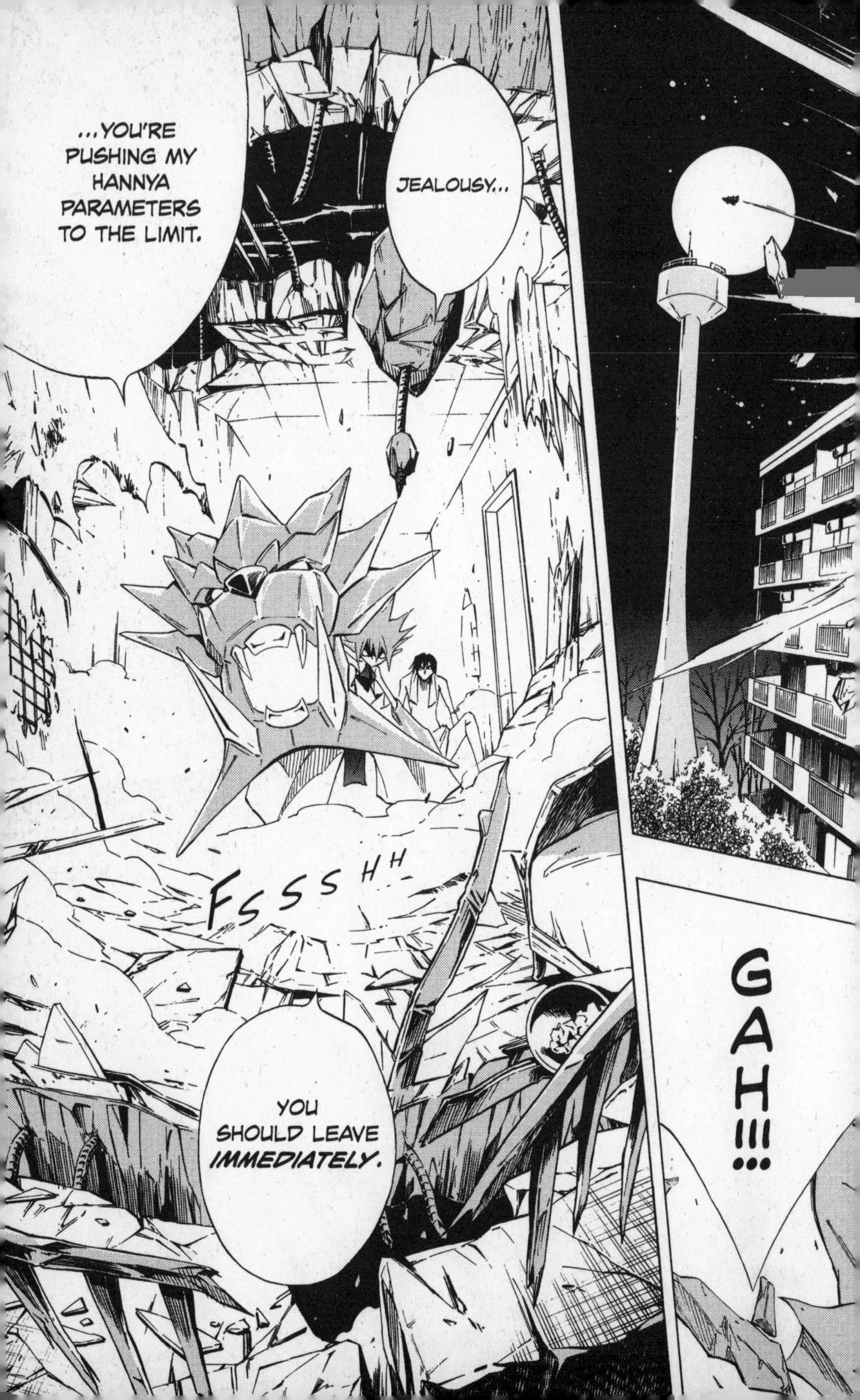
GAH!!!
JEALOUSY...
...YOU'RE PUSHING MY HANNYA PARAMETERS TO THE LIMIT.
FSSSHH
YOU SHOULD LEAVE *IMMEDIATELY*.

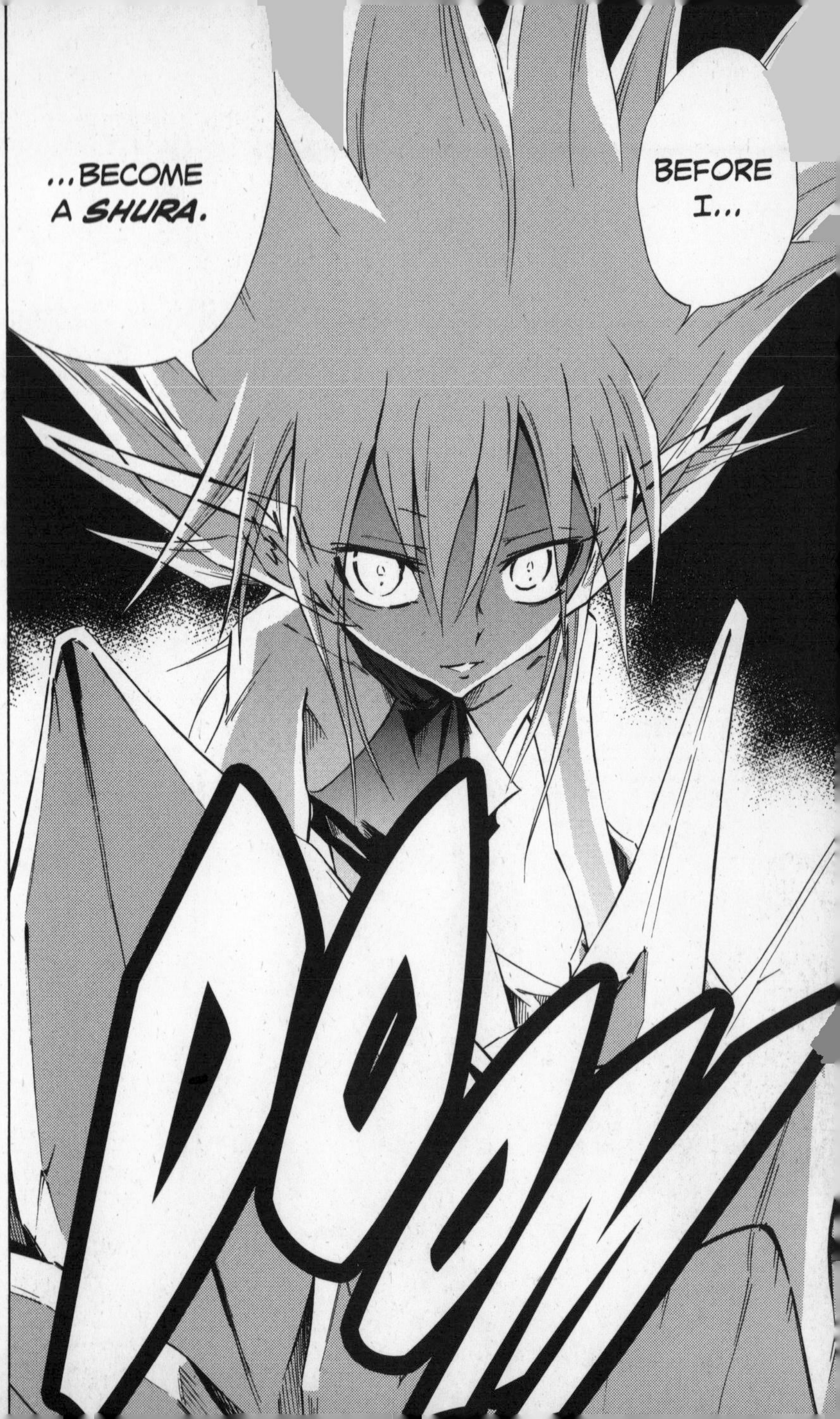
BEFORE I...
...BECOME A *SHURA*.
DOOM

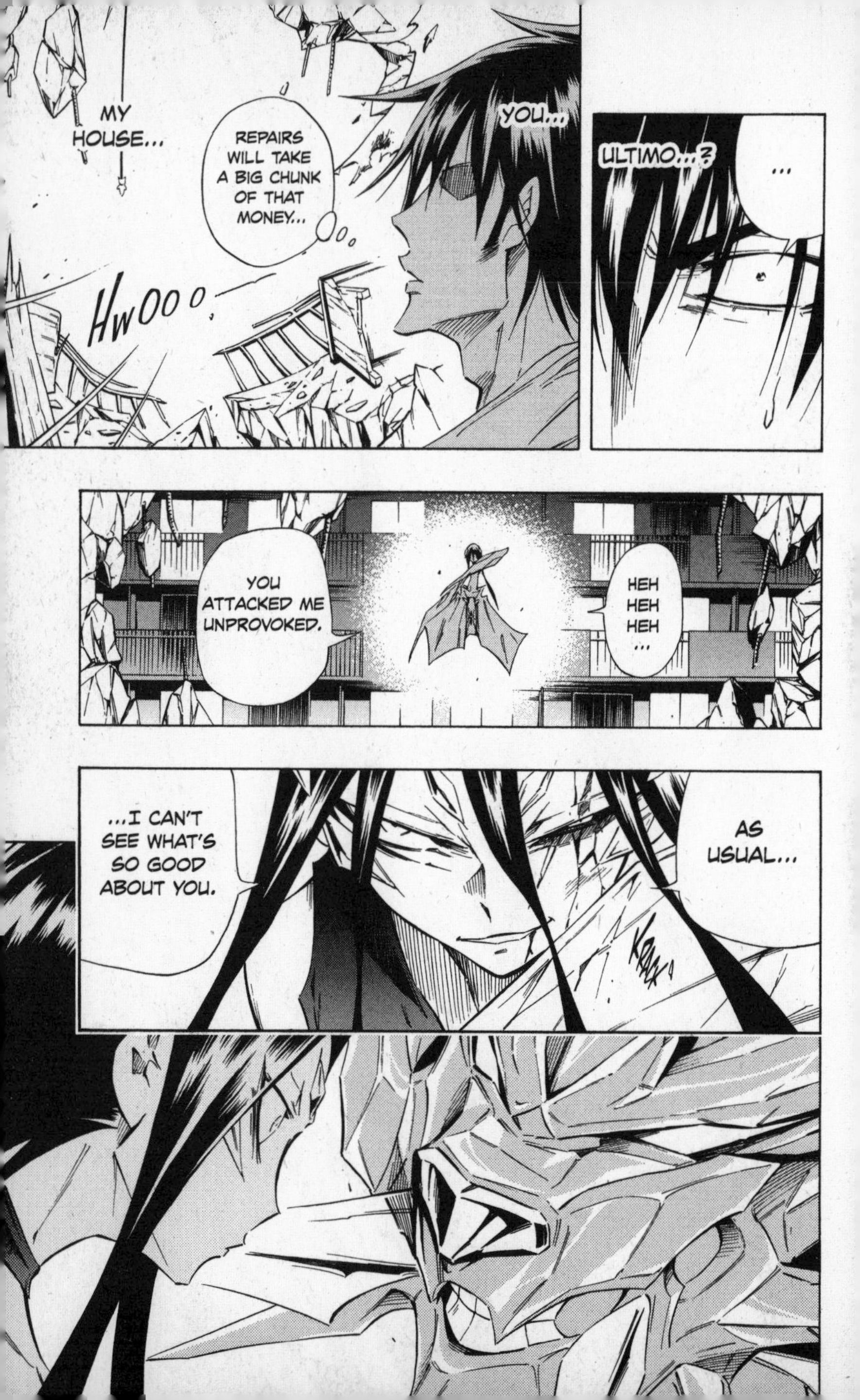
...
ULTIMO...?
YOU...
REPAIRS WILL TAKE A BIG CHUNK OF THAT MONEY...
MY HOUSE...
HWOOO
HEH HEH HEH ...
YOU ATTACKED ME UNPROVOKED.
AS USUAL...
KRACK
...I CAN'T SEE WHAT'S SO GOOD ABOUT YOU.

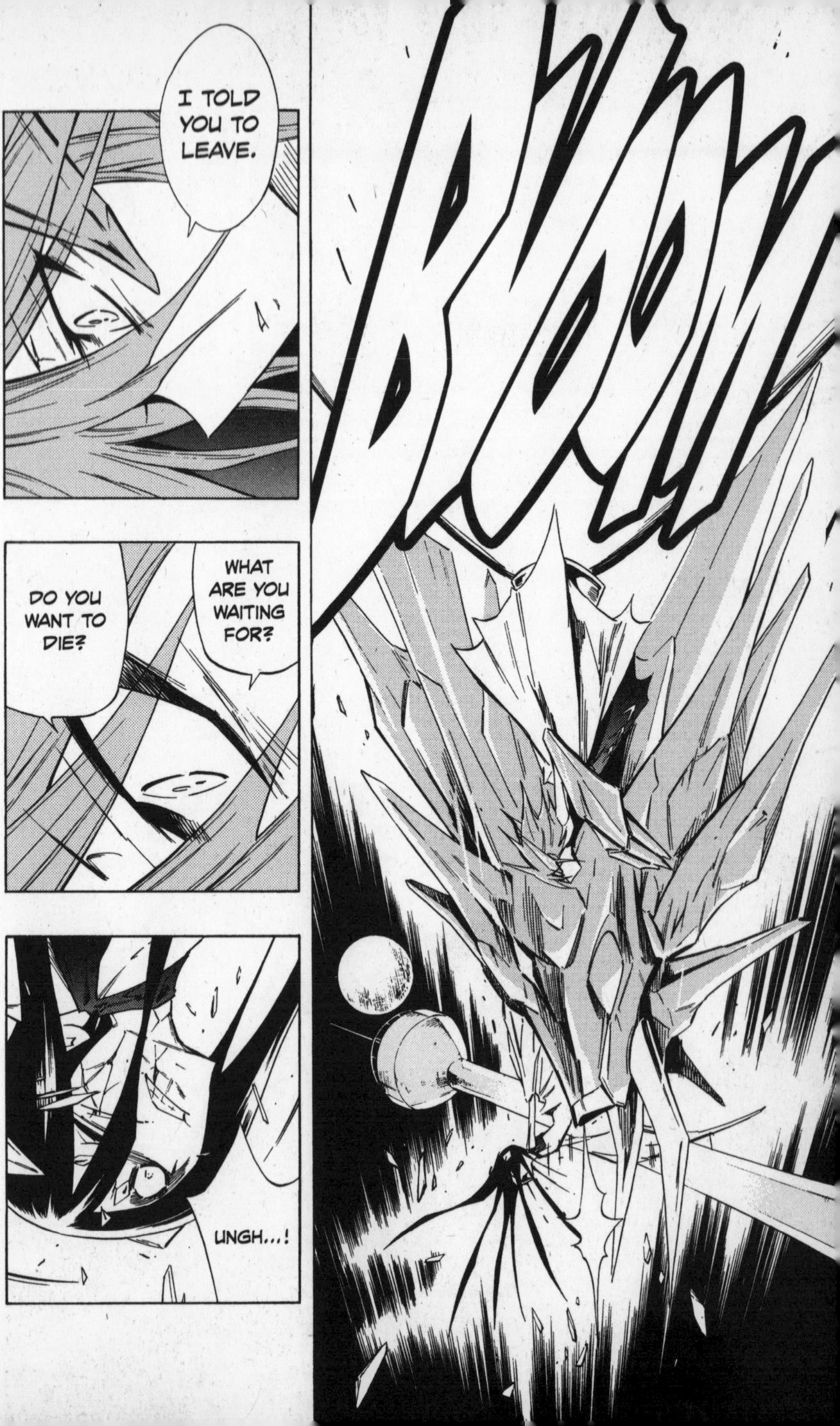
BOOM
I TOLD YOU TO LEAVE.
WHAT ARE YOU WAITING FOR?
DO YOU WANT TO DIE?
UNGH...!

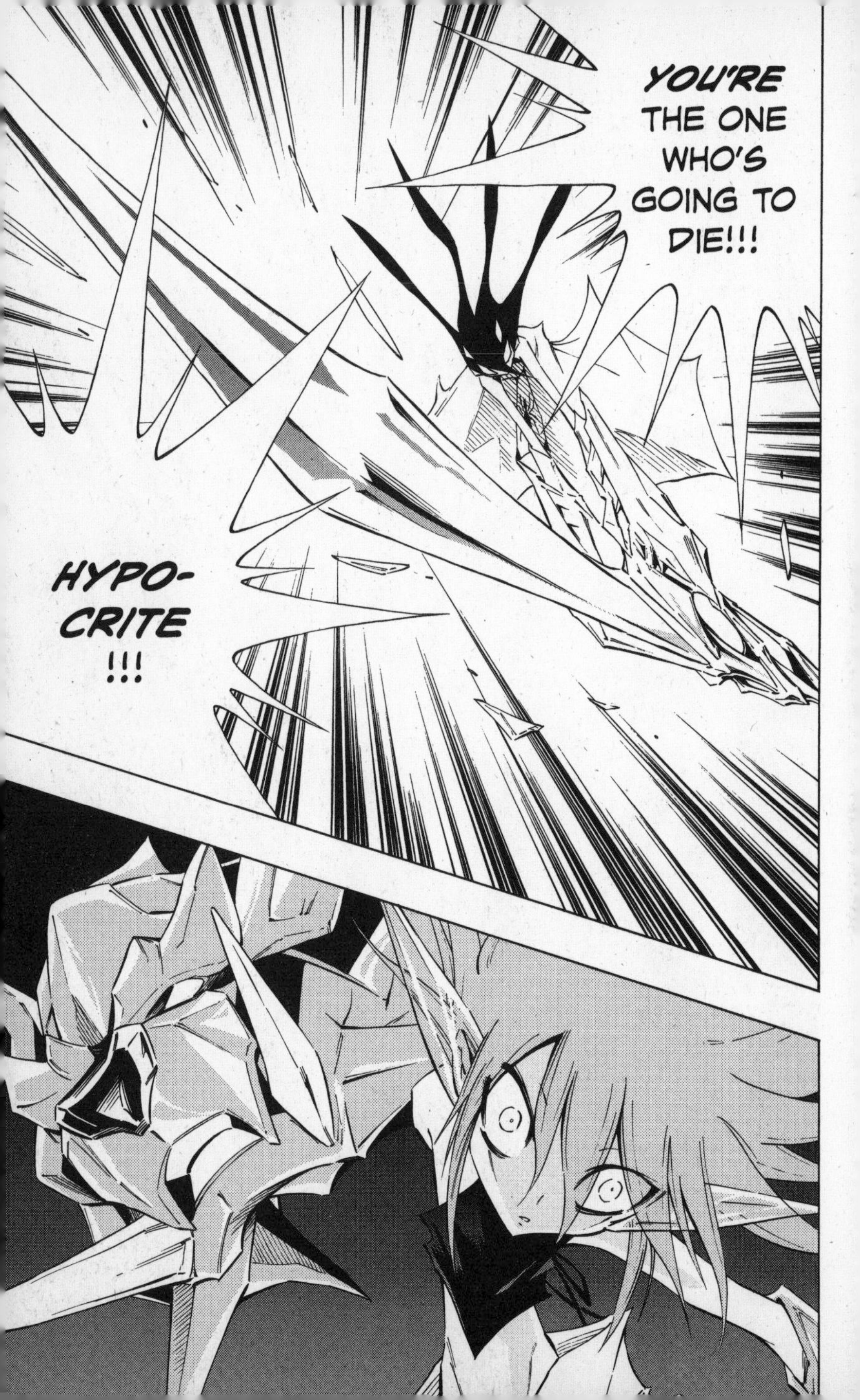
YOU'RE THE ONE WHO'S GOING TO DIE!!!
HYPO-CRITE !!!

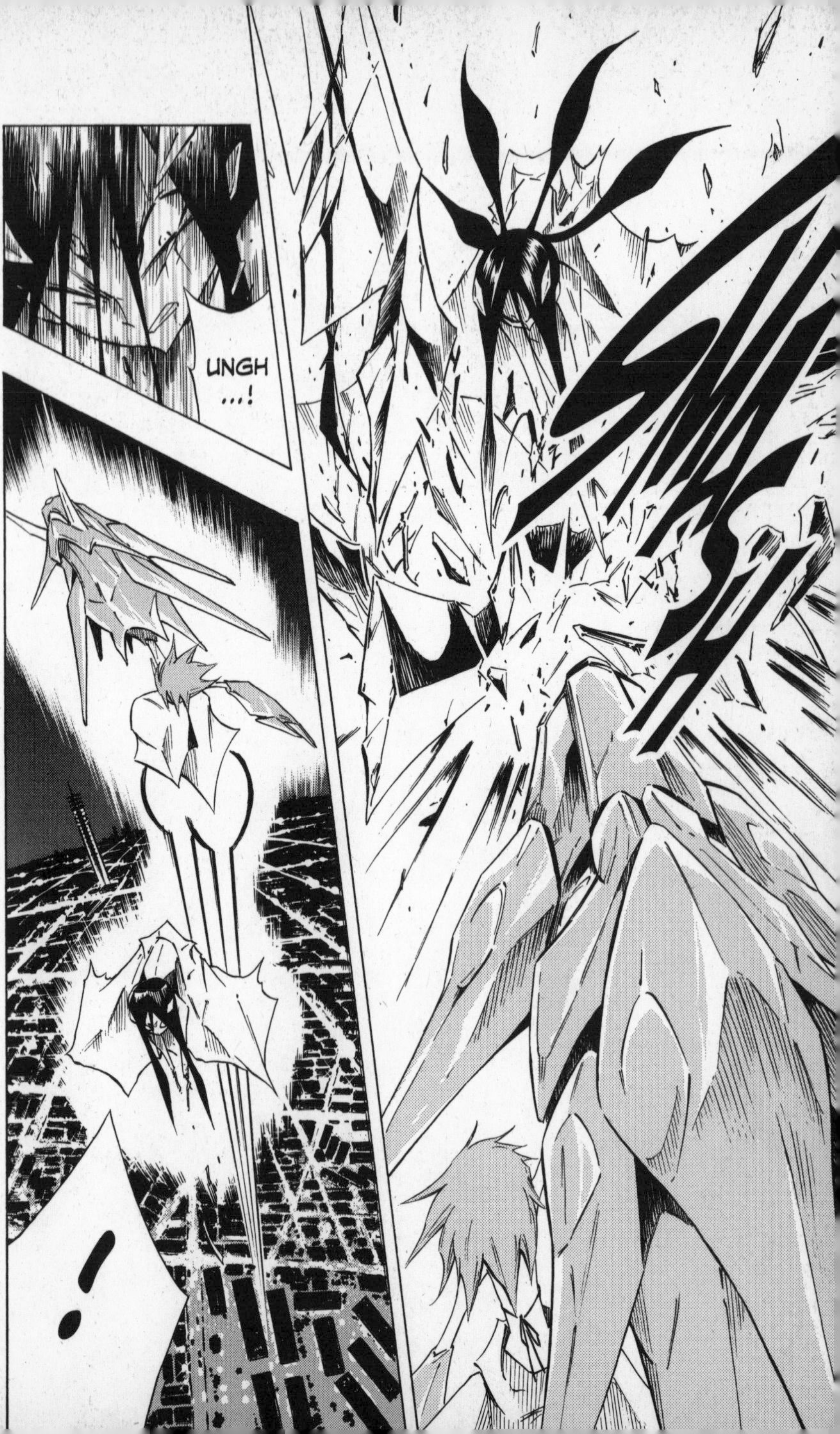
UNGH ...!
!

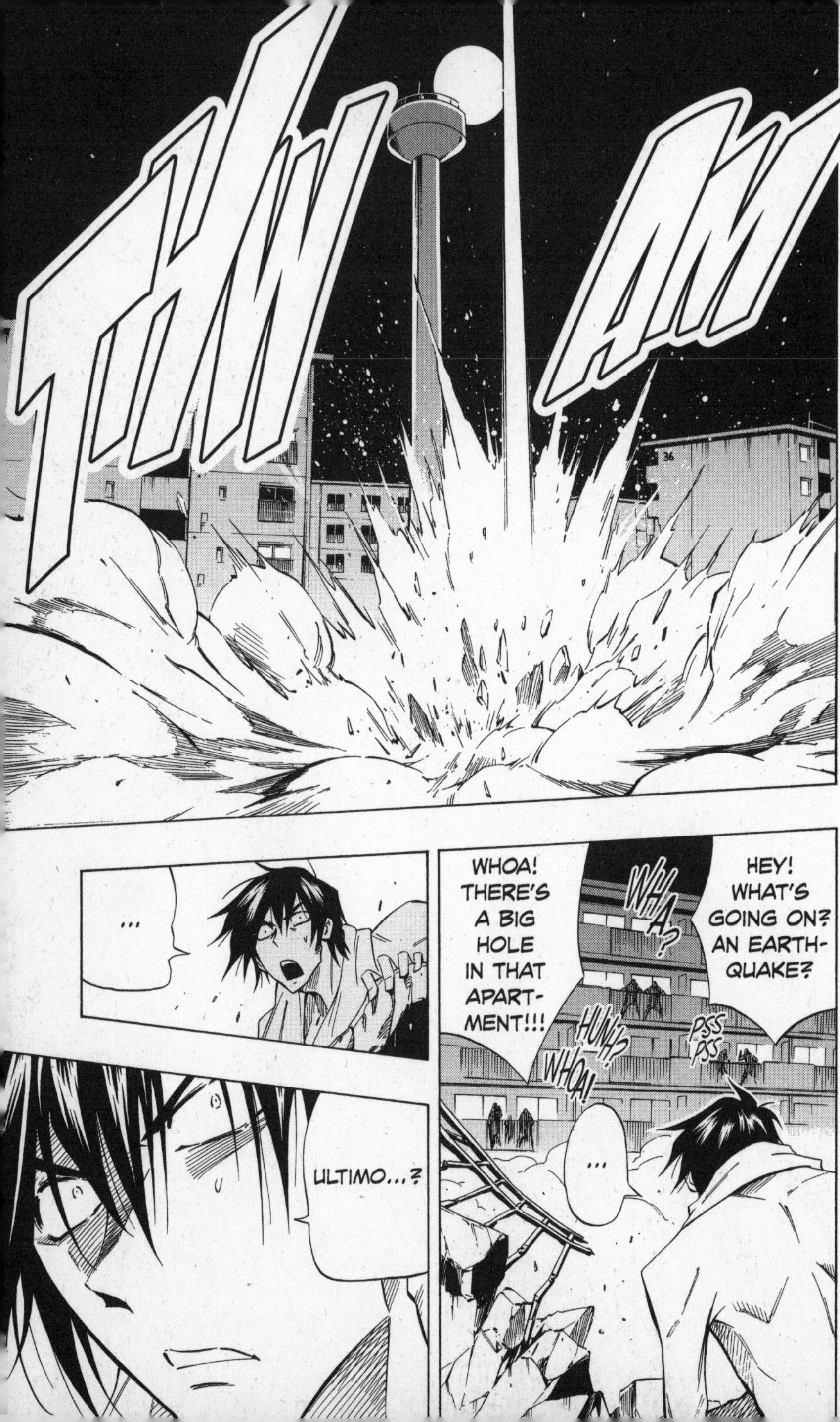
THWAM
HEY! WHAT'S GOING ON? AN EARTH-QUAKE?
WHA?
WHOA! THERE'S A BIG HOLE IN THAT APART-MENT!!!
PSS PSS
HUNH?!
WHOA!
...
...
ULTIMO...?

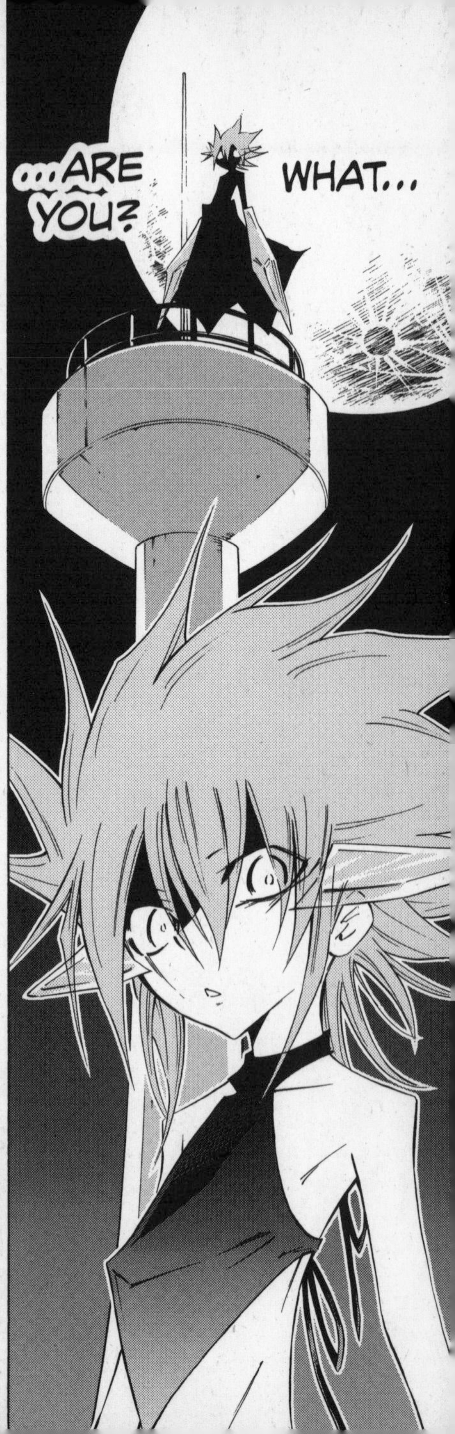
WHAT...
...ARE YOU?

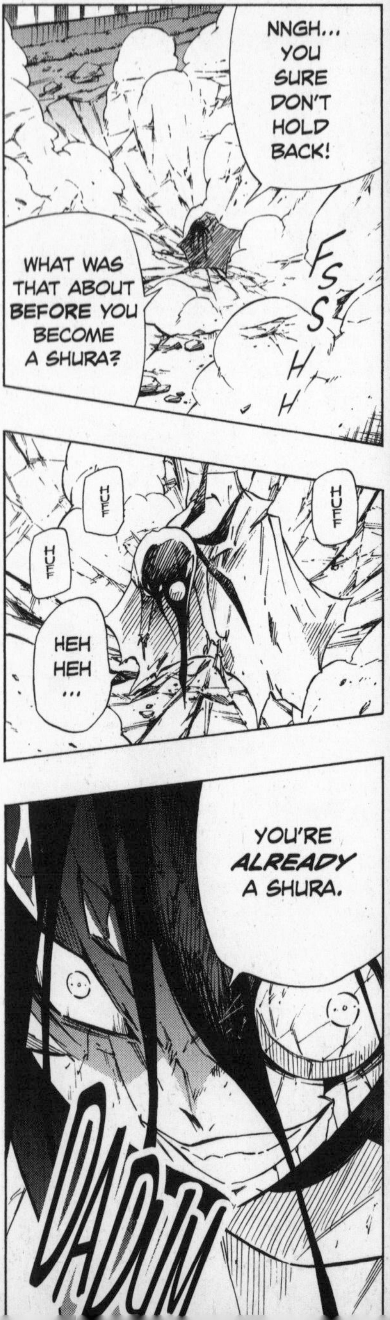
NNGH... YOU SURE DON'T HOLD BACK!
WHAT WAS THAT ABOUT BEFORE YOU BECOME A SHURA?
FSSHH
HUFF
HUFF
HEH HEH ...
YOU'RE *ALREADY* A SHURA.

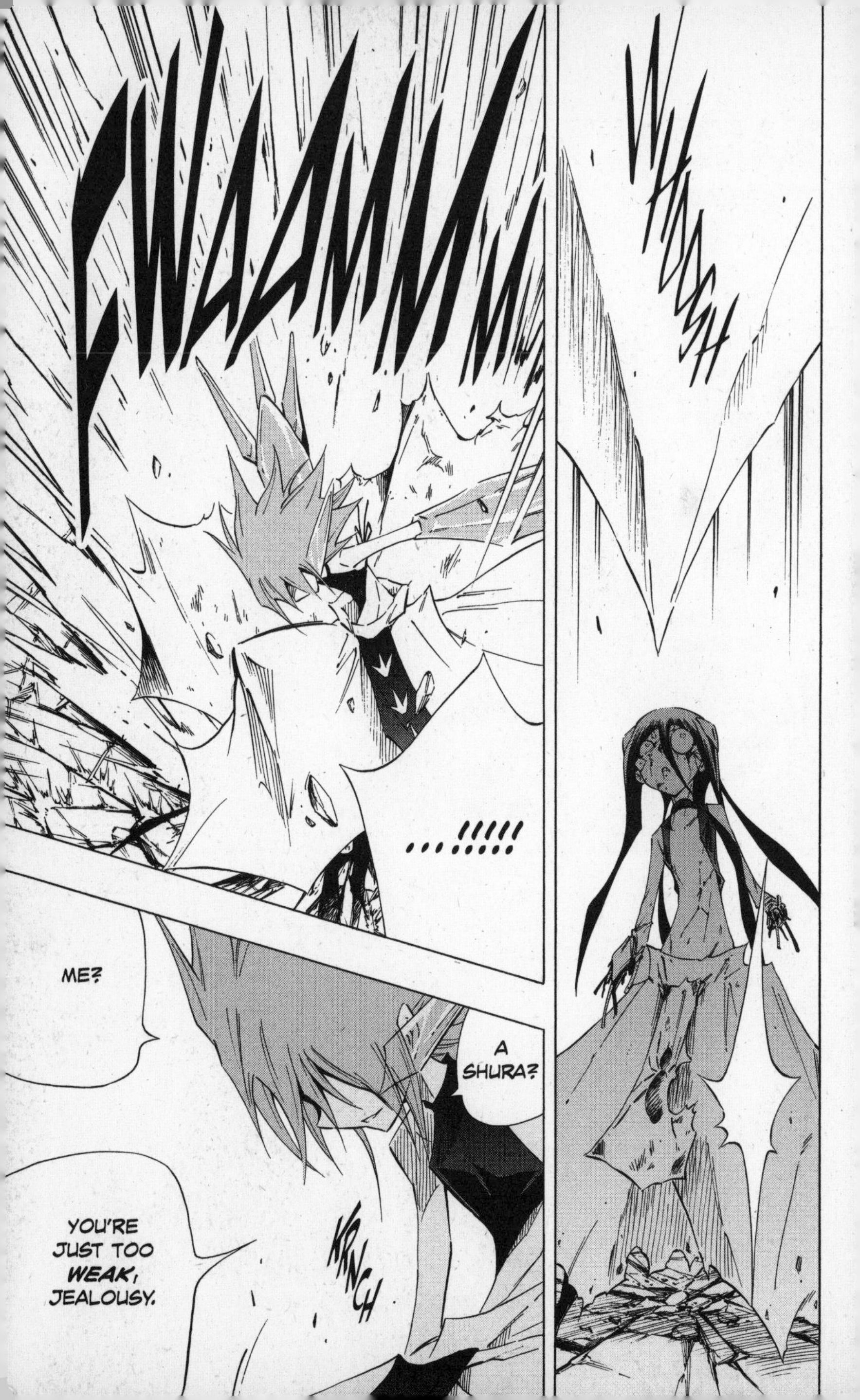
WHOOSH
CHWAMM
...!!!!!
A SHURA?
ME?
KRNCH
YOU'RE JUST TOO *WEAK*, JEALOUSY.

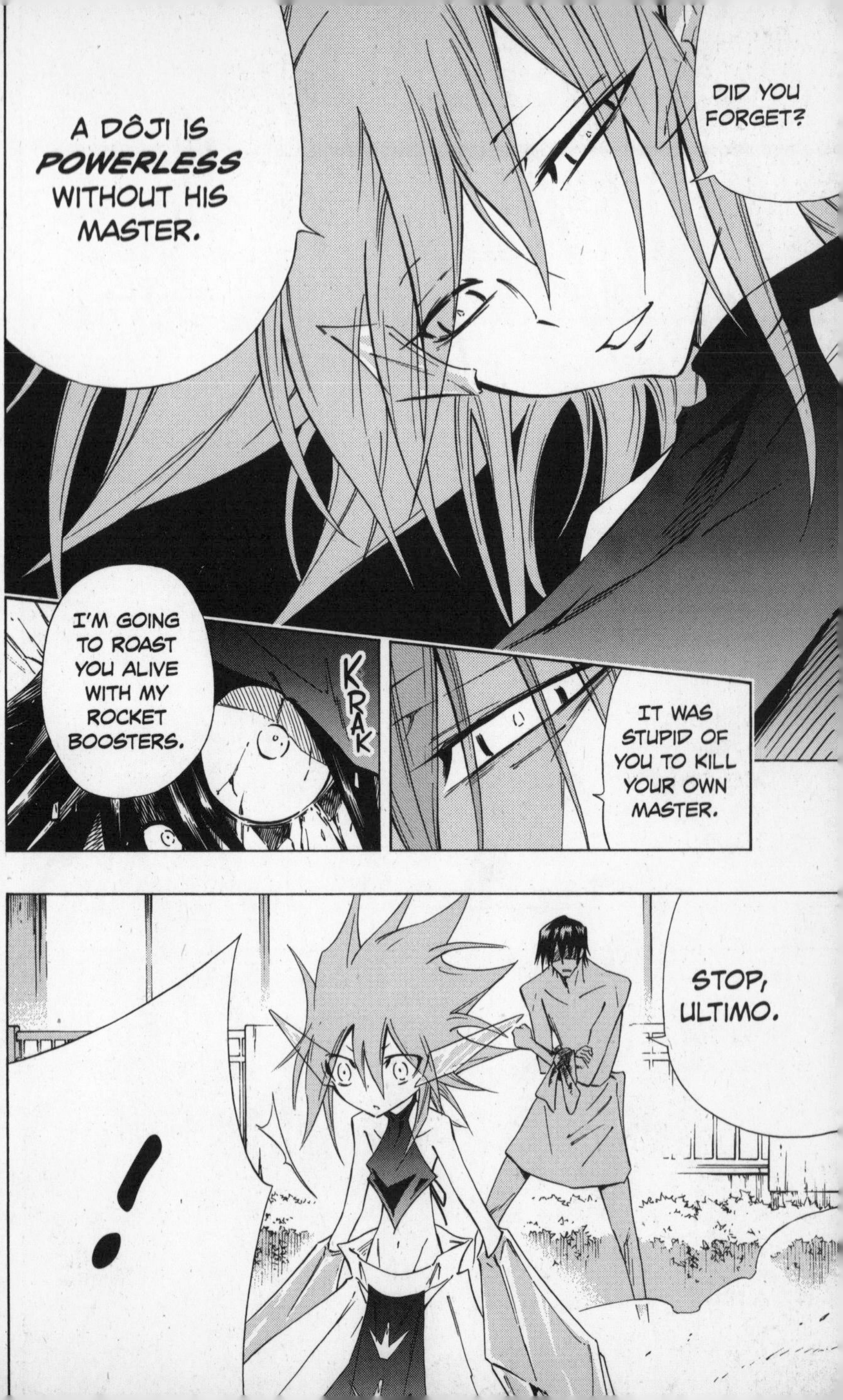
DID YOU FORGET?
A DÔJI IS *POWERLESS* WITHOUT HIS MASTER.
IT WAS STUPID OF YOU TO KILL YOUR OWN MASTER.
I'M GOING TO ROAST YOU ALIVE WITH MY ROCKET BOOSTERS.
KRAK
STOP, ULTIMO.
!

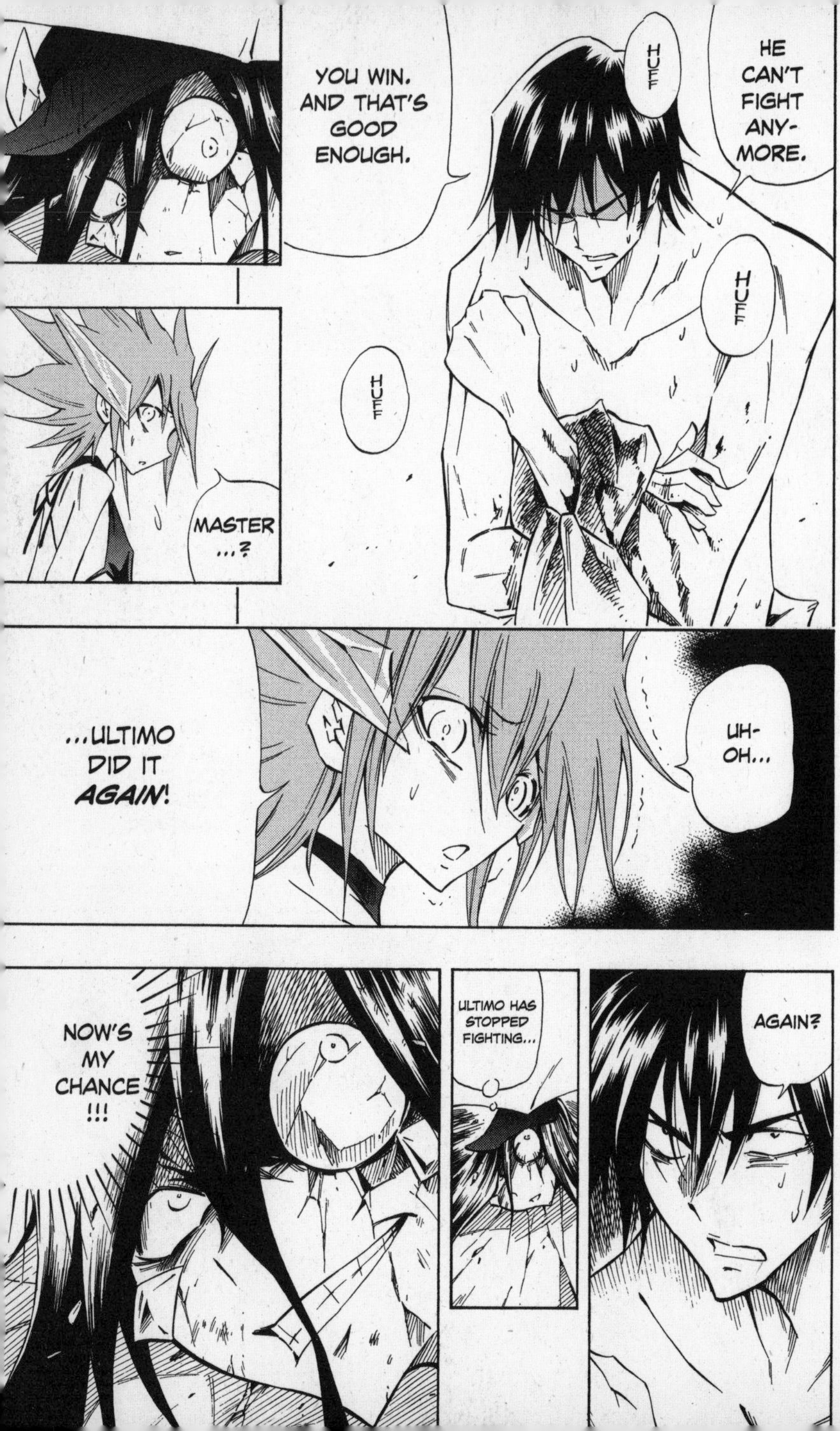
HE CAN'T FIGHT ANY-MORE.
HUFF
YOU WIN. AND THAT'S GOOD ENOUGH.
HUFF
HUFF
MASTER ...?
UH-OH...
...ULTIMO DID IT *AGAIN*!
AGAIN?
ULTIMO HAS STOPPED FIGHTING...
NOW'S MY CHANCE!!!

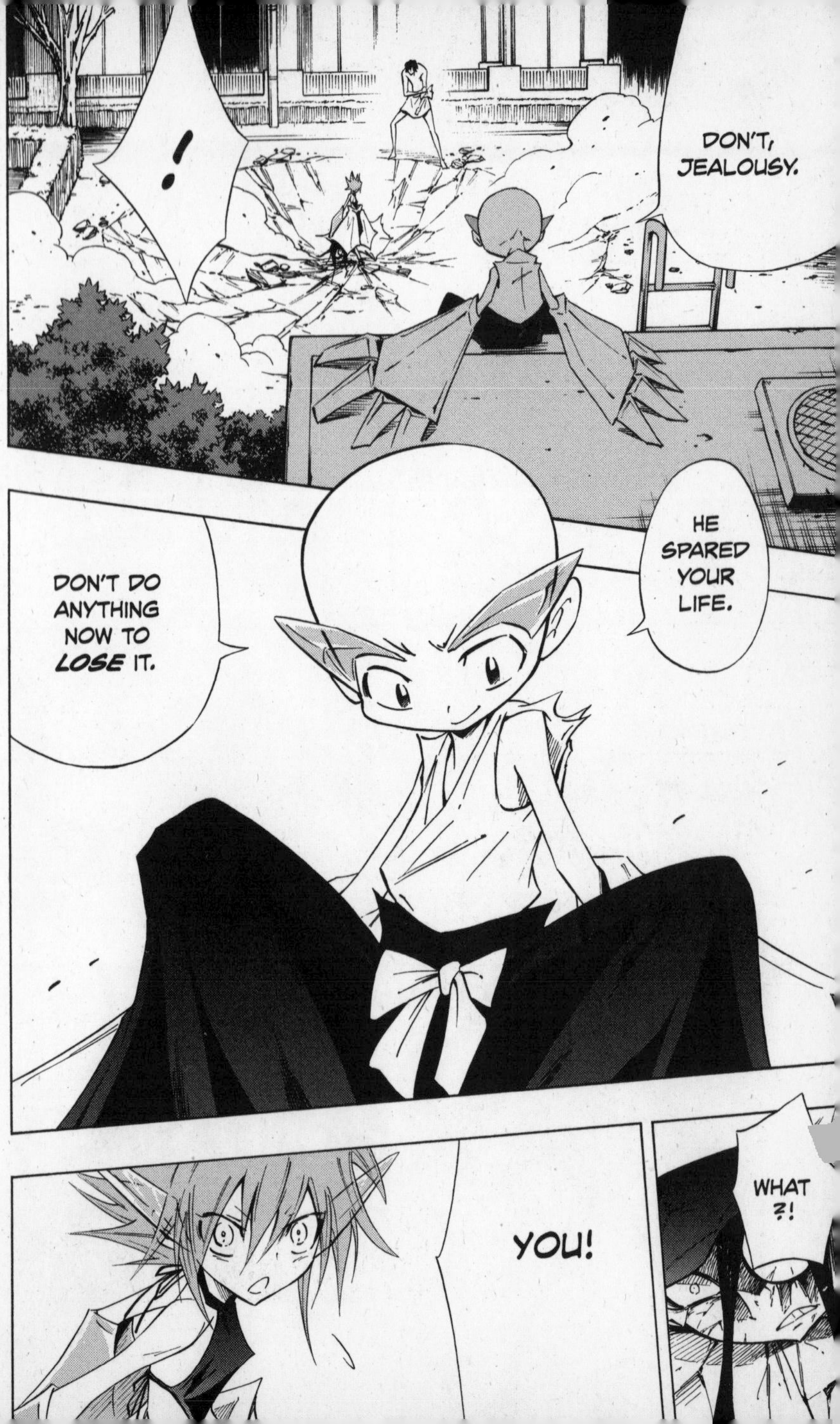
DON'T, JEALOUSY.
!
HE SPARED YOUR LIFE.
DON'T DO ANYTHING NOW TO *LOSE* IT.
WHAT?!
YOU!

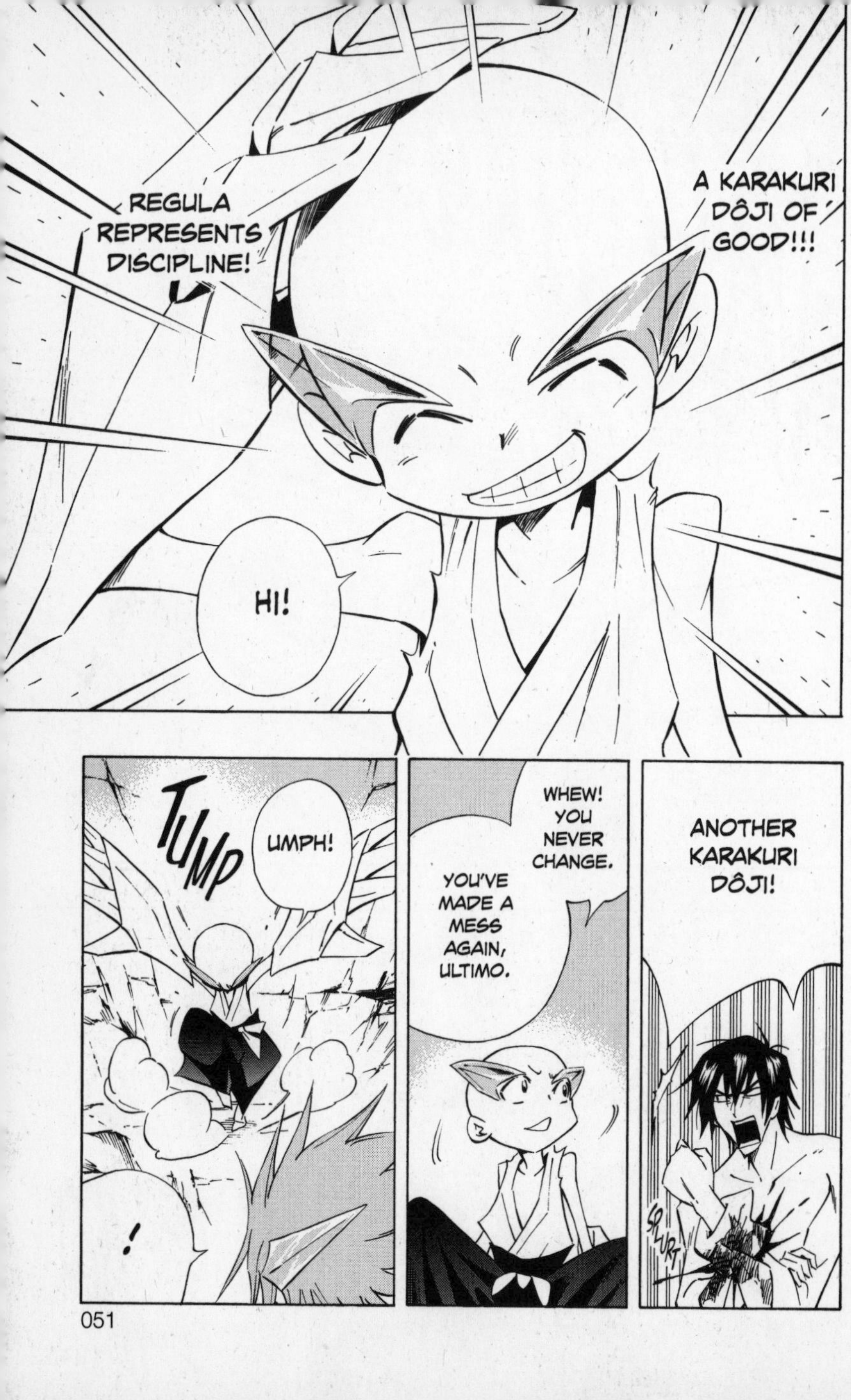
A KARAKURI DÔJI OF GOOD!!!
REGULA REPRESENTS DISCIPLINE!
HI!
ANOTHER KARAKURI DÔJI!
SPLURT
WHEW! YOU NEVER CHANGE.
YOU'VE MADE A MESS AGAIN, ULTIMO.
UMPH!
TUMP
!

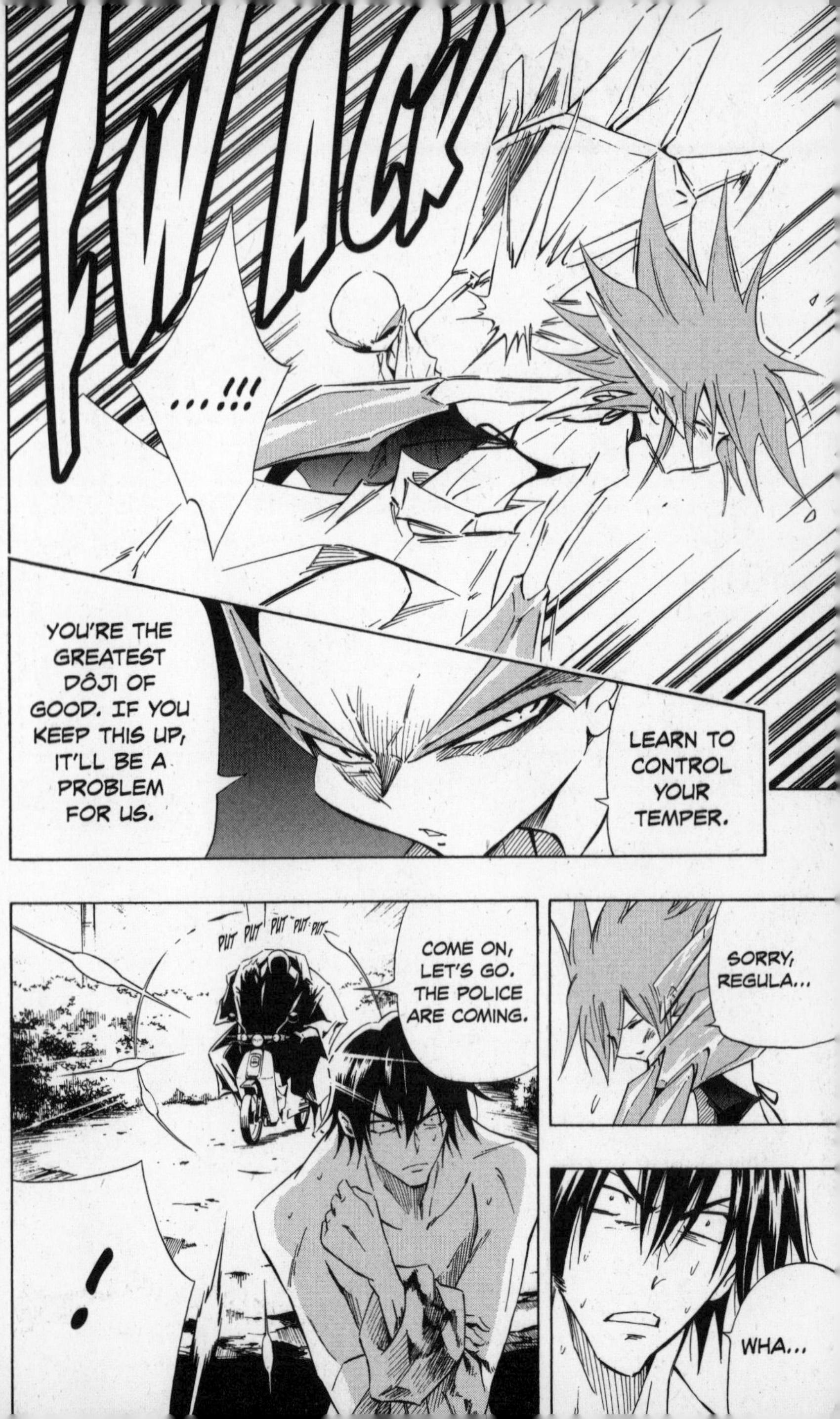
...!!!
LEARN TO CONTROL YOUR TEMPER.
YOU'RE THE GREATEST DÔJI OF GOOD. IF YOU KEEP THIS UP, IT'LL BE A PROBLEM FOR US.
SORRY, REGULA...
WHA...
PUT PUT PUT PUT PUT
COME ON, LET'S GO. THE POLICE ARE COMING.
!

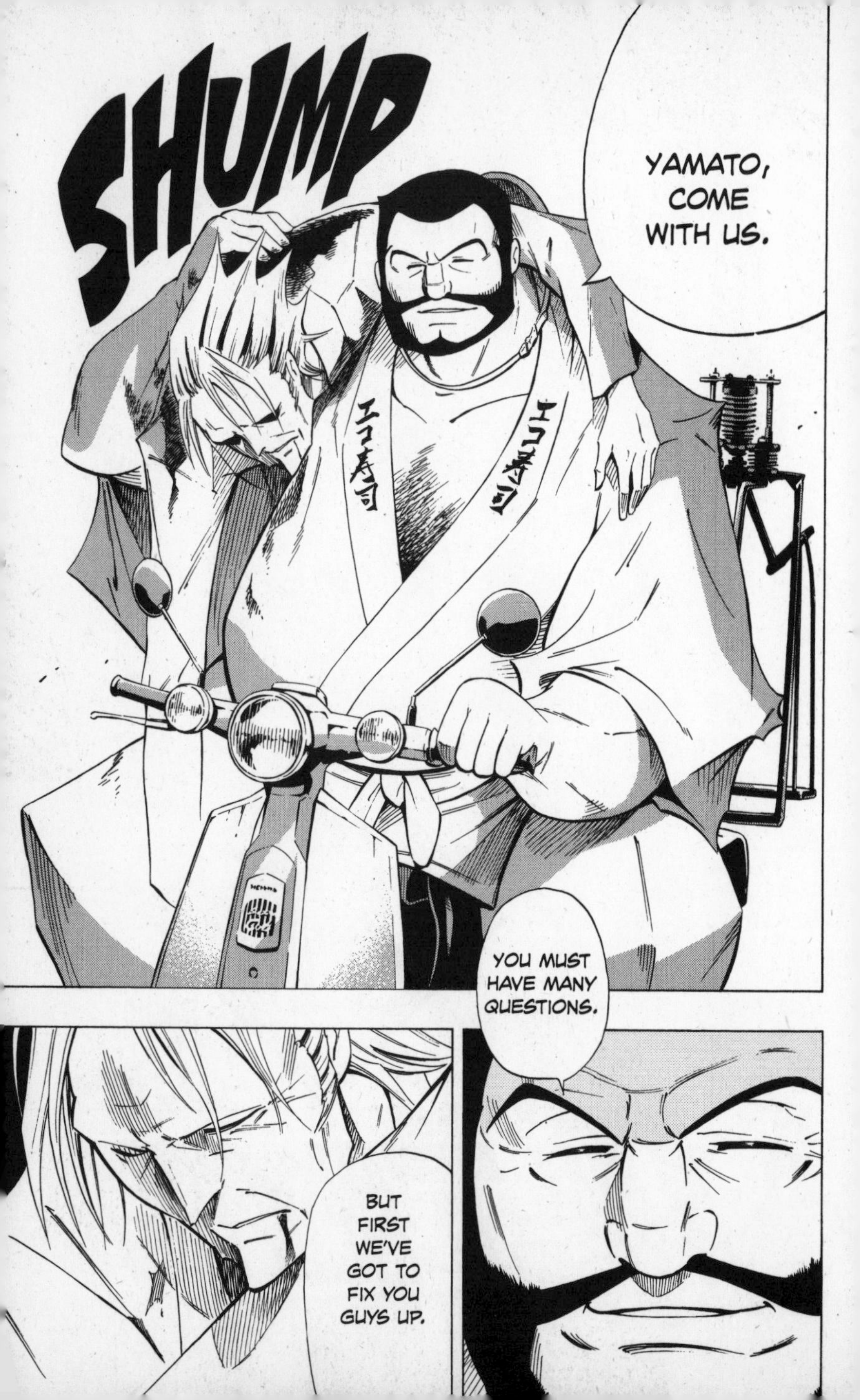
YAMATO, COME WITH US.
SHUMP
エコ寿司
エコ寿司
YOU MUST HAVE MANY QUESTIONS.
BUT FIRST WE'VE GOT TO FIX YOU GUYS UP.

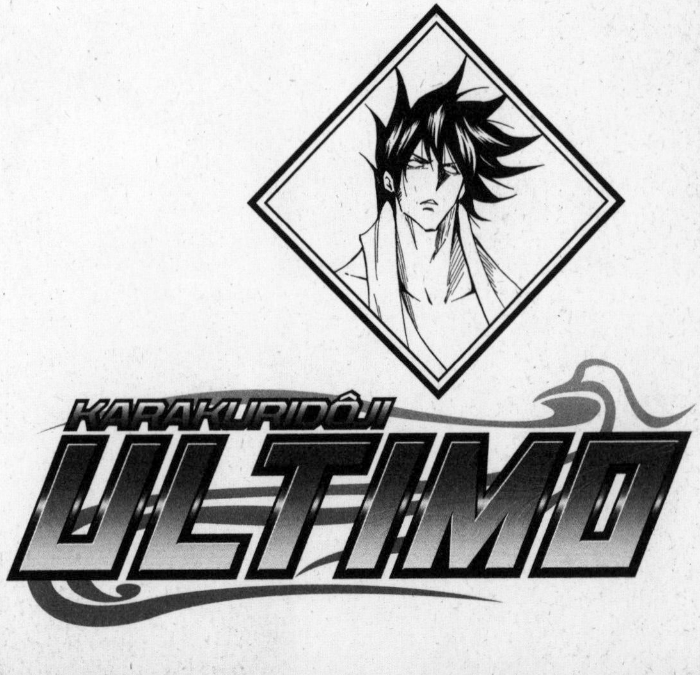

KARAKURIDÔJI
ULTIMO

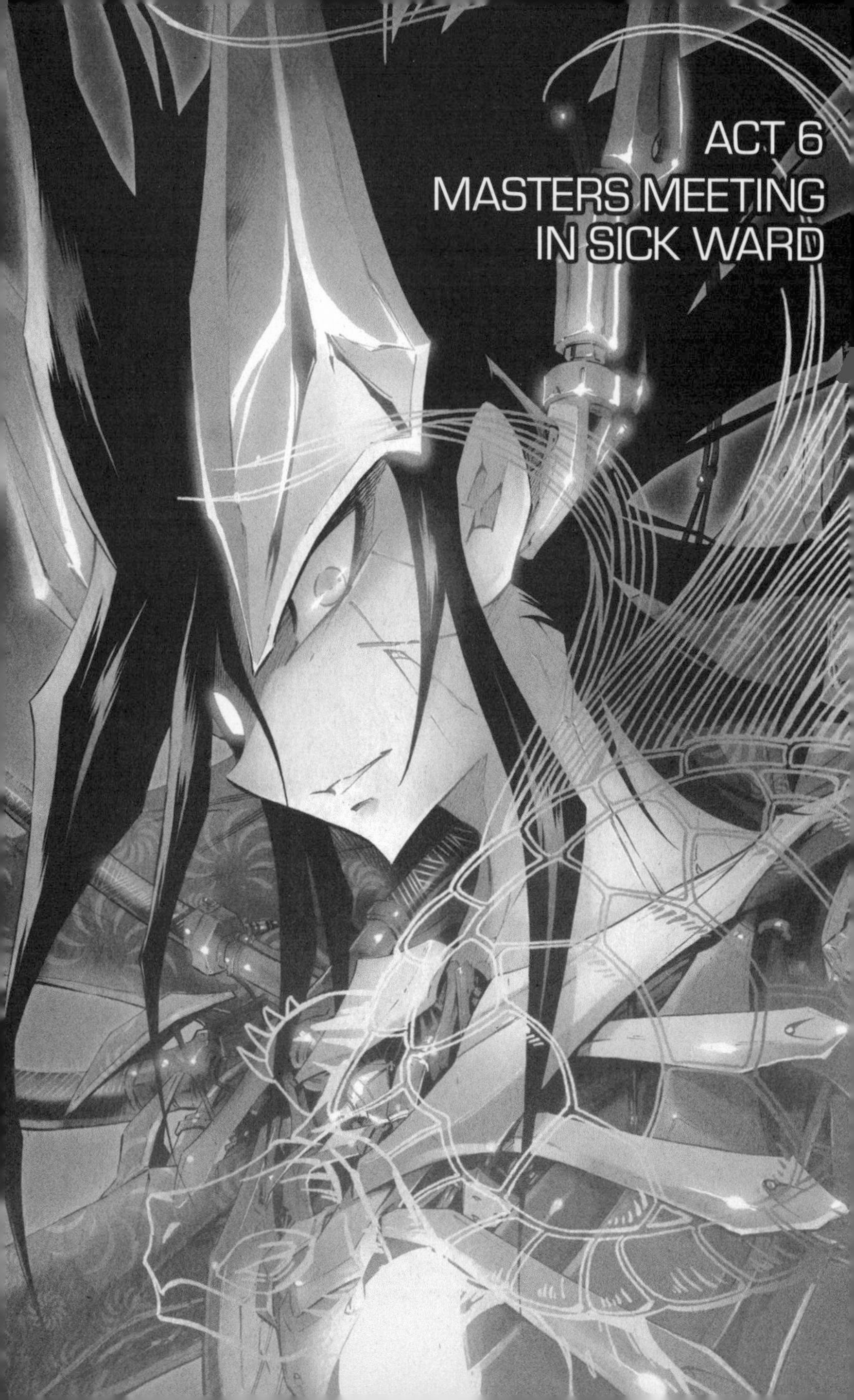
ACT 6
MASTERS MEETING
IN SICK WARD

KARAKURIDÔJI
ULTIMO

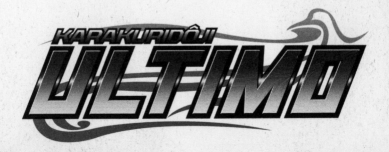

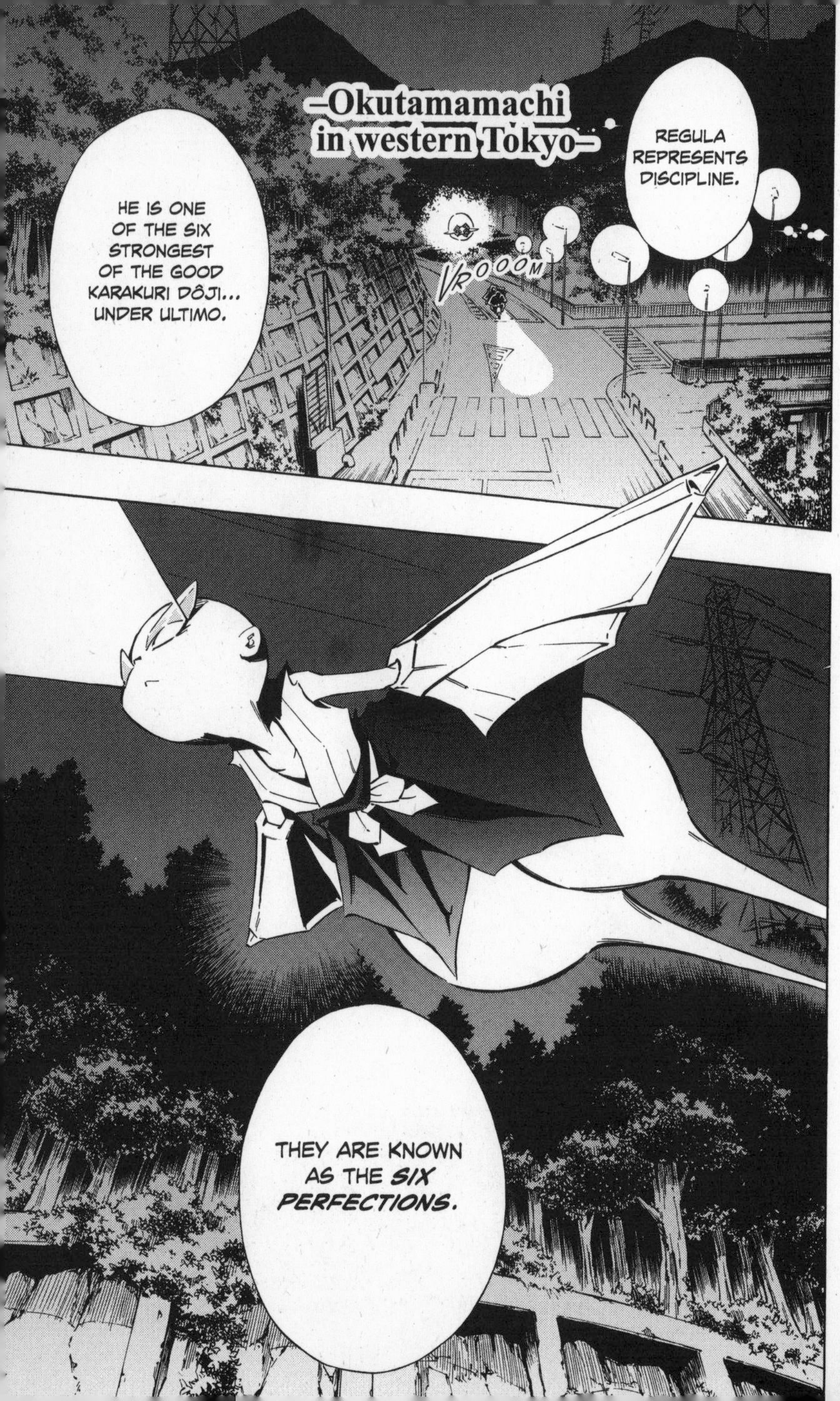
–Okutamamachi in western Tokyo–
REGULA REPRESENTS DISCIPLINE.
HE IS ONE OF THE SIX STRONGEST OF THE GOOD KARAKURI DÔJI... UNDER ULTIMO.
VROOOM
THEY ARE KNOWN AS THE *SIX PERFECTIONS*.

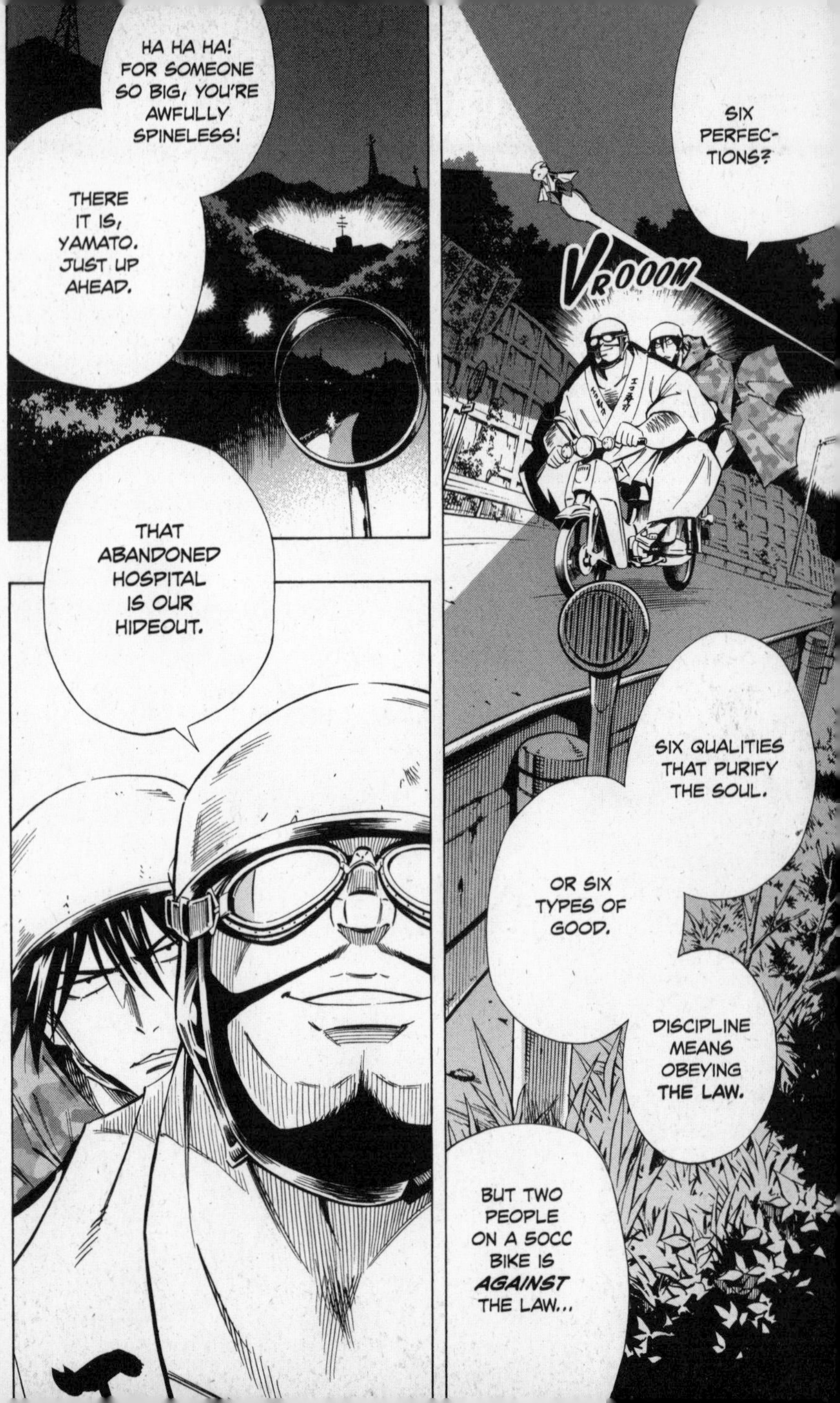
SIX PERFECTIONS?
VROOOM
SIX QUALITIES THAT PURIFY THE SOUL.
OR SIX TYPES OF GOOD.
DISCIPLINE MEANS OBEYING THE LAW.
BUT TWO PEOPLE ON A 50CC BIKE IS *AGAINST* THE LAW...
HA HA HA! FOR SOMEONE SO BIG, YOU'RE AWFULLY SPINELESS!
THERE IT IS, YAMATO. JUST UP AHEAD.
THAT ABANDONED HOSPITAL IS OUR HIDEOUT.

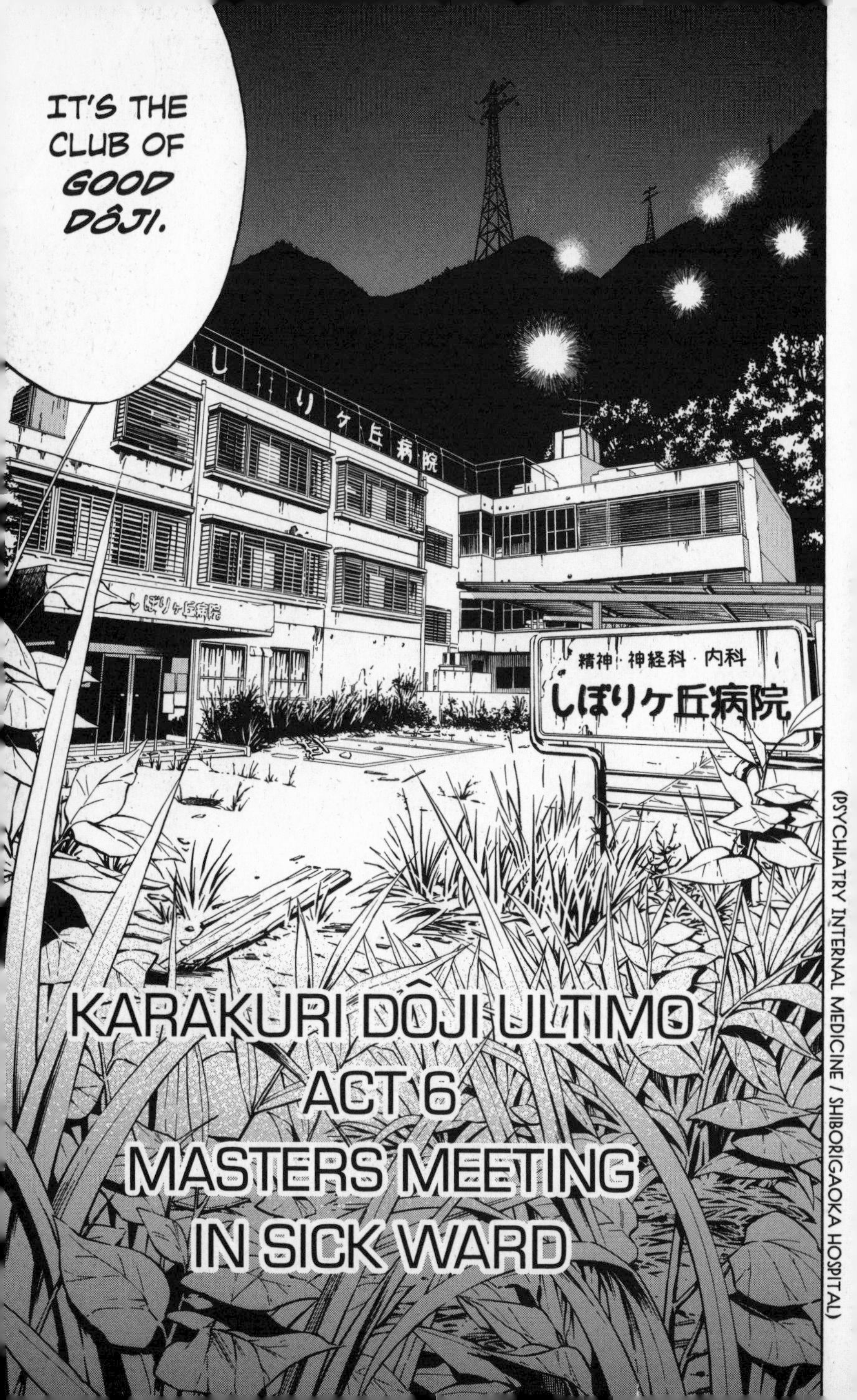

IT'S THE CLUB OF GOOD DÔJI.
しぼりヶ丘病院
精神·神経科·内科
しぼりヶ丘病院
(PSYCHIATRY INTERNAL MEDICINE / SHIBORIGAOKA HOSPITAL)
KARAKURI DÔJI ULTIMO
ACT 6
MASTERS MEETING
IN SICK WARD

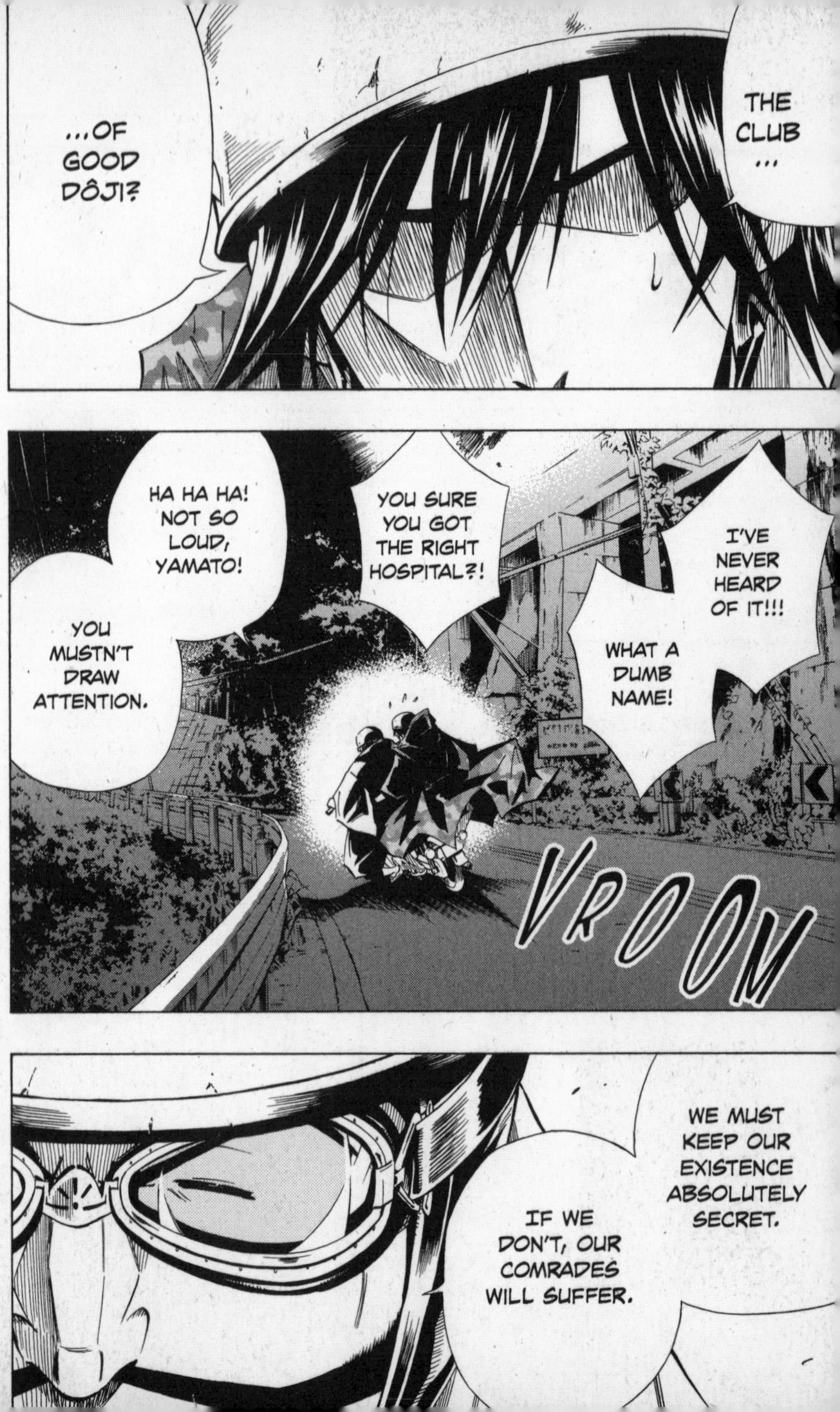
THE CLUB ...
...OF GOOD DÔJI?
I'VE NEVER HEARD OF IT!!!
WHAT A DUMB NAME!
YOU SURE YOU GOT THE RIGHT HOSPITAL?!
HA HA HA! NOT SO LOUD, YAMATO!
YOU MUSTN'T DRAW ATTENTION.
VROOM
WE MUST KEEP OUR EXISTENCE ABSOLUTELY SECRET.
IF WE DON'T, OUR COMRADES WILL SUFFER.

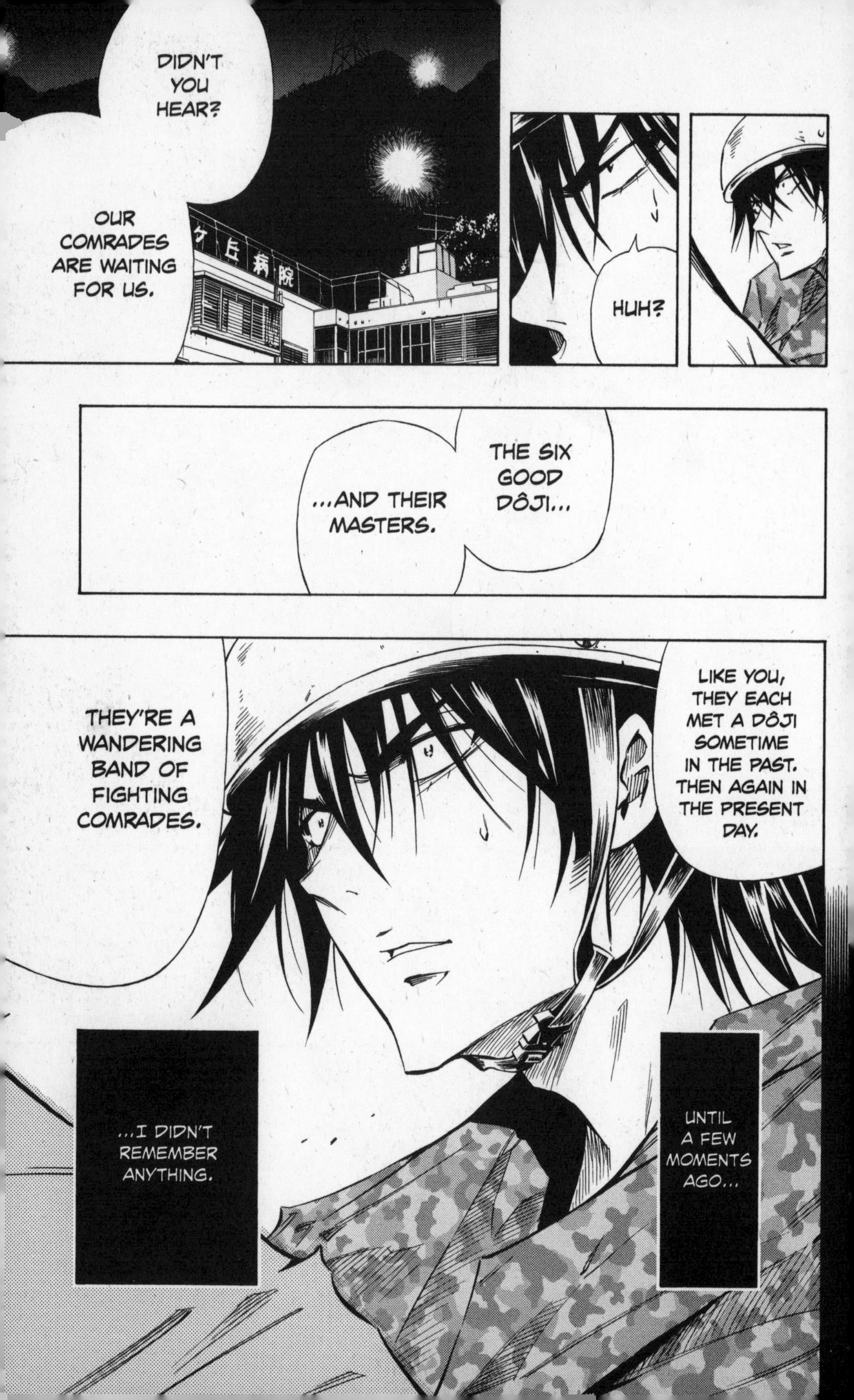
HUH?
DIDN'T YOU HEAR?
夕丘病院
OUR COMRADES ARE WAITING FOR US.
THE SIX GOOD DÔJI...
...AND THEIR MASTERS.
LIKE YOU, THEY EACH MET A DÔJI SOMETIME IN THE PAST. THEN AGAIN IN THE PRESENT DAY.
THEY'RE A WANDERING BAND OF FIGHTING COMRADES.
UNTIL A FEW MOMENTS AGO...
...I DIDN'T REMEMBER ANYTHING.

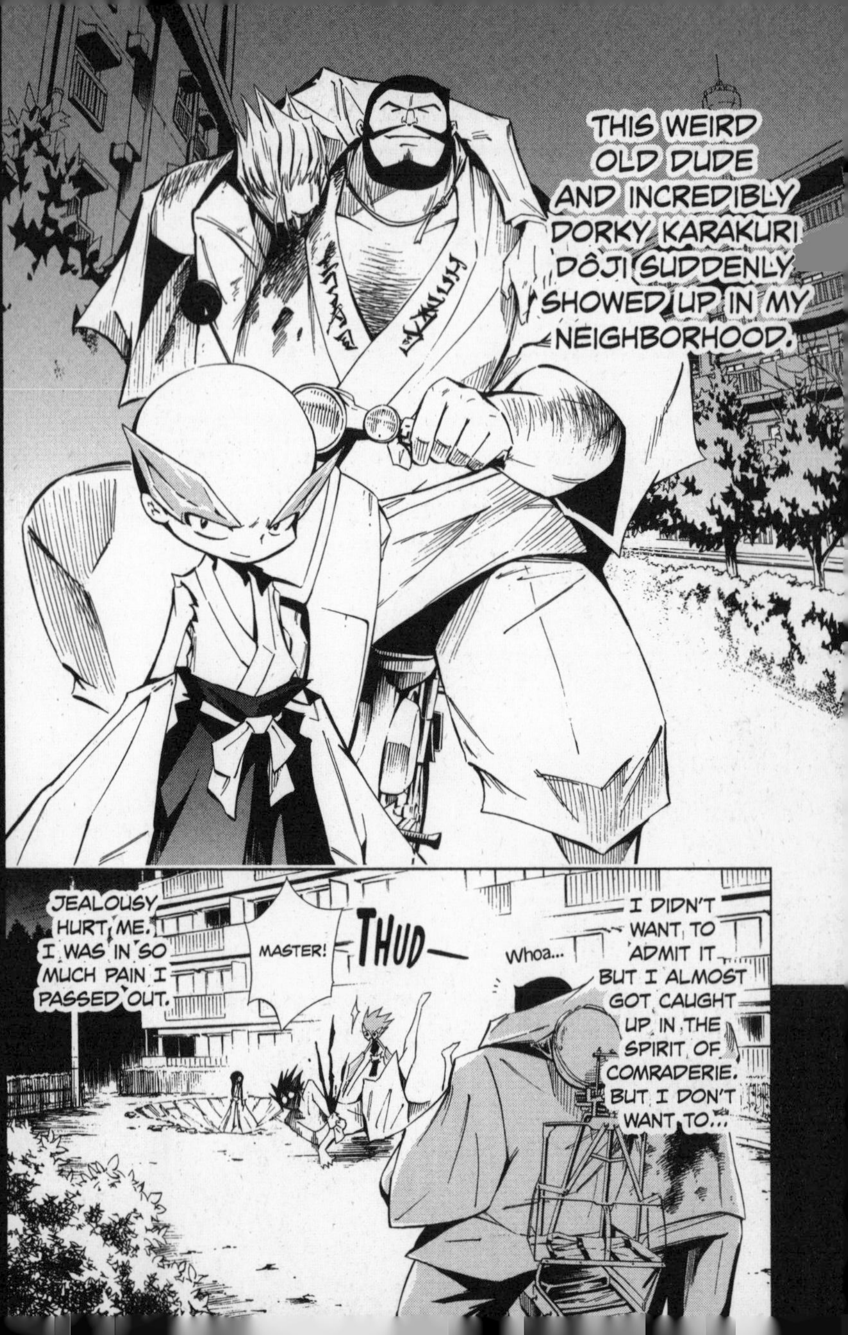
THIS WEIRD OLD DUDE AND INCREDIBLY DORKY KARAKURI DÔJI SUDDENLY SHOWED UP IN MY NEIGHBORHOOD.
I DIDN'T WANT TO ADMIT IT BUT I ALMOST GOT CAUGHT UP IN THE SPIRIT OF COMRADERIE. BUT I DON'T WANT TO...
Whoa...
THUD
MASTER!
JEALOUSY HURT ME. I WAS IN SO MUCH PAIN I PASSED OUT.

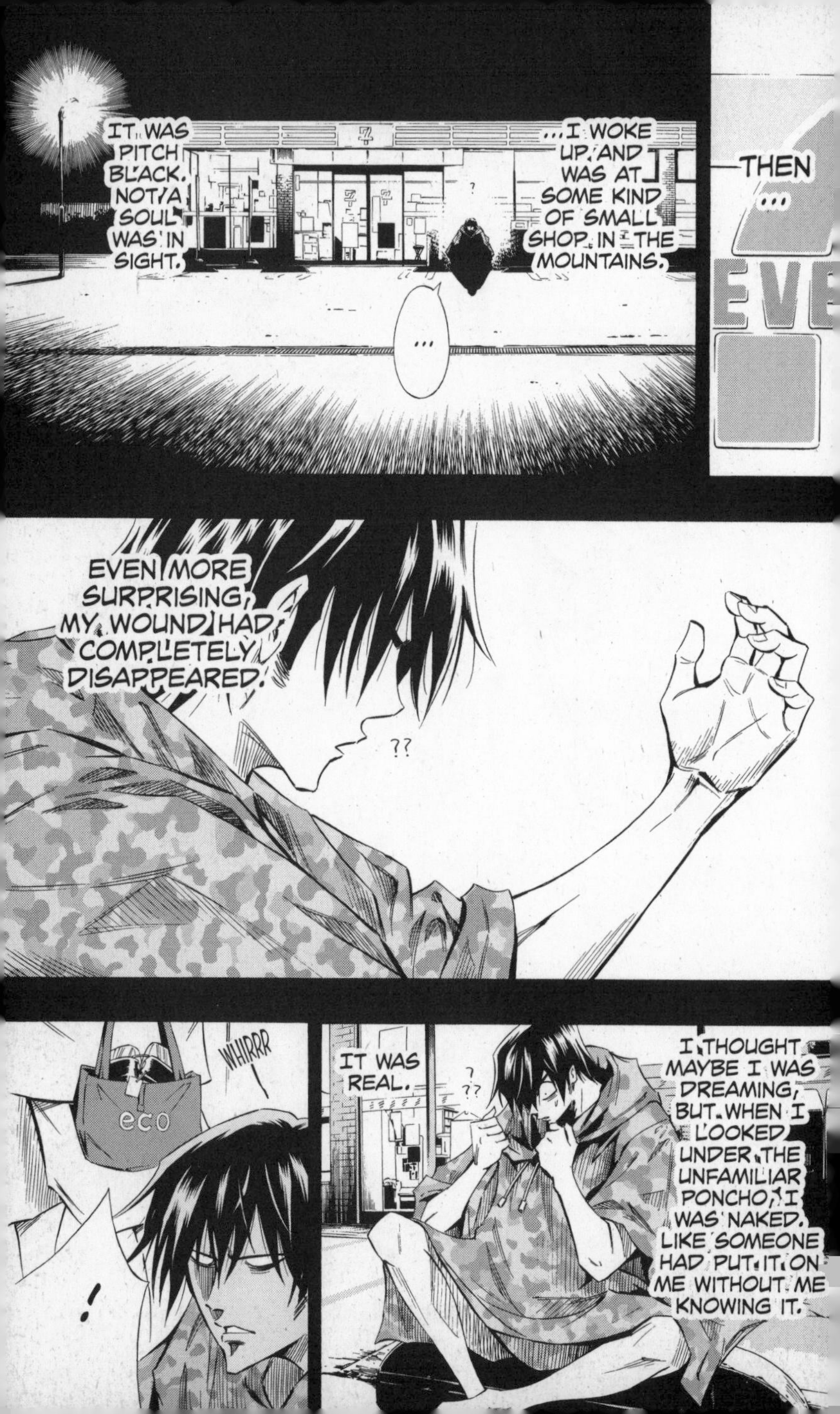
THEN...
EVE
...I WOKE UP, AND WAS AT SOME KIND OF SMALL SHOP IN THE MOUNTAINS.
IT WAS PITCH BLACK. NOT A SOUL WAS IN SIGHT.
...
EVEN MORE SURPRISING, MY WOUND HAD COMPLETELY DISAPPEARED.
??
I THOUGHT MAYBE I WAS DREAMING, BUT WHEN I LOOKED UNDER THE UNFAMILIAR PONCHO, I WAS NAKED. LIKE SOMEONE HAD PUT IT ON ME WITHOUT ME KNOWING IT.
? ??
IT WAS REAL.
WHIRRR
eco
!

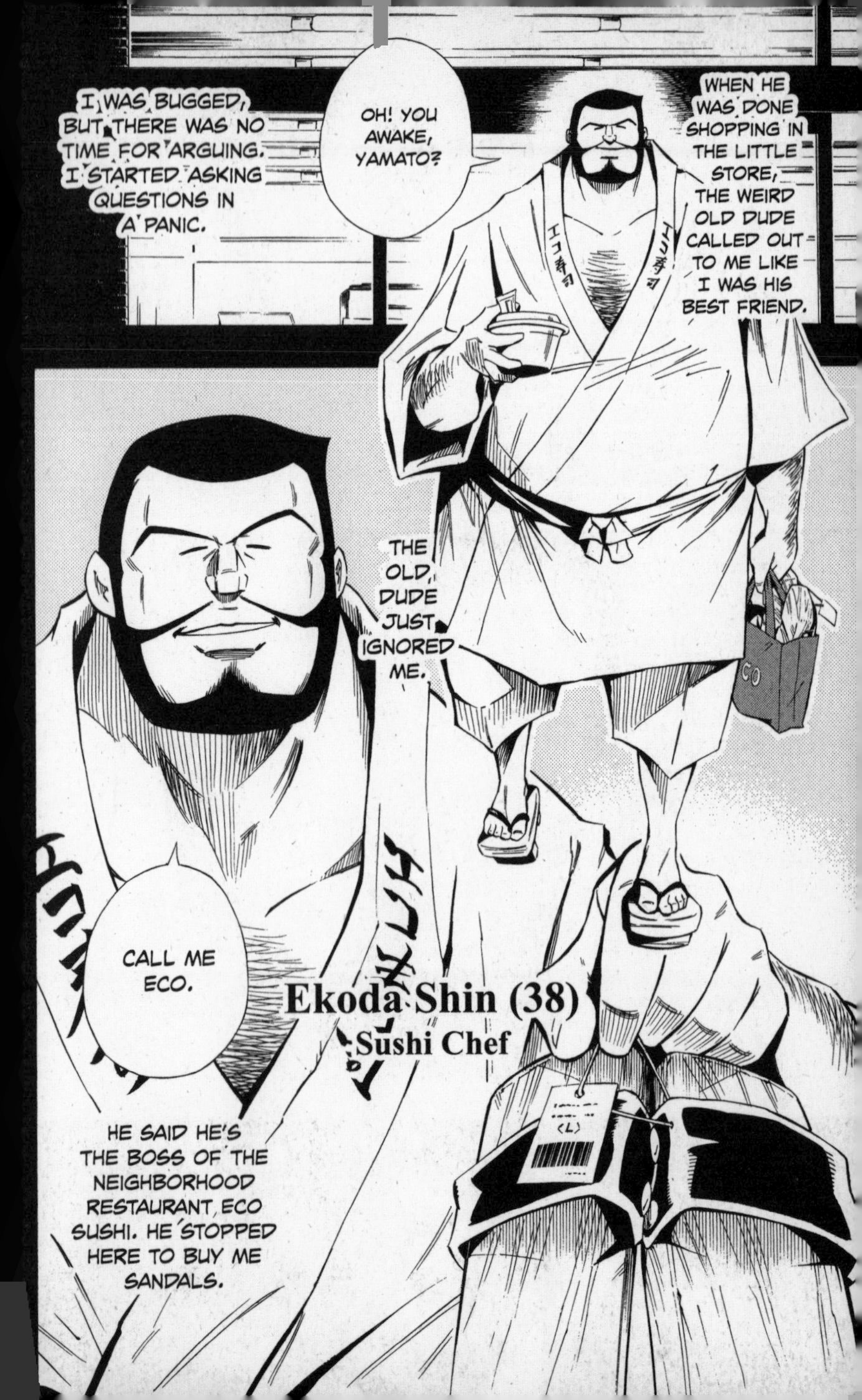
WHEN HE WAS DONE SHOPPING IN THE LITTLE STORE, THE WEIRD OLD DUDE CALLED OUT TO ME LIKE I WAS HIS BEST FRIEND.
OH! YOU AWAKE, YAMATO?
I WAS BUGGED, BUT THERE WAS NO TIME FOR ARGUING. I STARTED ASKING QUESTIONS IN A PANIC.
THE OLD DUDE JUST IGNORED ME.
CALL ME ECO.
Ekoda Shin (38)
Sushi Chef
HE SAID HE'S THE BOSS OF THE NEIGHBORHOOD RESTAURANT, ECO SUSHI. HE STOPPED HERE TO BUY ME SANDALS.

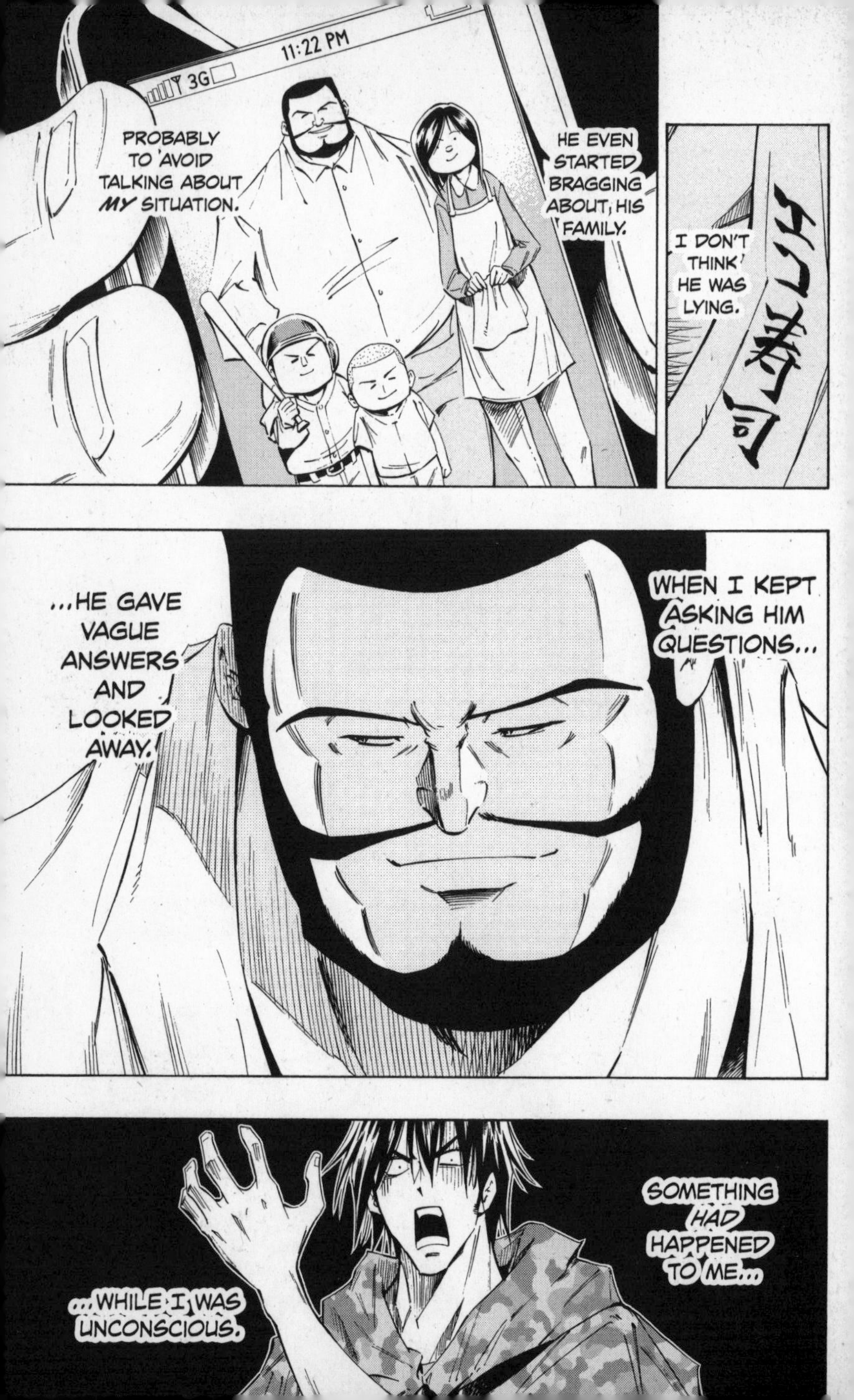
エコ寿司
I DON'T THINK HE WAS LYING.
11:22 PM
3G
HE EVEN STARTED BRAGGING ABOUT HIS FAMILY.
PROBABLY TO AVOID TALKING ABOUT MY SITUATION.
WHEN I KEPT ASKING HIM QUESTIONS...
...HE GAVE VAGUE ANSWERS AND LOOKED AWAY.
SOMETHING HAD HAPPENED TO ME...
...WHILE I WAS UNCONSCIOUS.

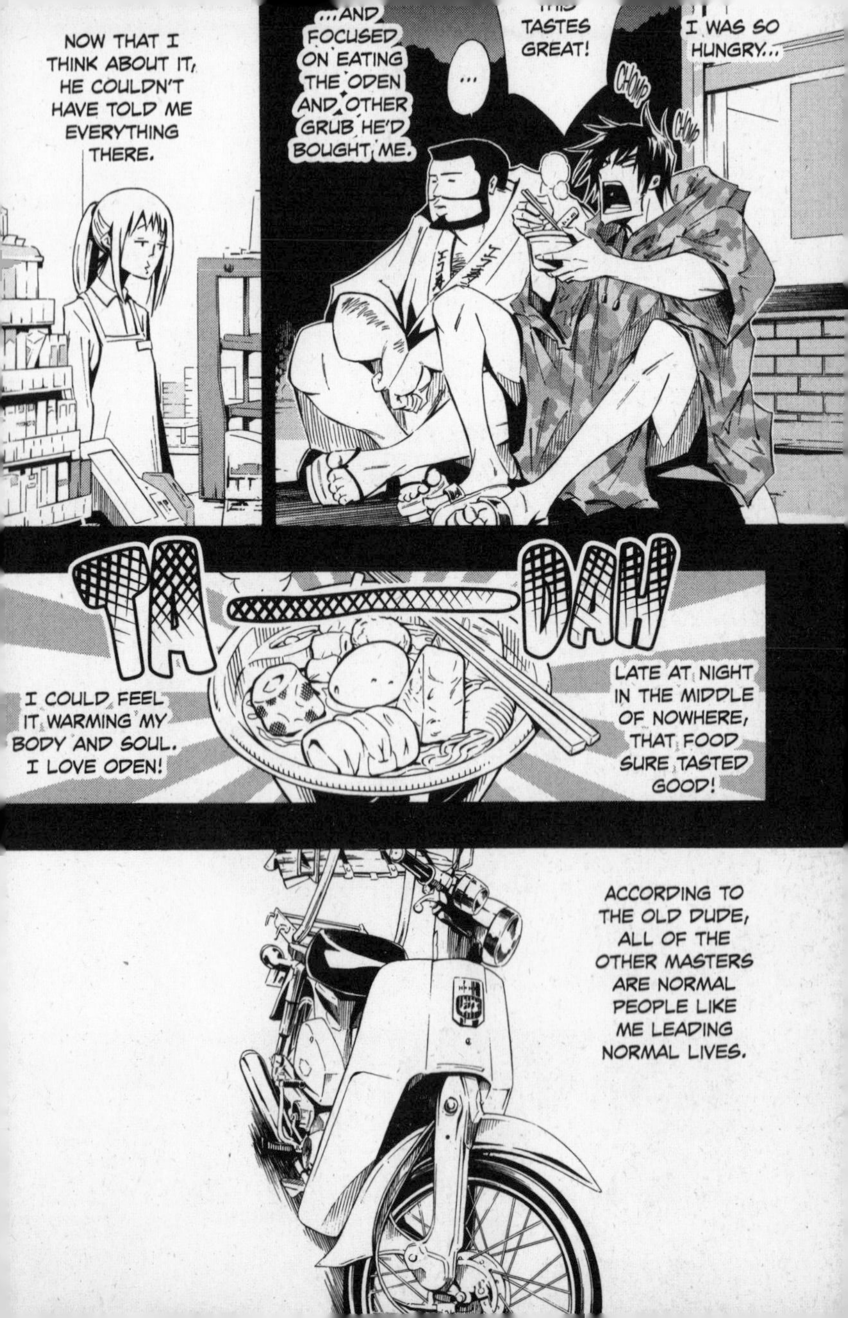
I WAS SO HUNGRY...
TASTES GREAT!
CHOMP
CHOMP
...
...AND FOCUSED ON EATING THE ODEN AND OTHER GRUB HE'D BOUGHT ME.
NOW THAT I THINK ABOUT IT, HE COULDN'T HAVE TOLD ME EVERYTHING THERE.
LATE AT NIGHT IN THE MIDDLE OF NOWHERE, THAT FOOD SURE TASTED GOOD!
TA—DAH
I COULD FEEL IT WARMING MY BODY AND SOUL. I LOVE ODEN!
ACCORDING TO THE OLD DUDE, ALL OF THE OTHER MASTERS ARE NORMAL PEOPLE LIKE ME LEADING NORMAL LIVES.

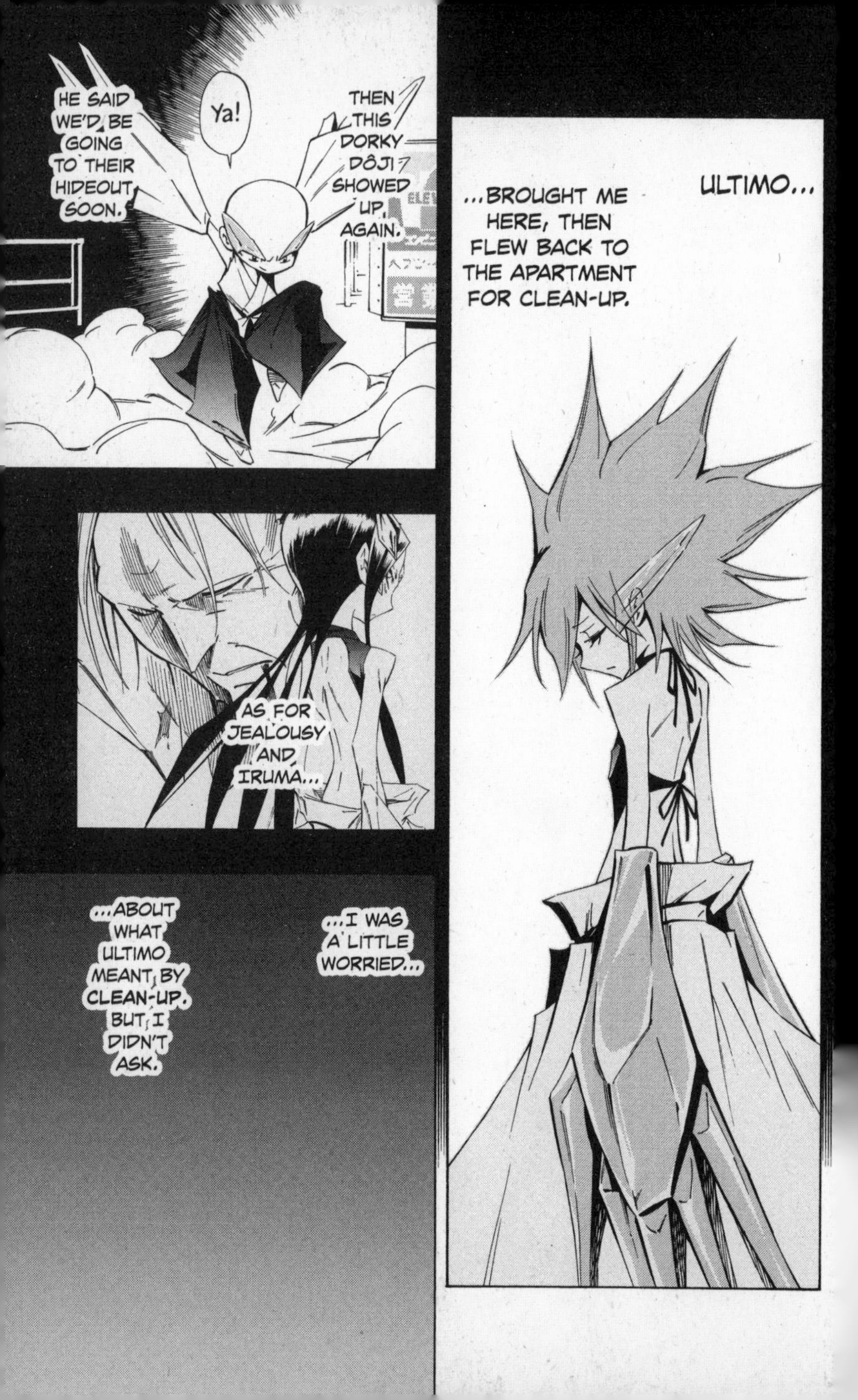
ULTIMO...
...BROUGHT ME HERE, THEN FLEW BACK TO THE APARTMENT FOR CLEAN-UP.
THEN THIS DORKY DÔJI SHOWED UP, AGAIN.
Ya!
HE SAID WE'D BE GOING TO THEIR HIDEOUT SOON.
AS FOR JEALOUSY AND IRUMA...
...I WAS A LITTLE WORRIED...
...ABOUT WHAT ULTIMO MEANT BY CLEAN-UP. BUT I DIDN'T ASK.

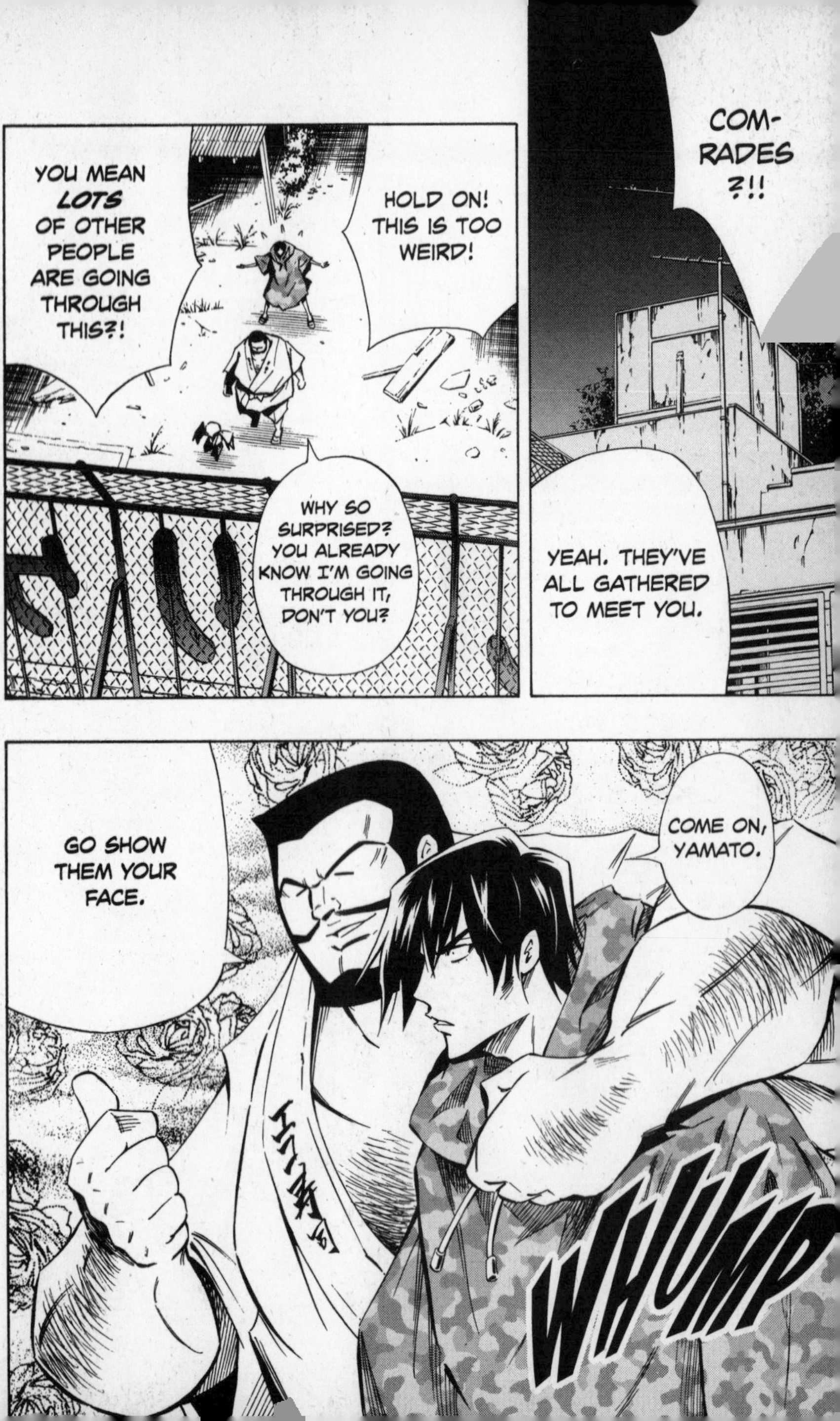
COM-RADES ?!!
YEAH. THEY'VE ALL GATHERED TO MEET YOU.
HOLD ON! THIS IS TOO WEIRD!
YOU MEAN *LOTS* OF OTHER PEOPLE ARE GOING THROUGH THIS?!
WHY SO SURPRISED? YOU ALREADY KNOW I'M GOING THROUGH IT, DON'T YOU?
COME ON, YAMATO.
GO SHOW THEM YOUR FACE.
WHUMP

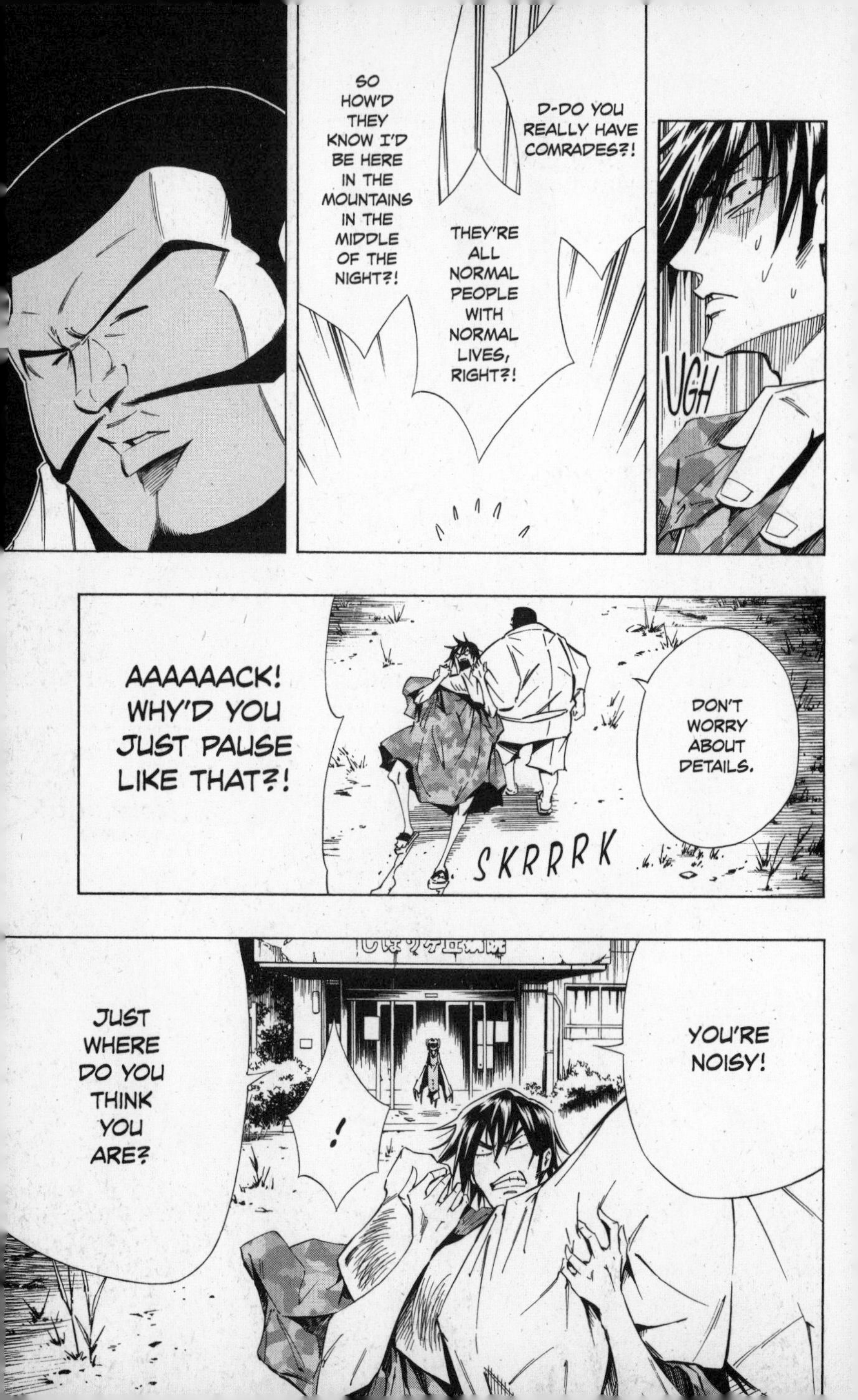
UGH
D-DO YOU REALLY HAVE COMRADES?!
THEY'RE ALL NORMAL PEOPLE WITH NORMAL LIVES, RIGHT?!
SO HOW'D THEY KNOW I'D BE HERE IN THE MOUNTAINS IN THE MIDDLE OF THE NIGHT?!
DON'T WORRY ABOUT DETAILS.
SKRRRK
AAAAAACK! WHY'D YOU JUST PAUSE LIKE THAT?!
YOU'RE NOISY!
!
JUST WHERE DO YOU THINK YOU ARE?

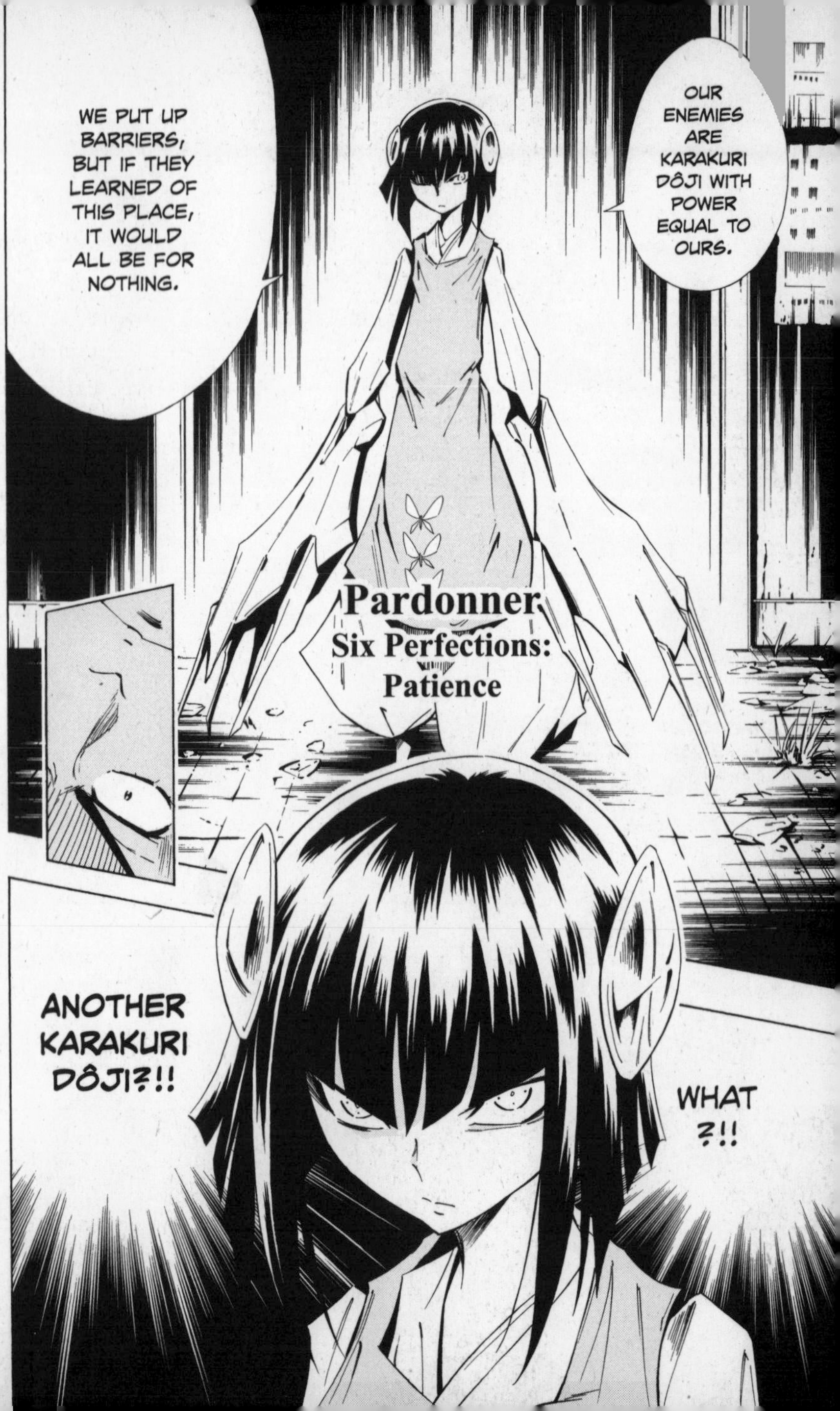
OUR ENEMIES ARE KARAKURI DÔJI WITH POWER EQUAL TO OURS.
WE PUT UP BARRIERS, BUT IF THEY LEARNED OF THIS PLACE, IT WOULD ALL BE FOR NOTHING.
Pardonner
Six Perfections: Patience
WHAT ?!!
ANOTHER KARAKURI DÔJI?!!

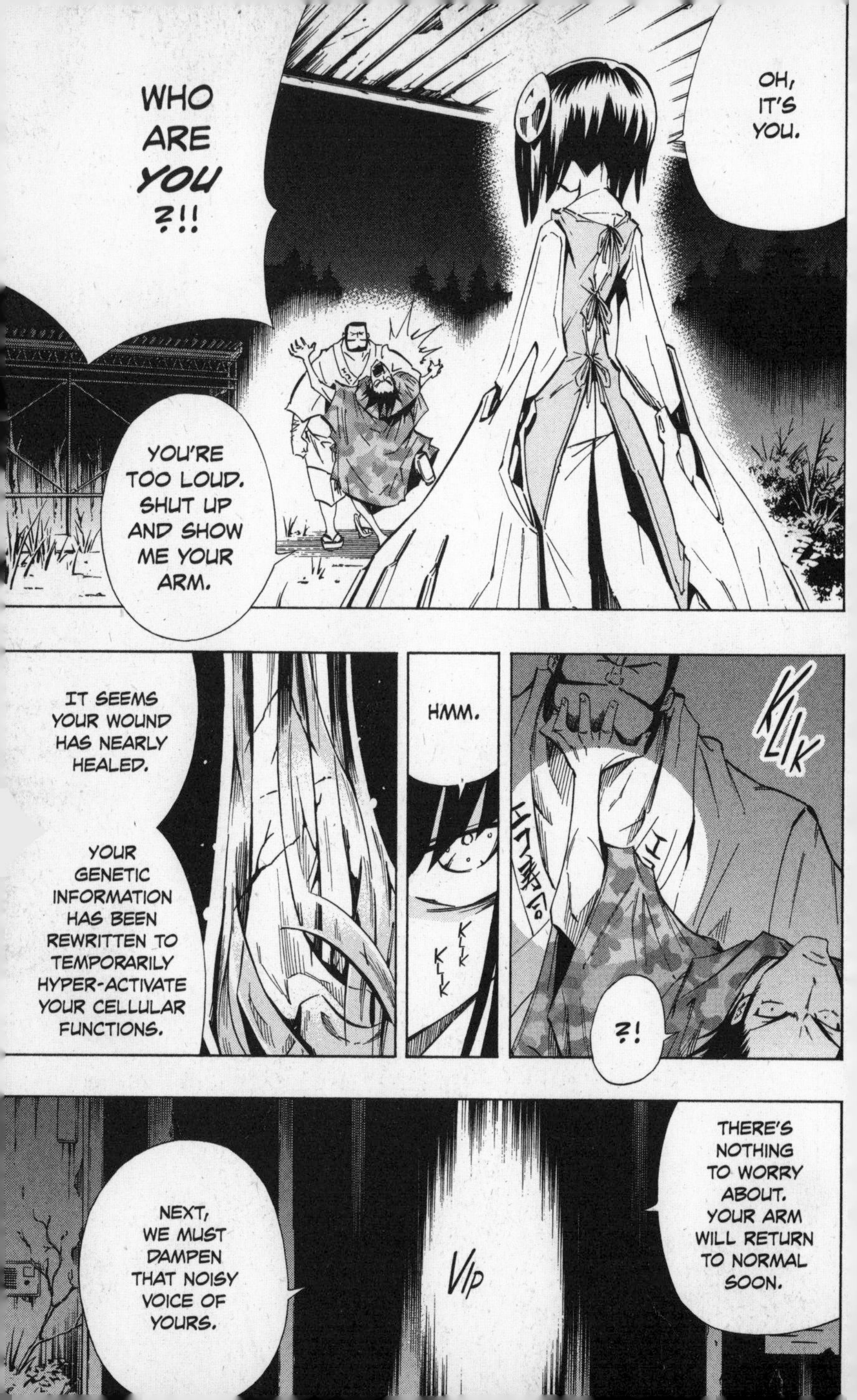
OH, IT'S YOU.
WHO ARE YOU ?!!
YOU'RE TOO LOUD. SHUT UP AND SHOW ME YOUR ARM.
KLIK
?!
HMM.
KLIK KLIK
IT SEEMS YOUR WOUND HAS NEARLY HEALED.
YOUR GENETIC INFORMATION HAS BEEN REWRITTEN TO TEMPORARILY HYPER-ACTIVATE YOUR CELLULAR FUNCTIONS.
THERE'S NOTHING TO WORRY ABOUT. YOUR ARM WILL RETURN TO NORMAL SOON.
VIP
NEXT, WE MUST DAMPEN THAT NOISY VOICE OF YOURS.

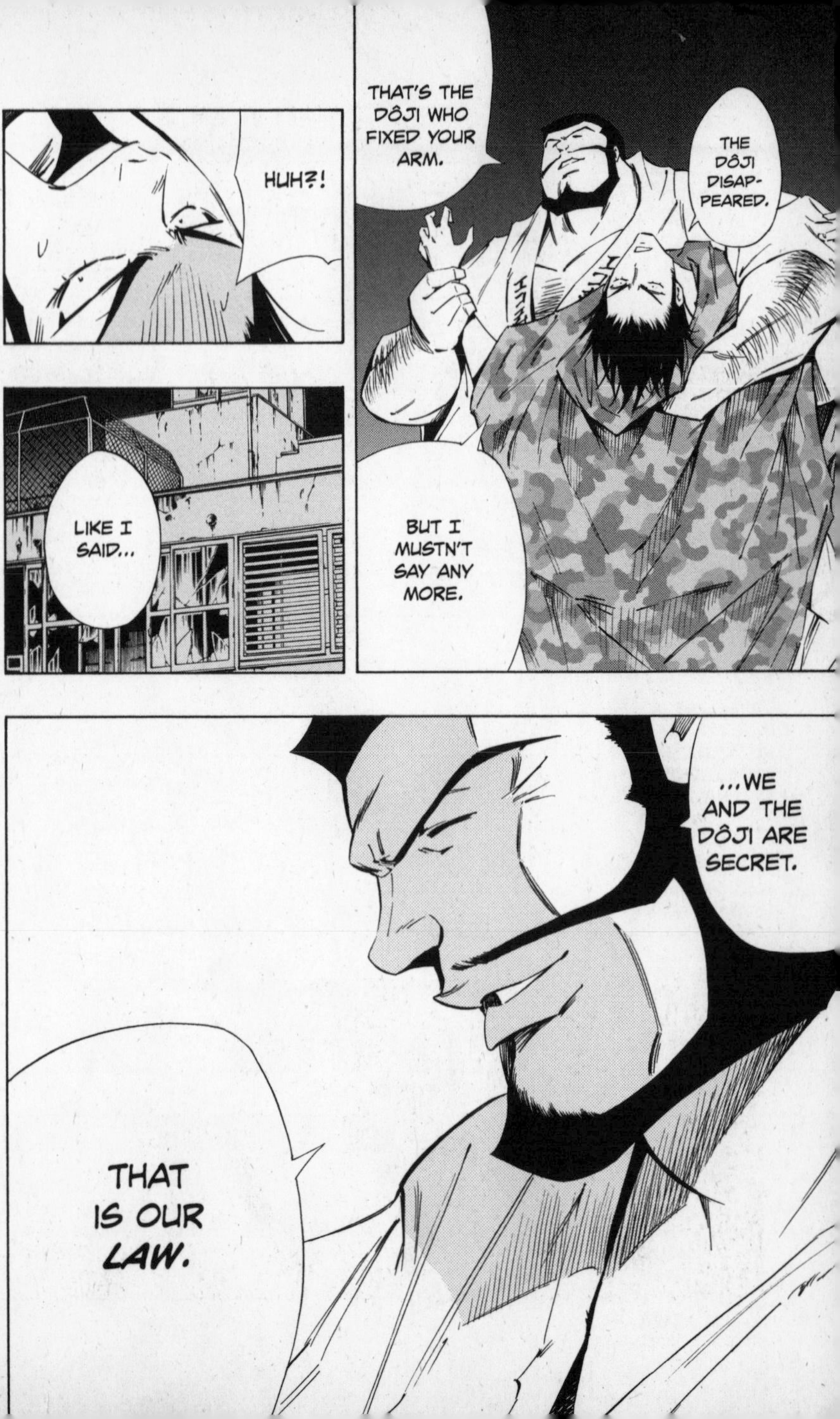
THE DÔJI DISAPPEARED.
THAT'S THE DÔJI WHO FIXED YOUR ARM.
BUT I MUSTN'T SAY ANY MORE.
HUH?!
LIKE I SAID...
...WE AND THE DÔJI ARE SECRET.
THAT IS OUR *LAW*.

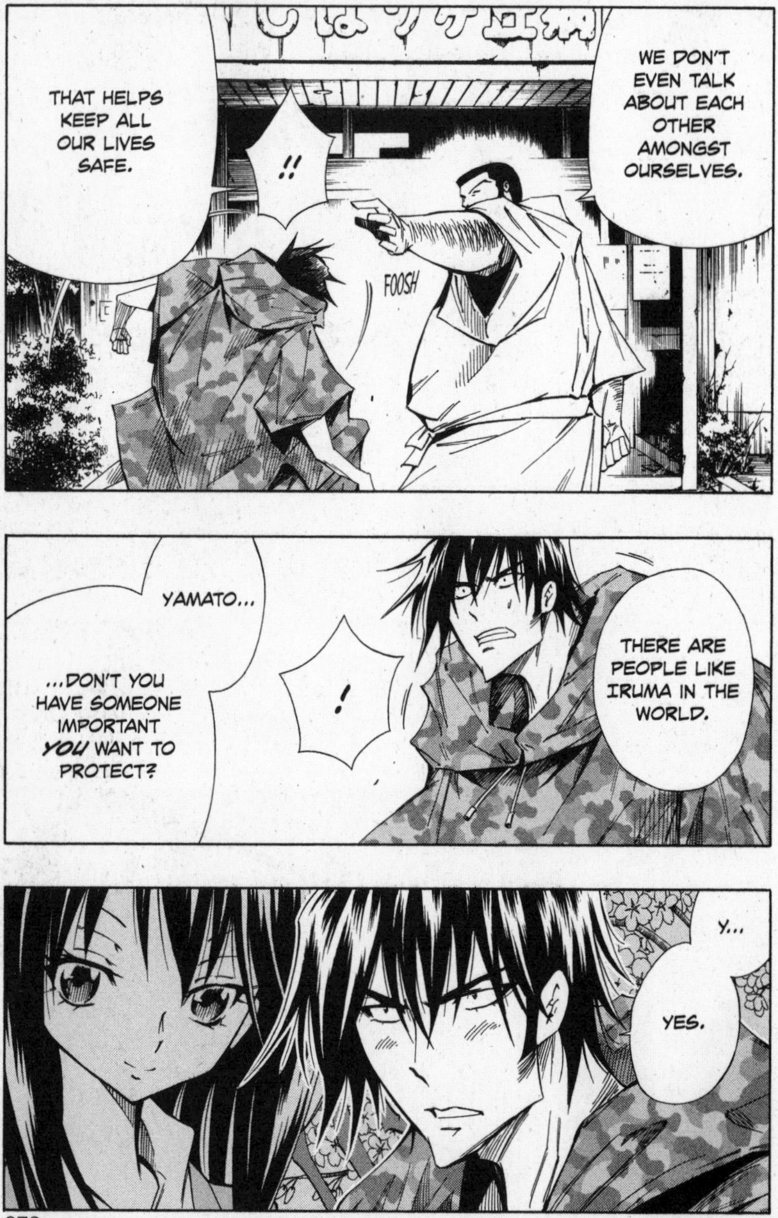

WE DON'T EVEN TALK ABOUT EACH OTHER AMONGST OURSELVES.
THAT HELPS KEEP ALL OUR LIVES SAFE.
!!
FOOSH
THERE ARE PEOPLE LIKE IRUMA IN THE WORLD.
YAMATO...
!
...DON'T YOU HAVE SOMEONE IMPORTANT *YOU* WANT TO PROTECT?
Y...
YES.

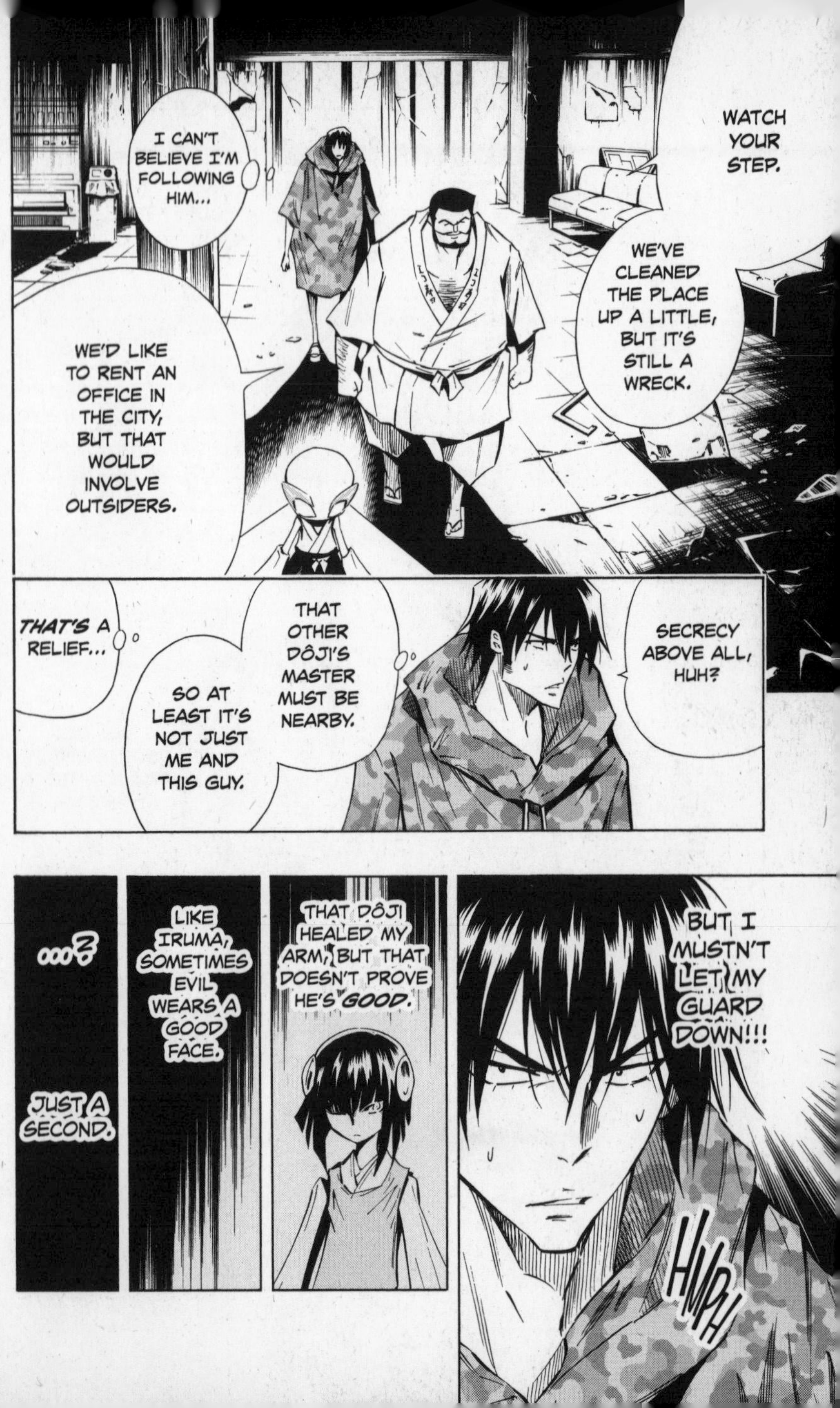
WATCH YOUR STEP.
WE'VE CLEANED THE PLACE UP A LITTLE, BUT IT'S STILL A WRECK.
I CAN'T BELIEVE I'M FOLLOWING HIM...
WE'D LIKE TO RENT AN OFFICE IN THE CITY, BUT THAT WOULD INVOLVE OUTSIDERS.
SECRECY ABOVE ALL, HUH?
THAT OTHER DÔJI'S MASTER MUST BE NEARBY.
SO AT LEAST IT'S NOT JUST ME AND THIS GUY.
THAT'S A RELIEF...
BUT I MUSTN'T LET MY GUARD DOWN!!!
HMPH!
THAT DÔJI HEALED MY ARM, BUT THAT DOESN'T PROVE HE'S *GOOD*.
LIKE IRUMA, SOMETIMES EVIL WEARS A GOOD FACE.
...?
JUST A SECOND.

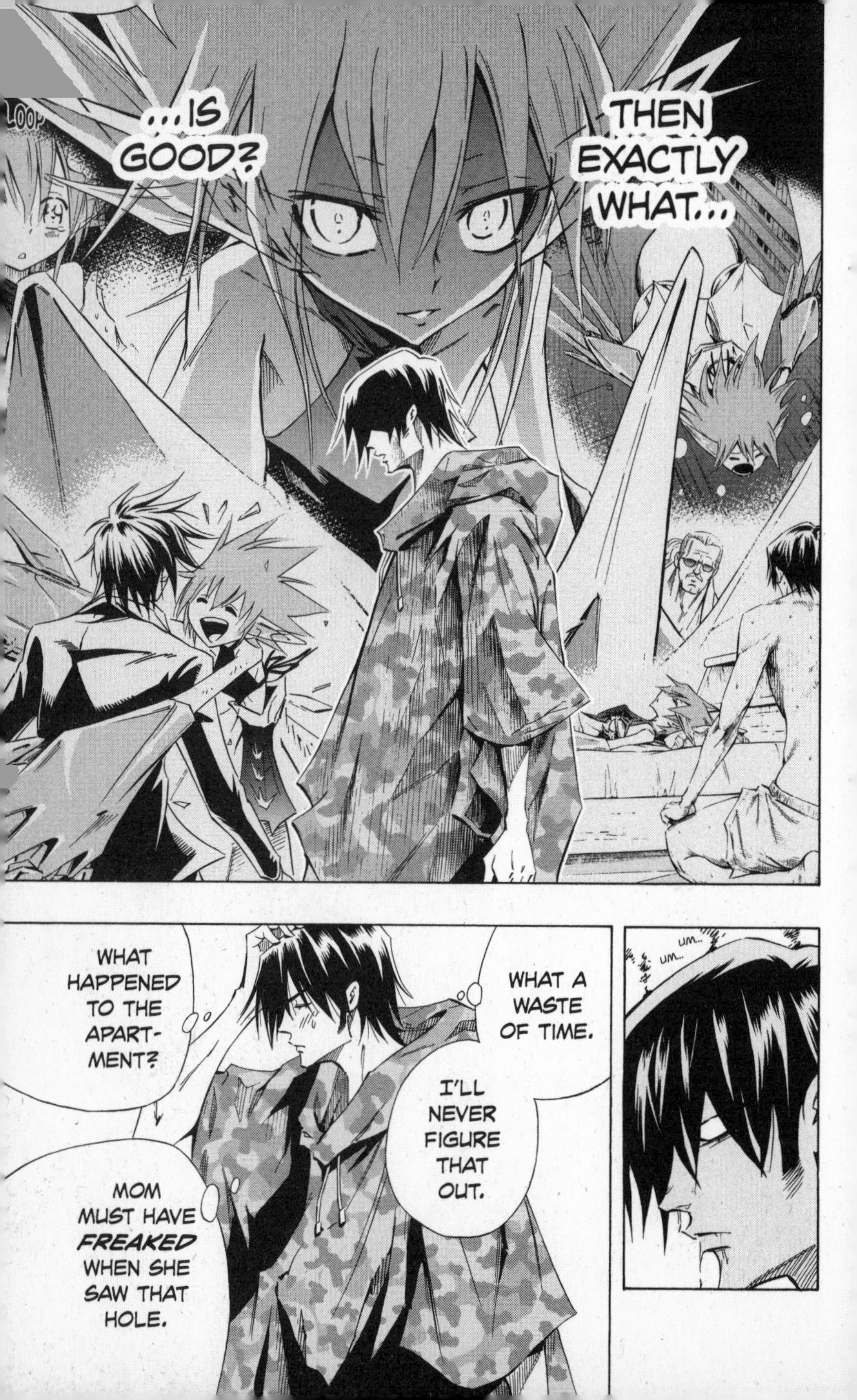
THEN EXACTLY WHAT...
...IS GOOD?
LOOP
um... um...
WHAT A WASTE OF TIME.
I'LL NEVER FIGURE THAT OUT.
WHAT HAPPENED TO THE APARTMENT?
MOM MUST HAVE *FREAKED* WHEN SHE SAW THAT HOLE.

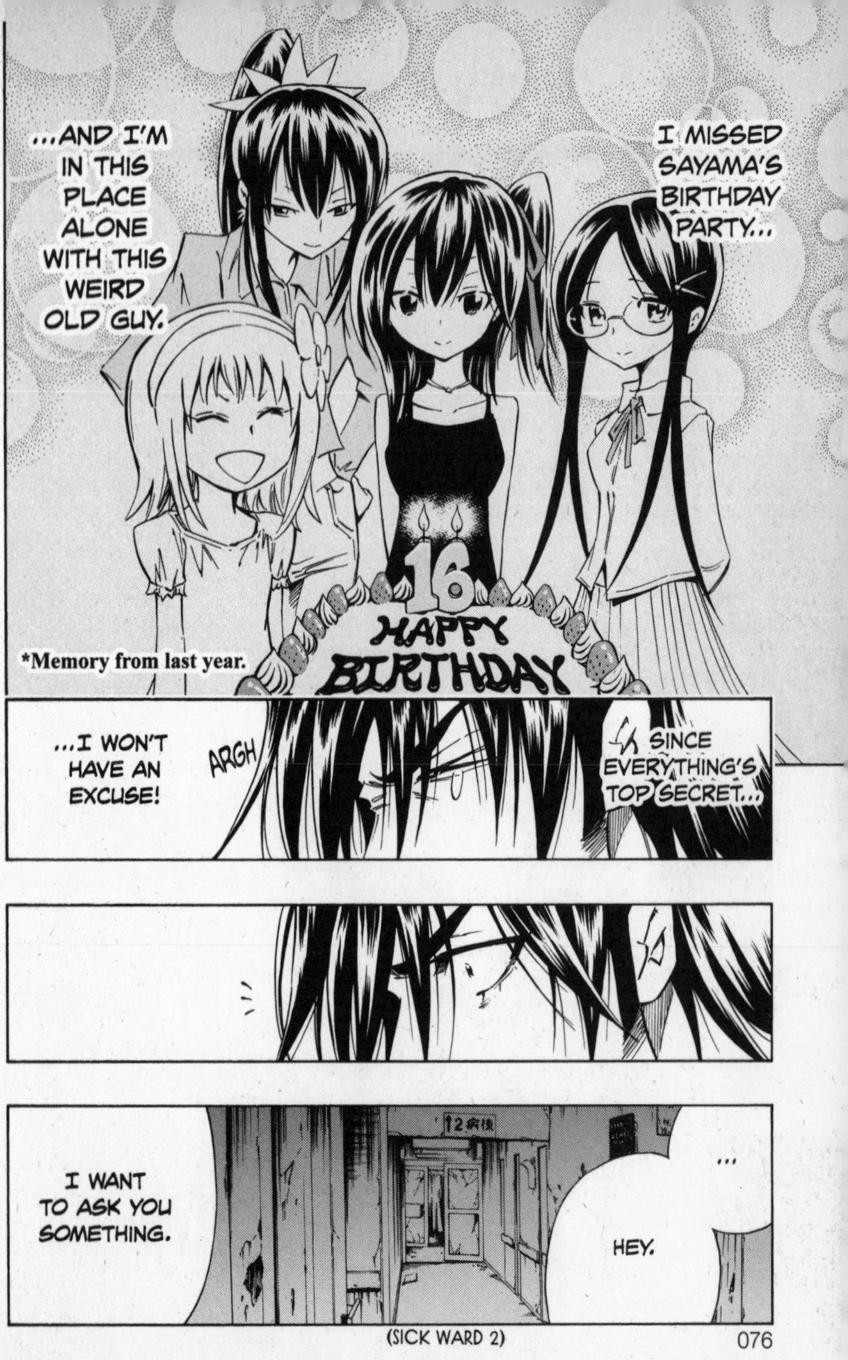
I MISSED SAYAMA'S BIRTHDAY PARTY...
...AND I'M IN THIS PLACE ALONE WITH THIS WEIRD OLD GUY.
16
HAPPY BIRTHDAY
*Memory from last year.
SINCE EVERYTHING'S TOP SECRET...
ARGH
...I WON'T HAVE AN EXCUSE!
...
HEY.
I WANT TO ASK YOU SOMETHING.
(SICK WARD 2)

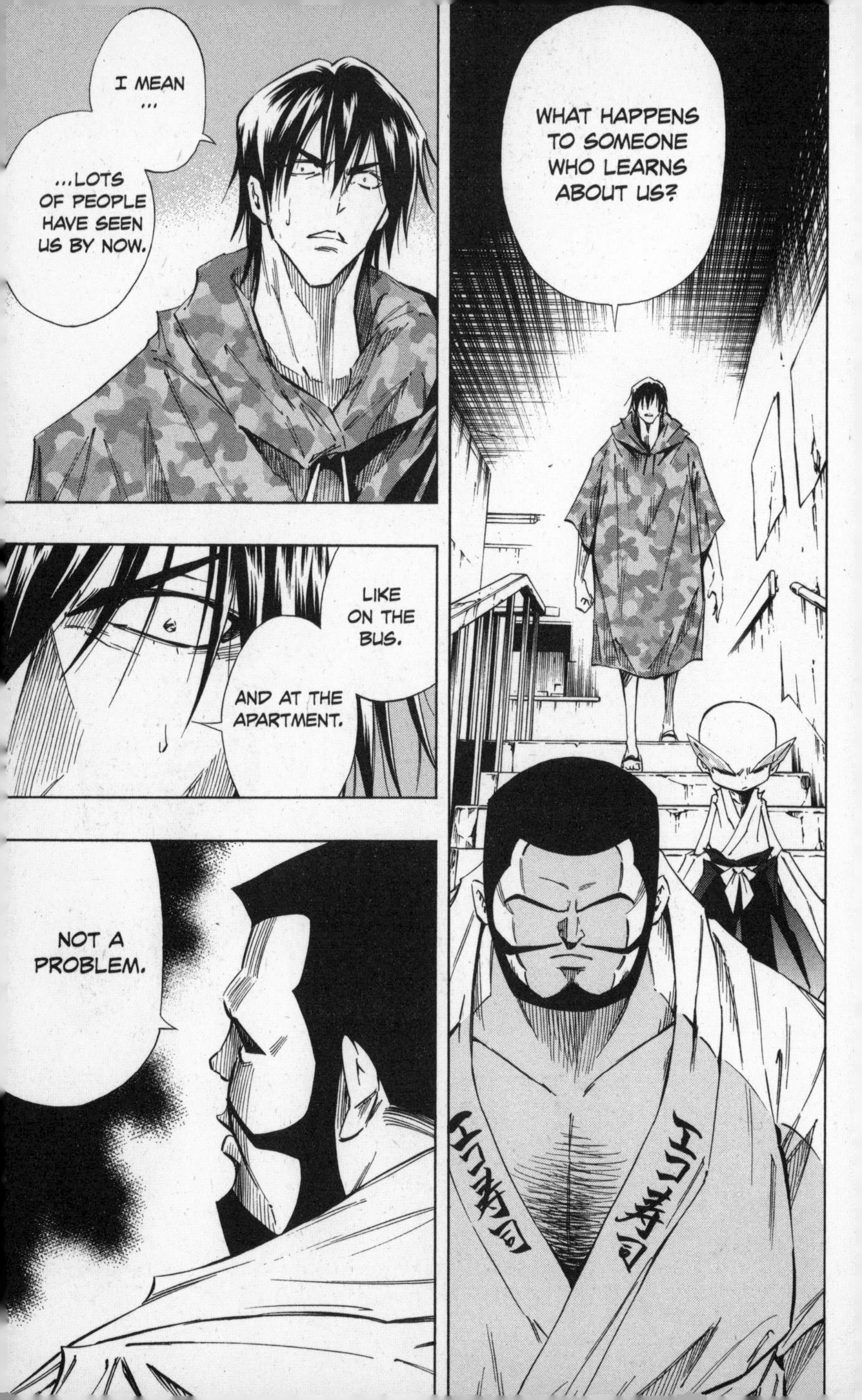
WHAT HAPPENS TO SOMEONE WHO LEARNS ABOUT US?
I MEAN ...
...LOTS OF PEOPLE HAVE SEEN US BY NOW.
LIKE ON THE BUS.
AND AT THE APARTMENT.
NOT A PROBLEM.

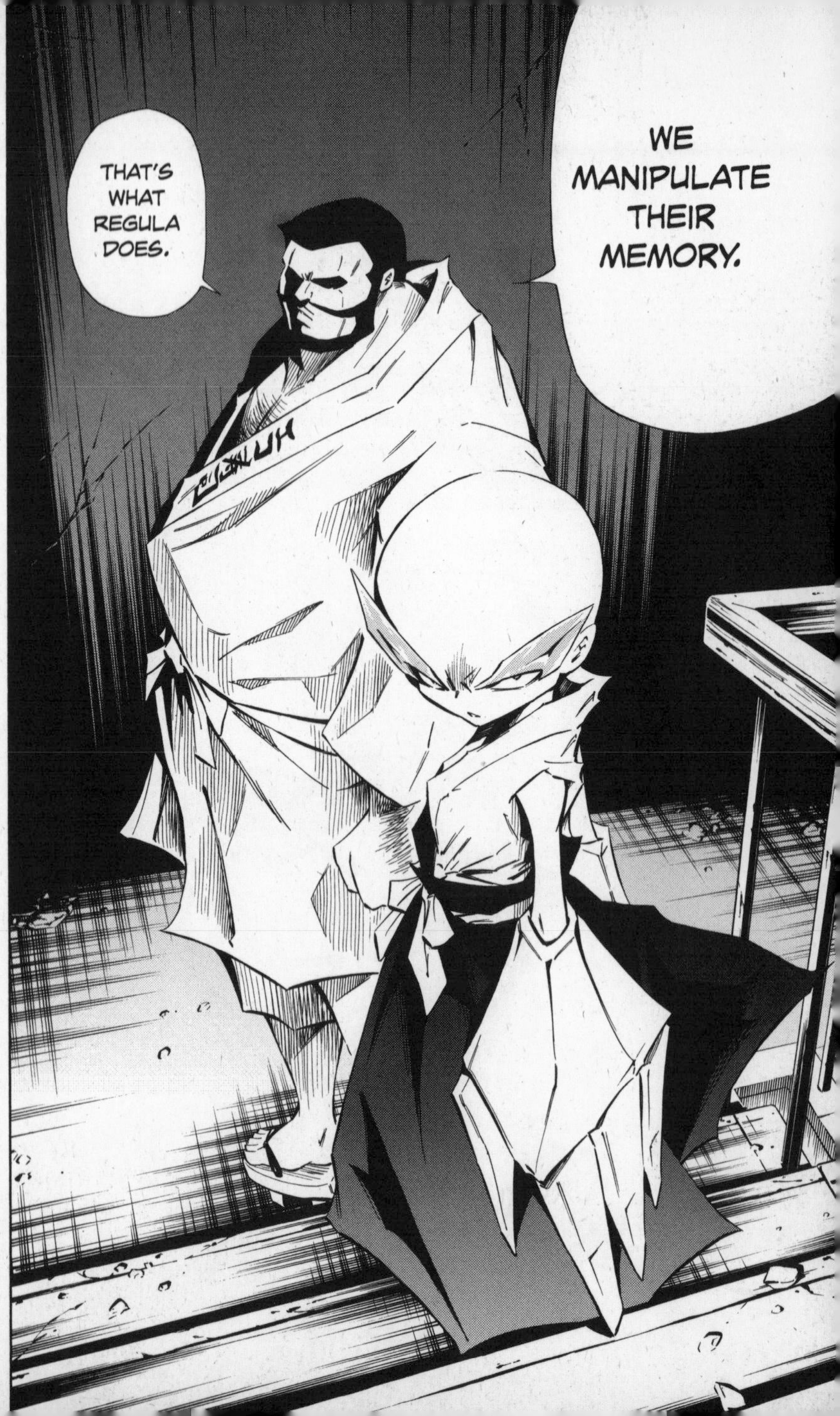
WE MANIPULATE THEIR MEMORY.
THAT'S WHAT REGULA DOES.

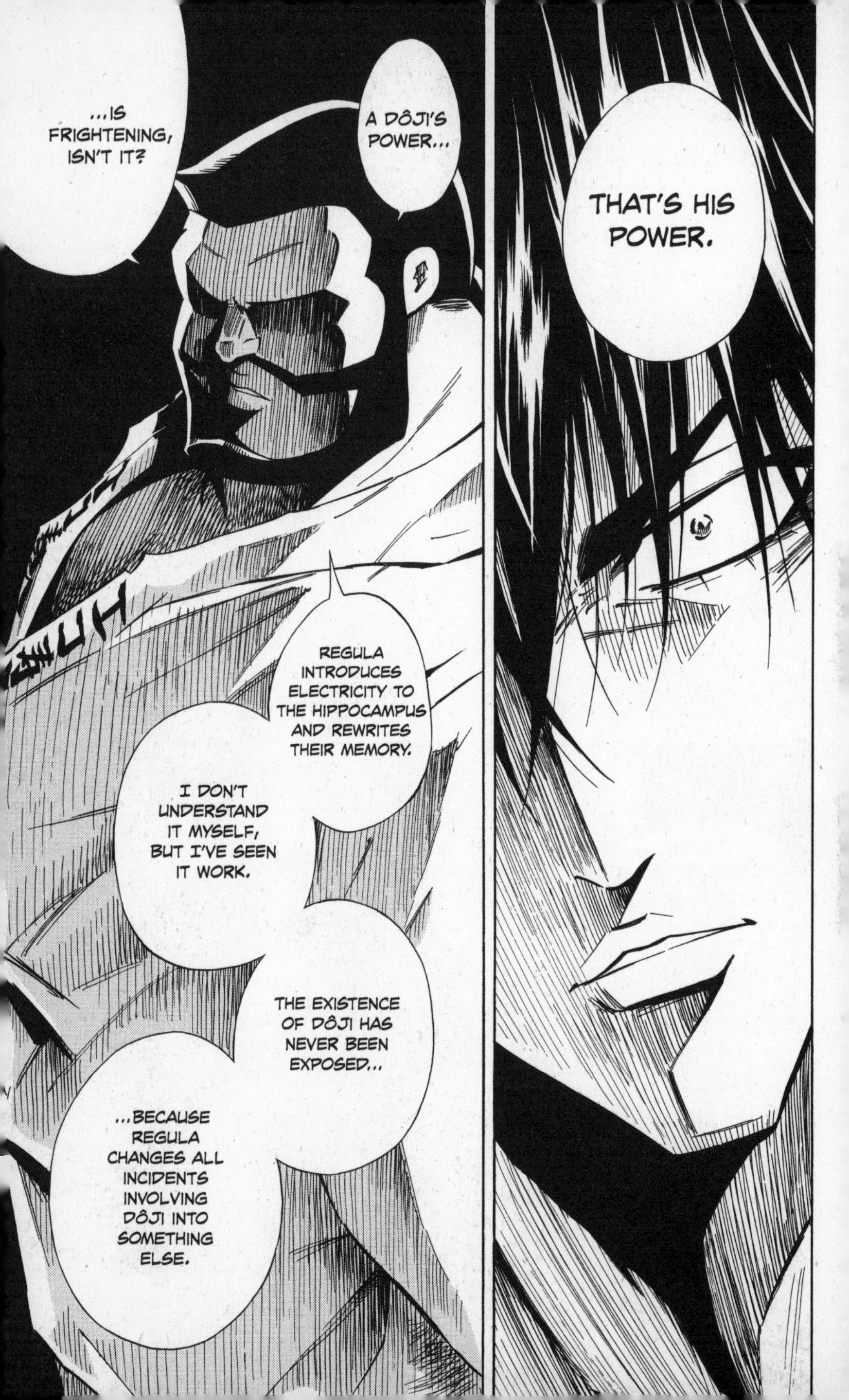
THAT'S HIS POWER.
A DÔJI'S POWER...
...IS FRIGHTENING, ISN'T IT?
REGULA INTRODUCES ELECTRICITY TO THE HIPPOCAMPUS AND REWRITES THEIR MEMORY.
I DON'T UNDERSTAND IT MYSELF, BUT I'VE SEEN IT WORK.
THE EXISTENCE OF DÔJI HAS NEVER BEEN EXPOSED...
...BECAUSE REGULA CHANGES ALL INCIDENTS INVOLVING DÔJI INTO SOMETHING ELSE.

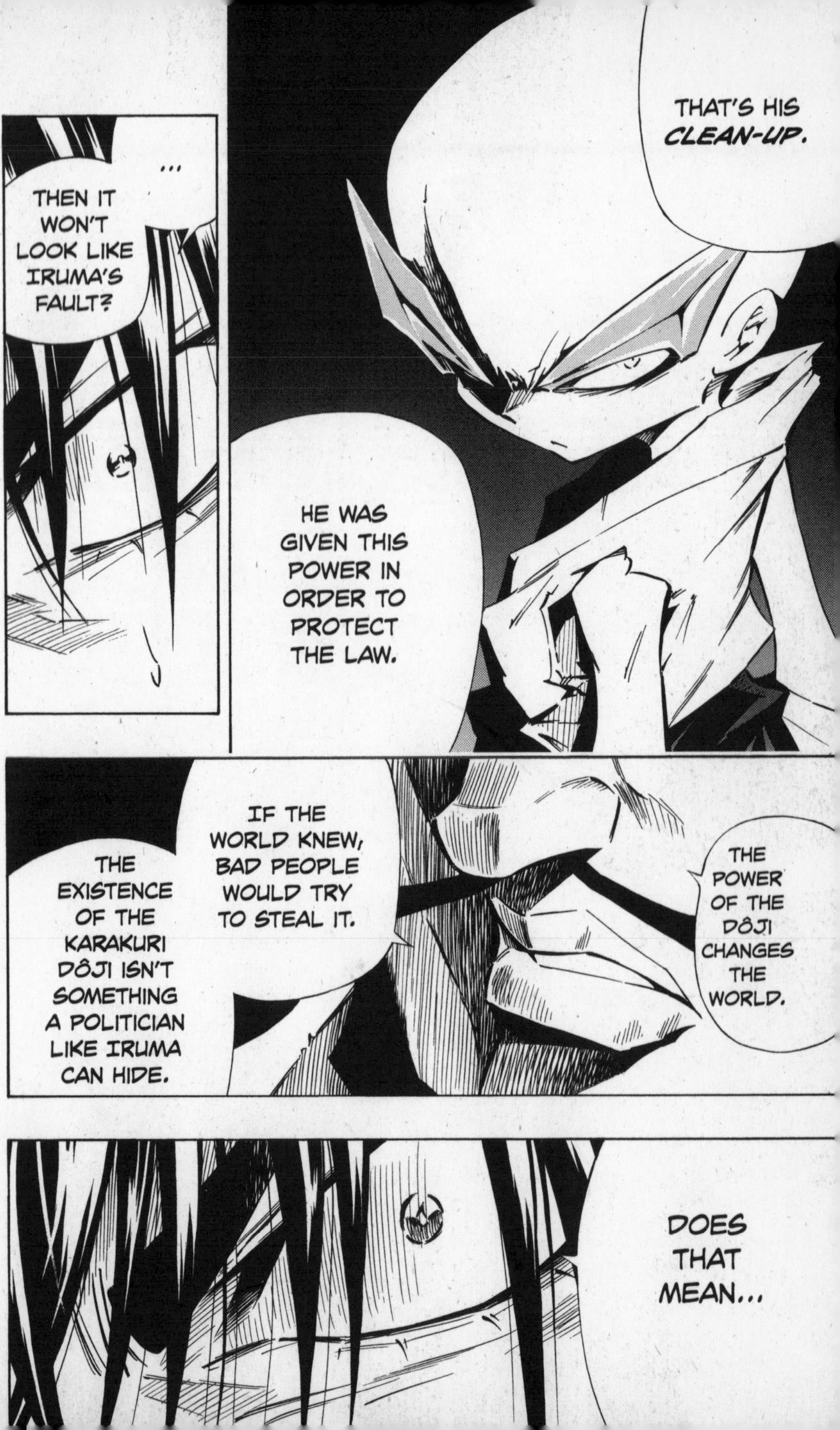
THAT'S HIS *CLEAN-UP*.
HE WAS GIVEN THIS POWER IN ORDER TO PROTECT THE LAW.
...
THEN IT WON'T LOOK LIKE IRUMA'S FAULT?
THE POWER OF THE DÔJI CHANGES THE WORLD.
IF THE WORLD KNEW, BAD PEOPLE WOULD TRY TO STEAL IT.
THE EXISTENCE OF THE KARAKURI DÔJI ISN'T SOMETHING A POLITICIAN LIKE IRUMA CAN HIDE.
DOES THAT MEAN...

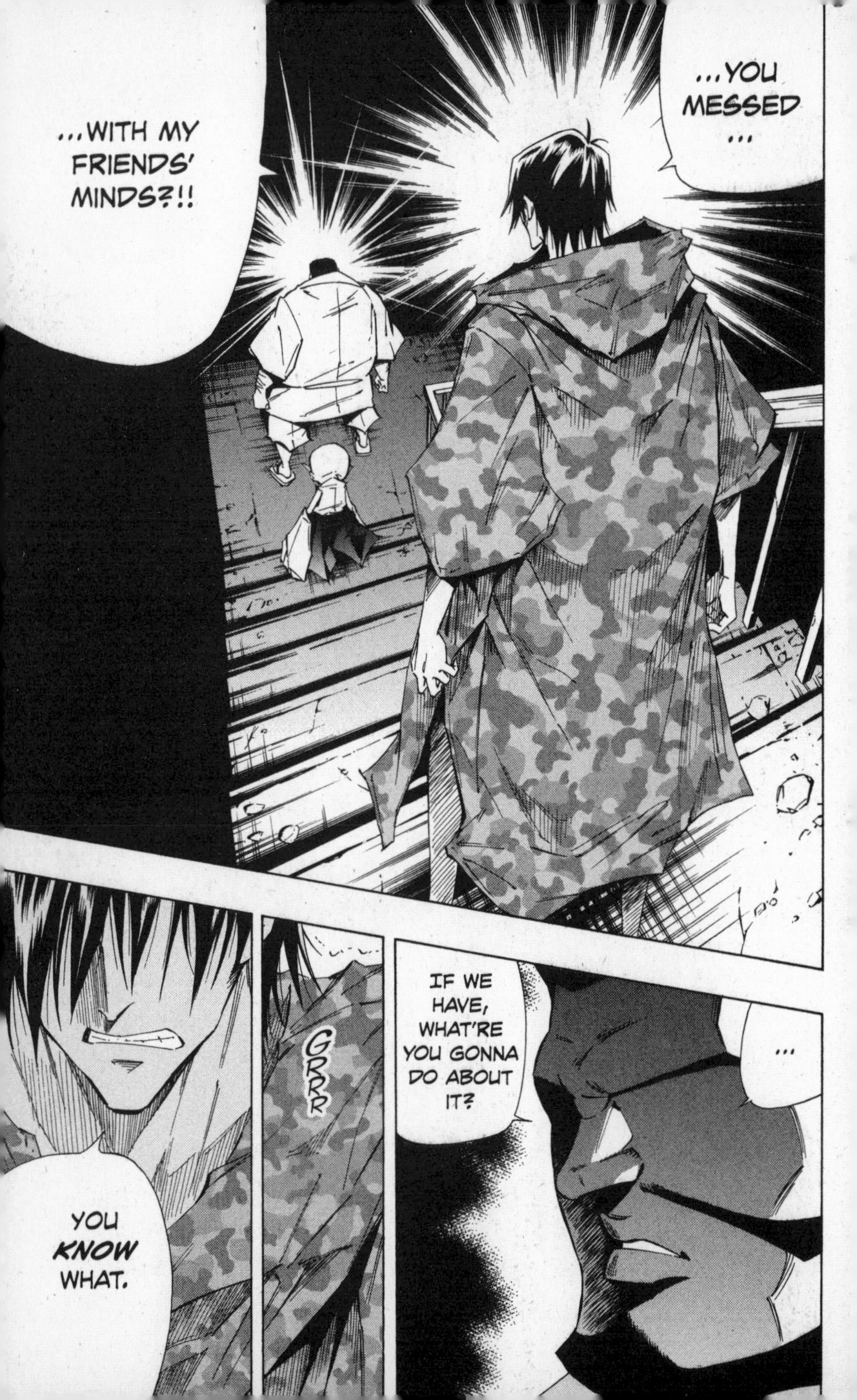
...YOU MESSED ...
...WITH MY FRIENDS' MINDS?!!
...
IF WE HAVE, WHAT'RE YOU GONNA DO ABOUT IT?
GRRR
YOU *KNOW* WHAT.

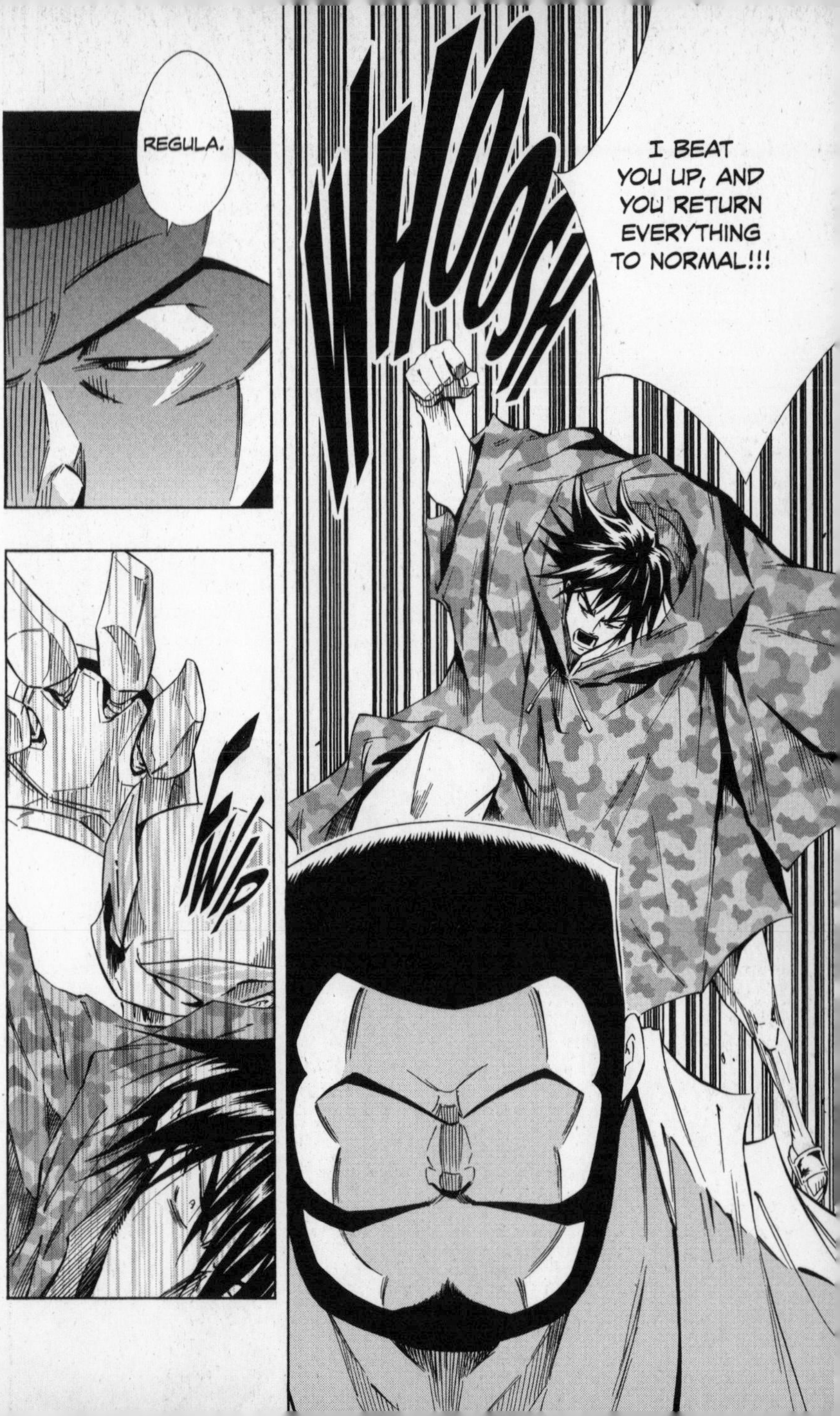
WHOOSH
I BEAT YOU UP, AND YOU RETURN EVERYTHING TO NORMAL!!!
REGULA.
FWIP

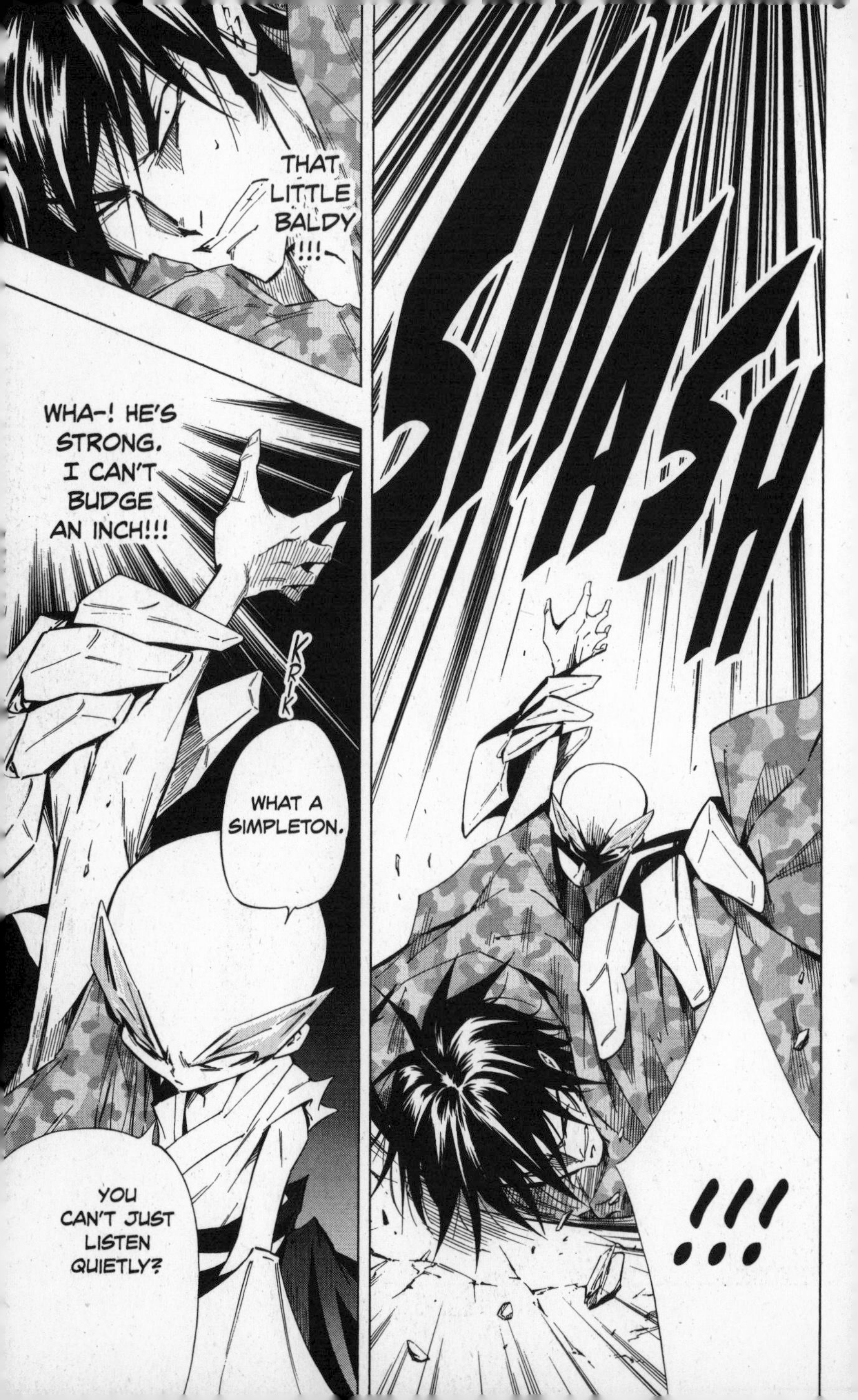
SHASH
!!!
THAT LITTLE BALDY!!!
WHA-! HE'S STRONG. I CAN'T BUDGE AN INCH!!!
KRIK
WHAT A SIMPLETON.
YOU CAN'T JUST LISTEN QUIETLY?

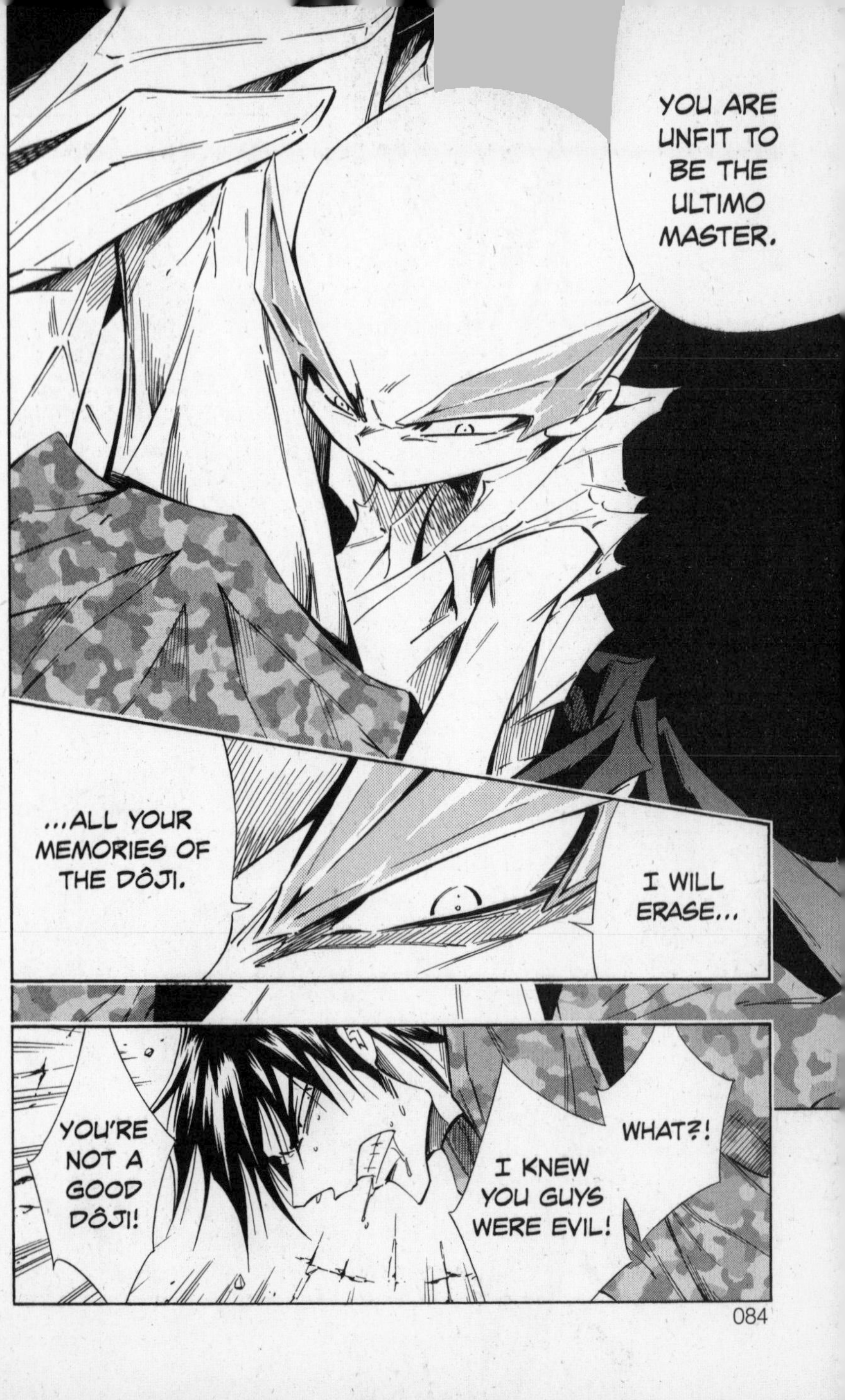
YOU ARE UNFIT TO BE THE ULTIMO MASTER.
I WILL ERASE...
...ALL YOUR MEMORIES OF THE DÔJI.
WHAT?!
I KNEW YOU GUYS WERE EVIL!
YOU'RE NOT A GOOD DÔJI!

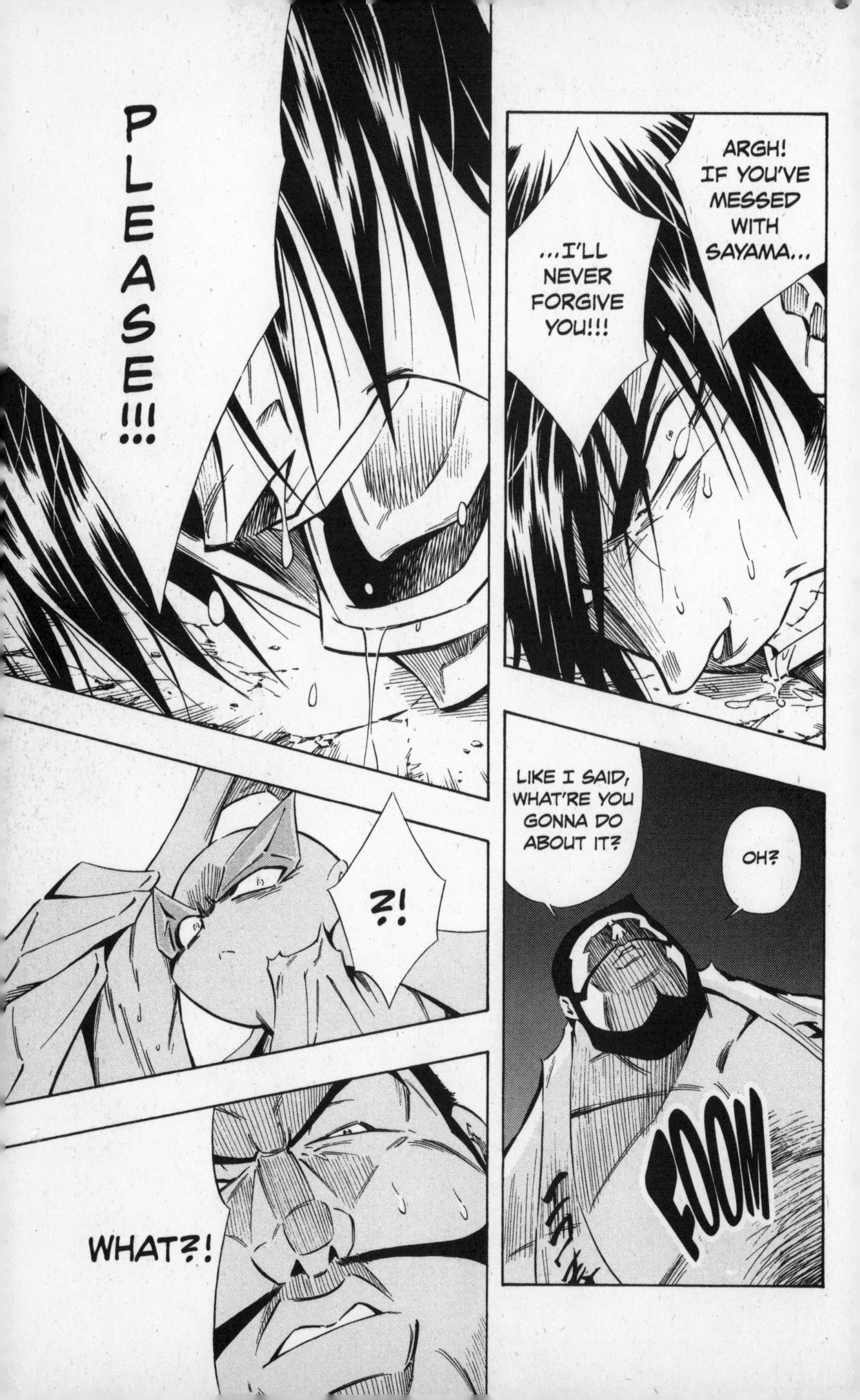
ARGH! IF YOU'VE MESSED WITH SAYAMA...
...I'LL NEVER FORGIVE YOU!!!
PLEASE!!!
LIKE I SAID, WHAT'RE YOU GONNA DO ABOUT IT?
OH?
FOOM
?!
WHAT?!

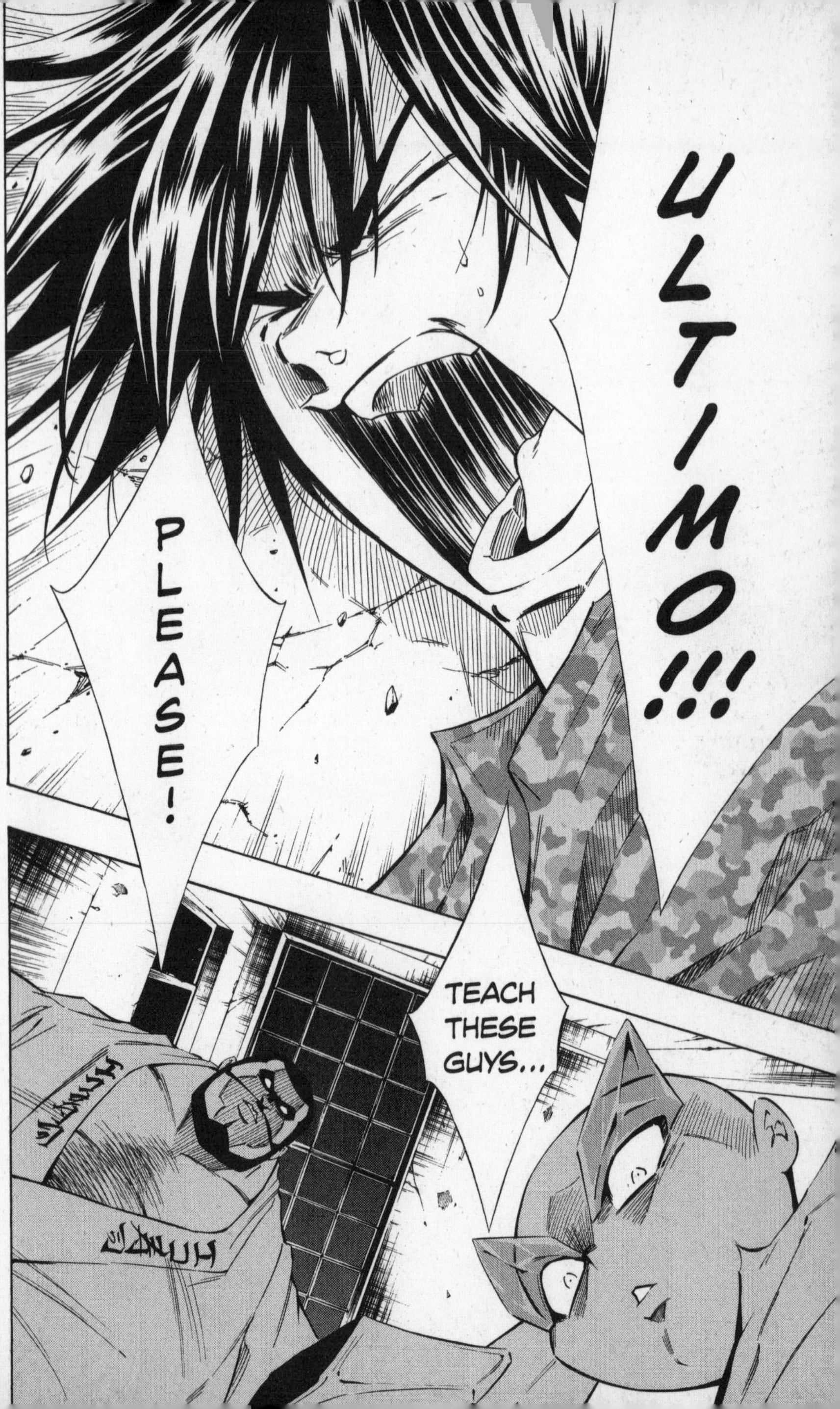
ULTIMO!!!
PLEASE!
TEACH THESE GUYS...

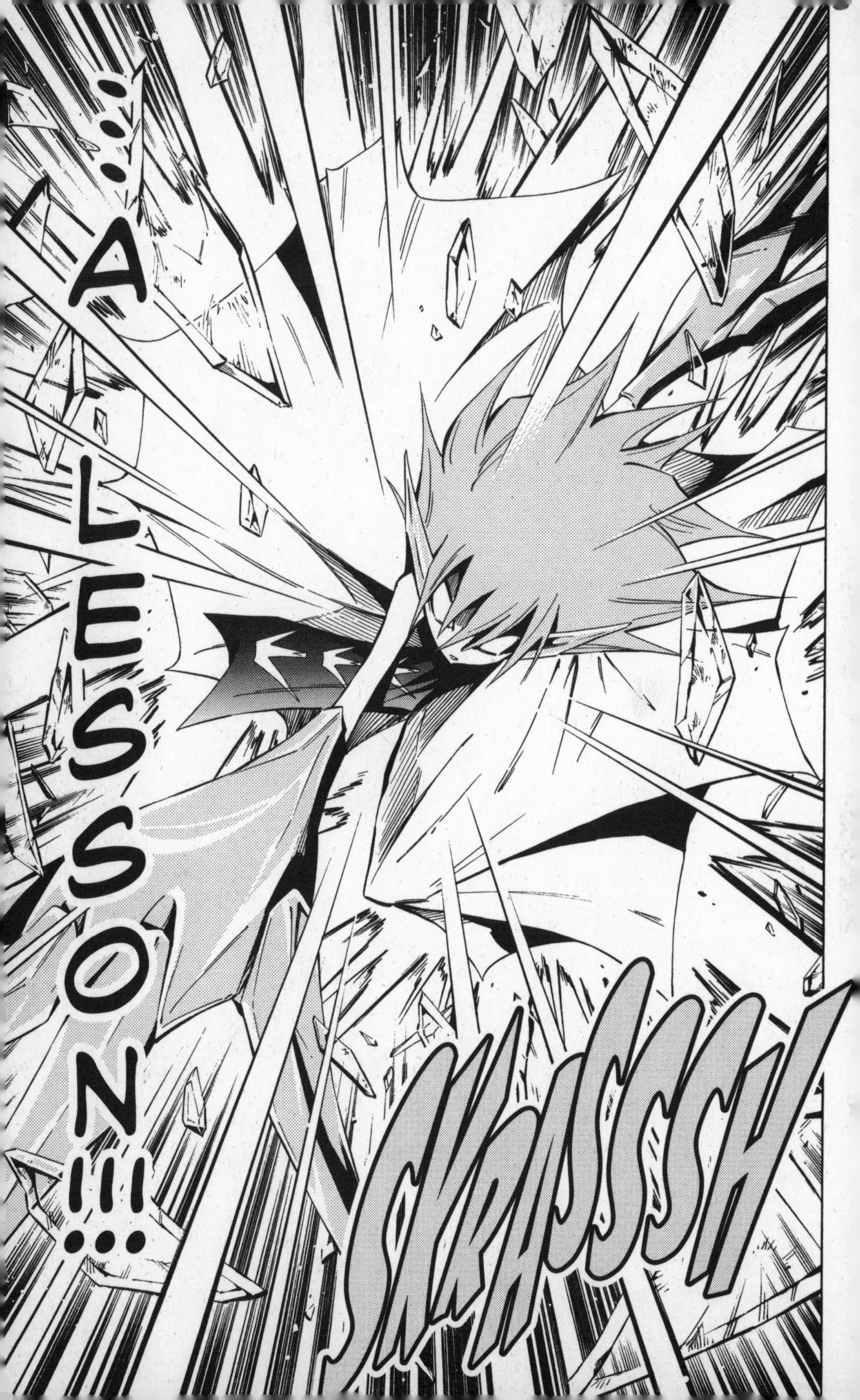
...A LESSON!!...
SHASSCH

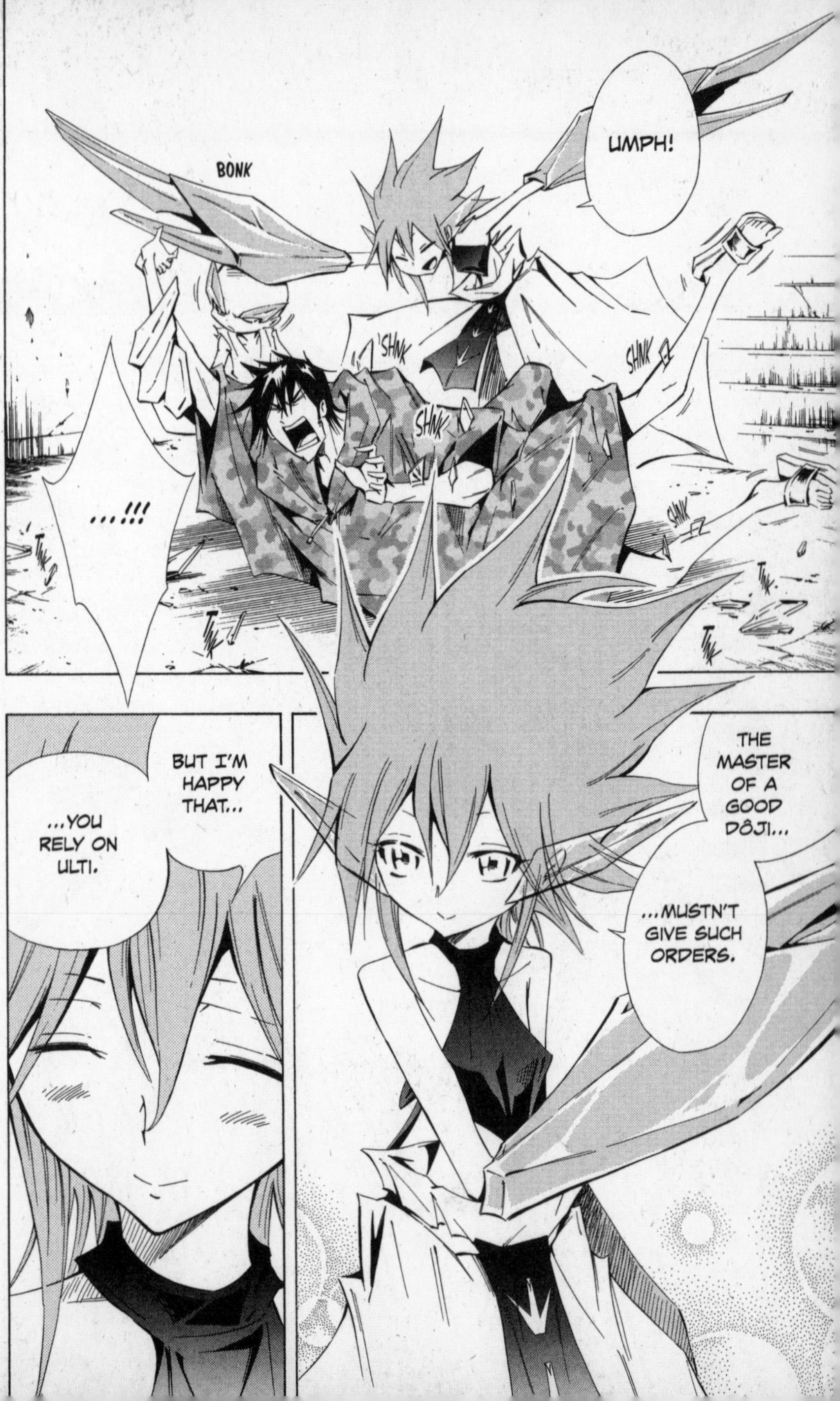
UMPH!
BONK
SHNK
SHNK
SHNK
SHNK
...!!!
TINK
TINK
TINK
TINK
THE MASTER OF A GOOD DÔJI...
...MUSTN'T GIVE SUCH ORDERS.
BUT I'M HAPPY THAT...
...YOU RELY ON ULTI.

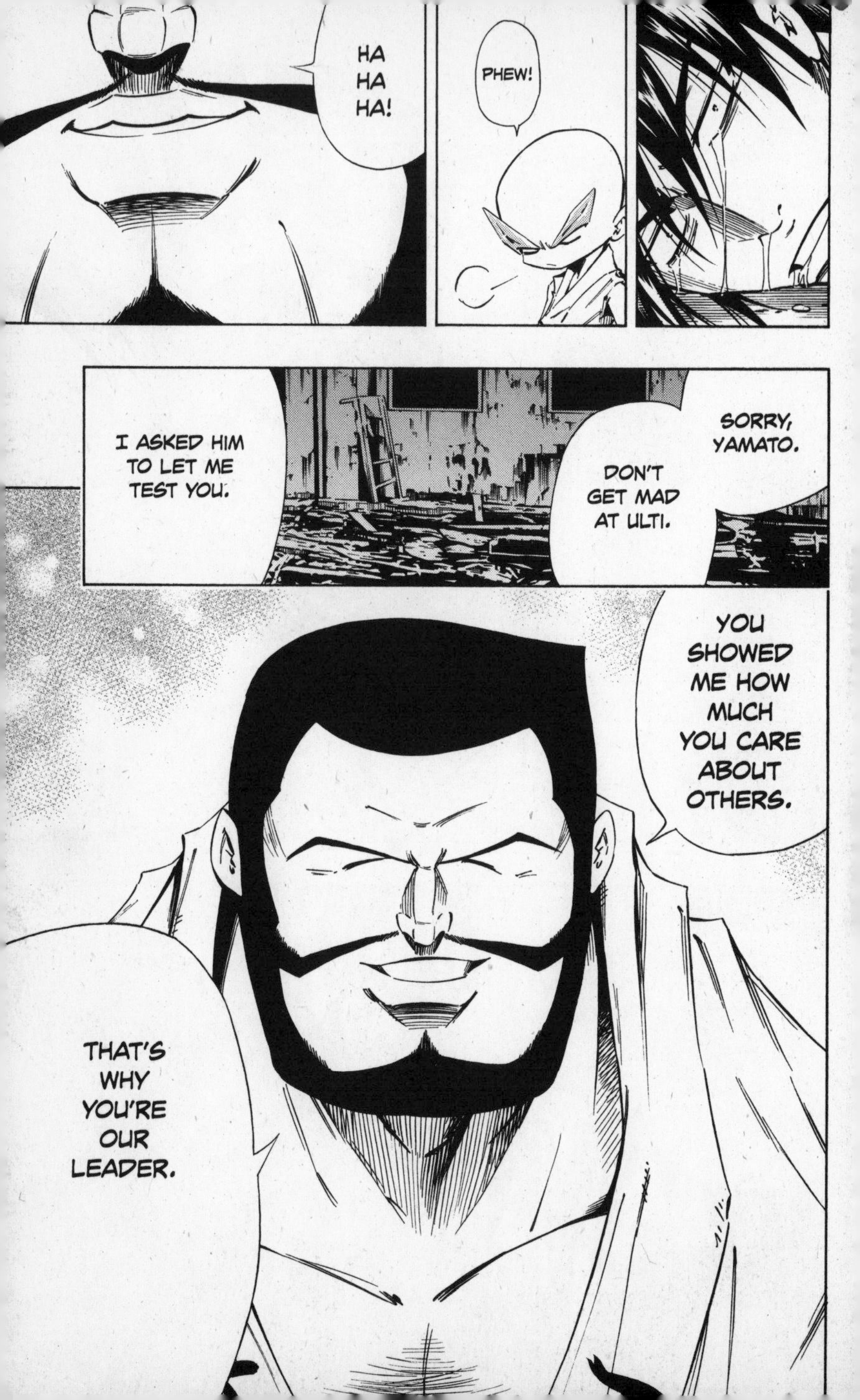
PHEW!
HA HA HA!
SORRY, YAMATO.
DON'T GET MAD AT ULTI.
I ASKED HIM TO LET ME TEST YOU.
YOU SHOWED ME HOW MUCH YOU CARE ABOUT OTHERS.
THAT'S WHY YOU'RE OUR LEADER.

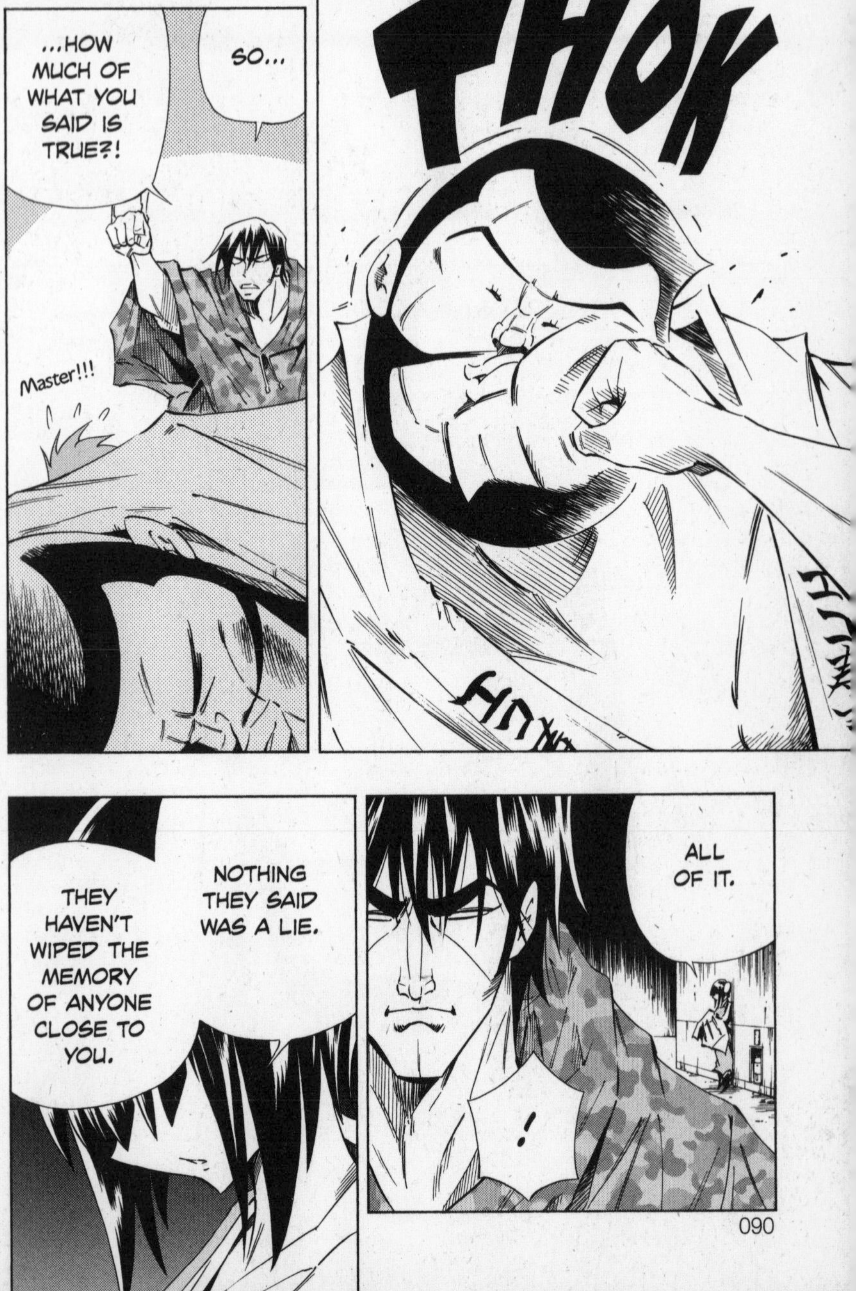
THOK
SO...
...HOW MUCH OF WHAT YOU SAID IS TRUE?!
Master!!!
ALL OF IT.
!
NOTHING THEY SAID WAS A LIE.
THEY HAVEN'T WIPED THE MEMORY OF ANYONE CLOSE TO YOU.

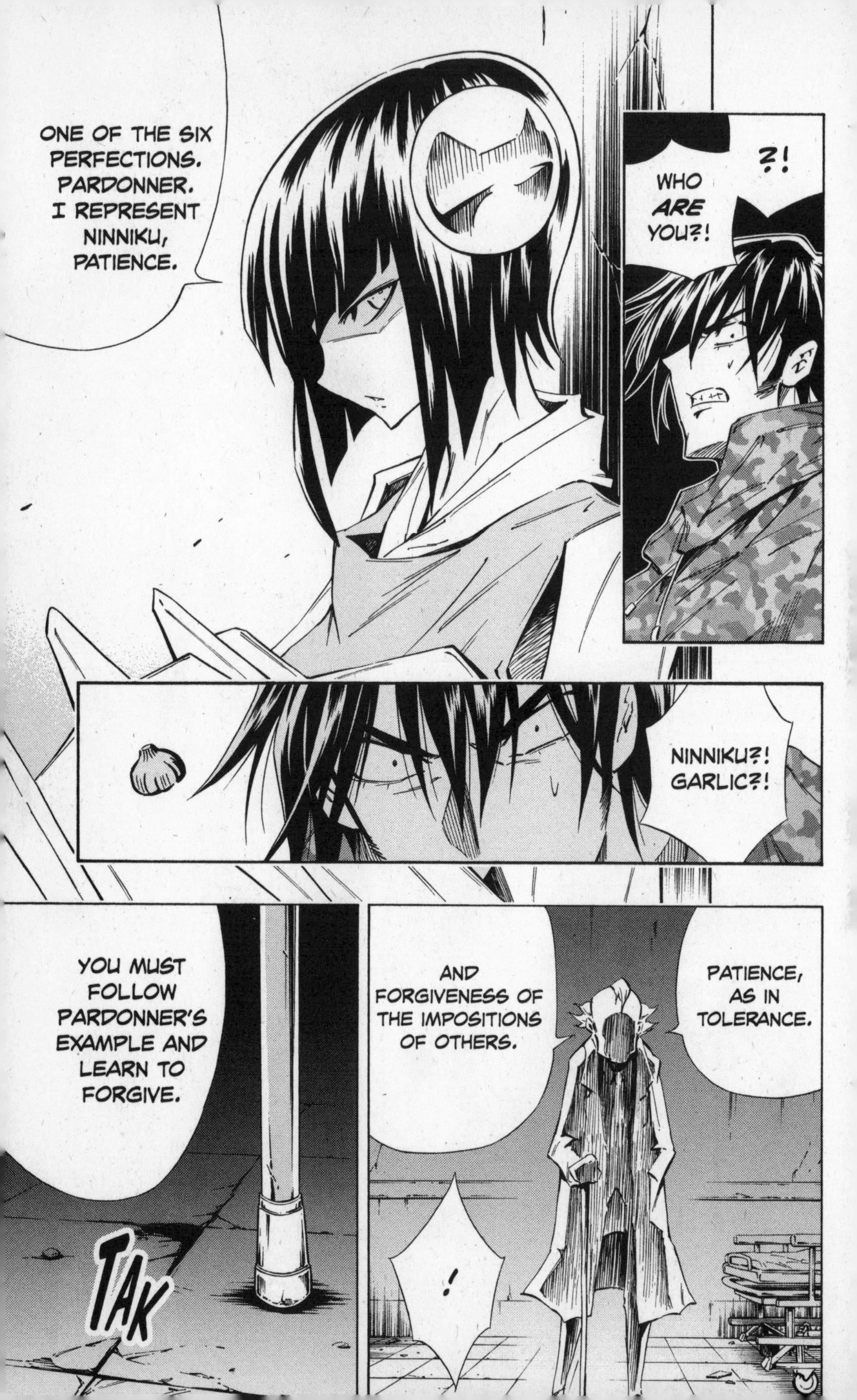
?!
WHO ARE YOU?!
ONE OF THE SIX PERFECTIONS. PARDONNER. I REPRESENT NINNIKU, PATIENCE.
NINNIKU?! GARLIC?!
PATIENCE, AS IN TOLERANCE.
AND FORGIVENESS OF THE IMPOSITIONS OF OTHERS.
!
YOU MUST FOLLOW PARDONNER'S EXAMPLE AND LEARN TO FORGIVE.
TAK

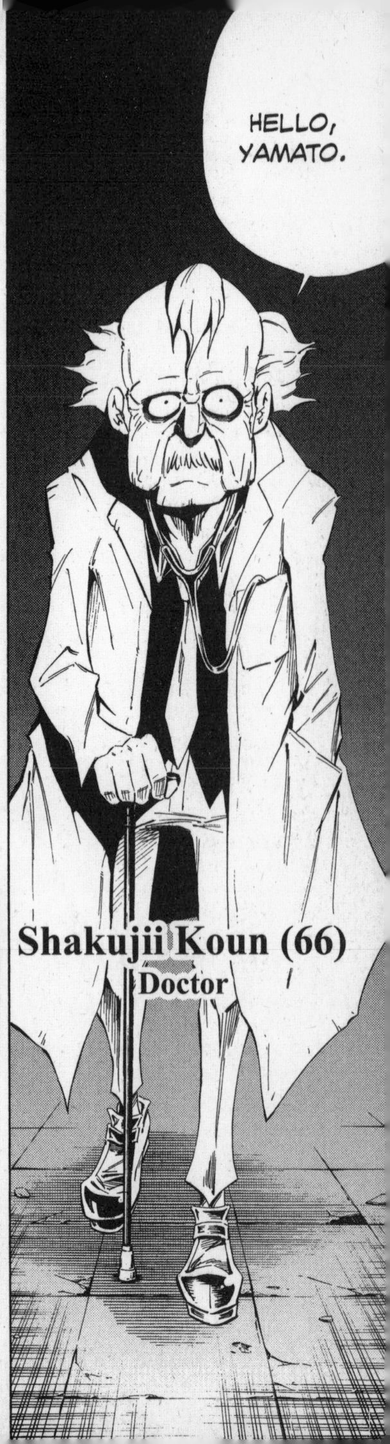
HELLO, YAMATO.
Shakujii Koun (66)
Doctor

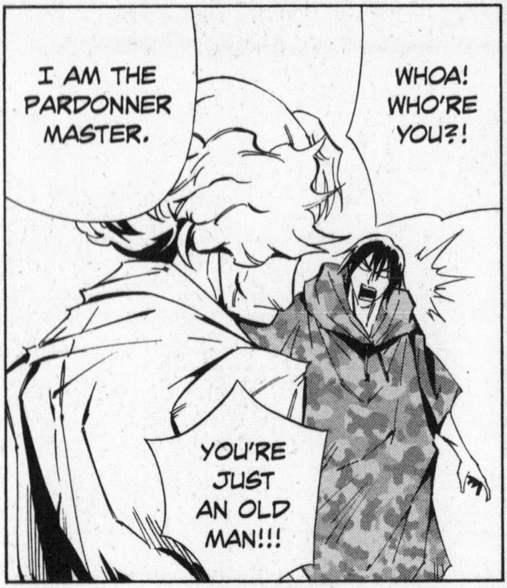
WHOA! WHO'RE YOU?!
I AM THE PARDONNER MASTER.
YOU'RE JUST AN OLD MAN!!!

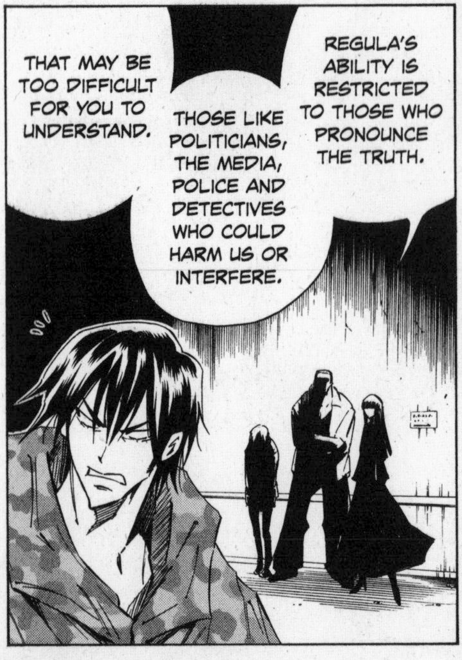
REGULA'S ABILITY IS RESTRICTED TO THOSE WHO PRONOUNCE THE TRUTH.
THOSE LIKE POLITICIANS, THE MEDIA, POLICE AND DETECTIVES WHO COULD HARM US OR INTERFERE.
THAT MAY BE TOO DIFFICULT FOR YOU TO UNDERSTAND.

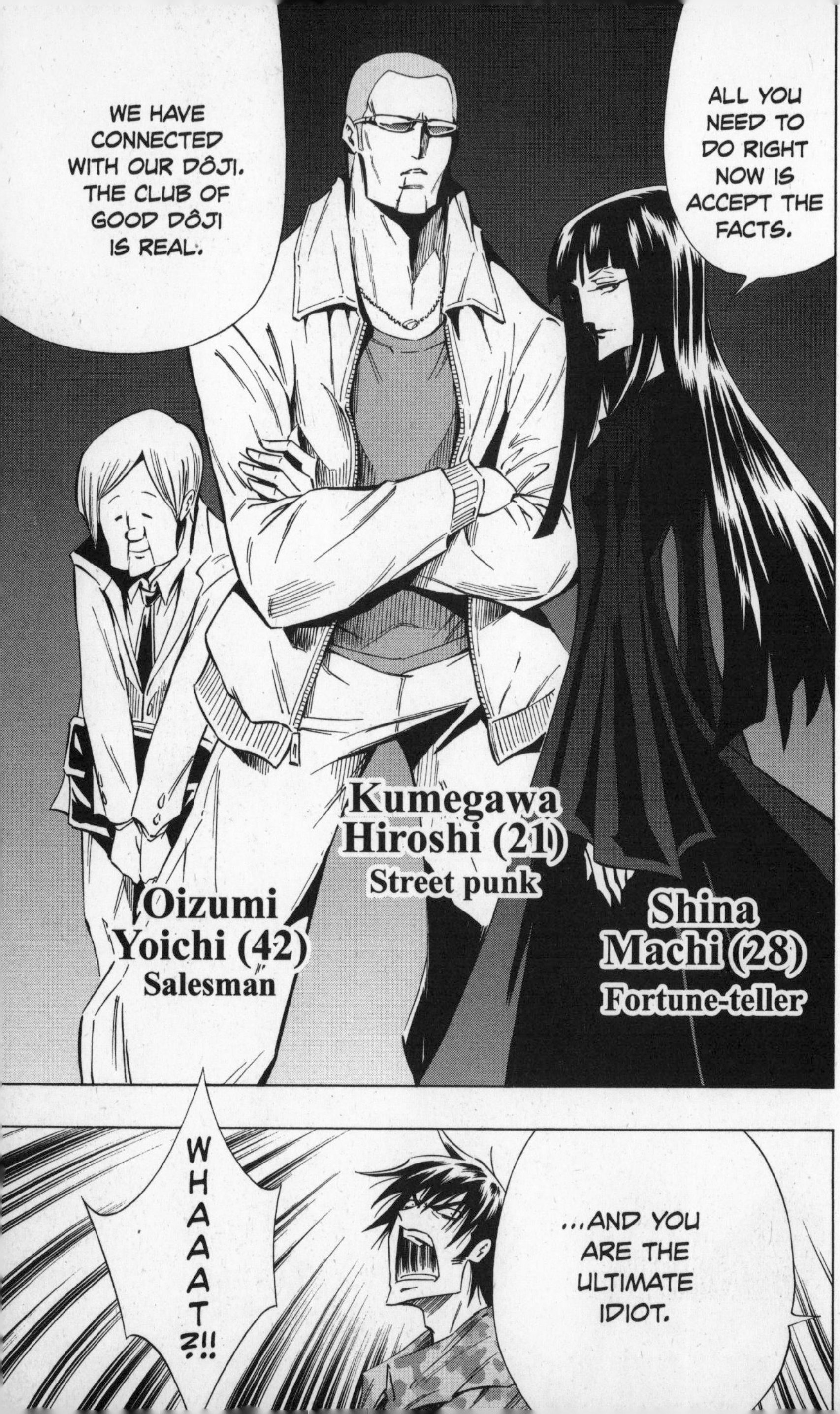
ALL YOU NEED TO DO RIGHT NOW IS ACCEPT THE FACTS.
WE HAVE CONNECTED WITH OUR DÔJI. THE CLUB OF GOOD DÔJI IS REAL.
Shina Machi (28) Fortune-teller
Kumegawa Hiroshi (21) Street punk
Oizumi Yoichi (42) Salesman
...AND YOU ARE THE ULTIMATE IDIOT.
WHAAAAT?!!

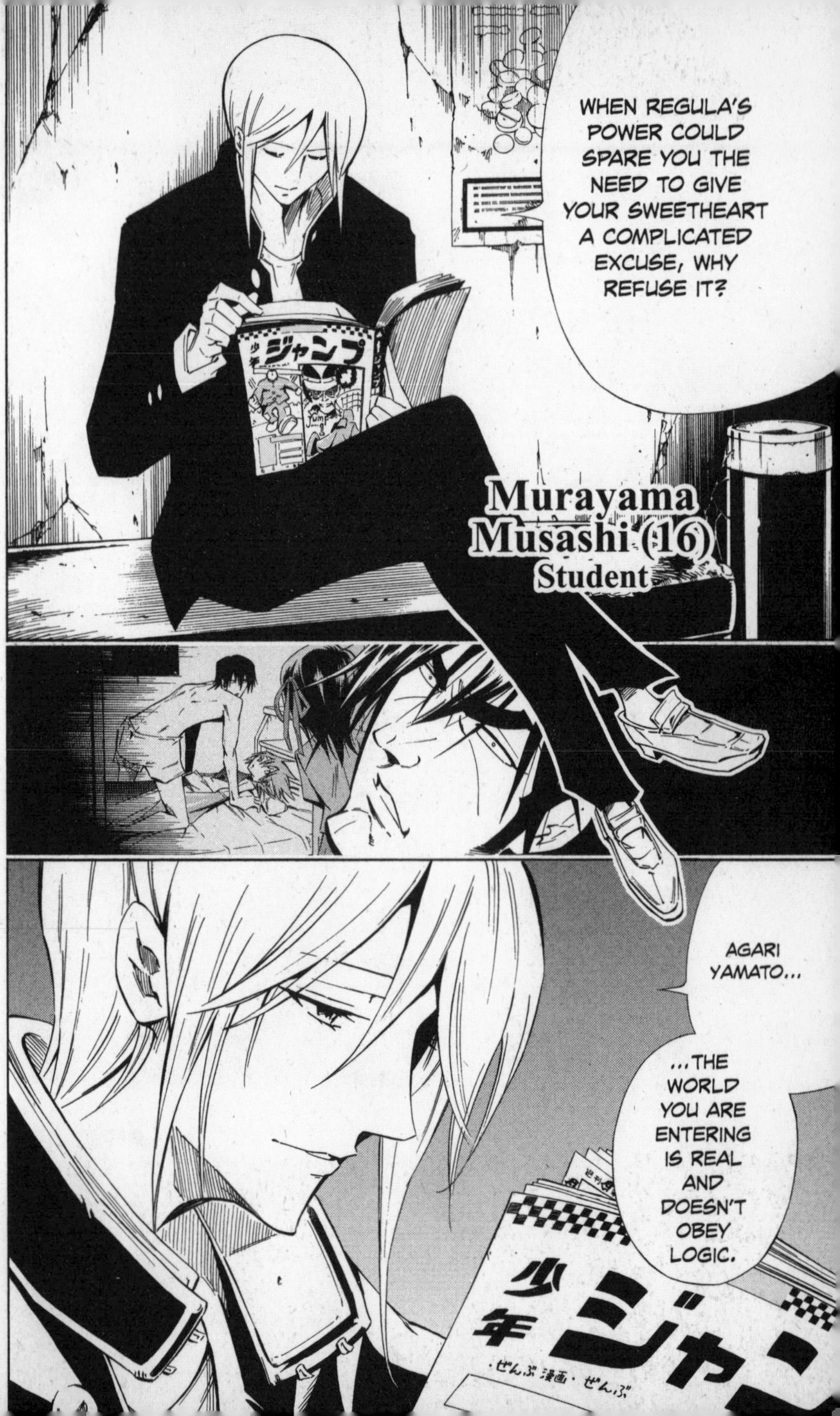
WHEN REGULA'S POWER COULD SPARE YOU THE NEED TO GIVE YOUR SWEETHEART A COMPLICATED EXCUSE, WHY REFUSE IT?
Murayama Musashi (16)
Student
AGARI YAMATO...
...THE WORLD YOU ARE ENTERING IS REAL AND DOESN'T OBEY LOGIC.

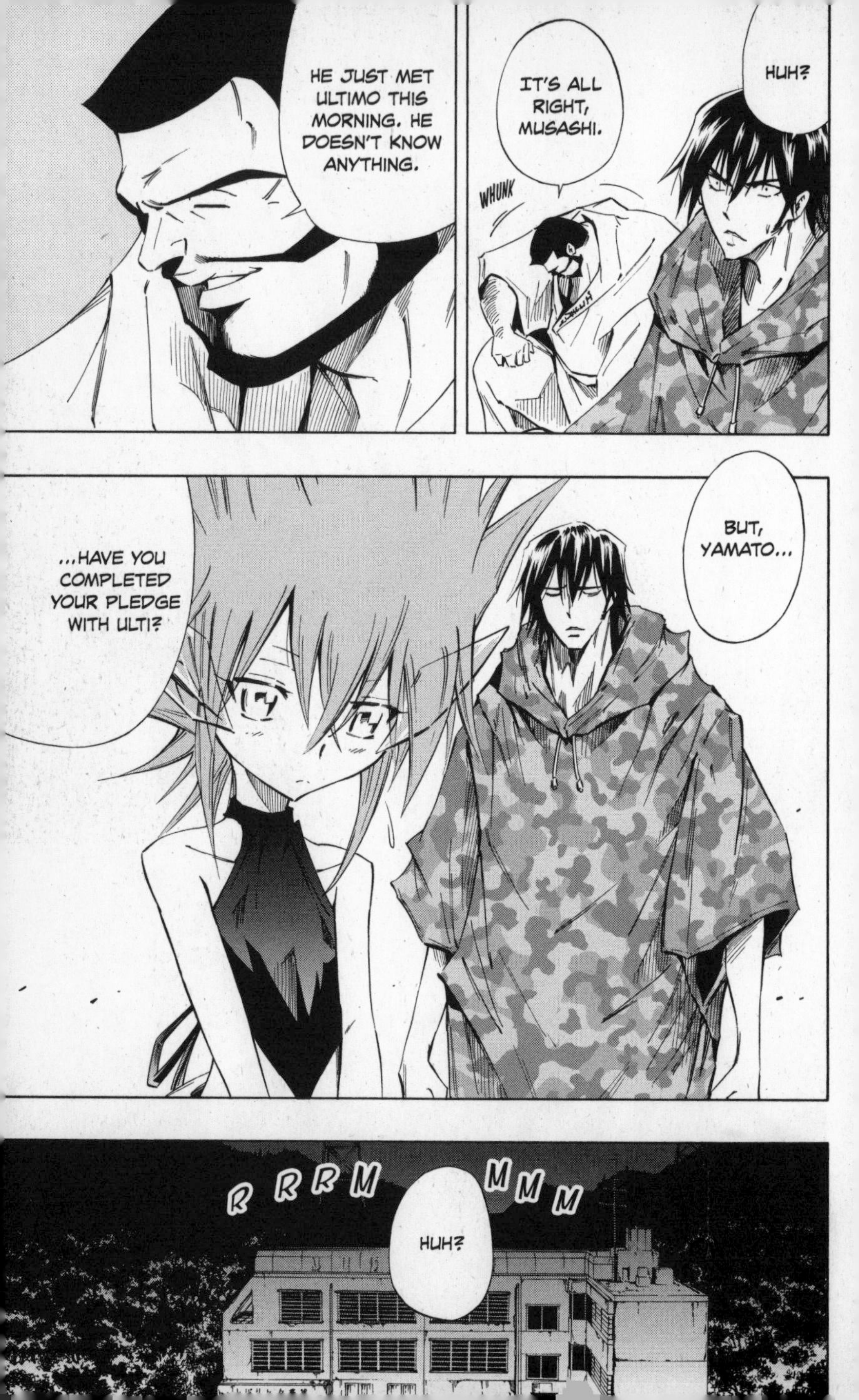
HUH?
IT'S ALL RIGHT, MUSASHI.
WHUNK
HE JUST MET ULTIMO THIS MORNING. HE DOESN'T KNOW ANYTHING.
BUT, YAMATO...
...HAVE YOU COMPLETED YOUR PLEDGE WITH ULTI?
RRRM MMM
HUH?

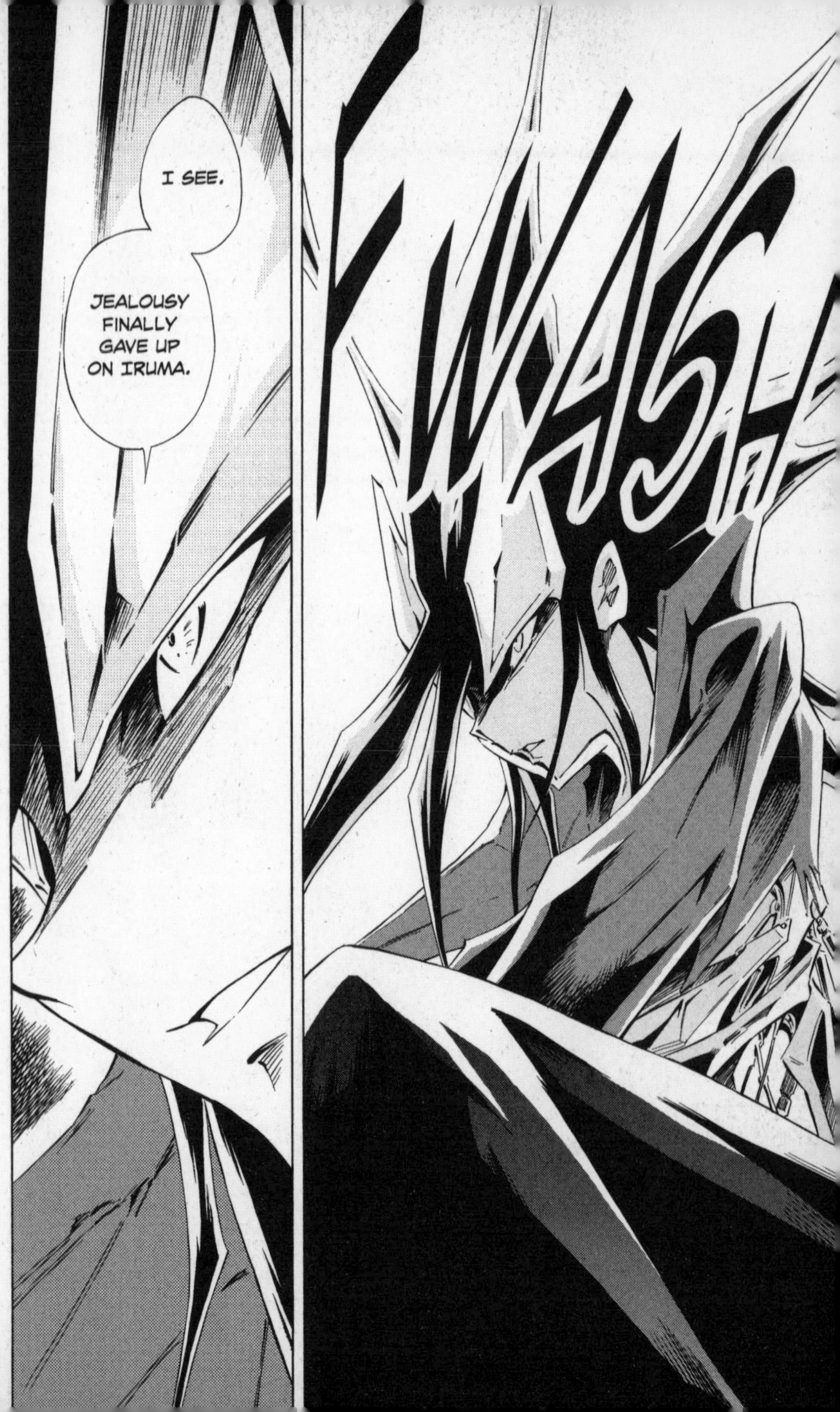
FWASH
I SEE.
JEALOUSY FINALLY GAVE UP ON IRUMA.

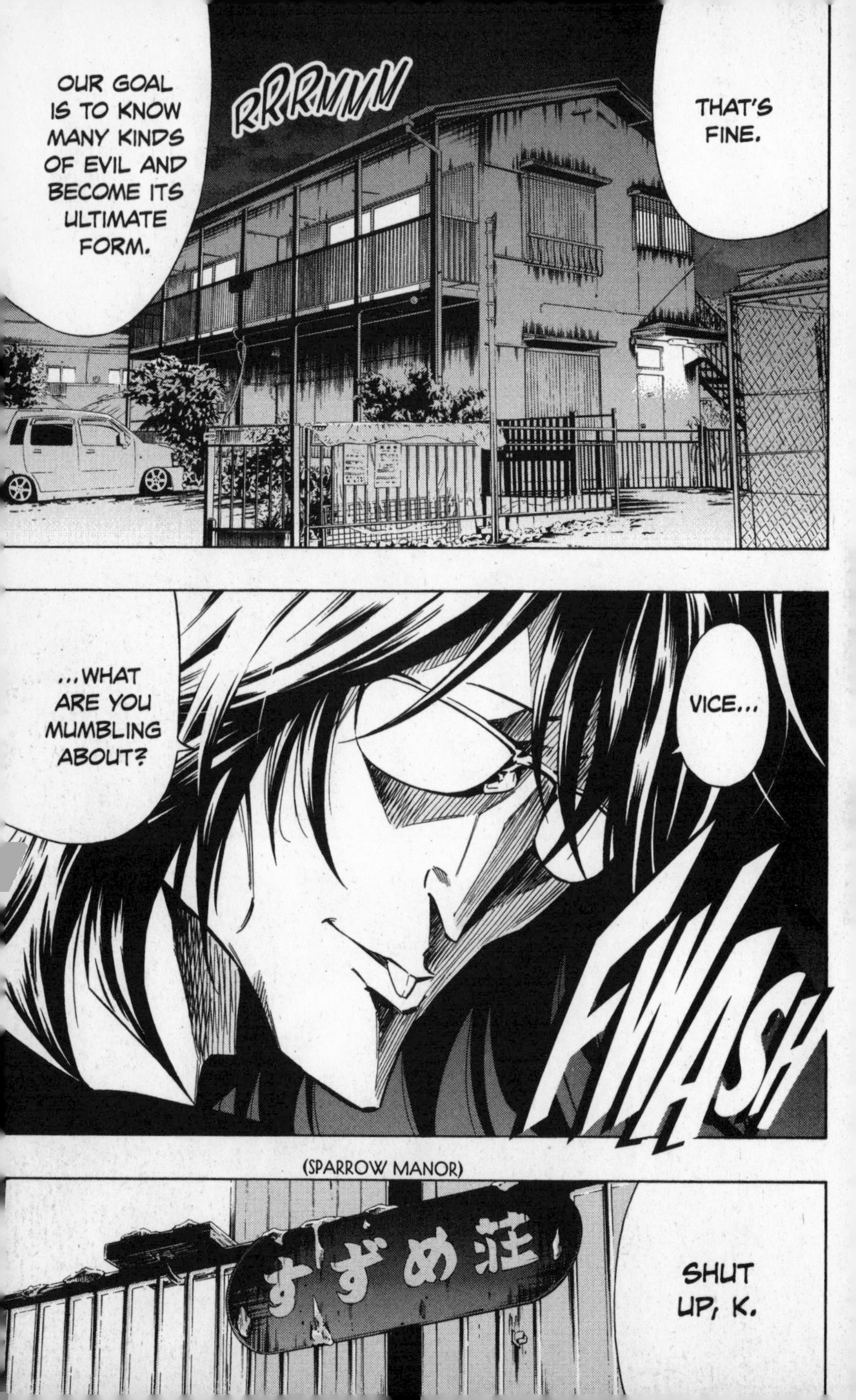
THAT'S FINE.
RRRMMM
OUR GOAL IS TO KNOW MANY KINDS OF EVIL AND BECOME ITS ULTIMATE FORM.
VICE...
...WHAT ARE YOU MUMBLING ABOUT?
FLASH
(SPARROW MANOR)
すずめ荘
SHUT UP, K.

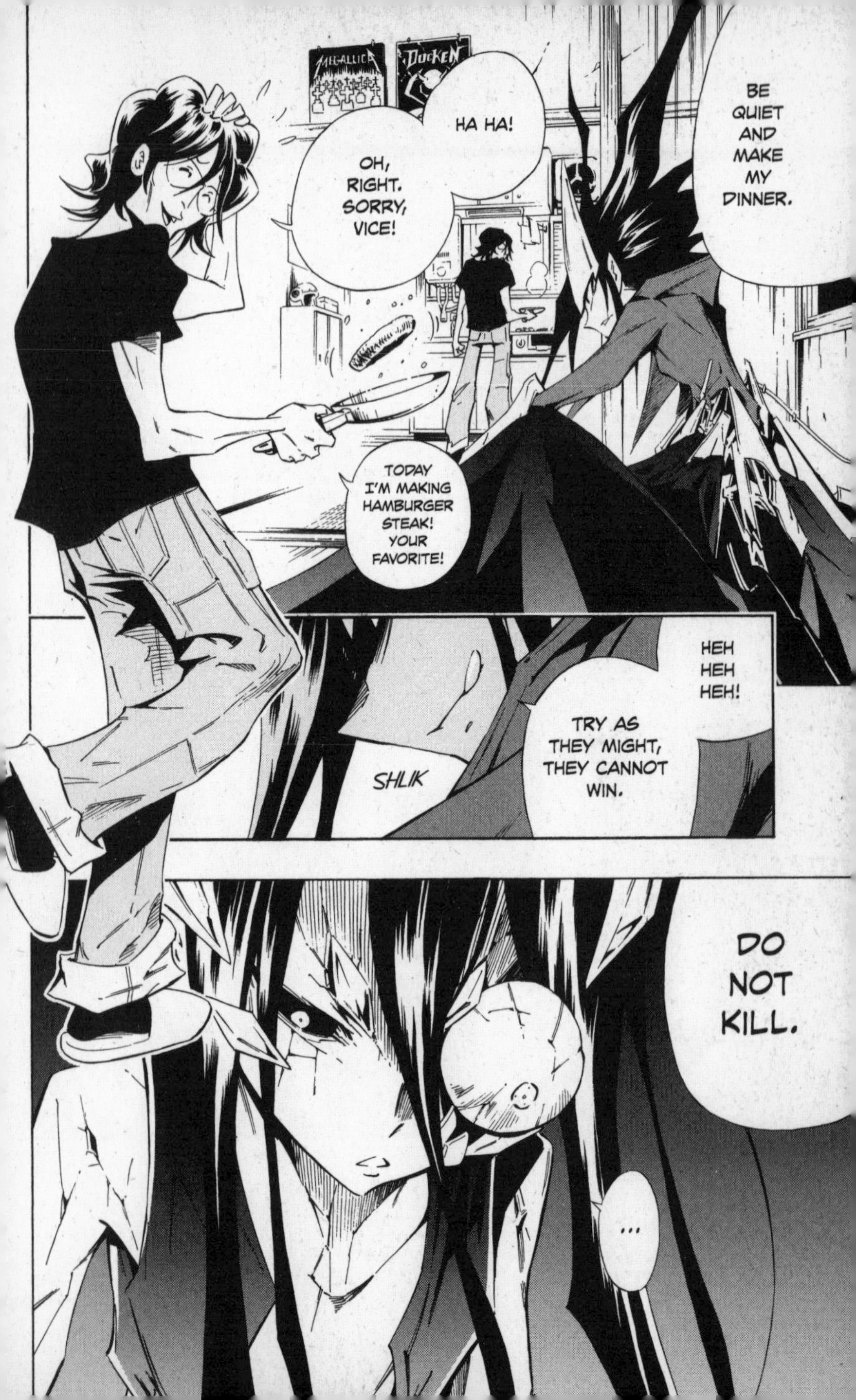
BE QUIET AND MAKE MY DINNER.
HA HA!
OH, RIGHT. SORRY, VICE!
TODAY I'M MAKING HAMBURGER STEAK! YOUR FAVORITE!
HEH HEH HEH!
TRY AS THEY MIGHT, THEY CANNOT WIN.
SHLIK
DO NOT KILL.
...

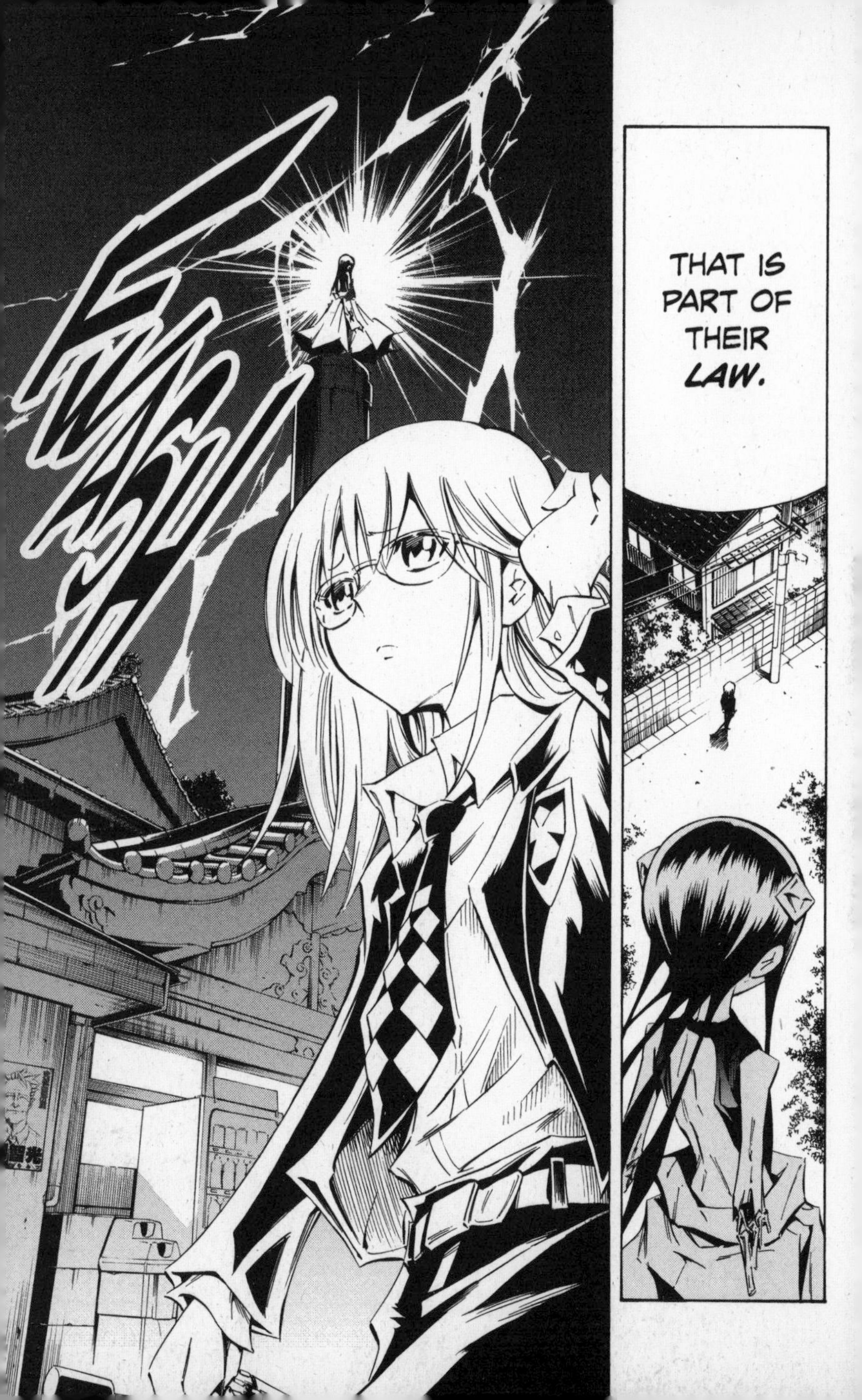
THAT IS PART OF THEIR LAW.

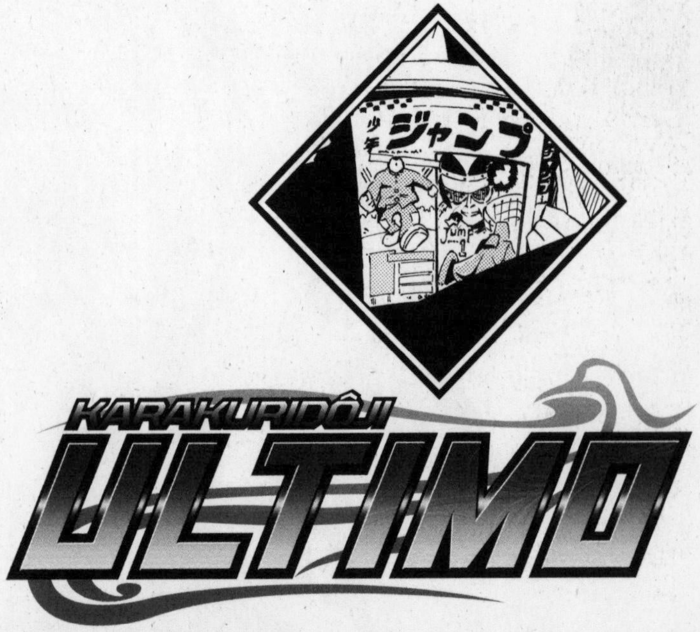
少年ジャンプ
Jump

KARAKURIDÔJI
ULTIMO

ACT 7 MR. BLOWN-TO-BITS

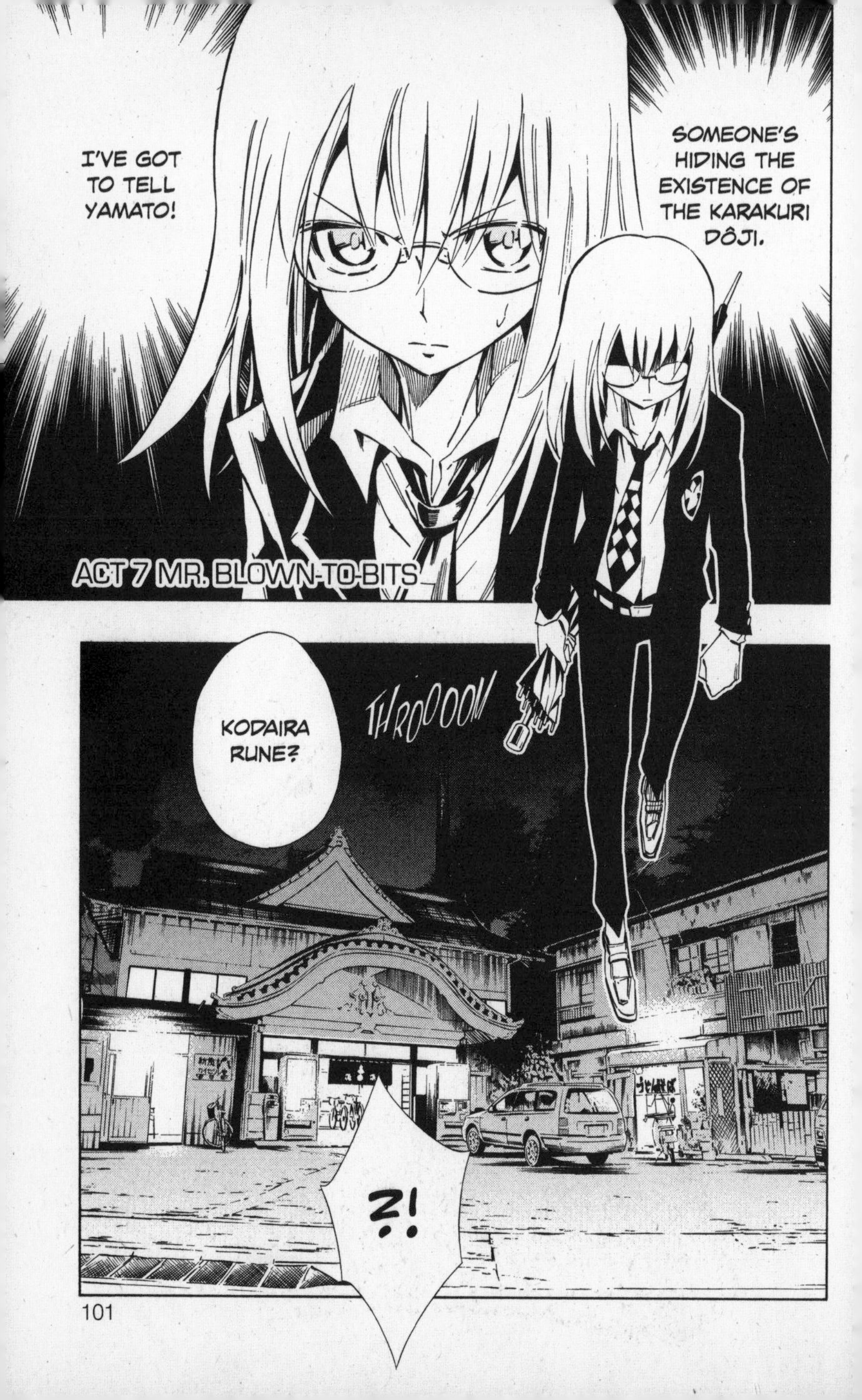
SOMEONE'S HIDING THE EXISTENCE OF THE KARAKURI DÔJI.
I'VE GOT TO TELL YAMATO!
THROOOOM
KODAIRA RUNE?
?!

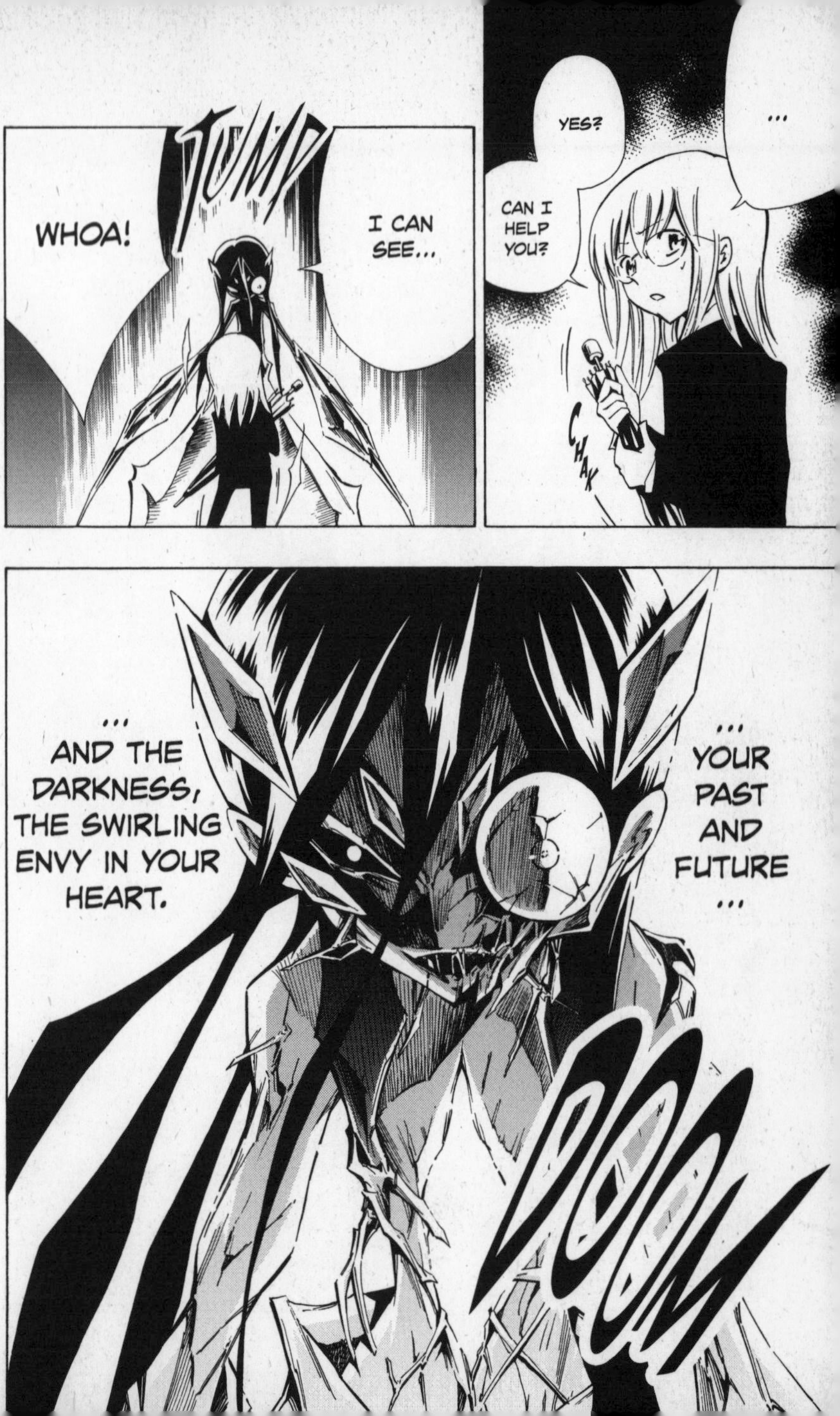
...
YES?
CAN I HELP YOU?
CHAK
JUMP
I CAN SEE...
WHOA!
... YOUR PAST AND FUTURE ...
... AND THE DARKNESS, THE SWIRLING ENVY IN YOUR HEART.
VOOM

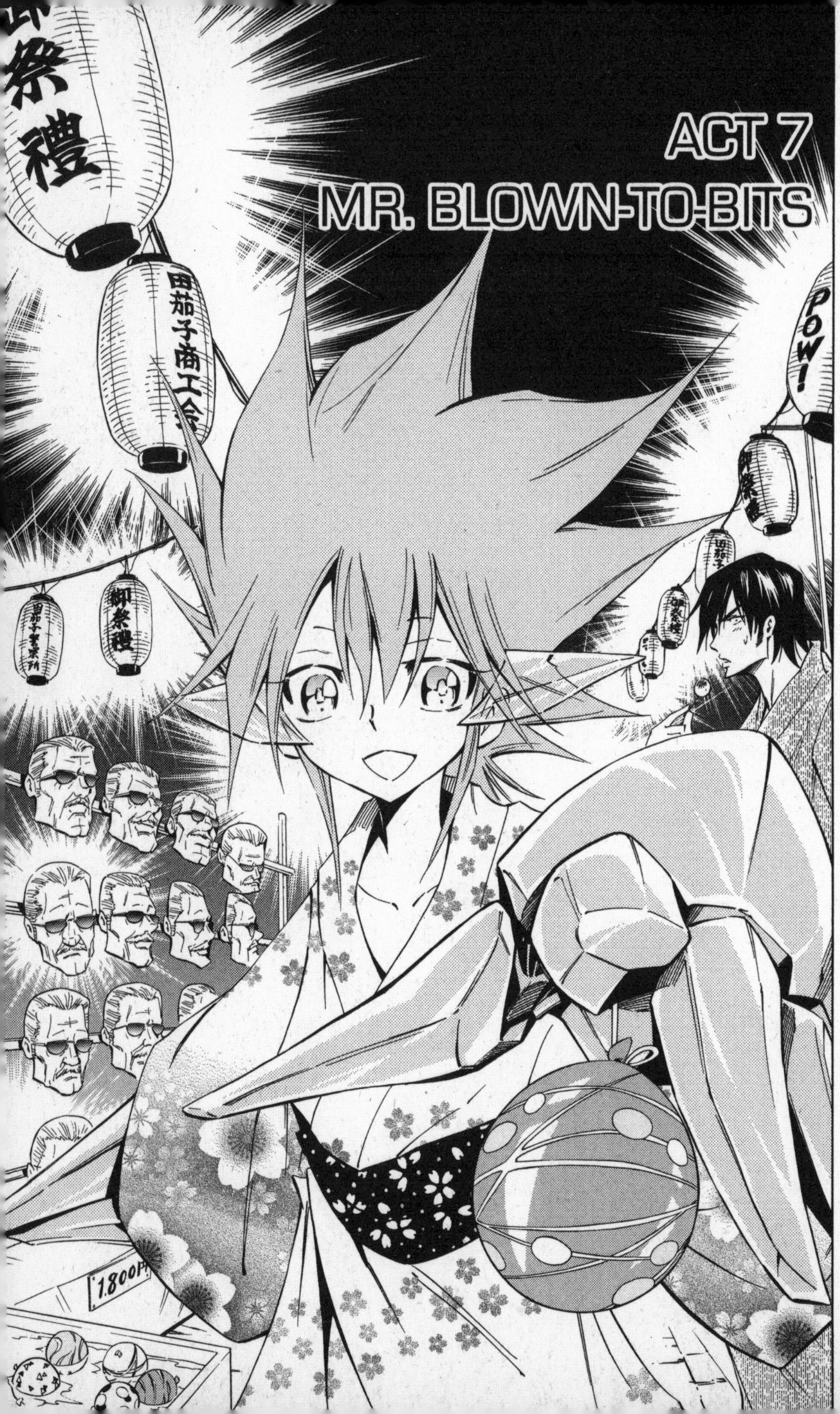
ACT 7
MR. BLOWN-TO-BITS
POW!
御祭禮
1,800円

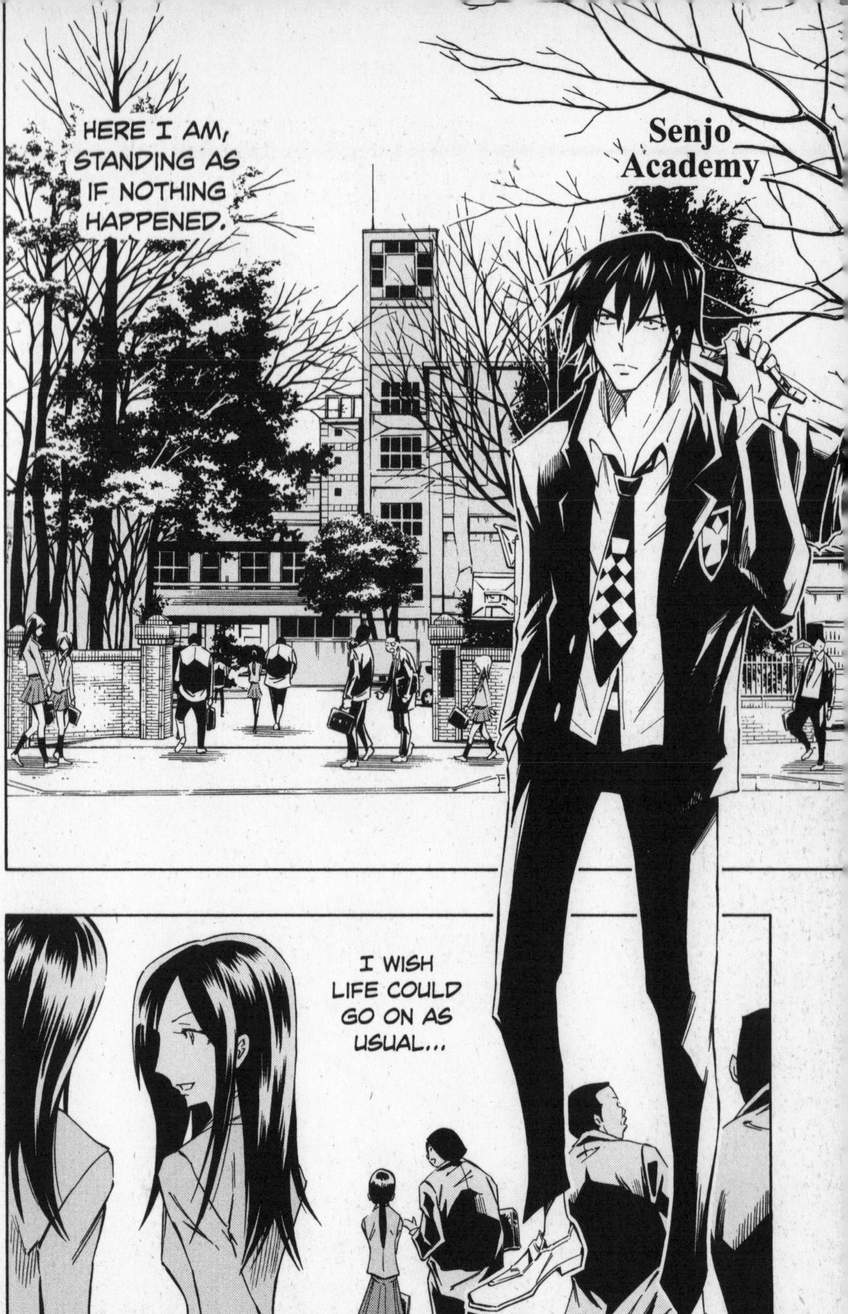
Senjo Academy
HERE I AM, STANDING AS IF NOTHING HAPPENED.
I WISH LIFE COULD GO ON AS USUAL...

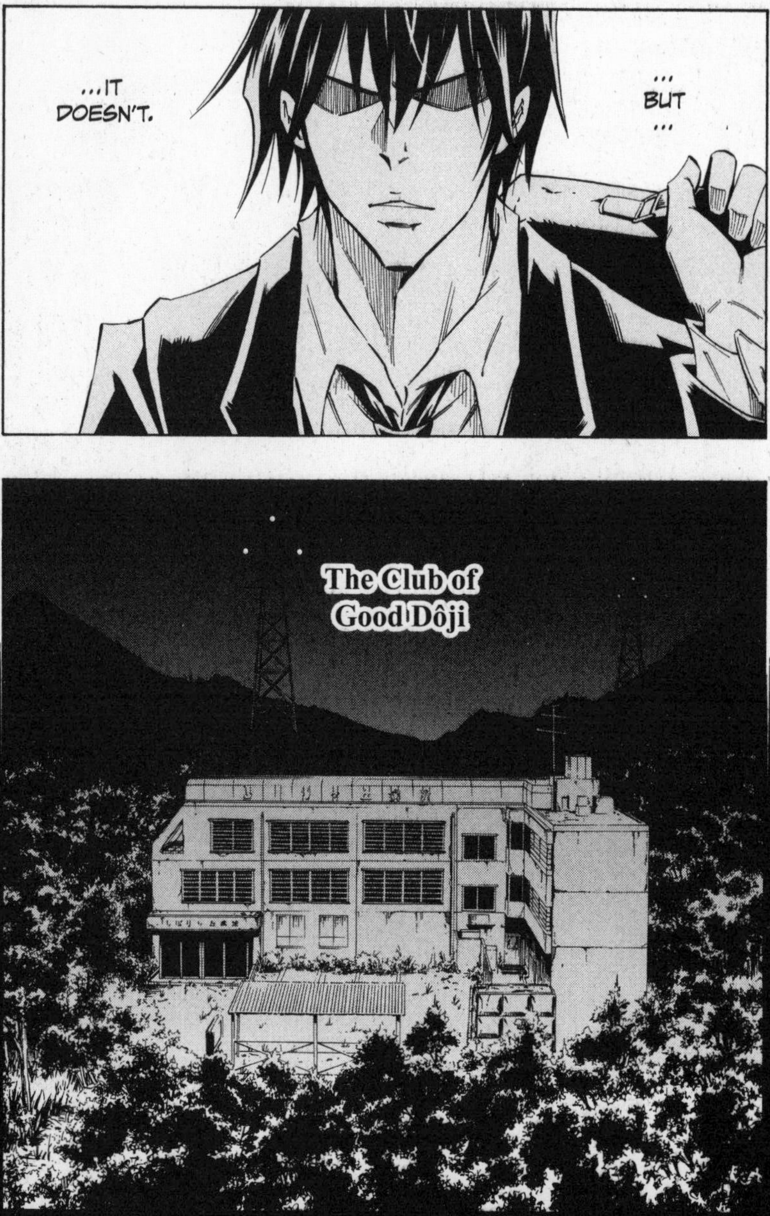
... BUT ...
...IT DOESN'T.
The Club of Good Dôji

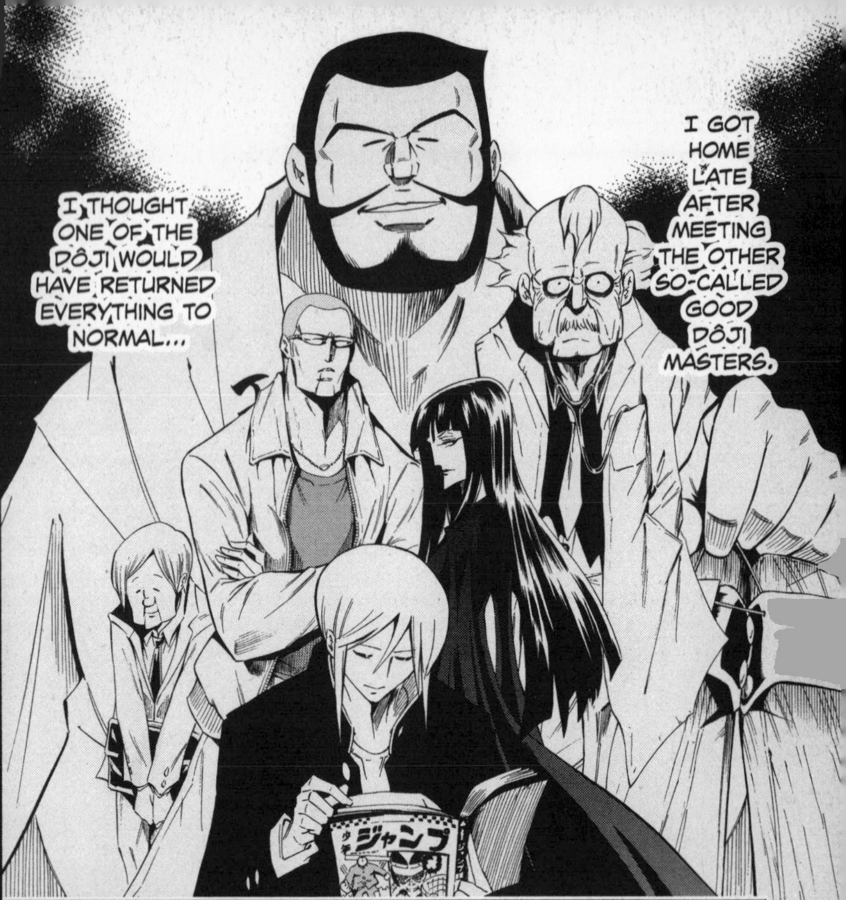
I GOT HOME LATE AFTER MEETING THE OTHER SO-CALLED GOOD DÔJI MASTERS.
I THOUGHT ONE OF THE DÔJI WOULD HAVE RETURNED EVERYTHING TO NORMAL...
少年ジャンプ

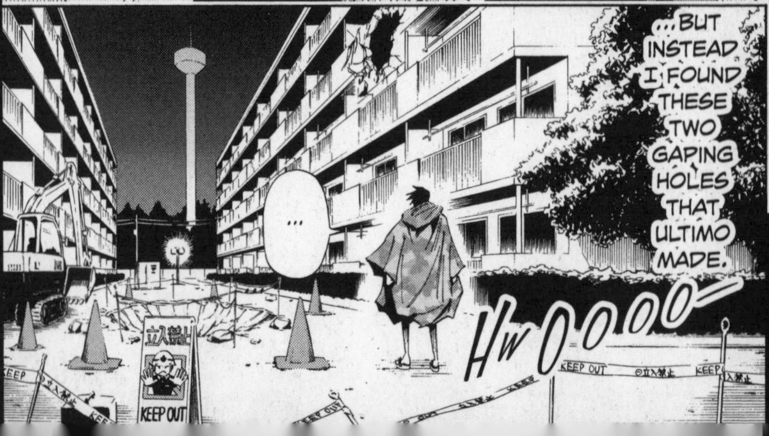
...BUT INSTEAD I FOUND THESE TWO GAPING HOLES THAT ULTIMO MADE.
...
HWOOOOO
立入禁止
KEEP OUT
KEEP OUT

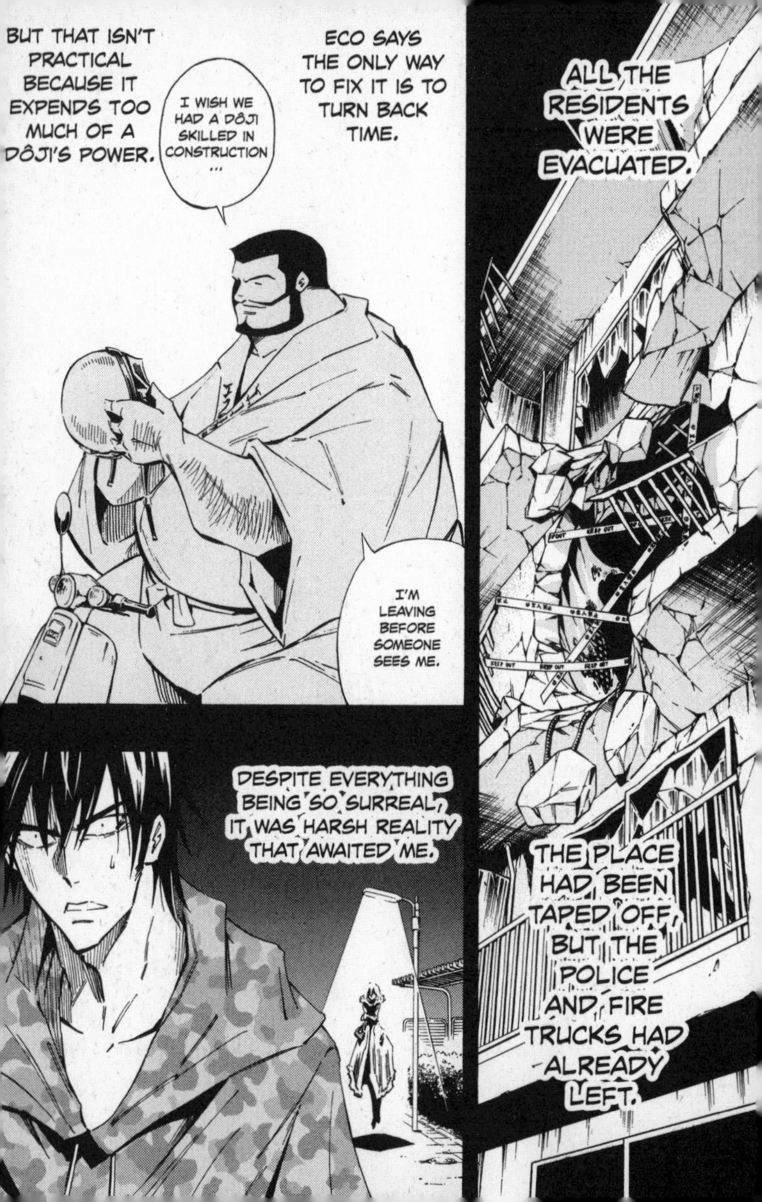
ALL THE RESIDENTS WERE EVACUATED.
THE PLACE HAD BEEN TAPED OFF, BUT THE POLICE AND FIRE TRUCKS HAD ALREADY LEFT.
KEEP OUT
ECO SAYS THE ONLY WAY TO FIX IT IS TO TURN BACK TIME.
BUT THAT ISN'T PRACTICAL BECAUSE IT EXPENDS TOO MUCH OF A DÔJI'S POWER.
I WISH WE HAD A DÔJI SKILLED IN CONSTRUCTION...
I'M LEAVING BEFORE SOMEONE SEES ME.
DESPITE EVERYTHING BEING SO SURREAL, IT WAS HARSH REALITY THAT AWAITED ME.

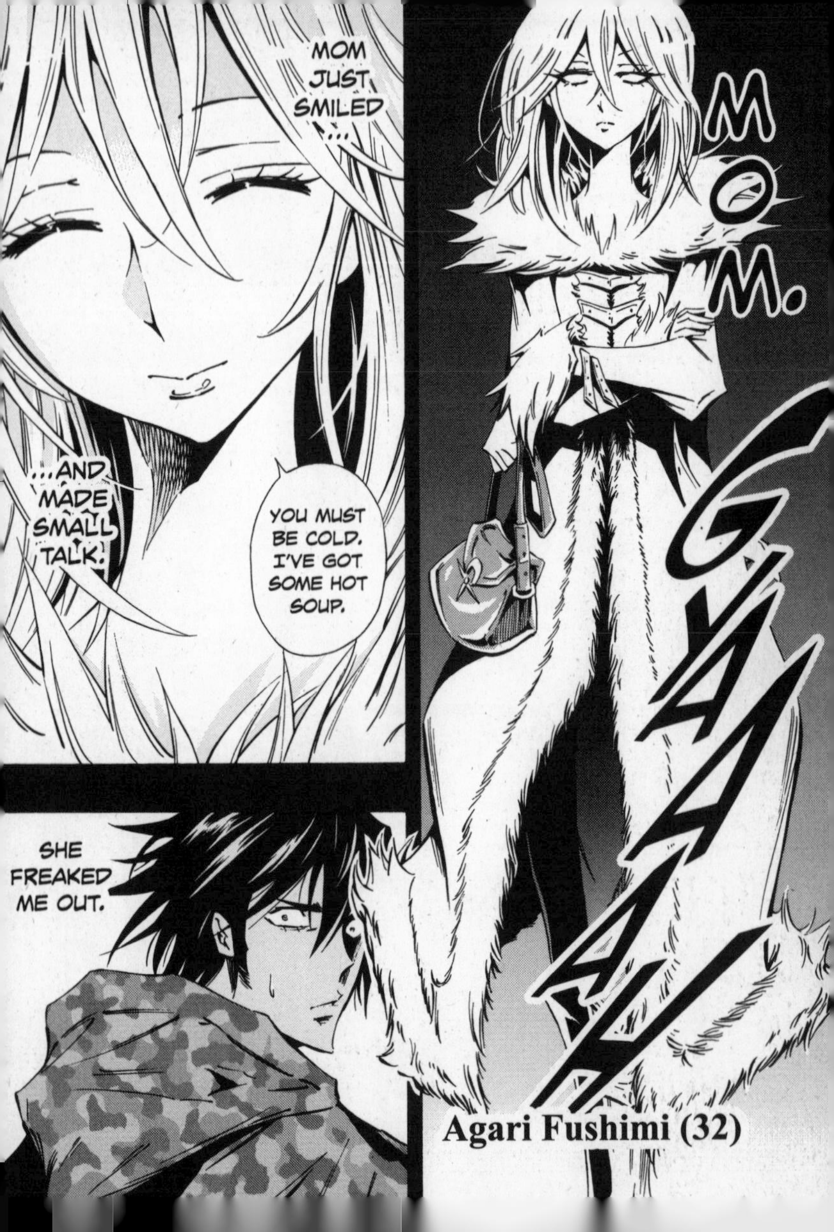
MOM.
GYAAAAH!
Agari Fushimi (32)
MOM JUST SMILED...
...AND MADE SMALL TALK.
YOU MUST BE COLD. I'VE GOT SOME HOT SOUP.
SHE FREAKED ME OUT.

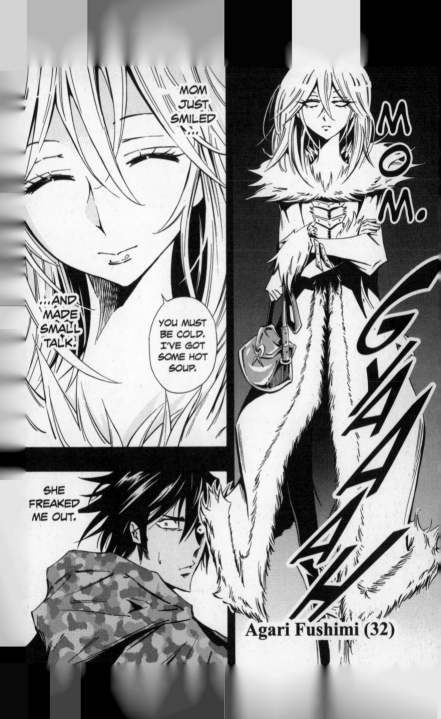

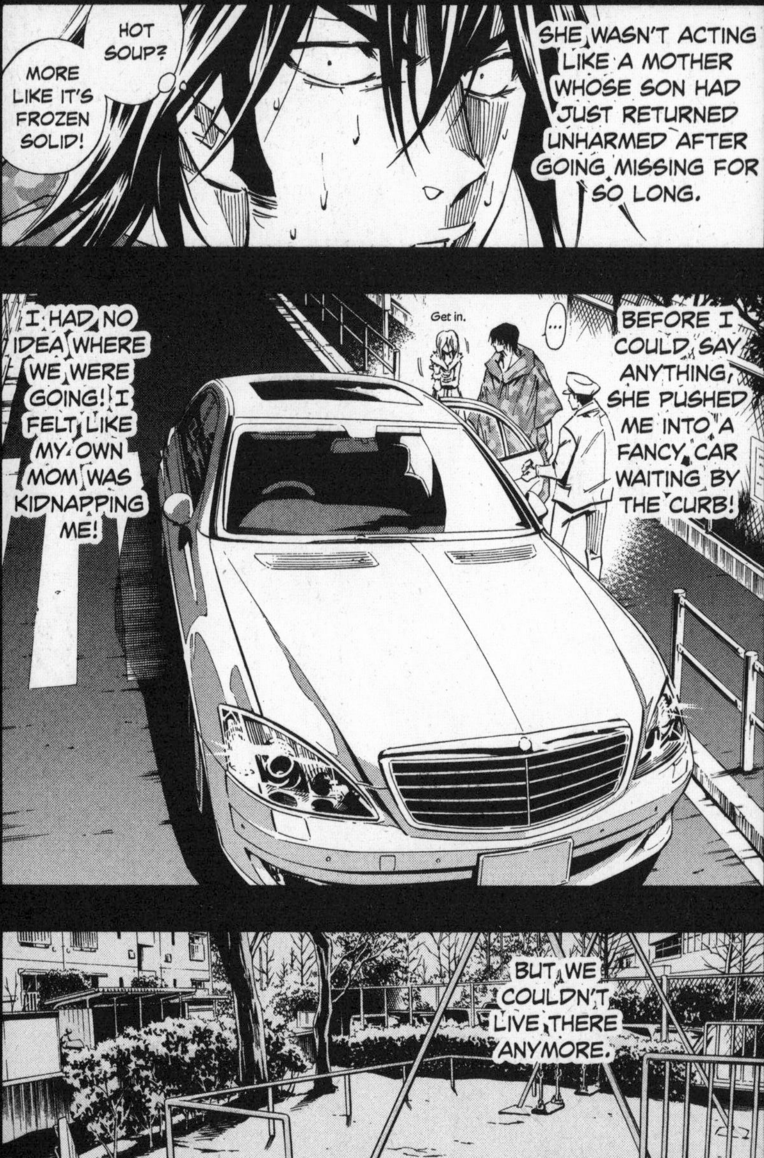
SHE WASN'T ACTING LIKE A MOTHER WHOSE SON HAD JUST RETURNED UNHARMED AFTER GOING MISSING FOR SO LONG.
HOT SOUP?
MORE LIKE IT'S FROZEN SOLID!
BEFORE I COULD SAY ANYTHING, SHE PUSHED ME INTO A FANCY CAR WAITING BY THE CURB!
...
Get in.
I HAD NO IDEA WHERE WE WERE GOING! I FELT LIKE MY OWN MOM WAS KIDNAPPING ME!
BUT WE COULDN'T LIVE THERE ANYMORE.

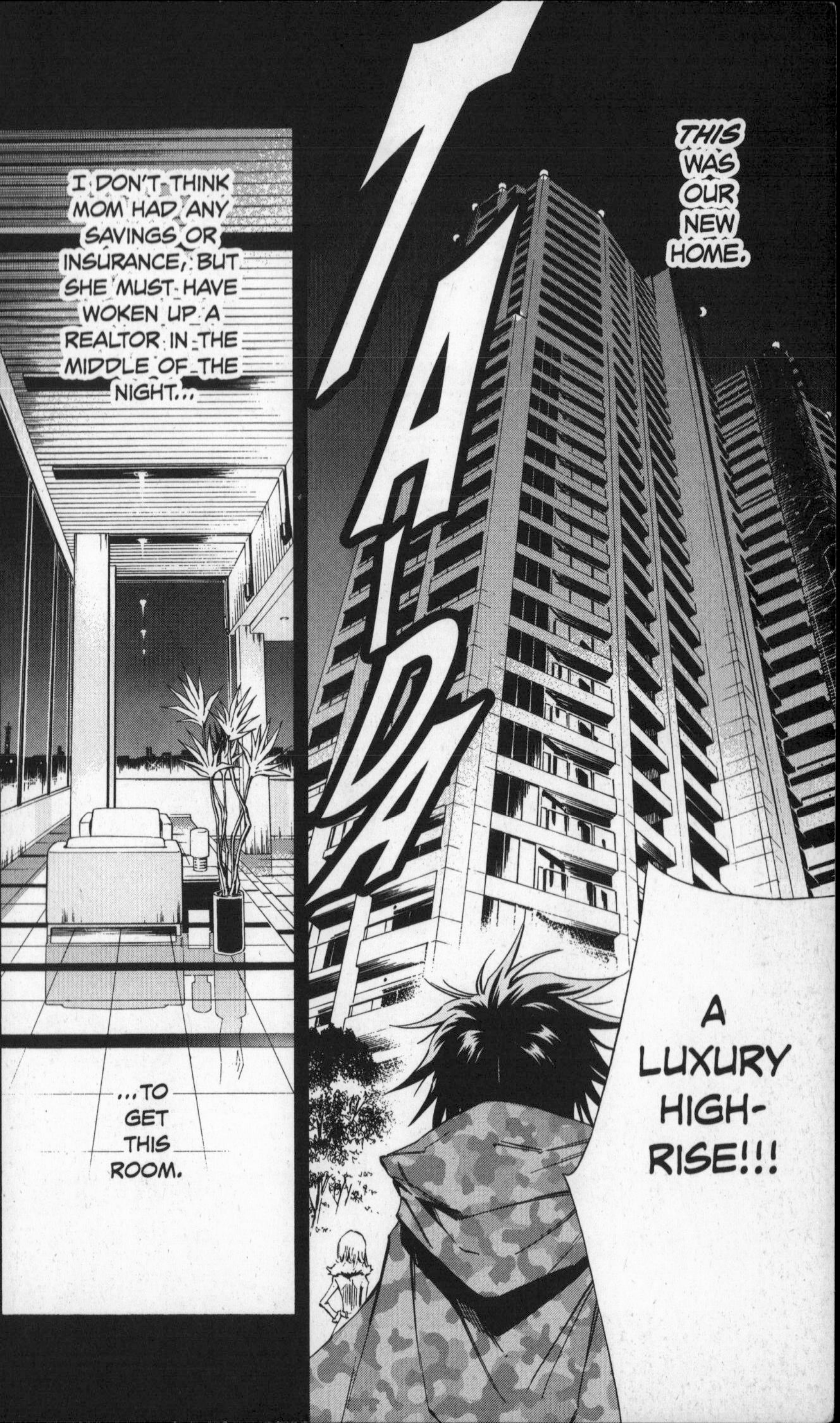
TA-DA
THIS WAS OUR NEW HOME.
A LUXURY HIGH-RISE!!!
I DON'T THINK MOM HAD ANY SAVINGS OR INSURANCE, BUT SHE MUST HAVE WOKEN UP A REALTOR IN THE MIDDLE OF THE NIGHT...
...TO GET THIS ROOM.

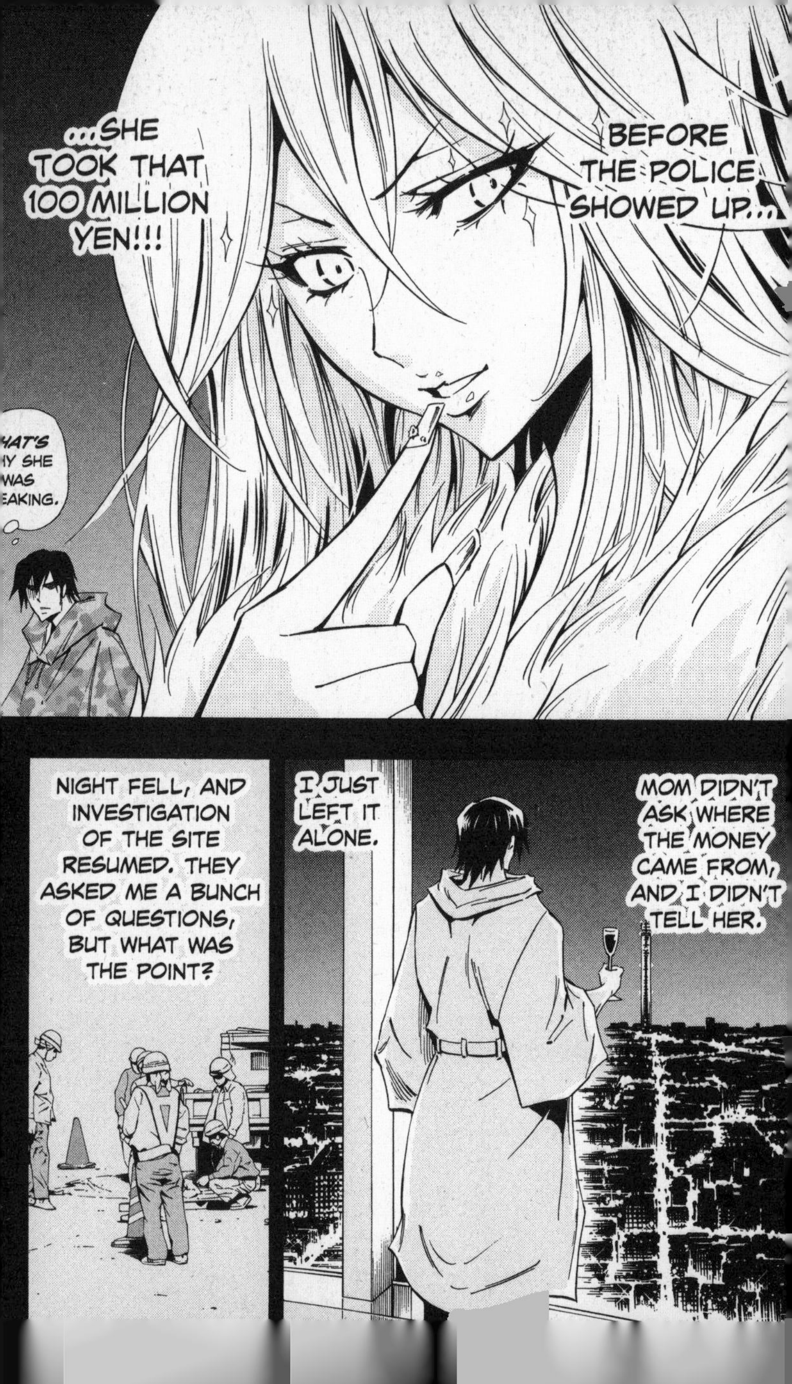
BEFORE THE POLICE SHOWED UP...
...SHE TOOK THAT 100 MILLION YEN!!!
HAT'S HY SHE WAS EAKING.
MOM DIDN'T ASK WHERE THE MONEY CAME FROM, AND I DIDN'T TELL HER.
I JUST LEFT IT ALONE.
NIGHT FELL, AND INVESTIGATION OF THE SITE RESUMED. THEY ASKED ME A BUNCH OF QUESTIONS, BUT WHAT WAS THE POINT?

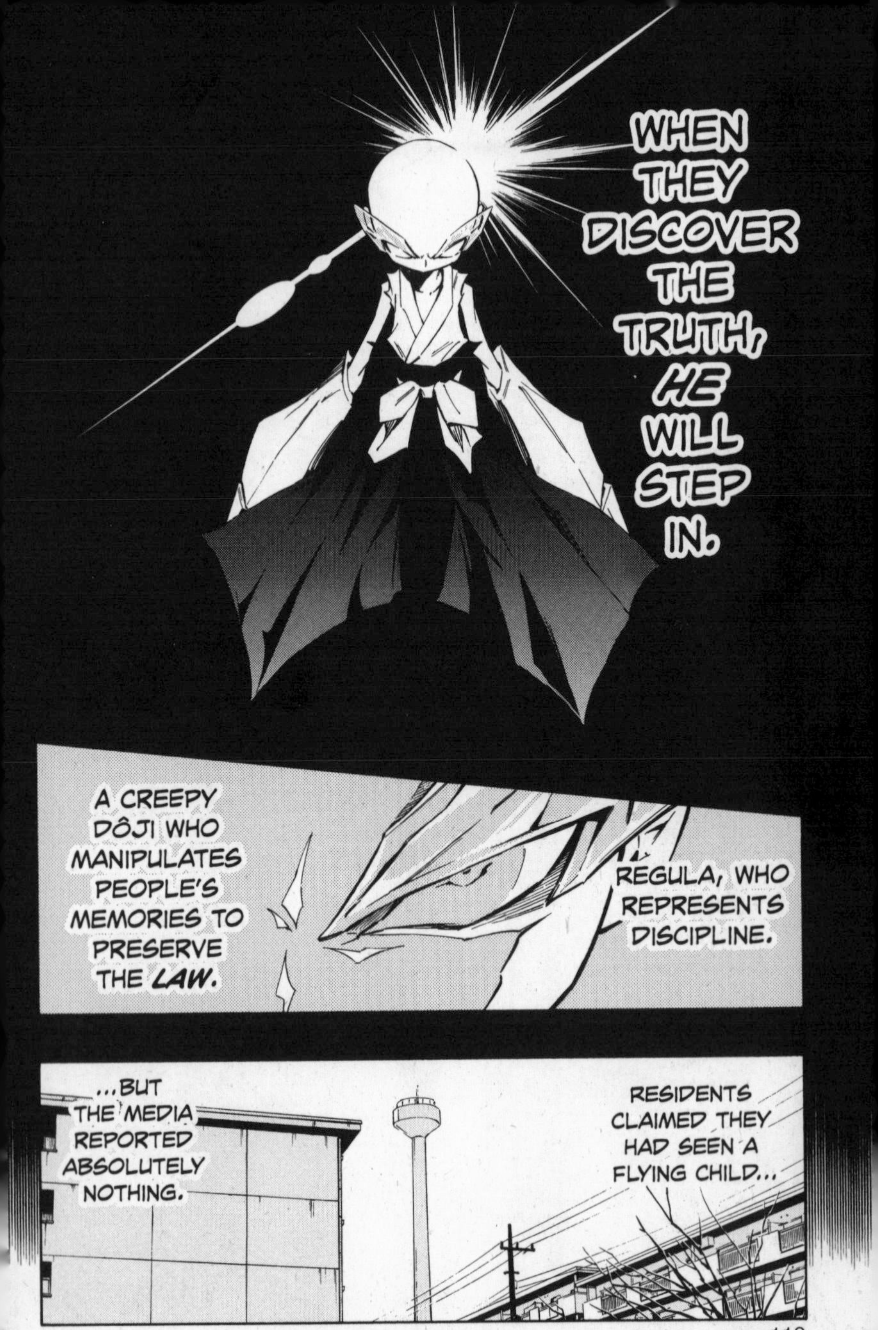
WHEN THEY DISCOVER THE TRUTH, HE WILL STEP IN.
REGULA, WHO REPRESENTS DISCIPLINE.
A CREEPY DÔJI WHO MANIPULATES PEOPLE'S MEMORIES TO PRESERVE THE LAW.
RESIDENTS CLAIMED THEY HAD SEEN A FLYING CHILD...
...BUT THE MEDIA REPORTED ABSOLUTELY NOTHING.

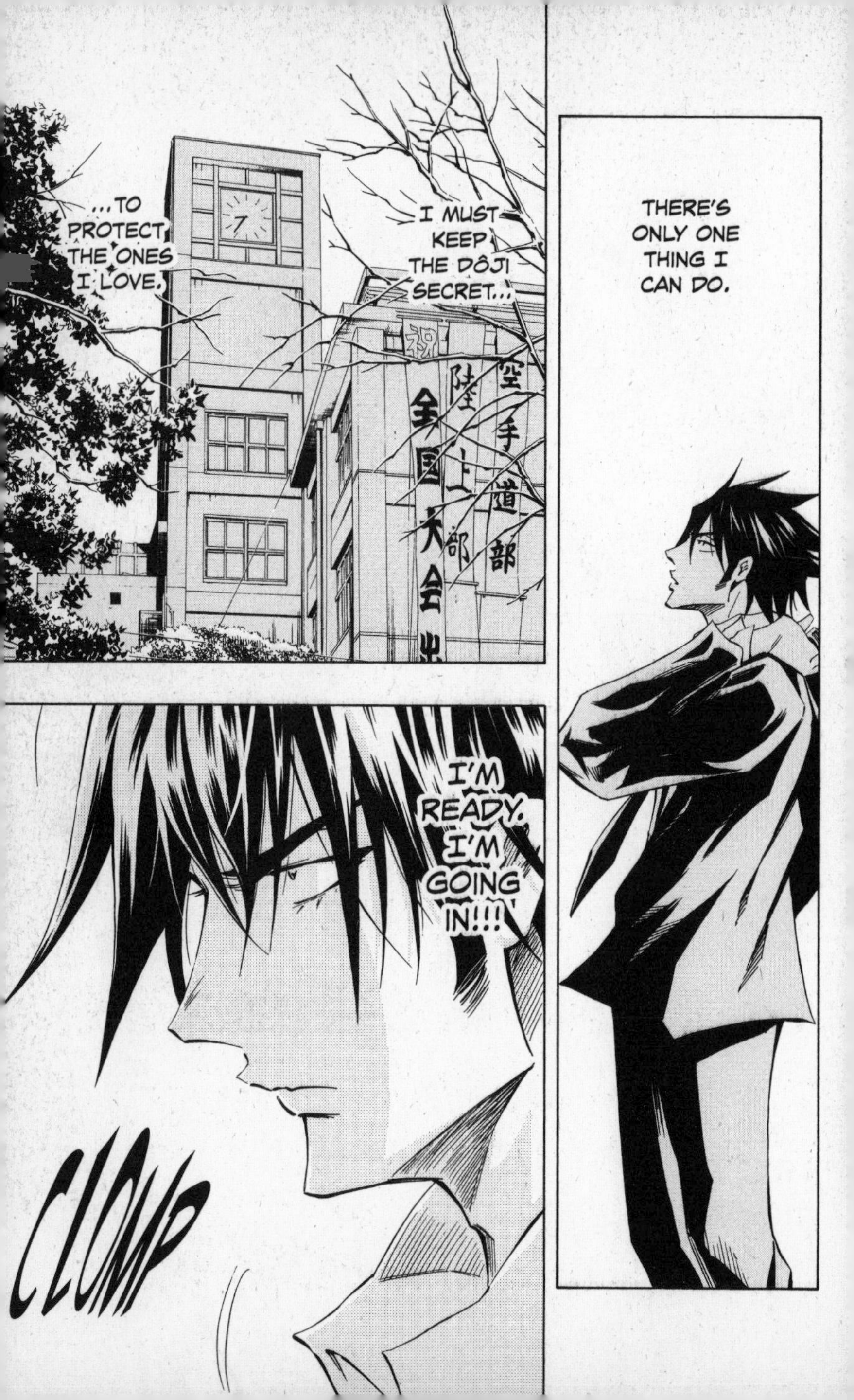
THERE'S ONLY ONE THING I CAN DO.
I MUST KEEP THE DÔJI SECRET...
...TO PROTECT THE ONES I LOVE.
祝
空手道部
陸上部
全国大会
I'M READY. I'M GOING IN!!!
CLOMP

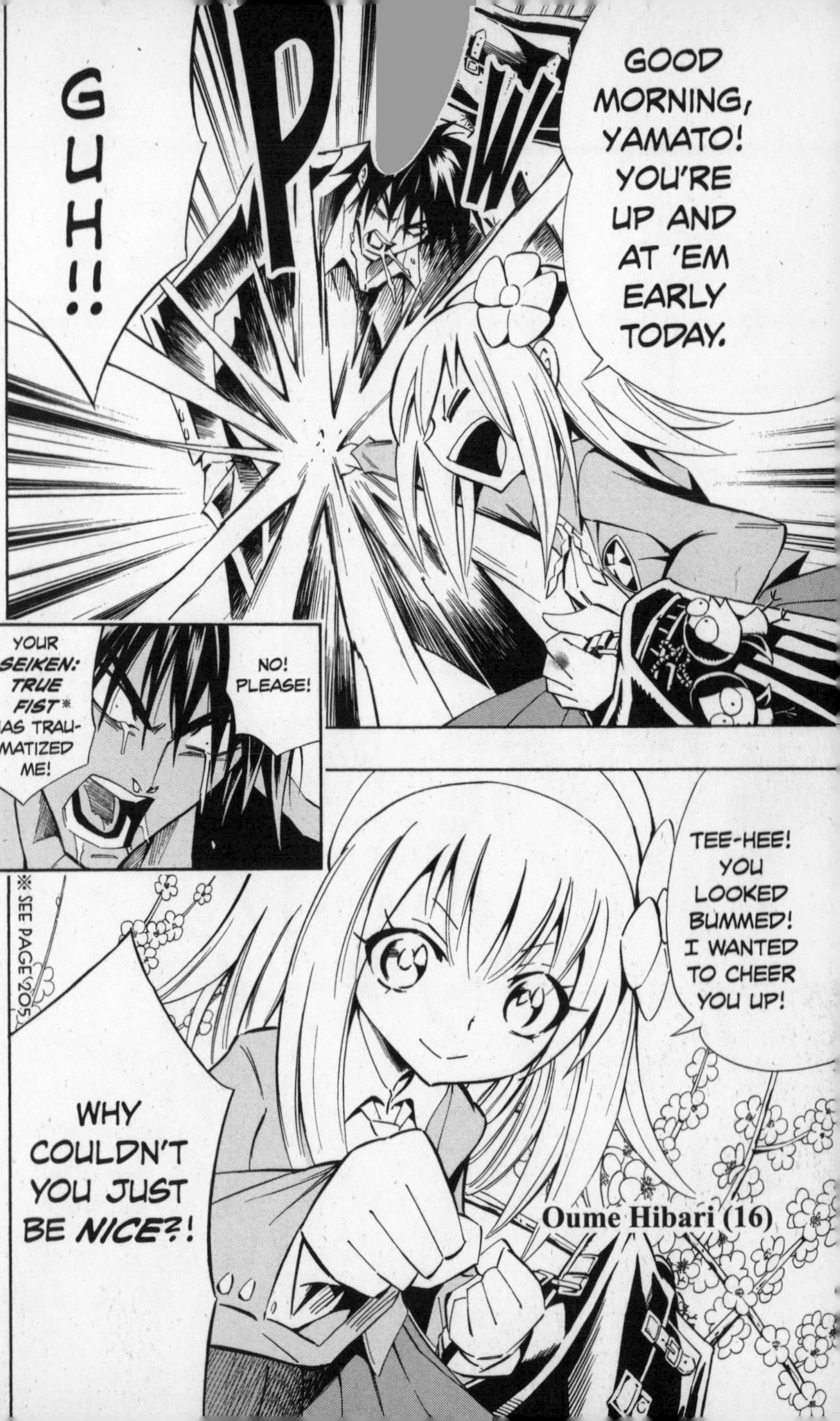
GOOD MORNING, YAMATO! YOU'RE UP AND AT 'EM EARLY TODAY.
GUH!!
NO! PLEASE!
YOUR SEIKEN: TRUE FIST※ HAS TRAUMATIZED ME!
TEE-HEE! YOU LOOKED BUMMED! I WANTED TO CHEER YOU UP!
WHY COULDN'T YOU JUST BE NICE?!
Oume Hibari (16)

※ SEE PAGE 205

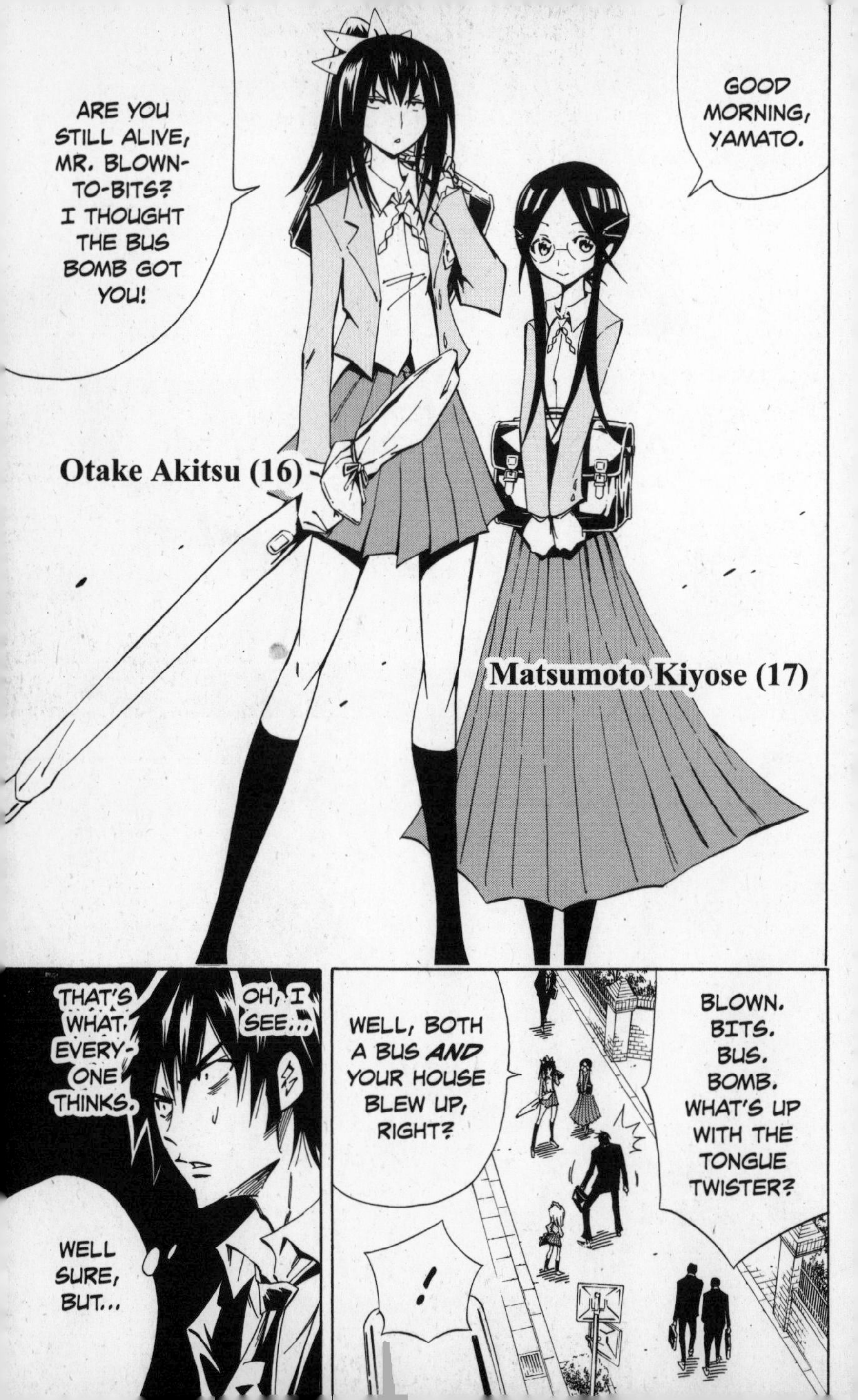
GOOD MORNING, YAMATO.
ARE YOU STILL ALIVE, MR. BLOWN-TO-BITS? I THOUGHT THE BUS BOMB GOT YOU!
Otake Akitsu (16)
Matsumoto Kiyose (17)
BLOWN. BITS. BUS. BOMB. WHAT'S UP WITH THE TONGUE TWISTER?
WELL, BOTH A BUS AND YOUR HOUSE BLEW UP, RIGHT?
!
OH, I SEE...
THAT'S WHAT EVERY-ONE THINKS.
WELL SURE, BUT...

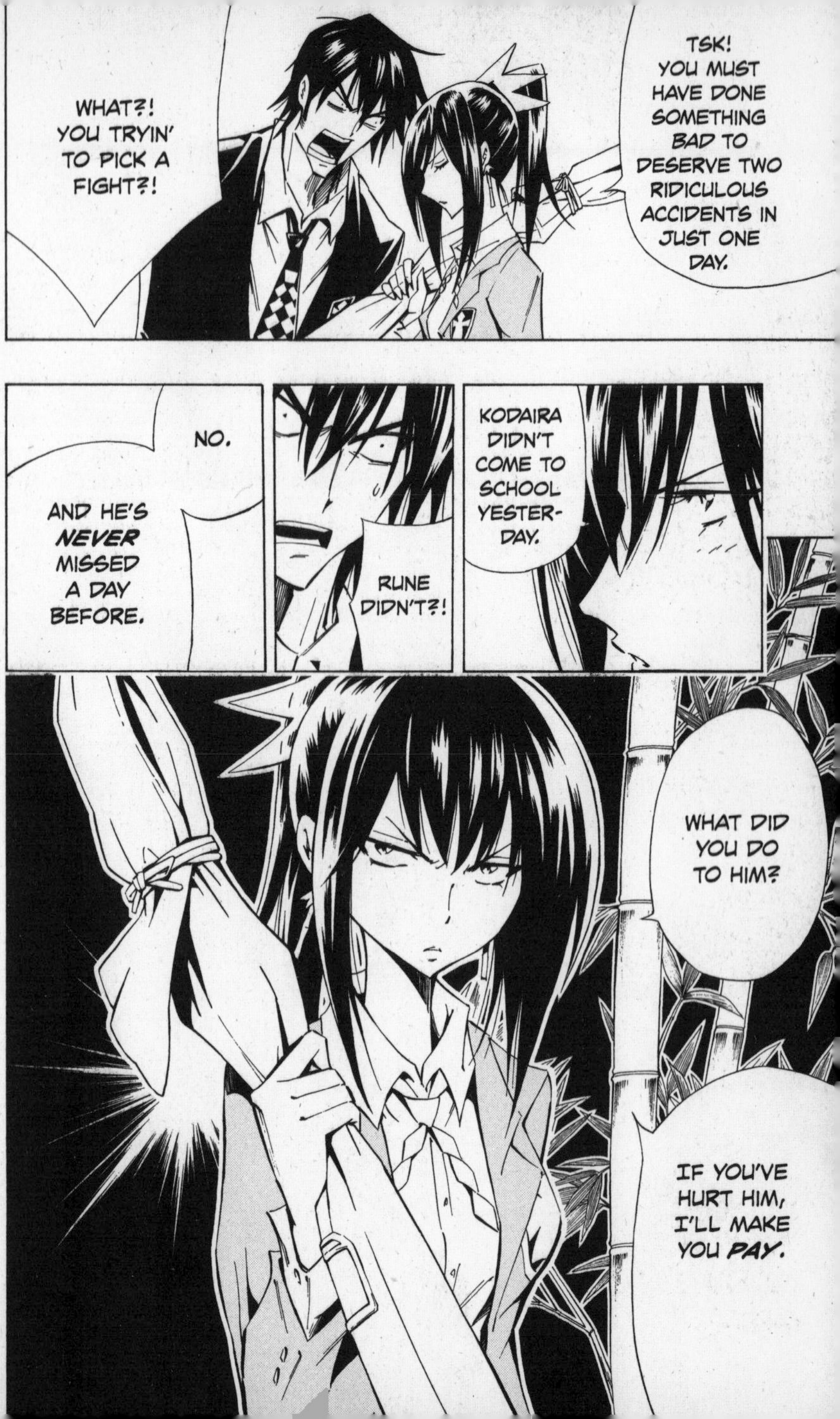
TSK! YOU MUST HAVE DONE SOMETHING BAD TO DESERVE TWO RIDICULOUS ACCIDENTS IN JUST ONE DAY.
WHAT?! YOU TRYIN' TO PICK A FIGHT?!
KODAIRA DIDN'T COME TO SCHOOL YESTER-DAY.
RUNE DIDN'T?!
NO.
AND HE'S *NEVER* MISSED A DAY BEFORE.
WHAT DID YOU DO TO HIM?
IF YOU'VE HURT HIM, I'LL MAKE YOU *PAY*.

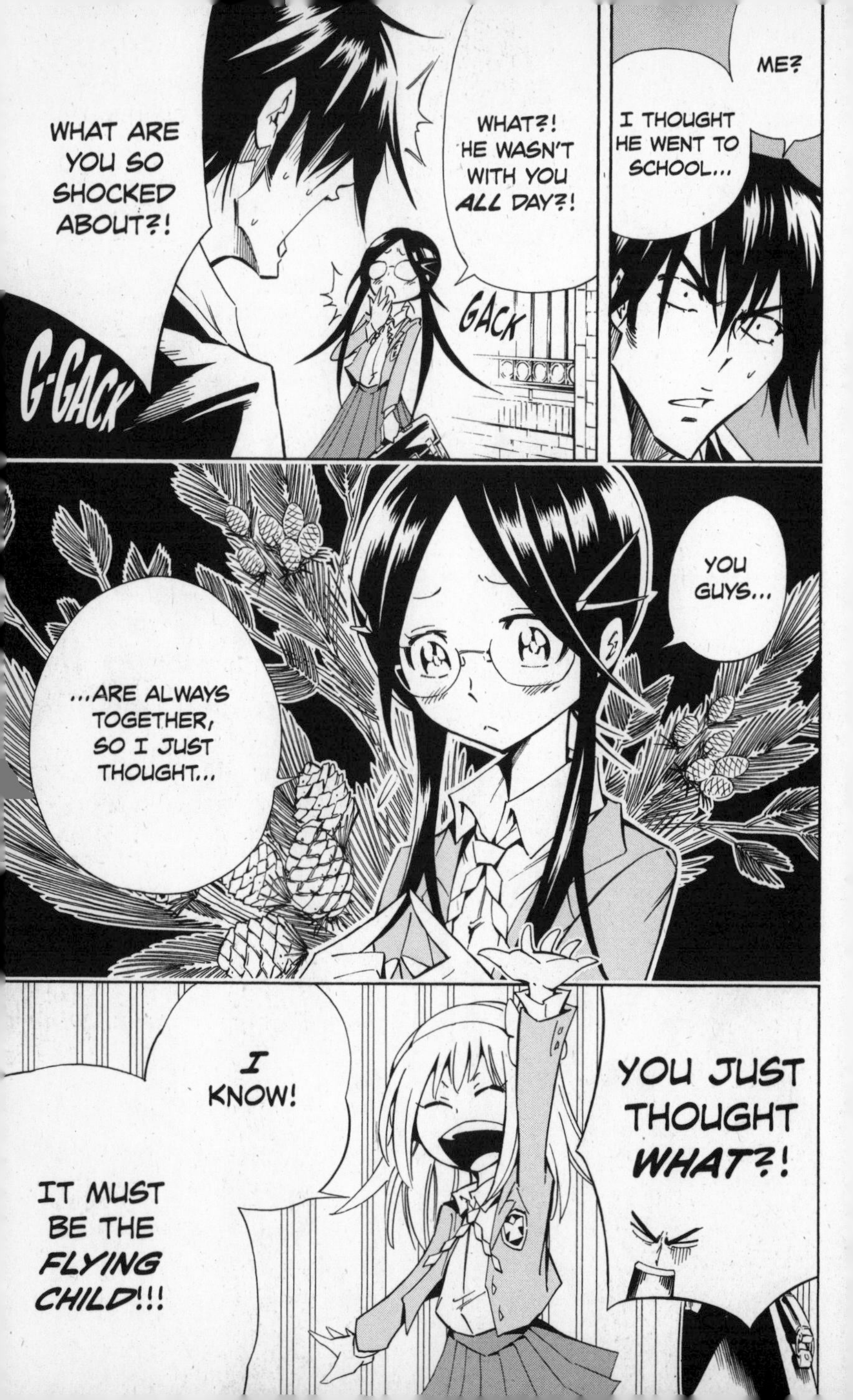
ME?
I THOUGHT HE WENT TO SCHOOL...
WHAT?! HE WASN'T WITH YOU ALL DAY?!
GACK
WHAT ARE YOU SO SHOCKED ABOUT?!
G-GACK
YOU GUYS...
...ARE ALWAYS TOGETHER, SO I JUST THOUGHT...
YOU JUST THOUGHT WHAT?!
I KNOW!
IT MUST BE THE FLYING CHILD!!!

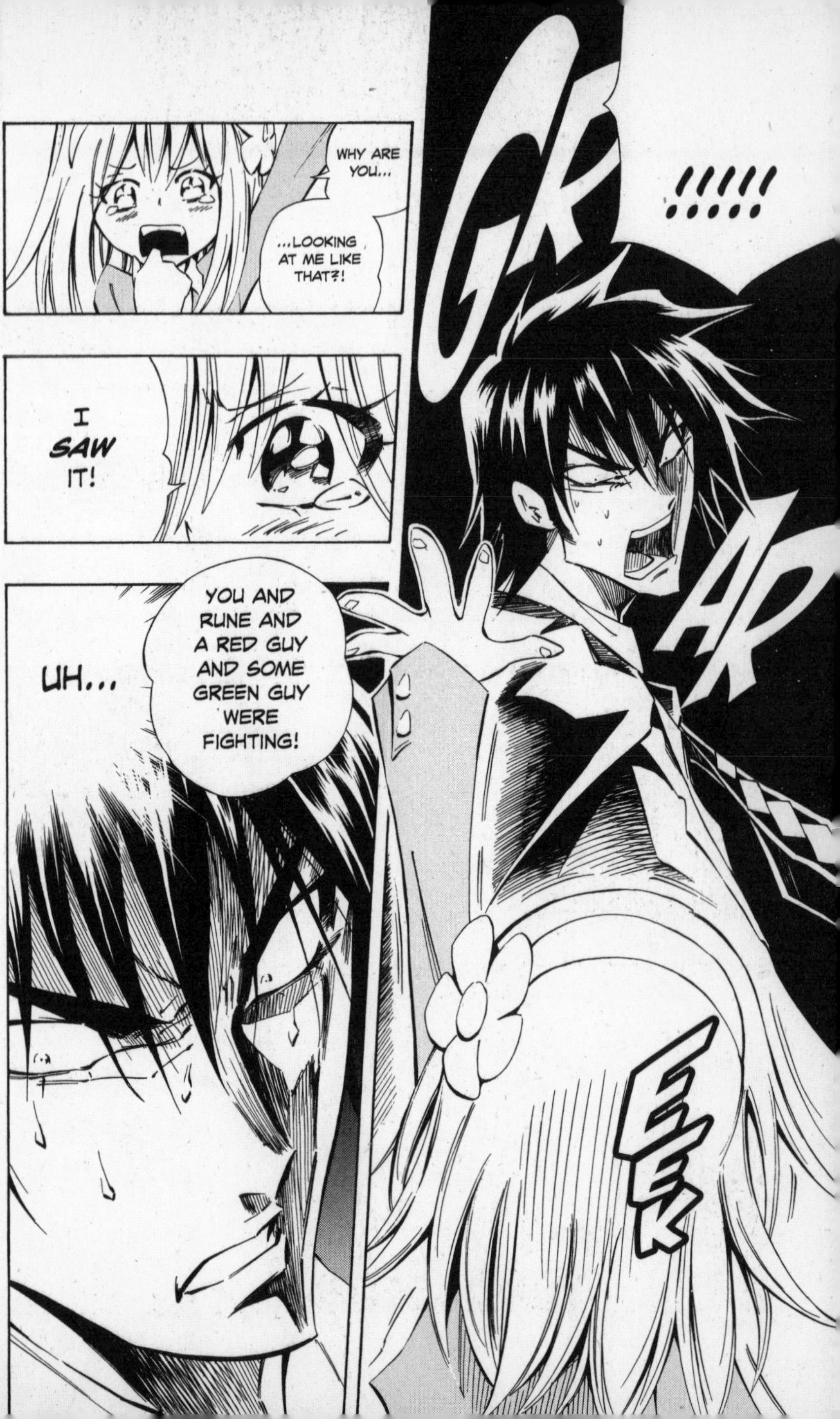
WHY ARE YOU...
...LOOKING AT ME LIKE THAT?!
I SAW IT!
YOU AND RUNE AND A RED GUY AND SOME GREEN GUY WERE FIGHTING!
UH...
GRAR
!!!!!
EEEK

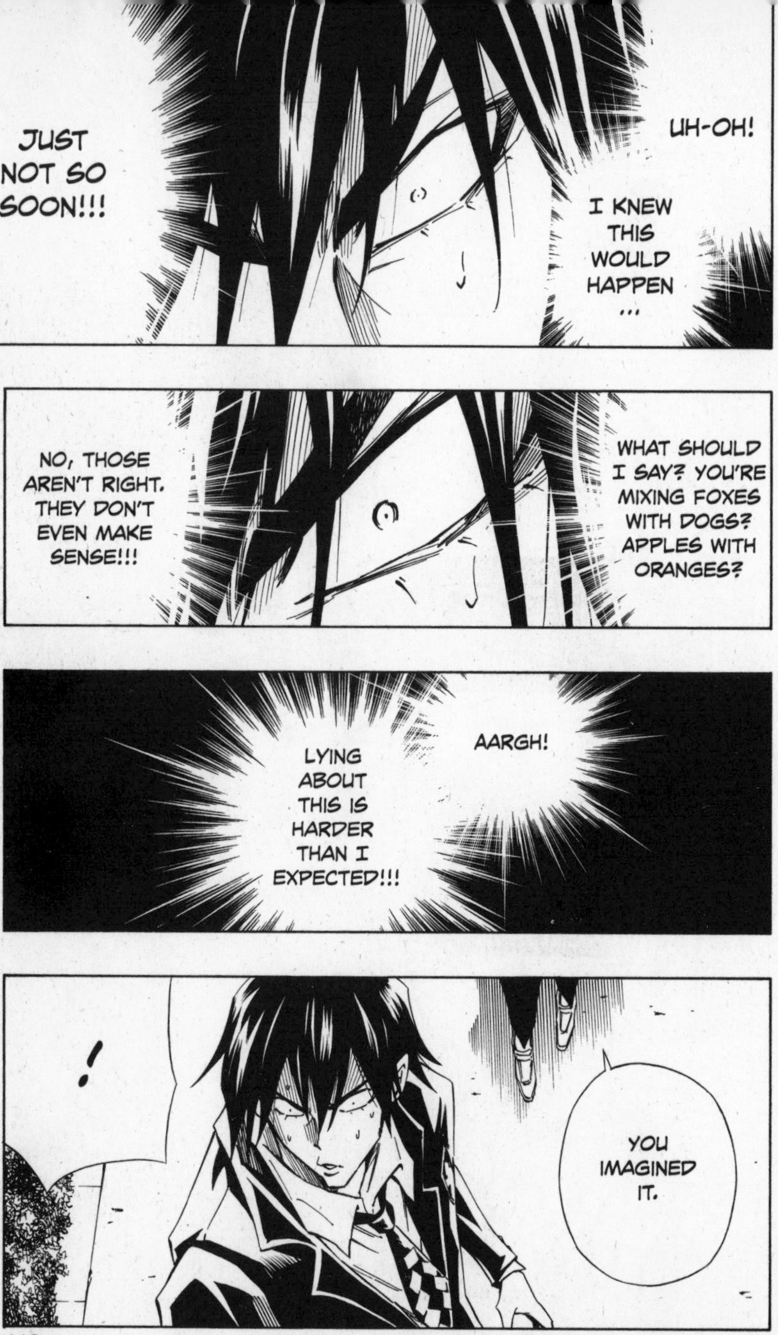
UH-OH!
I KNEW THIS WOULD HAPPEN ...
JUST NOT SO SOON!!!
WHAT SHOULD I SAY? YOU'RE MIXING FOXES WITH DOGS? APPLES WITH ORANGES?
NO, THOSE AREN'T RIGHT. THEY DON'T EVEN MAKE SENSE!!!
AARGH!
LYING ABOUT THIS IS HARDER THAN I EXPECTED!!!
YOU IMAGINED IT.
!

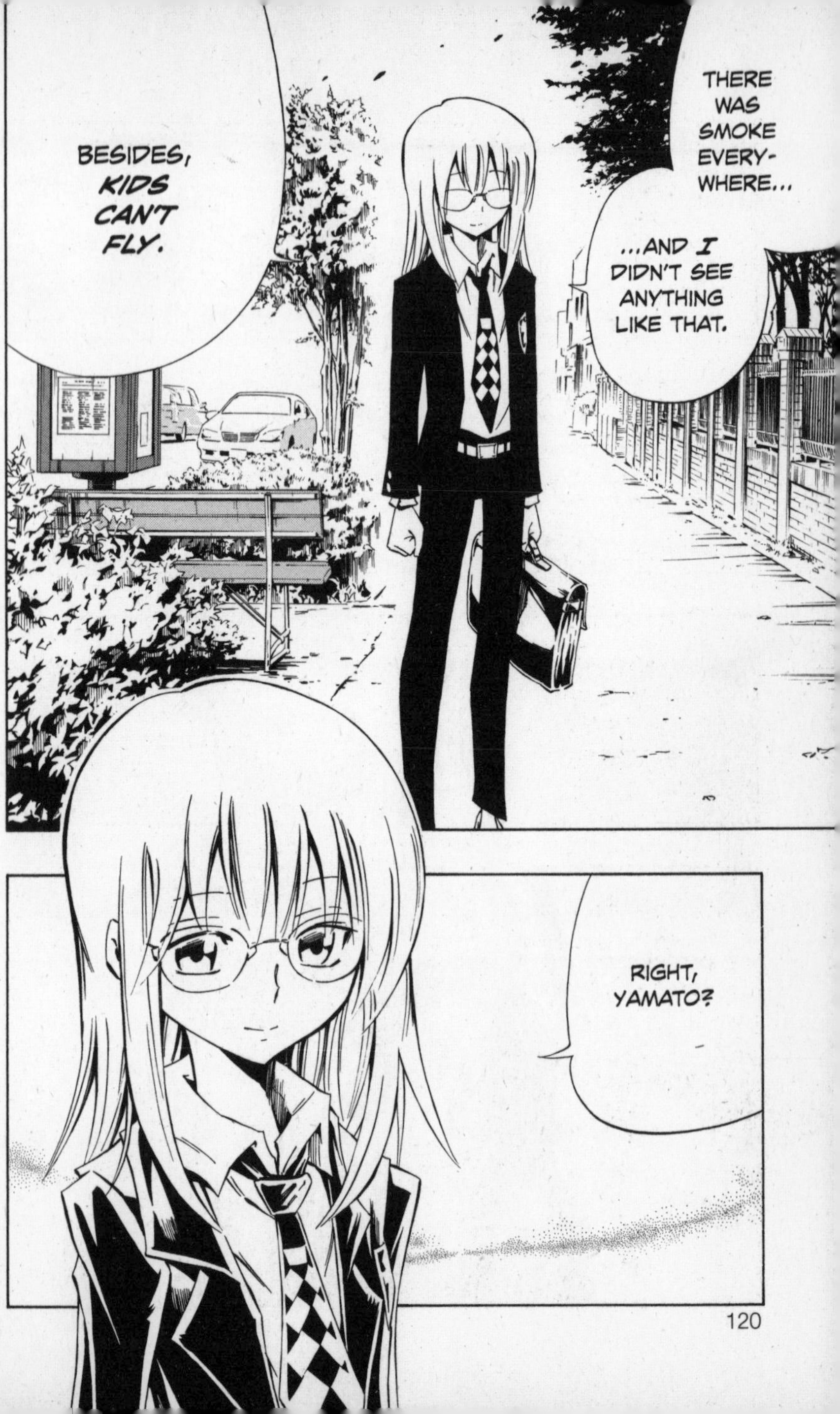
THERE WAS SMOKE EVERY-WHERE...
...AND I DIDN'T SEE ANYTHING LIKE THAT.
BESIDES, KIDS CAN'T FLY.
RIGHT, YAMATO?

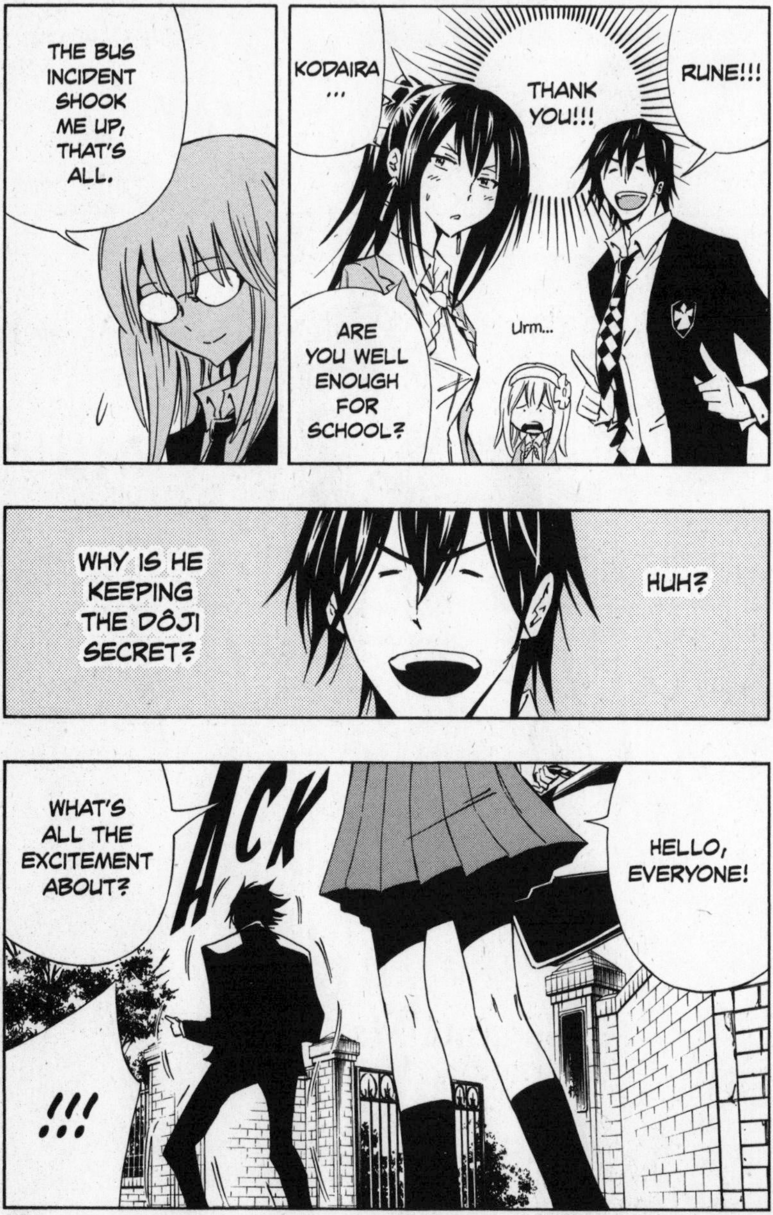

RUNE!!!
THANK YOU!!!
KODAIRA...
Urm...
ARE YOU WELL ENOUGH FOR SCHOOL?
THE BUS INCIDENT SHOOK ME UP, THAT'S ALL.
HUH?
WHY IS HE KEEPING THE DÔJI SECRET?
HELLO, EVERYONE!
ACK
WHAT'S ALL THE EXCITEMENT ABOUT?
!!!

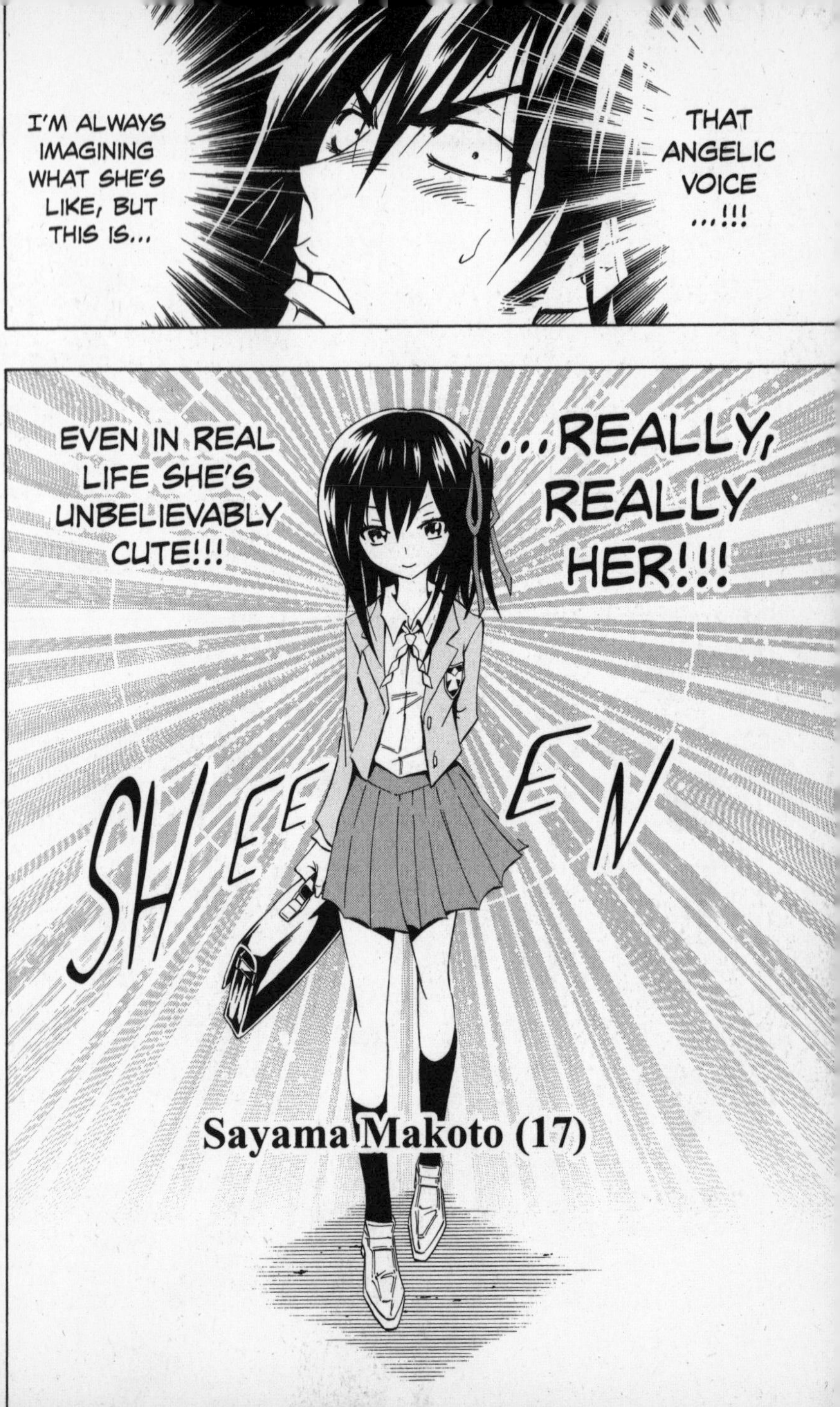
THAT ANGELIC VOICE ...!!!
I'M ALWAYS IMAGINING WHAT SHE'S LIKE, BUT THIS IS...
...REALLY, REALLY HER!!!
EVEN IN REAL LIFE SHE'S UNBELIEVABLY CUTE!!!
SHEEEN
Sayama Makoto (17)

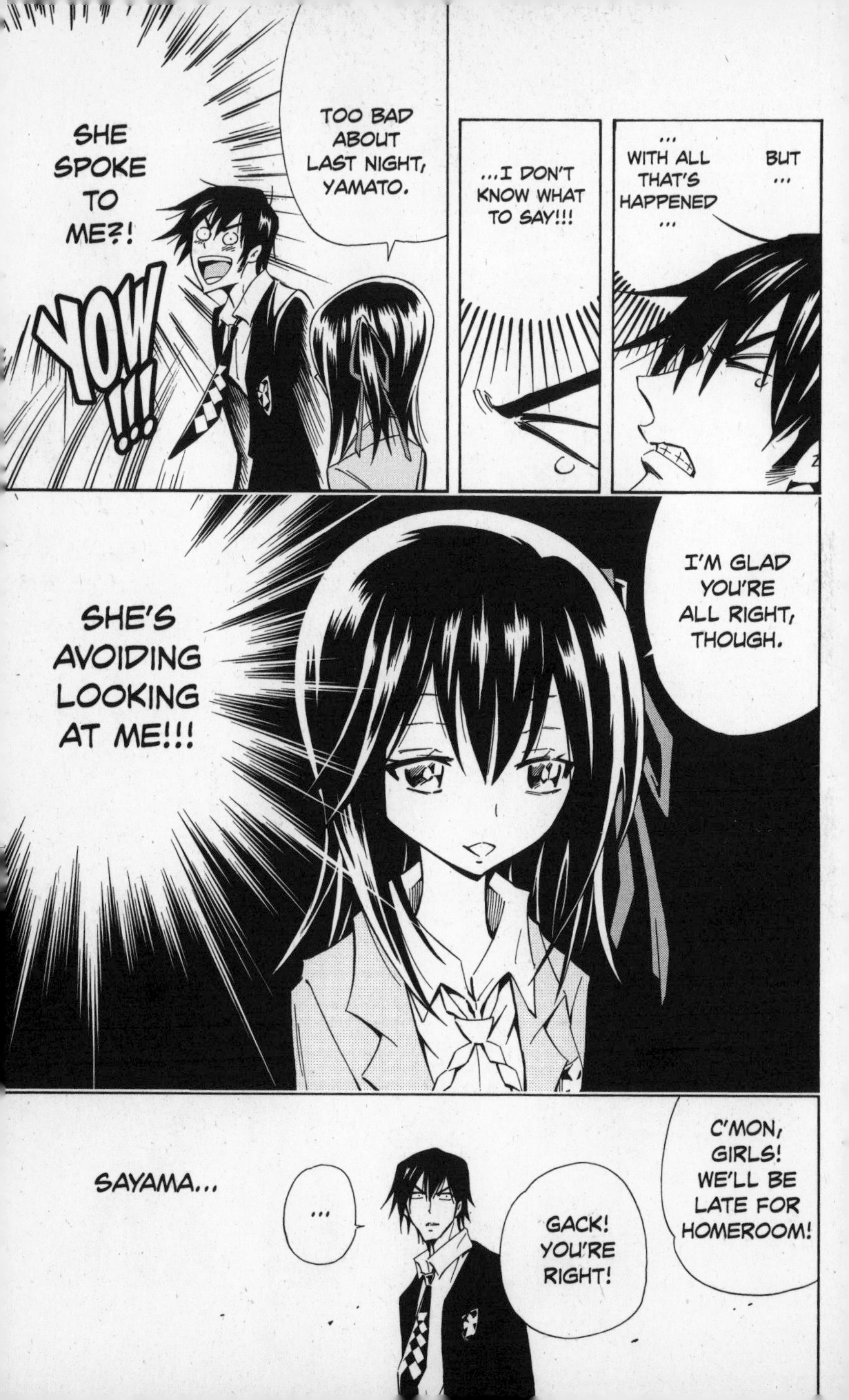
BUT ...
... WITH ALL THAT'S HAPPENED ...
...I DON'T KNOW WHAT TO SAY!!!
TOO BAD ABOUT LAST NIGHT, YAMATO.
SHE SPOKE TO ME?!
YOW!!!...
I'M GLAD YOU'RE ALL RIGHT, THOUGH.
SHE'S AVOIDING LOOKING AT ME!!!
C'MON, GIRLS! WE'LL BE LATE FOR HOMEROOM!
GACK! YOU'RE RIGHT!
...
SAYAMA...

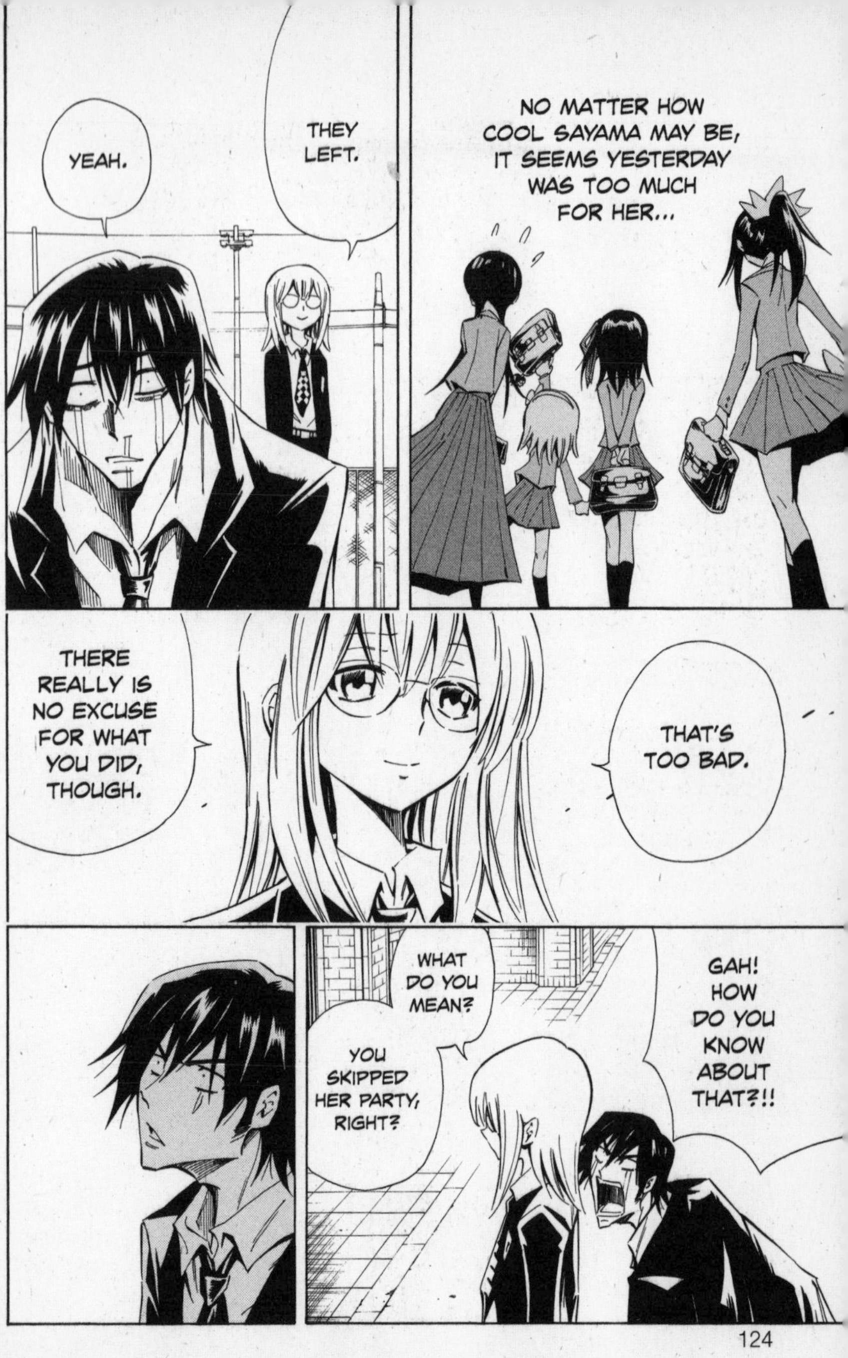
NO MATTER HOW COOL SAYAMA MAY BE, IT SEEMS YESTERDAY WAS TOO MUCH FOR HER...
THEY LEFT.
YEAH.
THAT'S TOO BAD.
THERE REALLY IS NO EXCUSE FOR WHAT YOU DID, THOUGH.
WHAT DO YOU MEAN?
YOU SKIPPED HER PARTY, RIGHT?
GAH! HOW DO YOU KNOW ABOUT THAT?!!

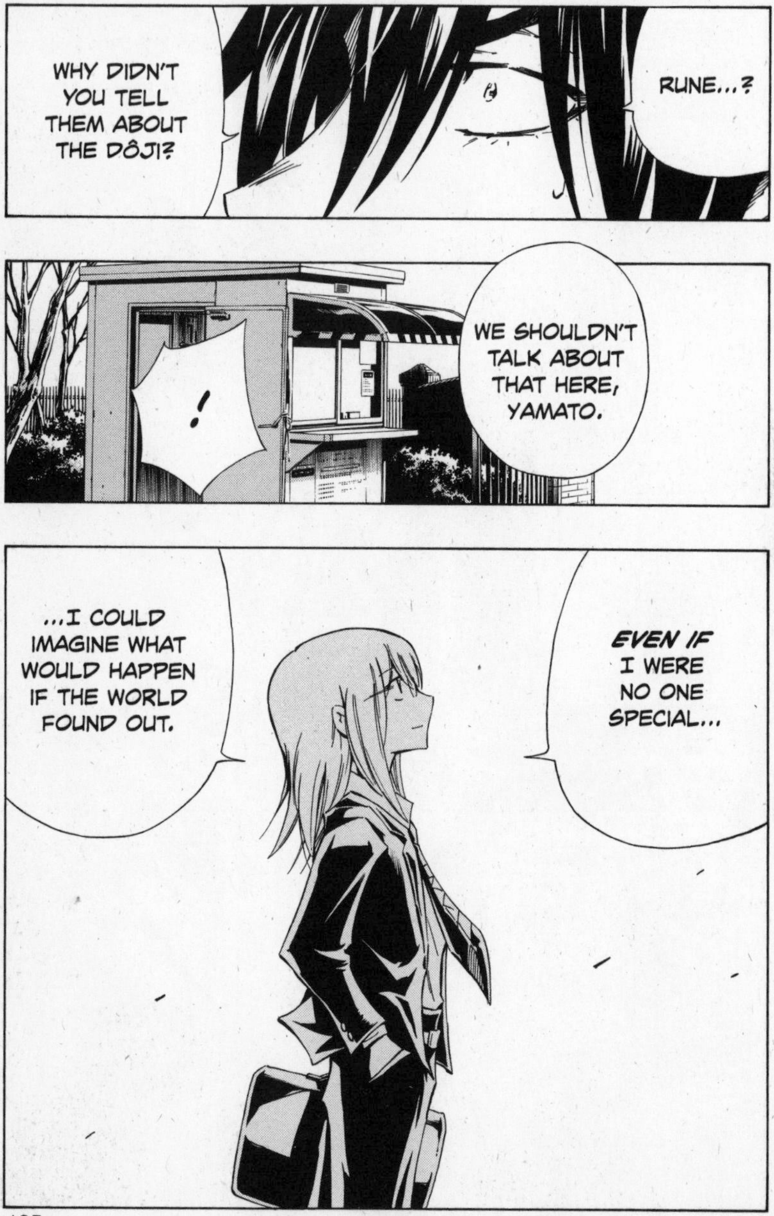
RUNE...?
WHY DIDN'T YOU TELL THEM ABOUT THE DÔJI?
WE SHOULDN'T TALK ABOUT THAT HERE, YAMATO.
!
EVEN IF I WERE NO ONE SPECIAL...
...I COULD IMAGINE WHAT WOULD HAPPEN IF THE WORLD FOUND OUT.

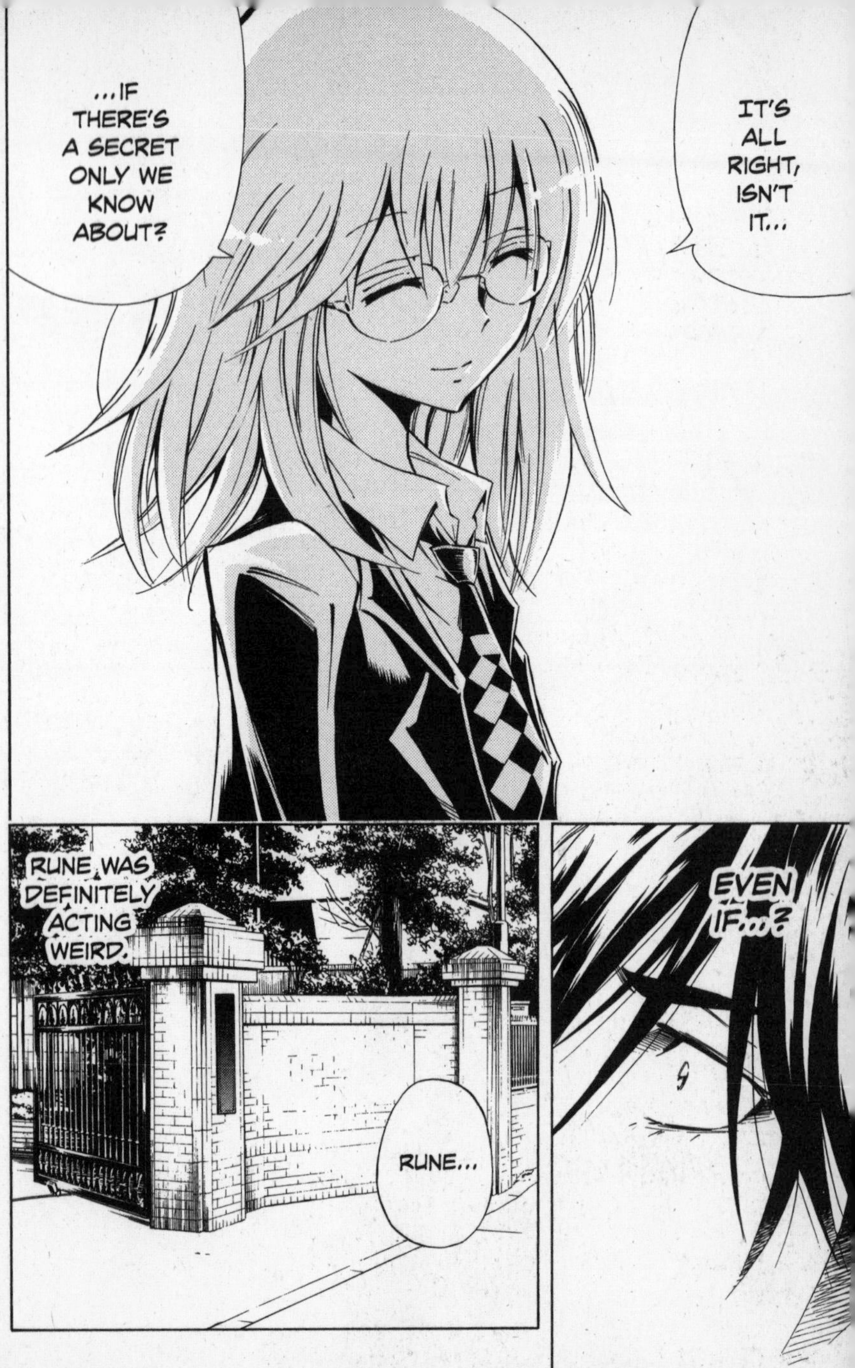
IT'S ALL RIGHT, ISN'T IT...
...IF THERE'S A SECRET ONLY WE KNOW ABOUT?
EVEN IF...?
RUNE WAS DEFINITELY ACTING WEIRD.
RUNE...

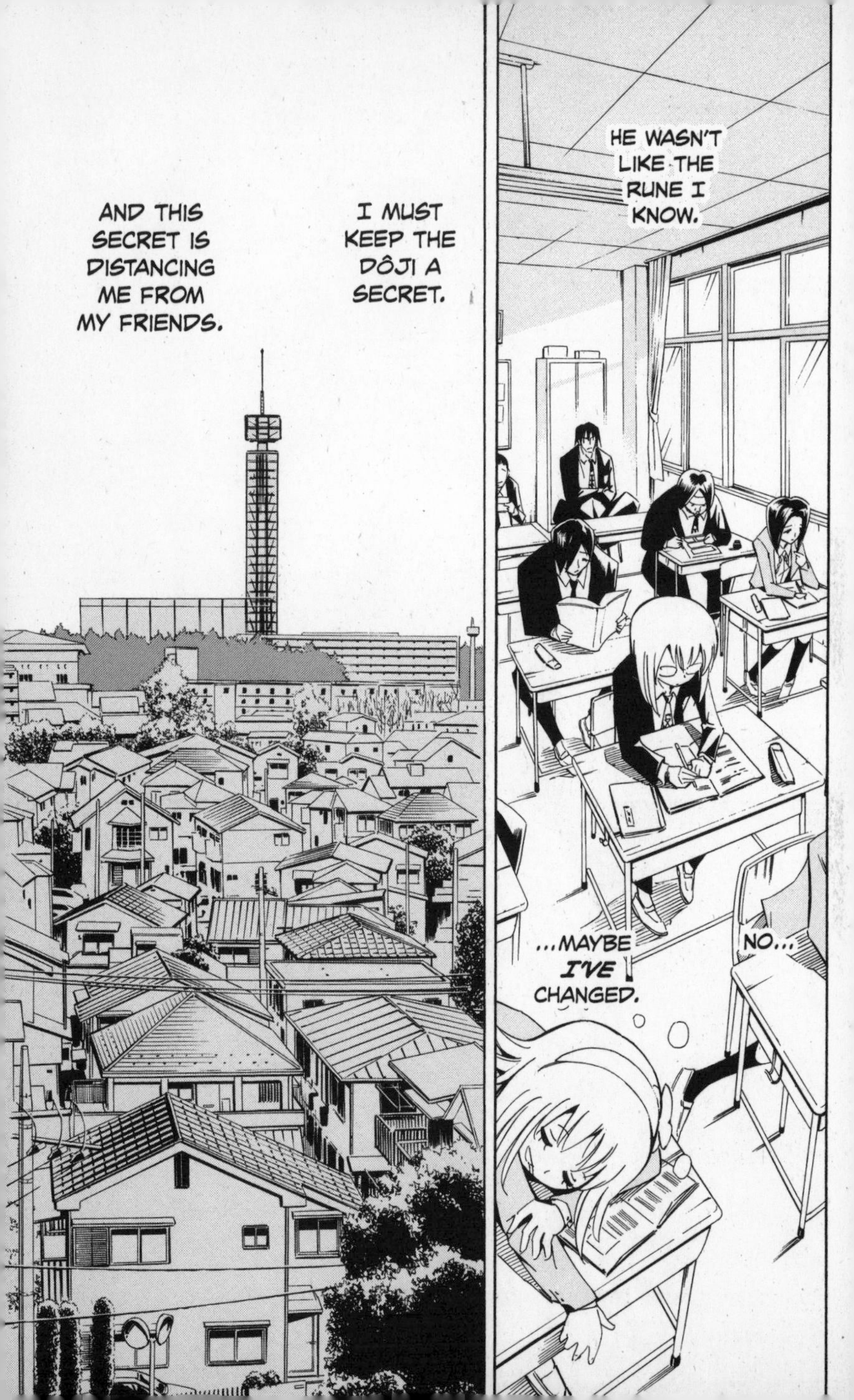
HE WASN'T LIKE THE RUNE I KNOW.
NO...
...MAYBE I'VE CHANGED.
I MUST KEEP THE DÔJI A SECRET.
AND THIS SECRET IS DISTANCING ME FROM MY FRIENDS.

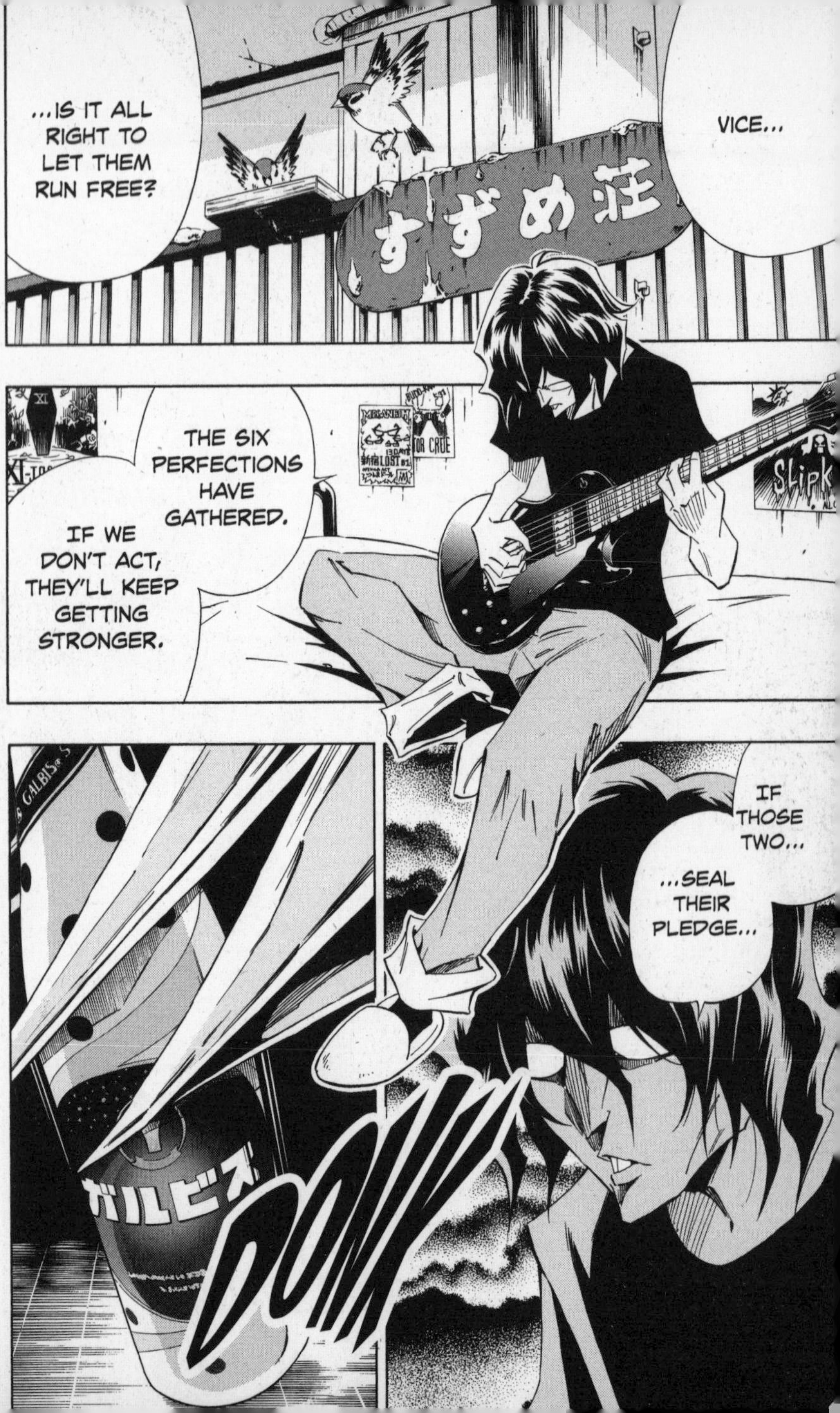
VICE...
...IS IT ALL RIGHT TO LET THEM RUN FREE?
すずめ荘
THE SIX PERFECTIONS HAVE GATHERED.
IF WE DON'T ACT, THEY'LL KEEP GETTING STRONGER.
IF THOSE TWO...
...SEAL THEIR PLEDGE...
GALBIS
ガルビス

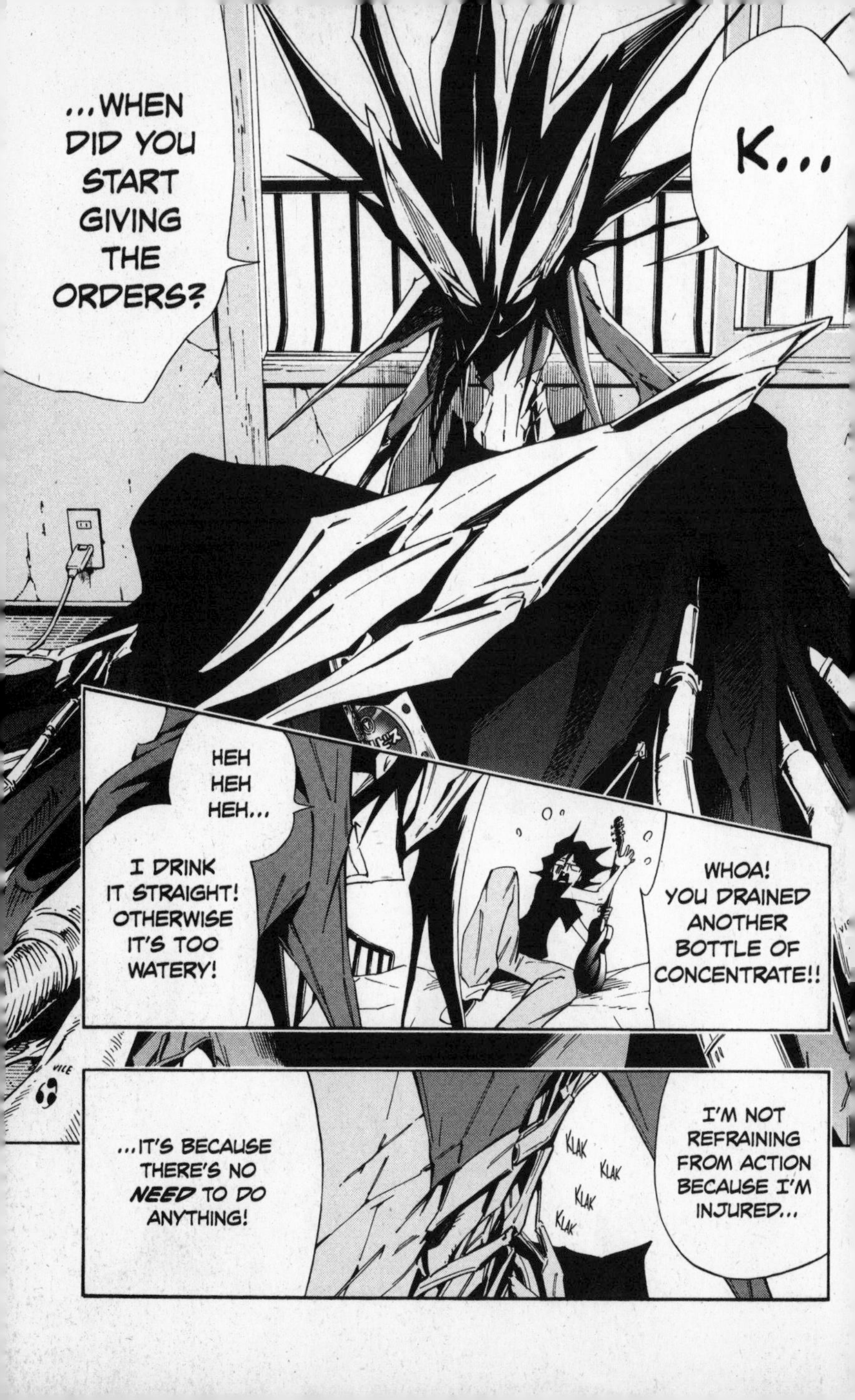
K...
...WHEN DID YOU START GIVING THE ORDERS?
WHOA! YOU DRAINED ANOTHER BOTTLE OF CONCENTRATE!!
HEH HEH HEH...
I DRINK IT STRAIGHT! OTHERWISE IT'S TOO WATERY!
I'M NOT REFRAINING FROM ACTION BECAUSE I'M INJURED...
KLAK KLAK KLAK KLAK
...IT'S BECAUSE THERE'S NO NEED TO DO ANYTHING!

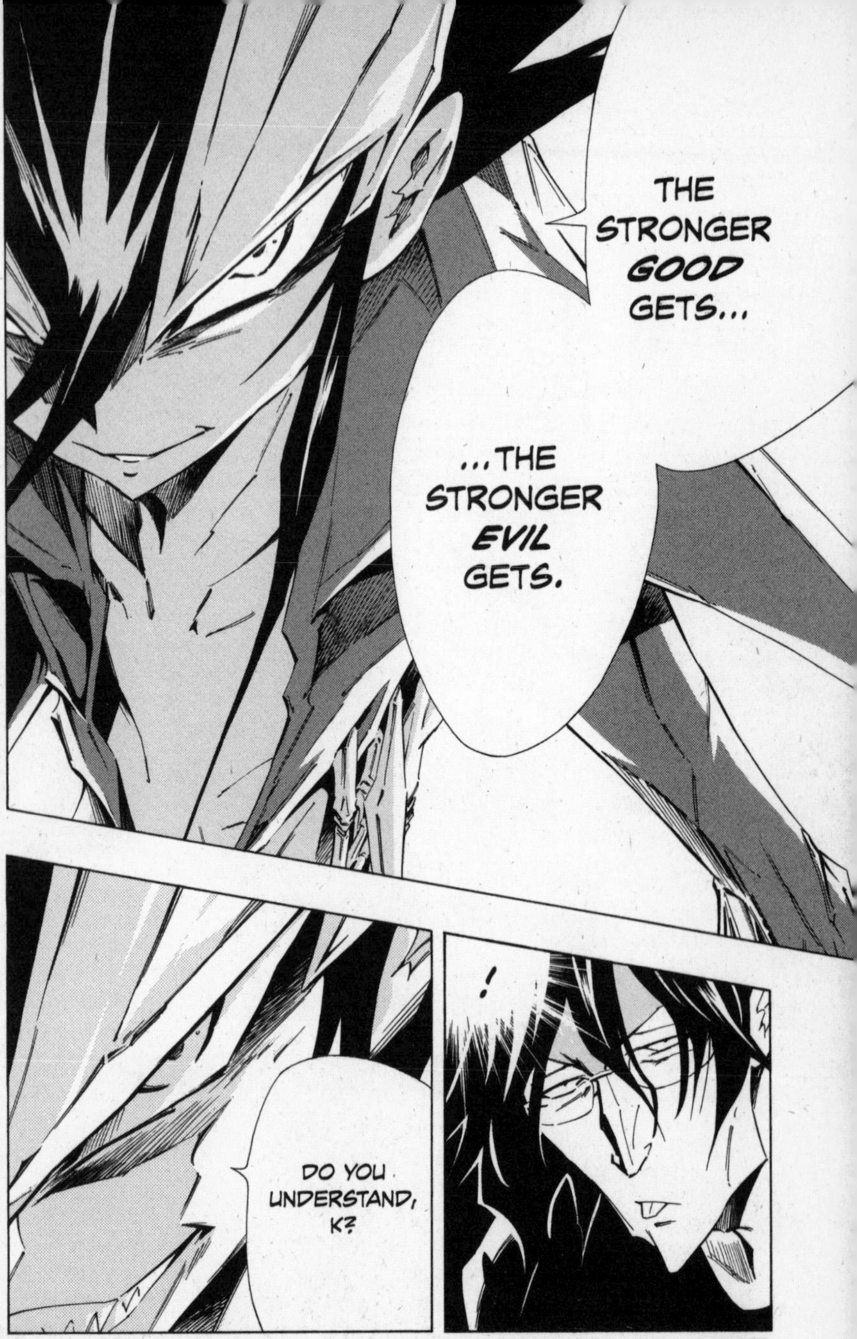
THE STRONGER GOOD GETS...
...THE STRONGER EVIL GETS.
!
DO YOU UNDERSTAND, K?

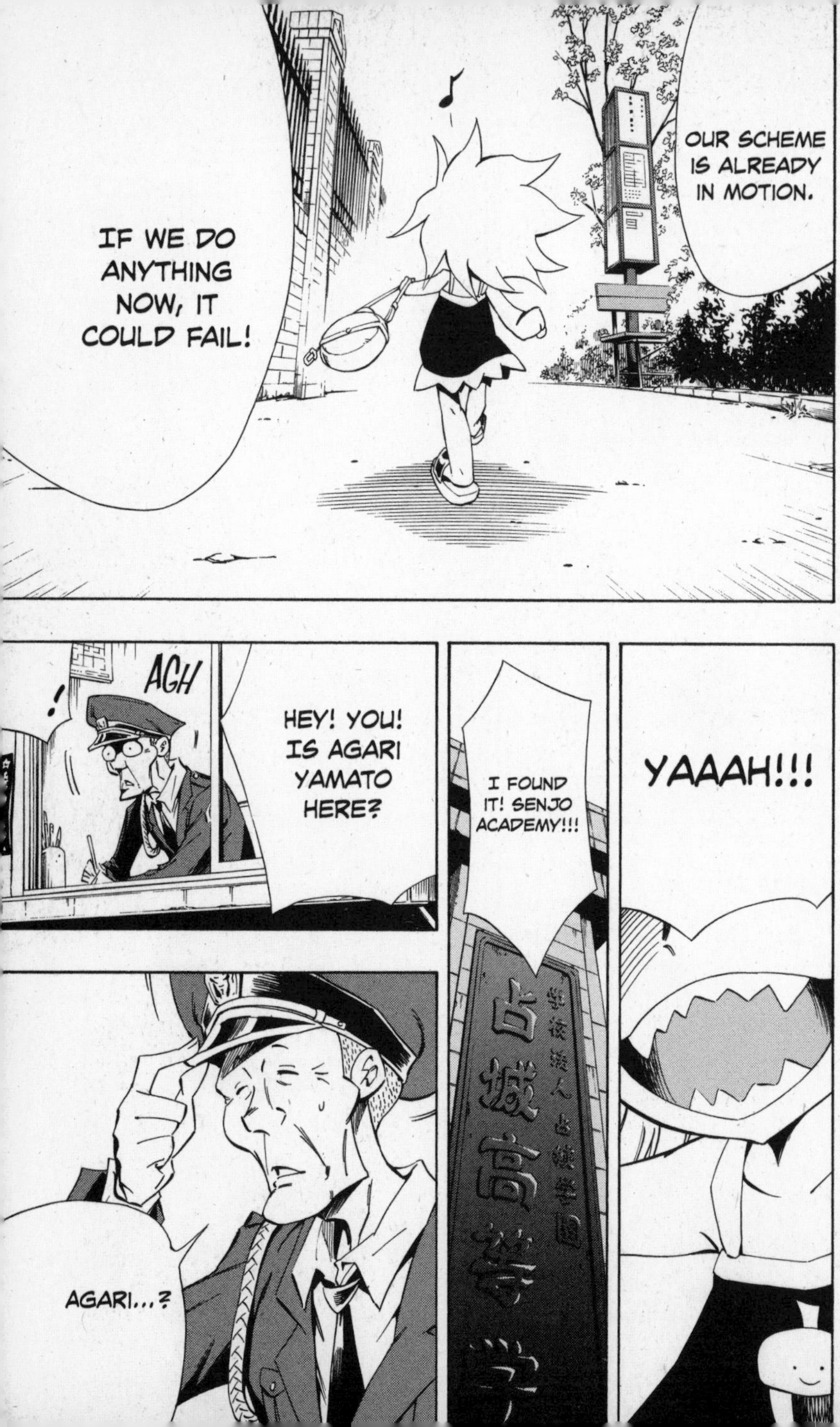
OUR SCHEME IS ALREADY IN MOTION.
IF WE DO ANYTHING NOW, IT COULD FAIL!
YAAAH!!!
I FOUND IT! SENJO ACADEMY!!!
占城高等学
AGH
HEY! YOU! IS AGARI YAMATO HERE?
AGARI...?

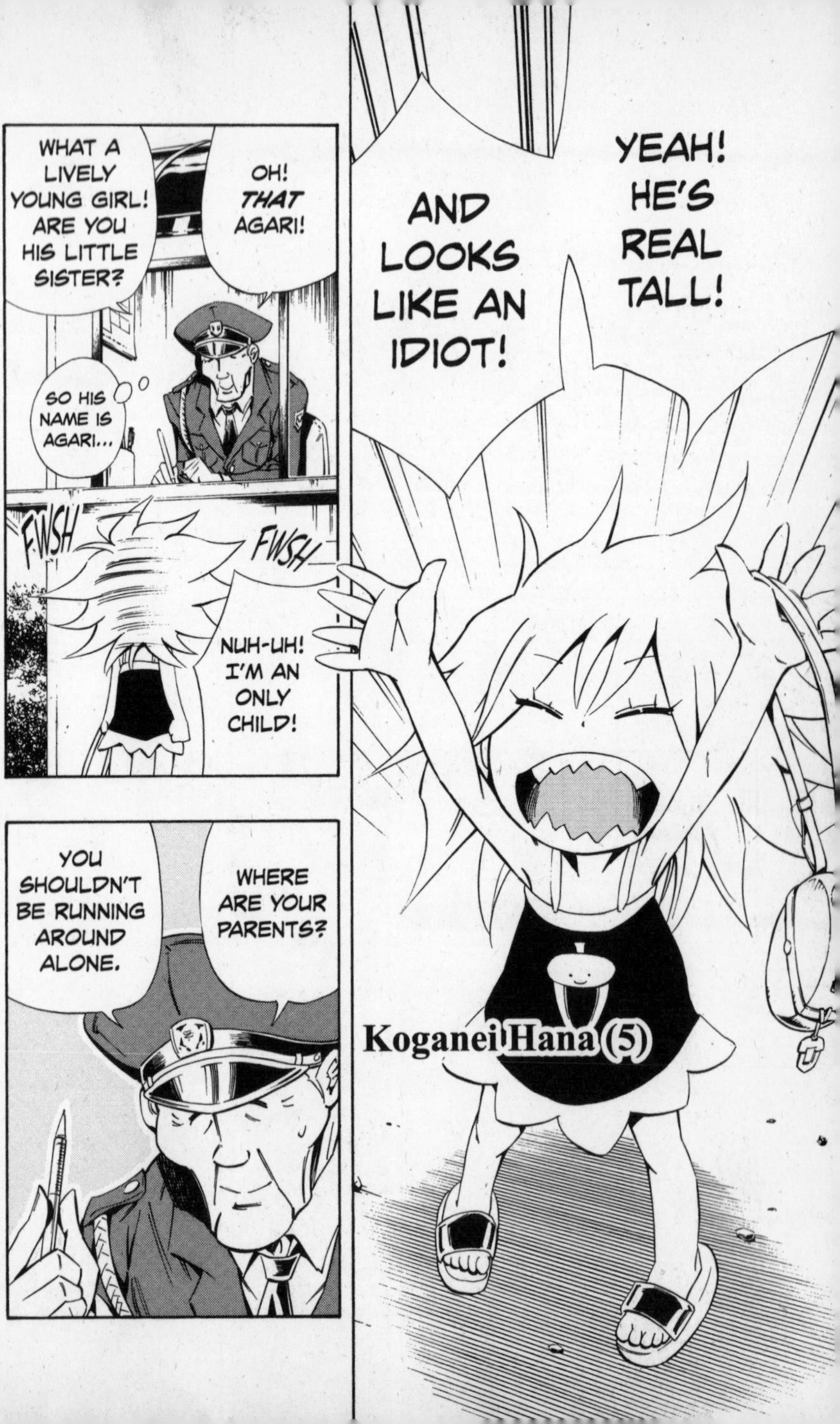
YEAH! HE'S REAL TALL!
AND LOOKS LIKE AN IDIOT!
Koganei Hana (5)
OH! *THAT* AGARI!
WHAT A LIVELY YOUNG GIRL! ARE YOU HIS LITTLE SISTER?
SO HIS NAME IS AGARI...
FWSH
FWSH
NUH-UH! I'M AN ONLY CHILD!
WHERE ARE YOUR PARENTS?
YOU SHOULDN'T BE RUNNING AROUND ALONE.

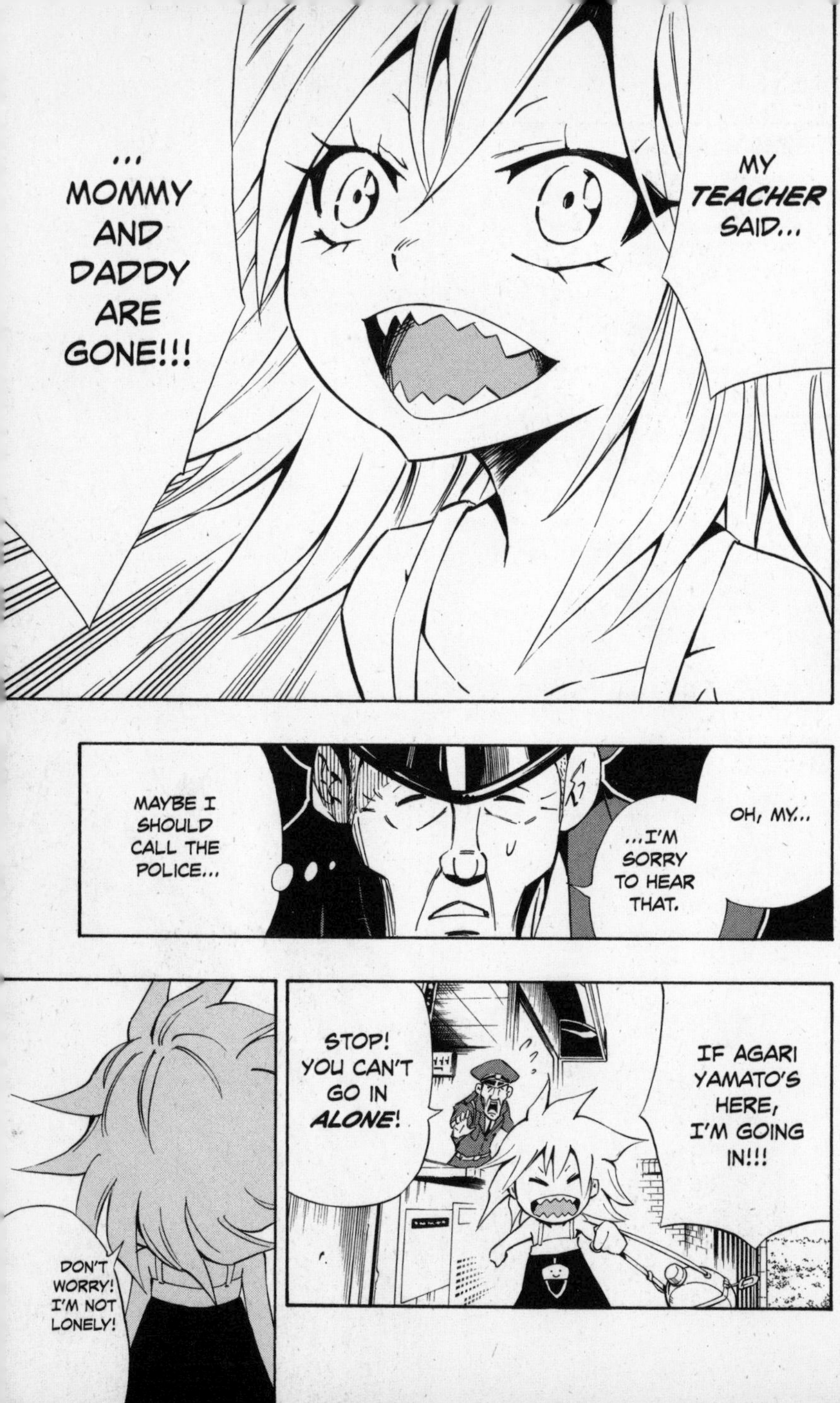
MY *TEACHER* SAID...
... MOMMY AND DADDY ARE GONE!!!
OH, MY...
...I'M SORRY TO HEAR THAT.
MAYBE I SHOULD CALL THE POLICE...
IF AGARI YAMATO'S HERE, I'M GOING IN!!!
STOP! YOU CAN'T GO IN *ALONE*!
DON'T WORRY! I'M NOT LONELY!

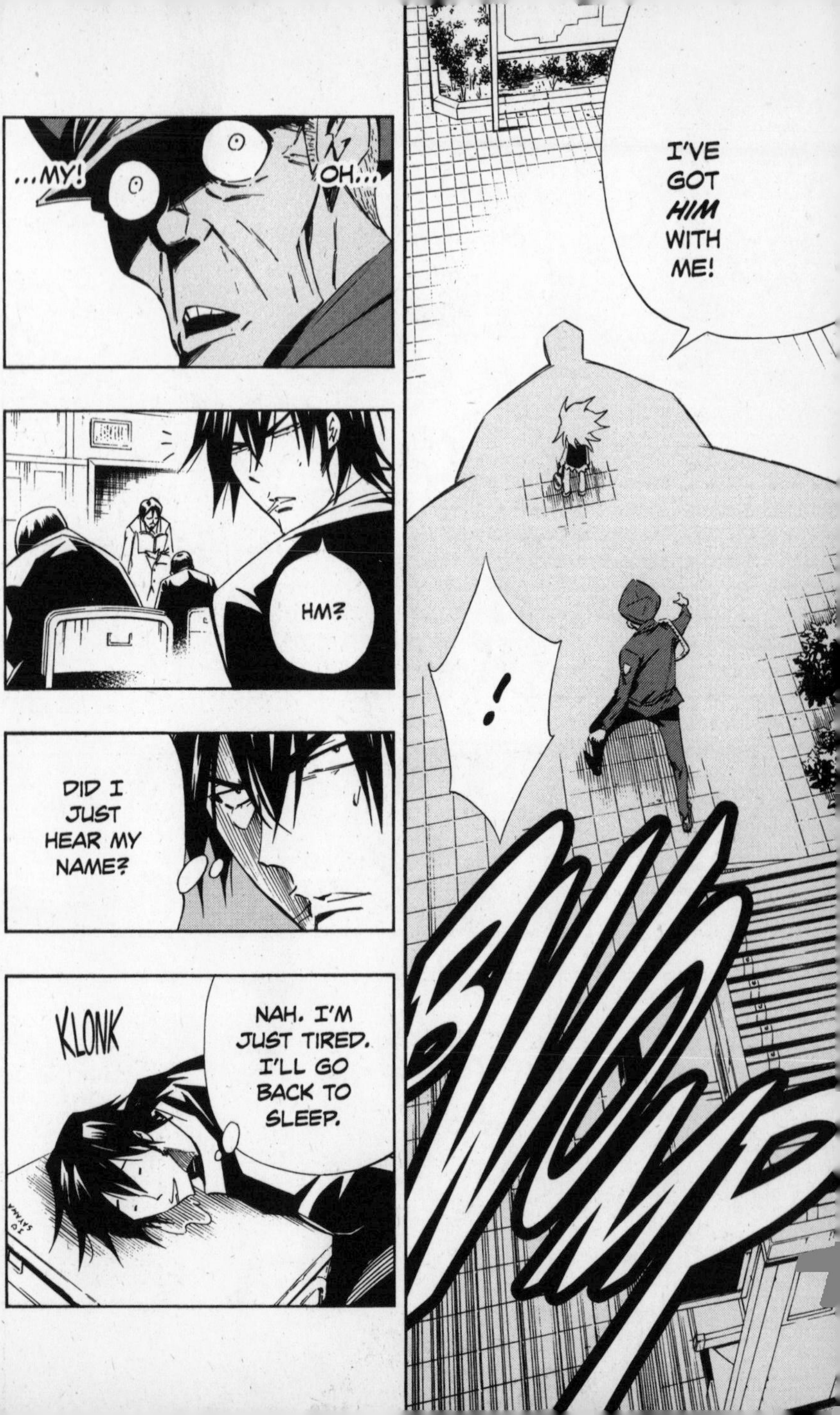
I'VE GOT *HIM* WITH ME!
!
OH...
...MY!
HM?
DID I JUST HEAR MY NAME?
NAH. I'M JUST TIRED. I'LL GO BACK TO SLEEP.
KLONK

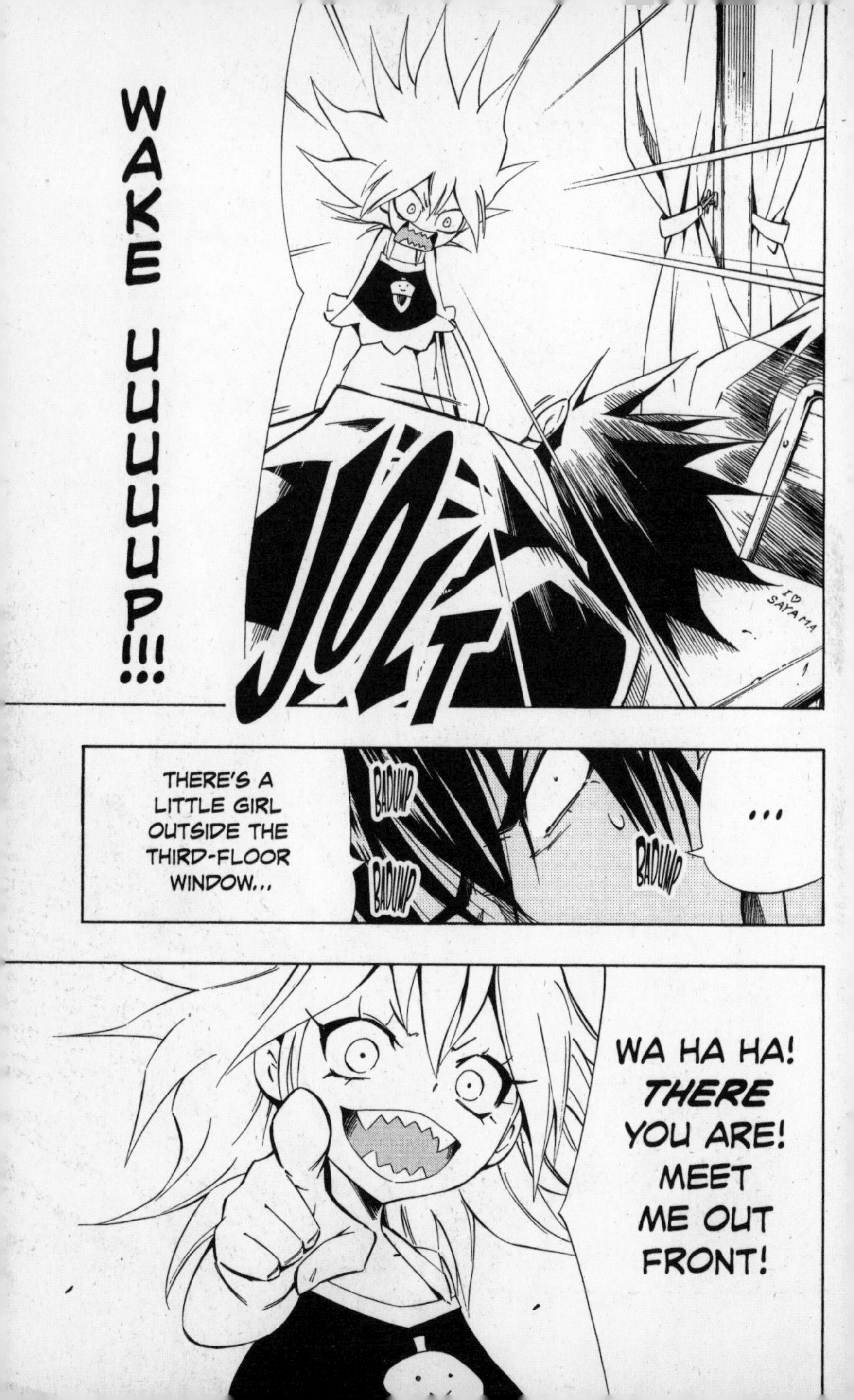
WAKE UUUUUP!!!
JOLT
I♡ SAYAMA
...
BADUMP
BADUMP
BADUMP
THERE'S A LITTLE GIRL OUTSIDE THE THIRD-FLOOR WINDOW...
WA HA HA! *THERE* YOU ARE! MEET ME OUT FRONT!

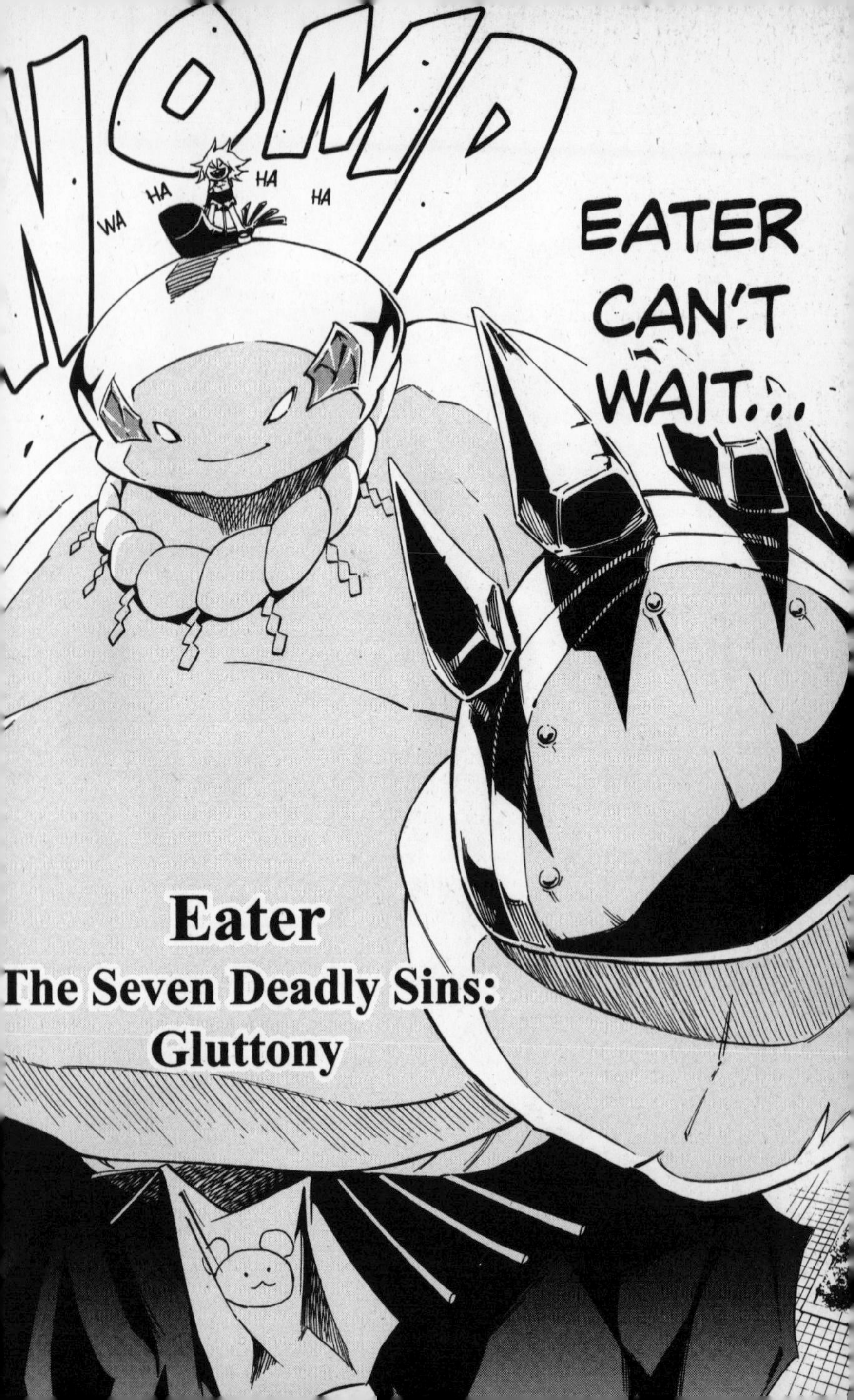
NOMP
WA HA HA HA
EATER CAN'T WAIT...
Eater
The Seven Deadly Sins: Gluttony

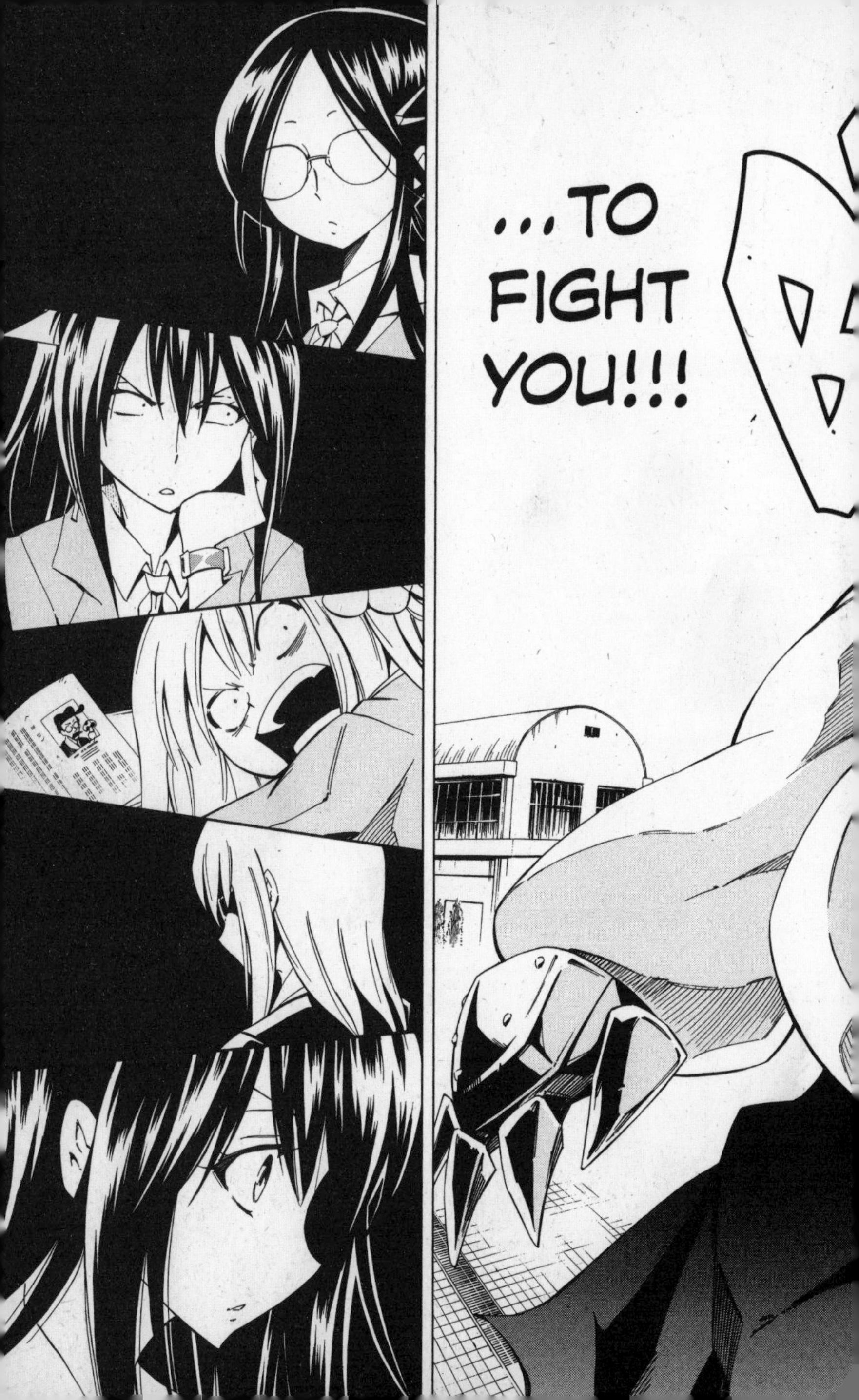
...TO FIGHT YOU!!!

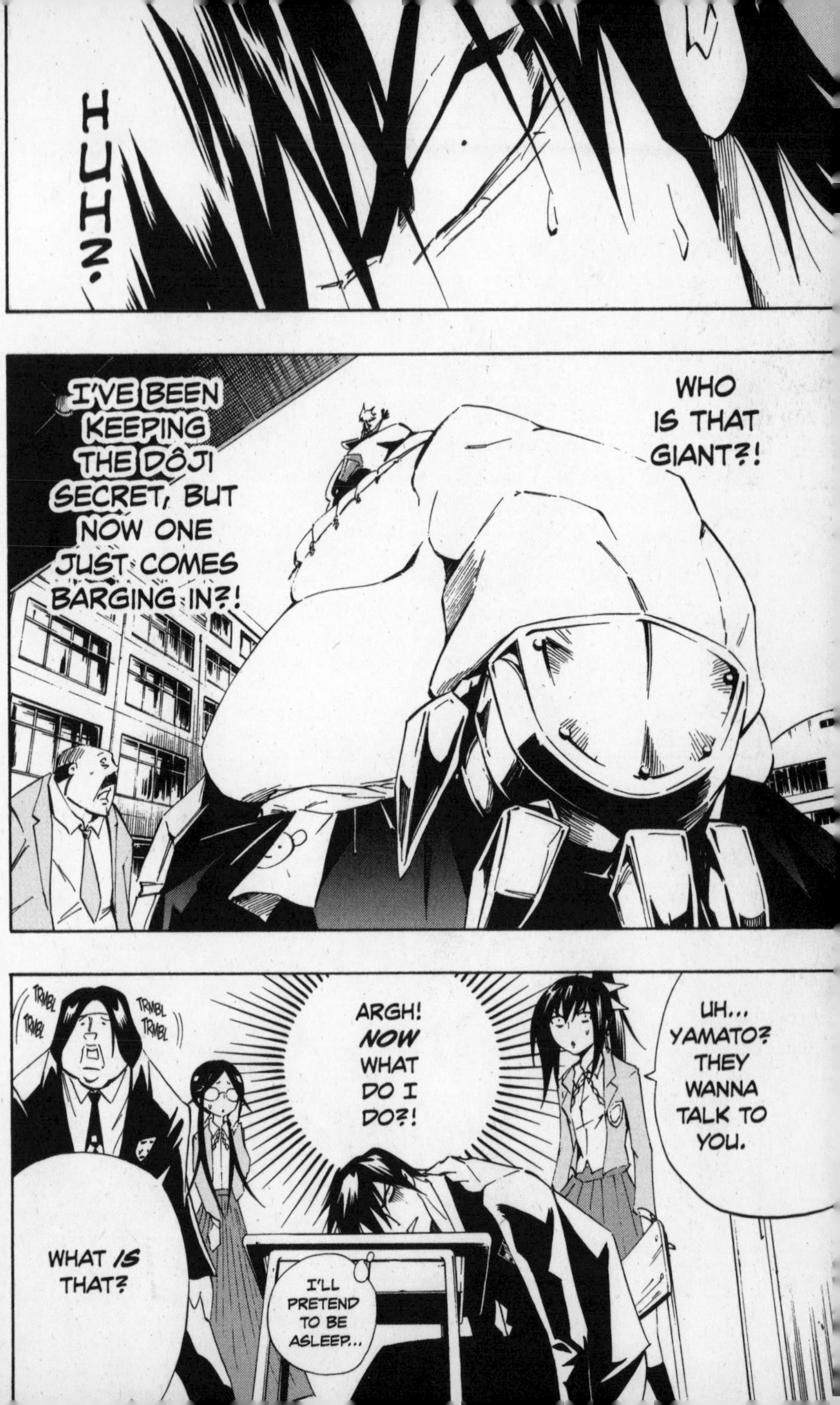
HUH?
WHO IS THAT GIANT?!
I'VE BEEN KEEPING THE DÔJI SECRET, BUT NOW ONE JUST COMES BARGING IN?!
UH... YAMATO? THEY WANNA TALK TO YOU.
ARGH! *NOW* WHAT DO I DO?!
TRMBL TRMBL
TRMBL TRMBL
I'LL PRETEND TO BE ASLEEP...
WHAT *IS* THAT?

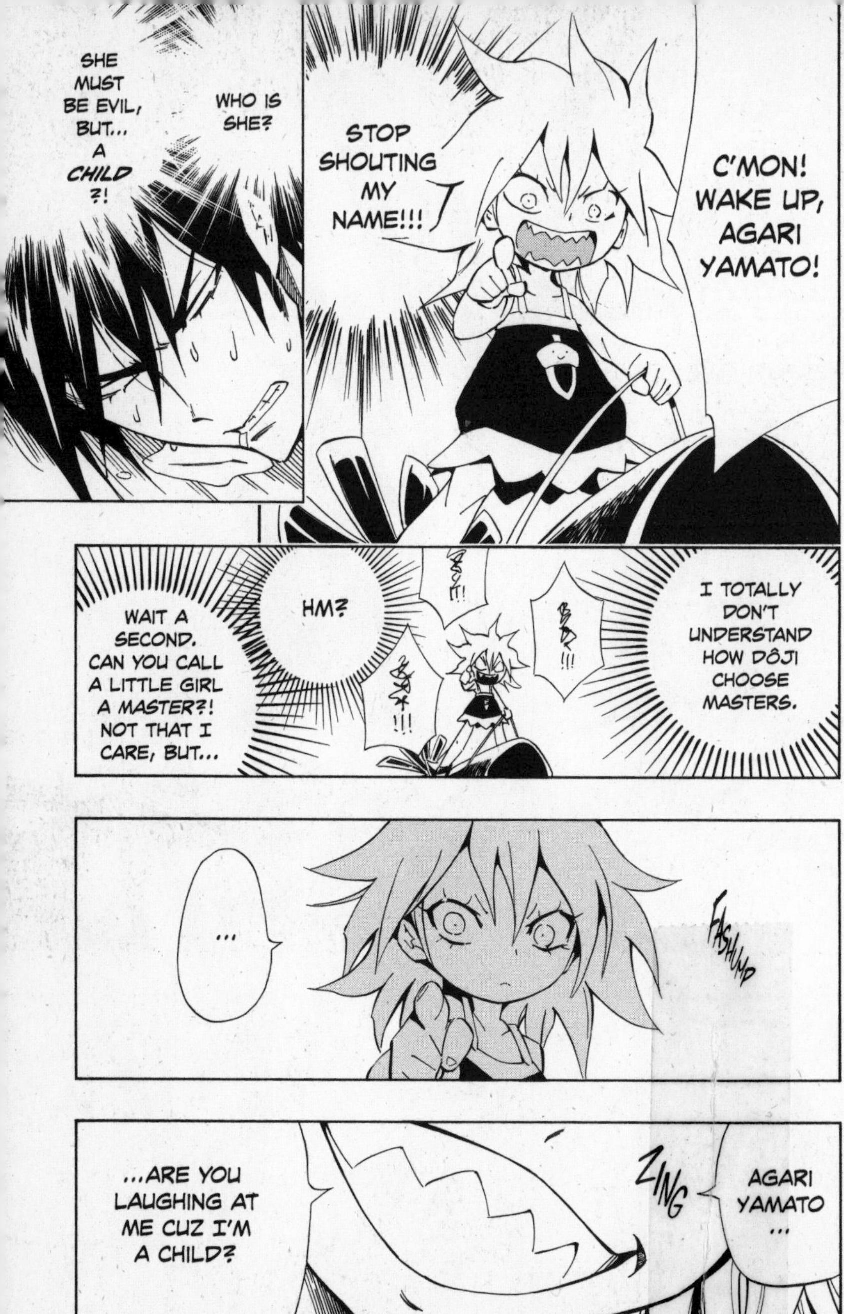
C'MON! WAKE UP, AGARI YAMATO!
STOP SHOUTING MY NAME!!!
WHO IS SHE?
SHE MUST BE EVIL, BUT... A CHILD?!
I TOTALLY DON'T UNDERSTAND HOW DÔJI CHOOSE MASTERS.
HM?
WAIT A SECOND. CAN YOU CALL A LITTLE GIRL A MASTER?! NOT THAT I CARE, BUT...
FASHUMP
...
AGARI YAMATO ...
ZING
...ARE YOU LAUGHING AT ME CUZ I'M A CHILD?

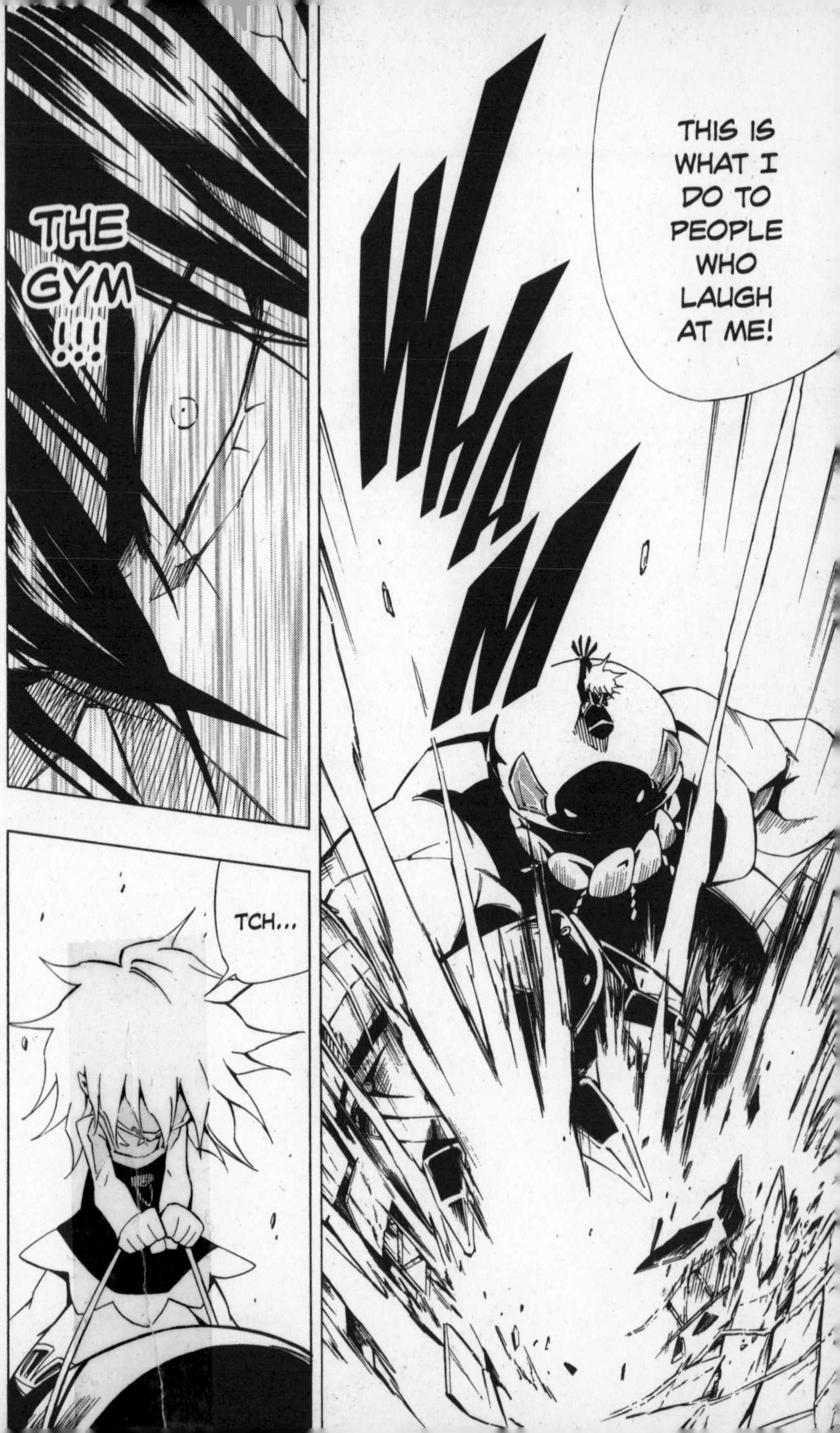
THIS IS WHAT I DO TO PEOPLE WHO LAUGH AT ME!
WHAM
THE GYM!!!
TCH...

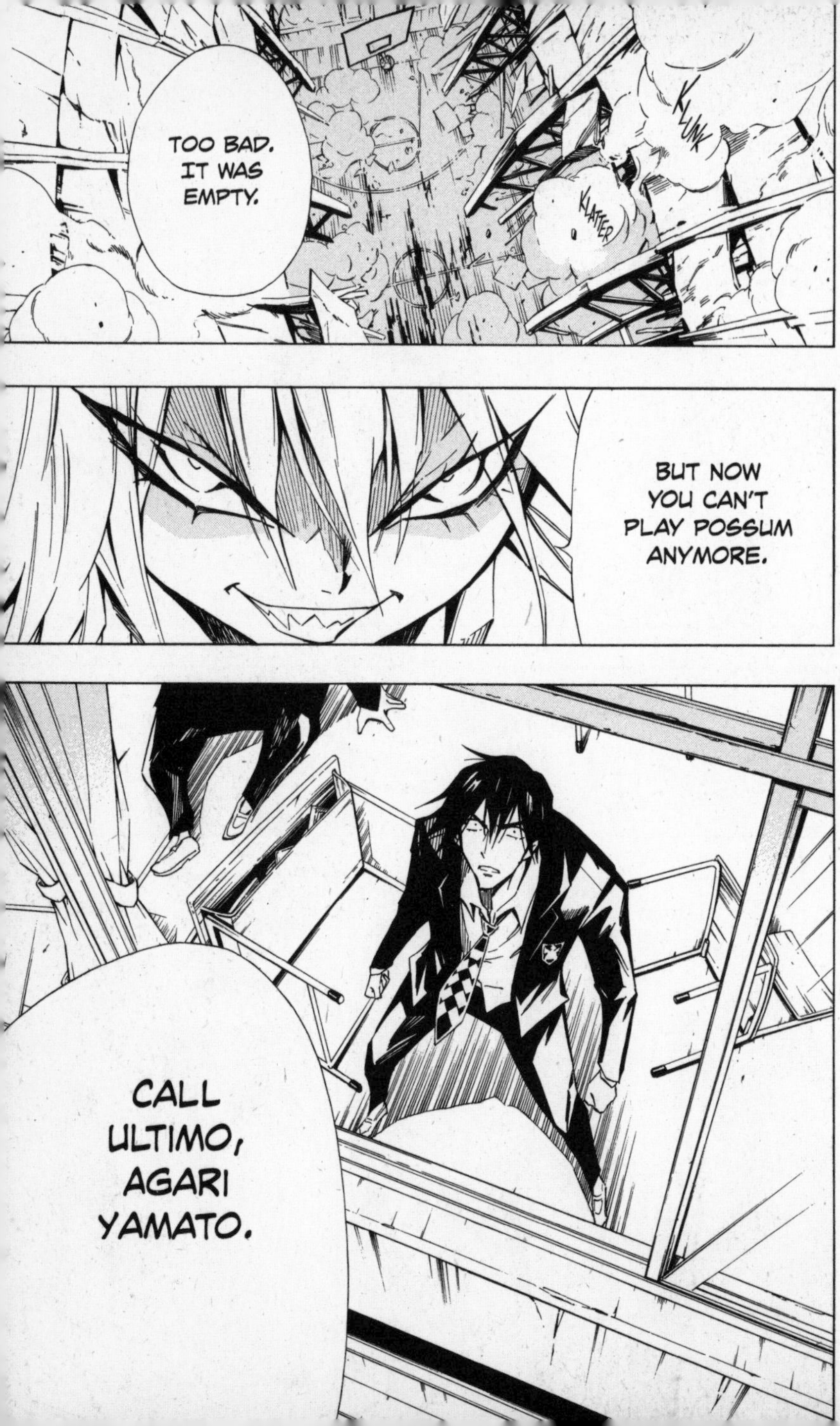
KLUNK
KLATTER
TOO BAD. IT WAS EMPTY.
BUT NOW YOU CAN'T PLAY POSSUM ANYMORE.
CALL ULTIMO, AGARI YAMATO.

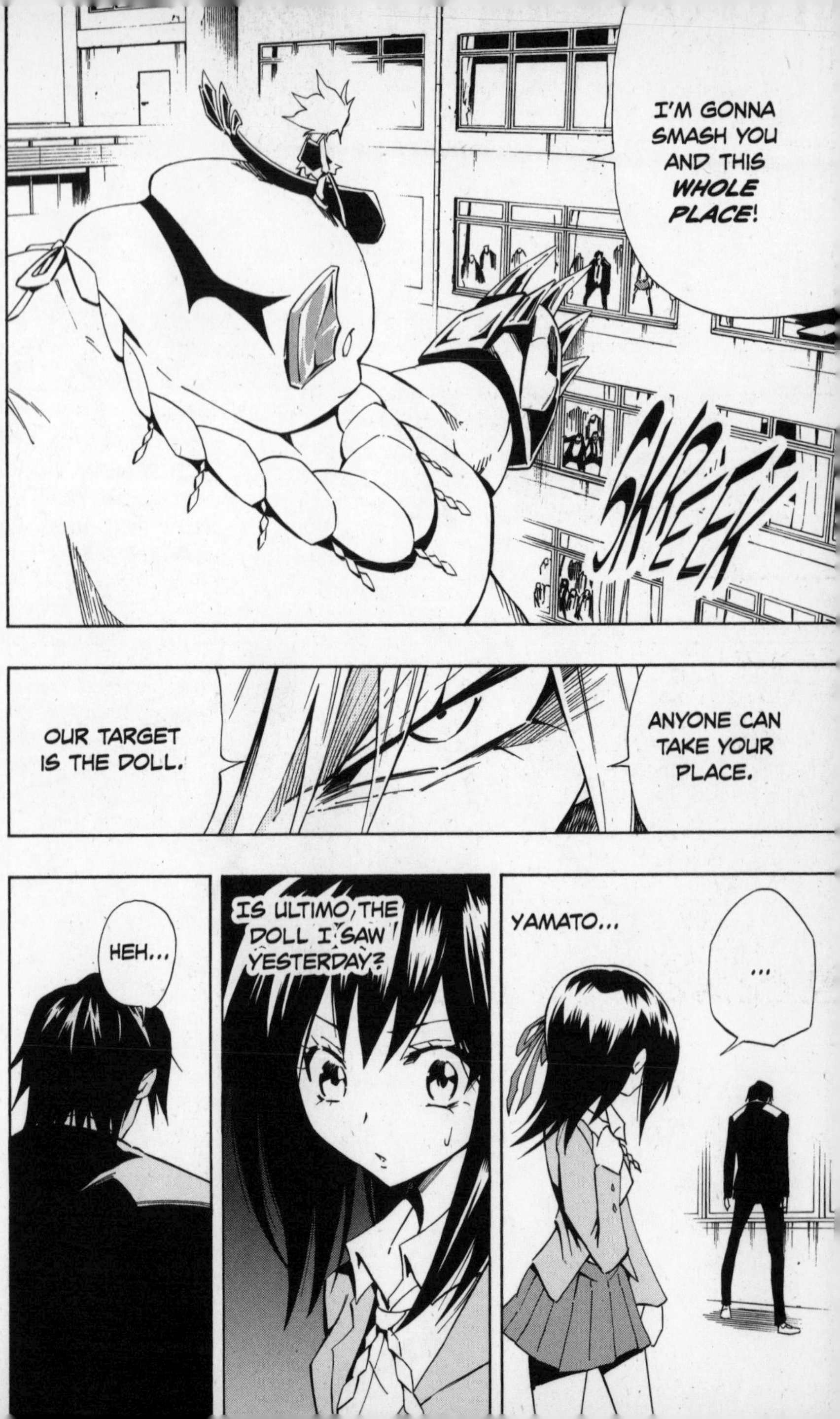
I'M GONNA SMASH YOU AND THIS *WHOLE PLACE!*
SKREEK
ANYONE CAN TAKE YOUR PLACE.
OUR TARGET IS THE DOLL.
YAMATO...
...
IS ULTIMO, THE DOLL I SAW YESTERDAY?
HEH...

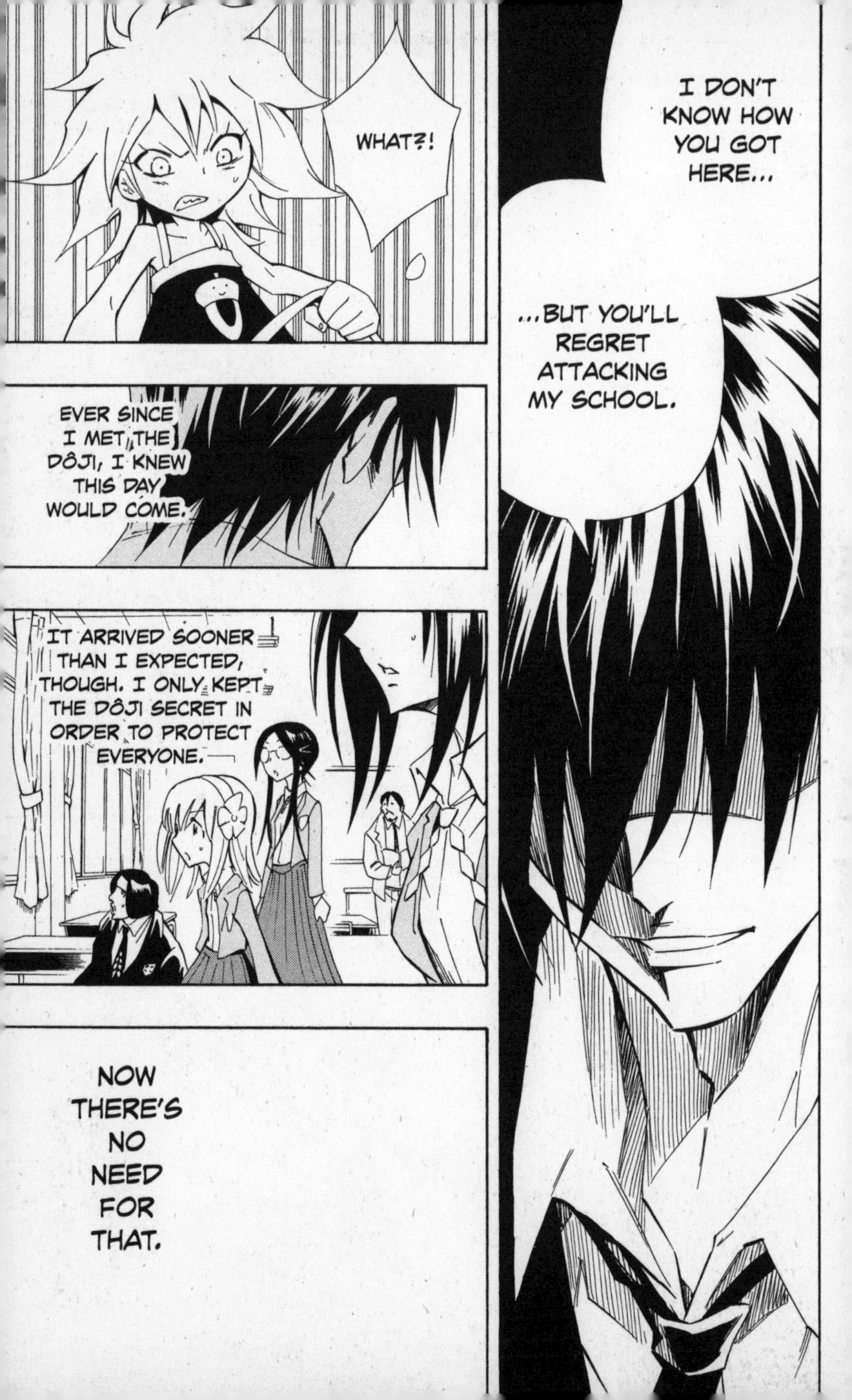
I DON'T KNOW HOW YOU GOT HERE...
...BUT YOU'LL REGRET ATTACKING MY SCHOOL.
WHAT?!
EVER SINCE I MET THE DÔJI, I KNEW THIS DAY WOULD COME.
IT ARRIVED SOONER THAN I EXPECTED, THOUGH. I ONLY KEPT THE DÔJI SECRET IN ORDER TO PROTECT EVERYONE.
NOW THERE'S NO NEED FOR THAT.

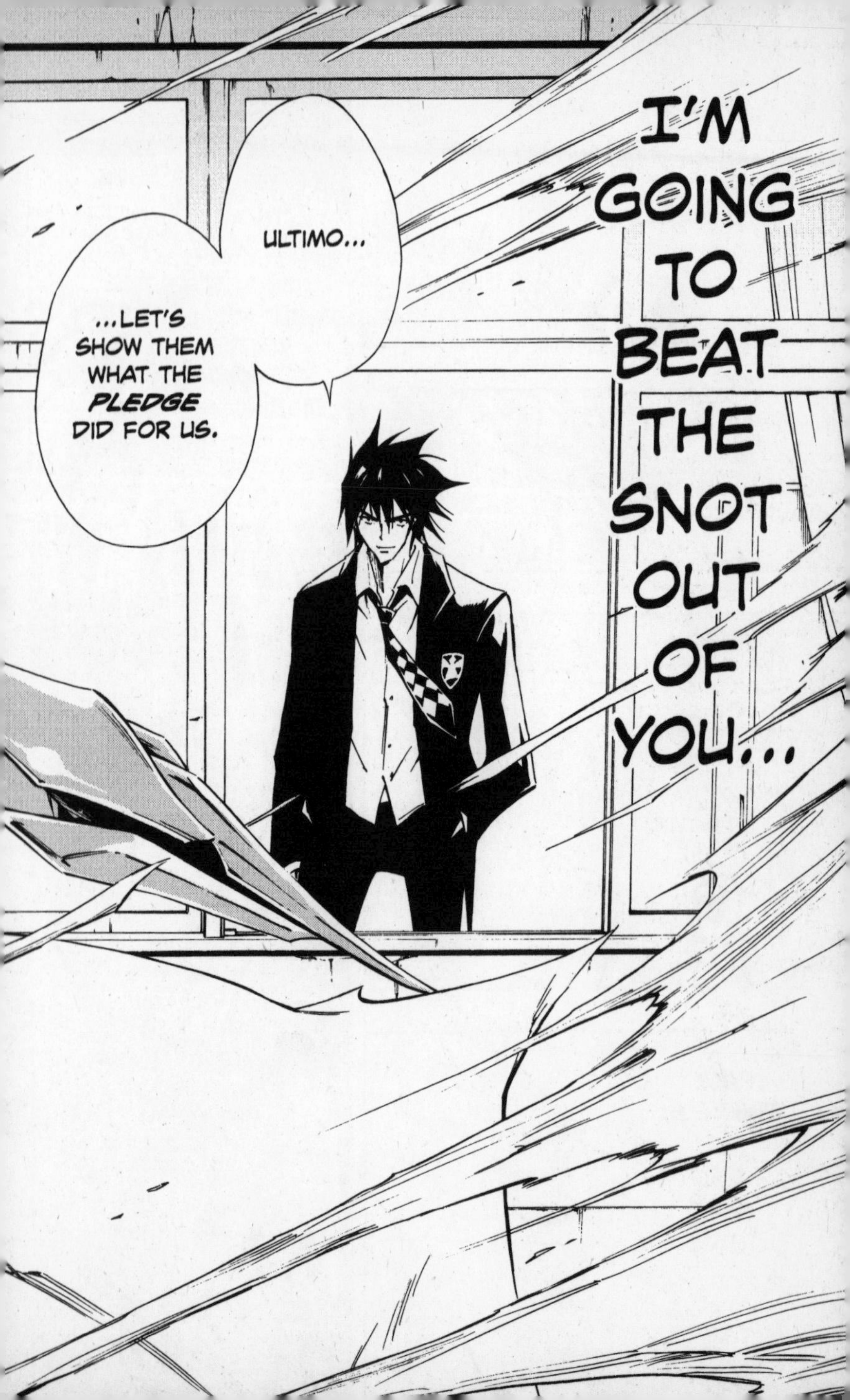
I'M GOING TO BEAT THE SNOT OUT OF YOU...
ULTIMO...
...LET'S SHOW THEM WHAT THE *PLEDGE* DID FOR US.

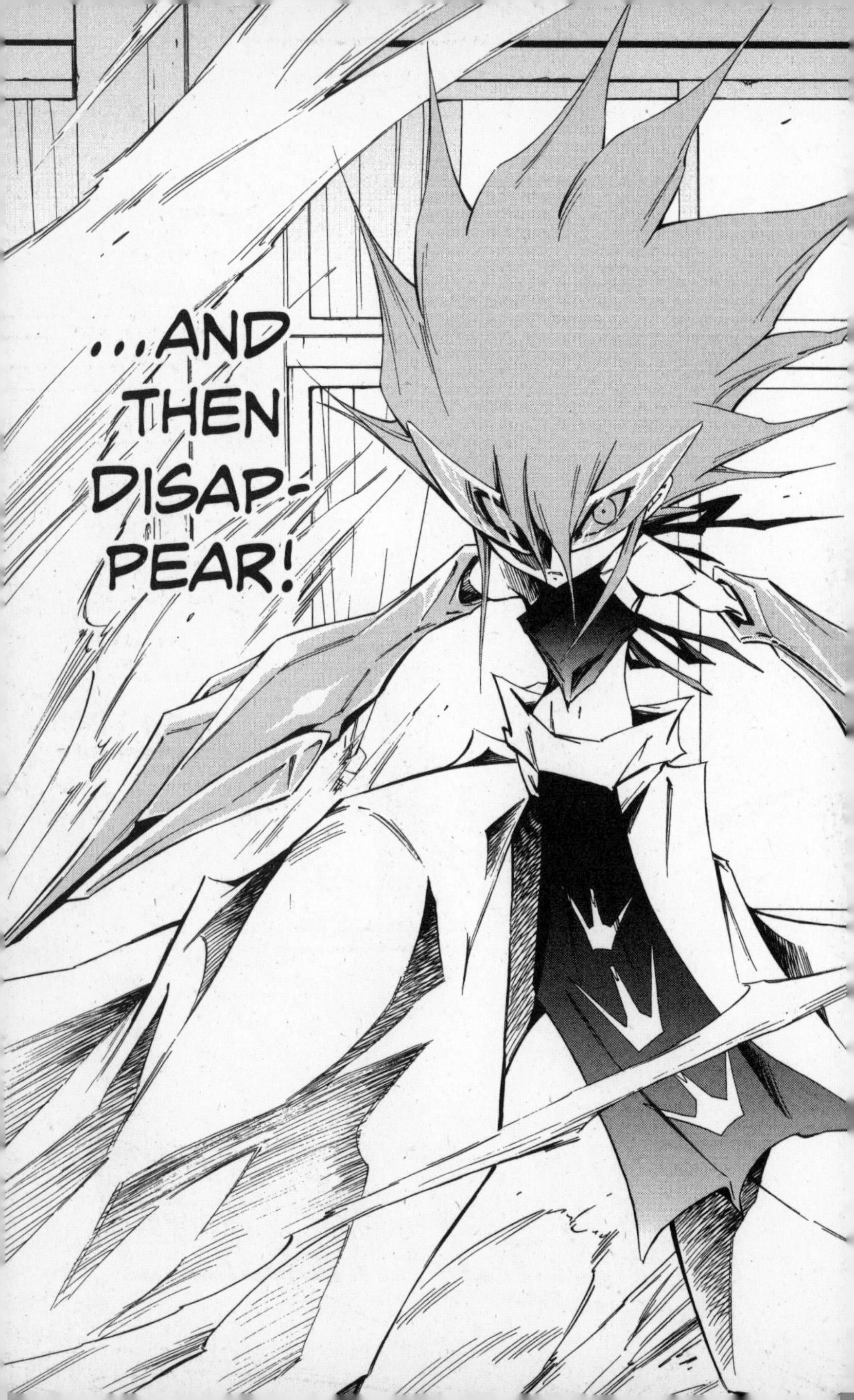
...AND THEN DISAP-PEAR!

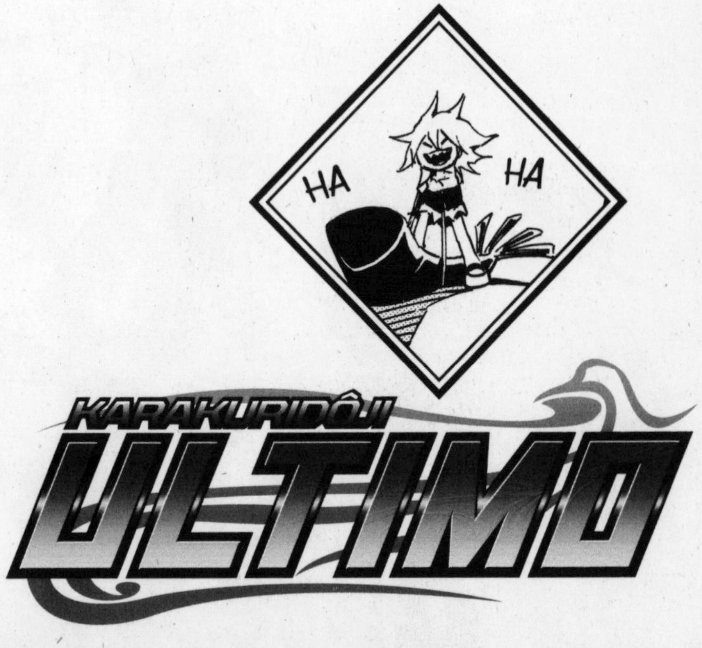
HA
HA

KARAKURIDÔJI
ULTIMO

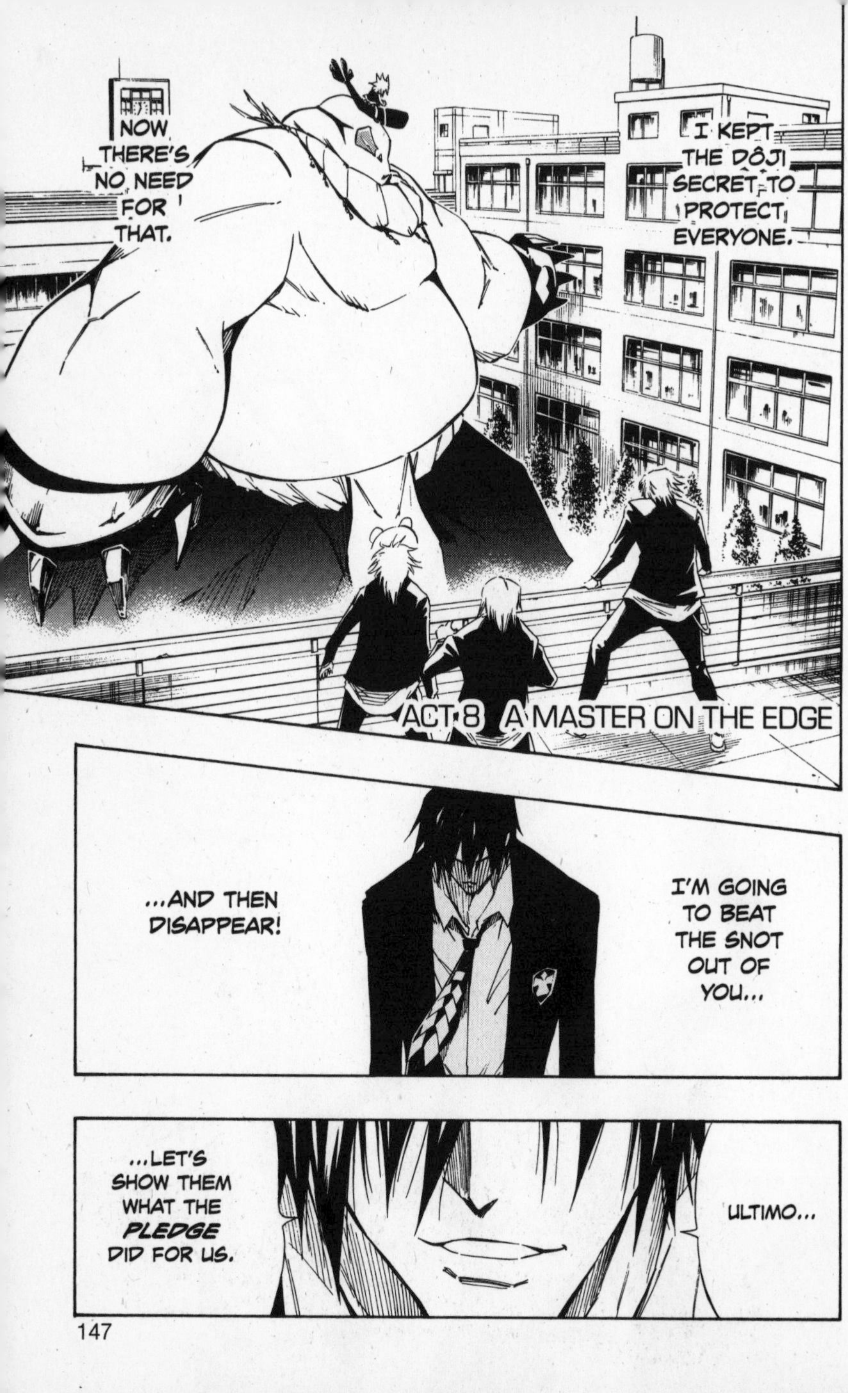
I KEPT THE DÔJI SECRET TO PROTECT EVERYONE.
NOW THERE'S NO NEED FOR THAT.
ACT 8 A MASTER ON THE EDGE
I'M GOING TO BEAT THE SNOT OUT OF YOU...
...AND THEN DISAPPEAR!
ULTIMO...
...LET'S SHOW THEM WHAT THE *PLEDGE* DID FOR US.

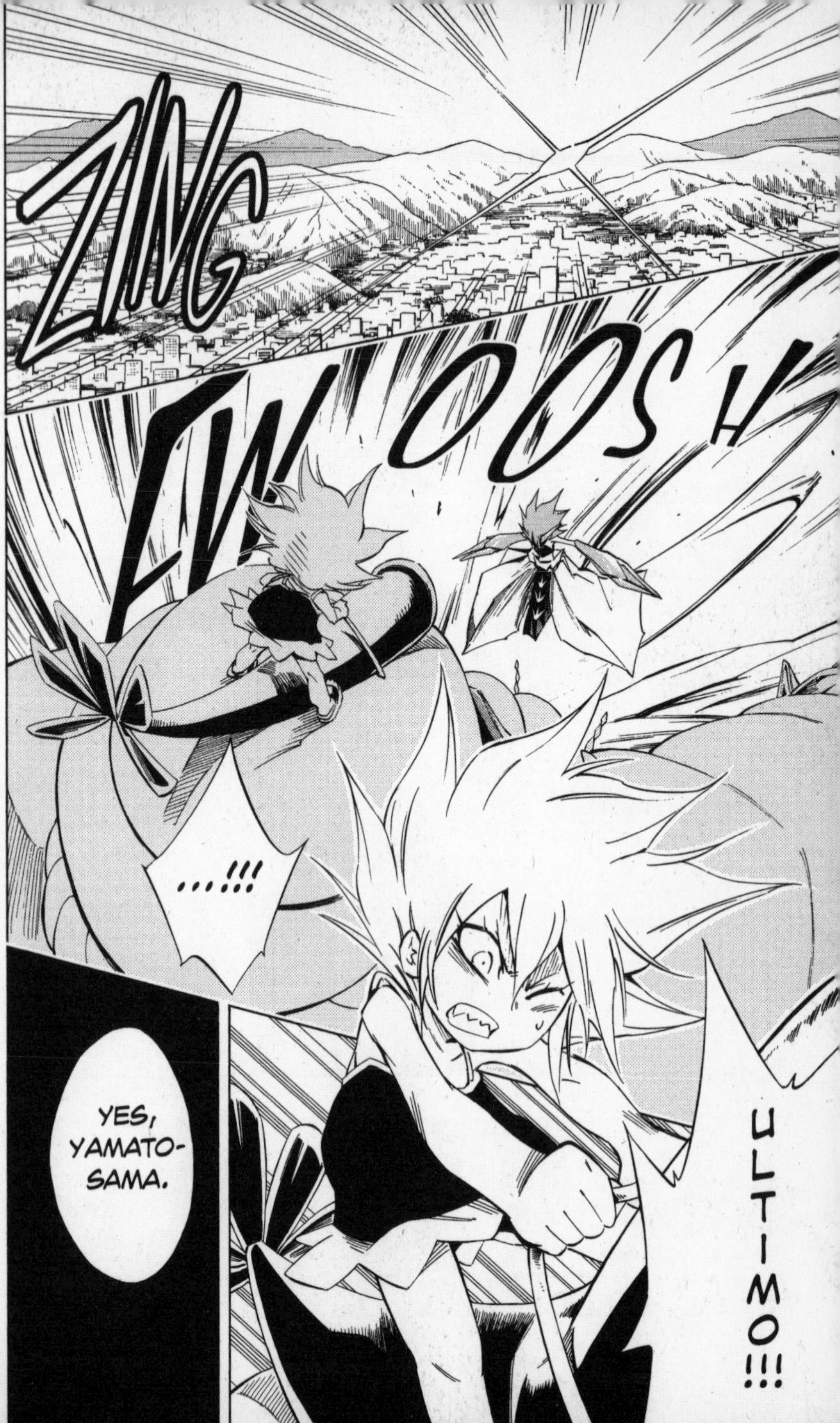
ZING
WHOOSH
...!!!
ULTIMO!!!
YES, YAMATO-SAMA.

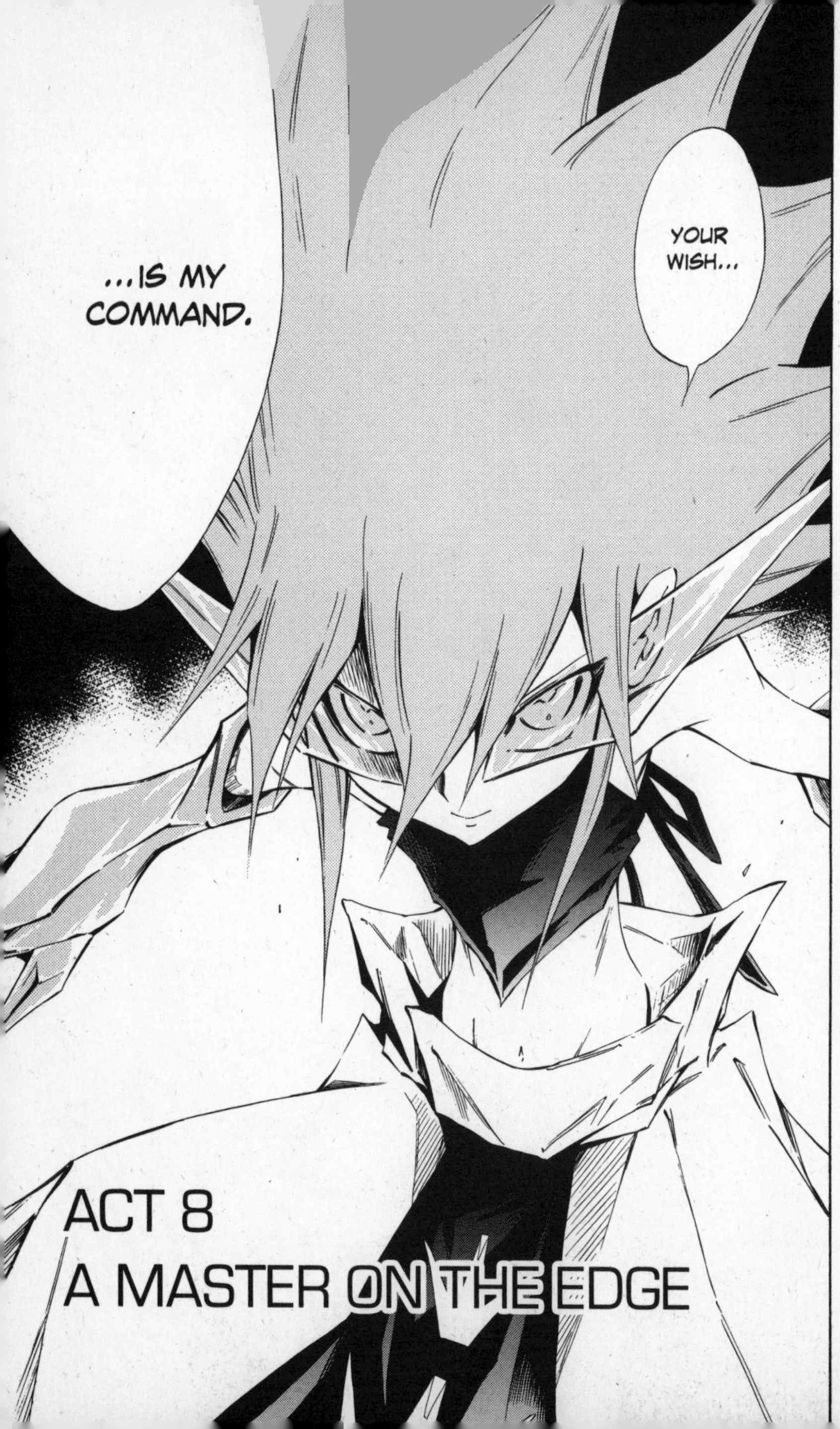
YOUR WISH...
...IS MY COMMAND.
ACT 8
A MASTER ON THE EDGE

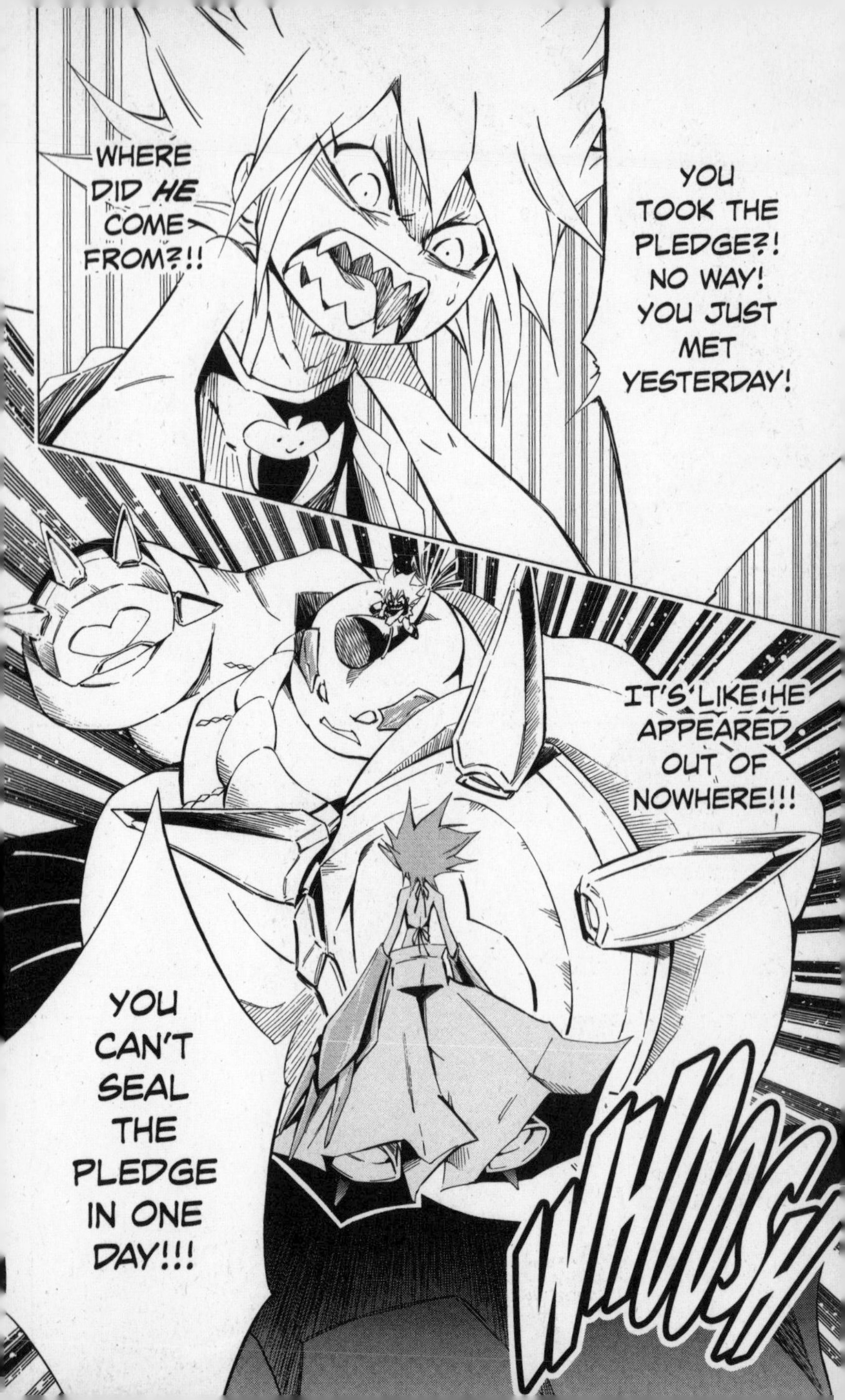
YOU TOOK THE PLEDGE?! NO WAY! YOU JUST MET YESTERDAY!
WHERE DID *HE* COME FROM?!!
IT'S LIKE HE APPEARED OUT OF NOWHERE!!!
YOU CAN'T SEAL THE PLEDGE IN ONE DAY!!!

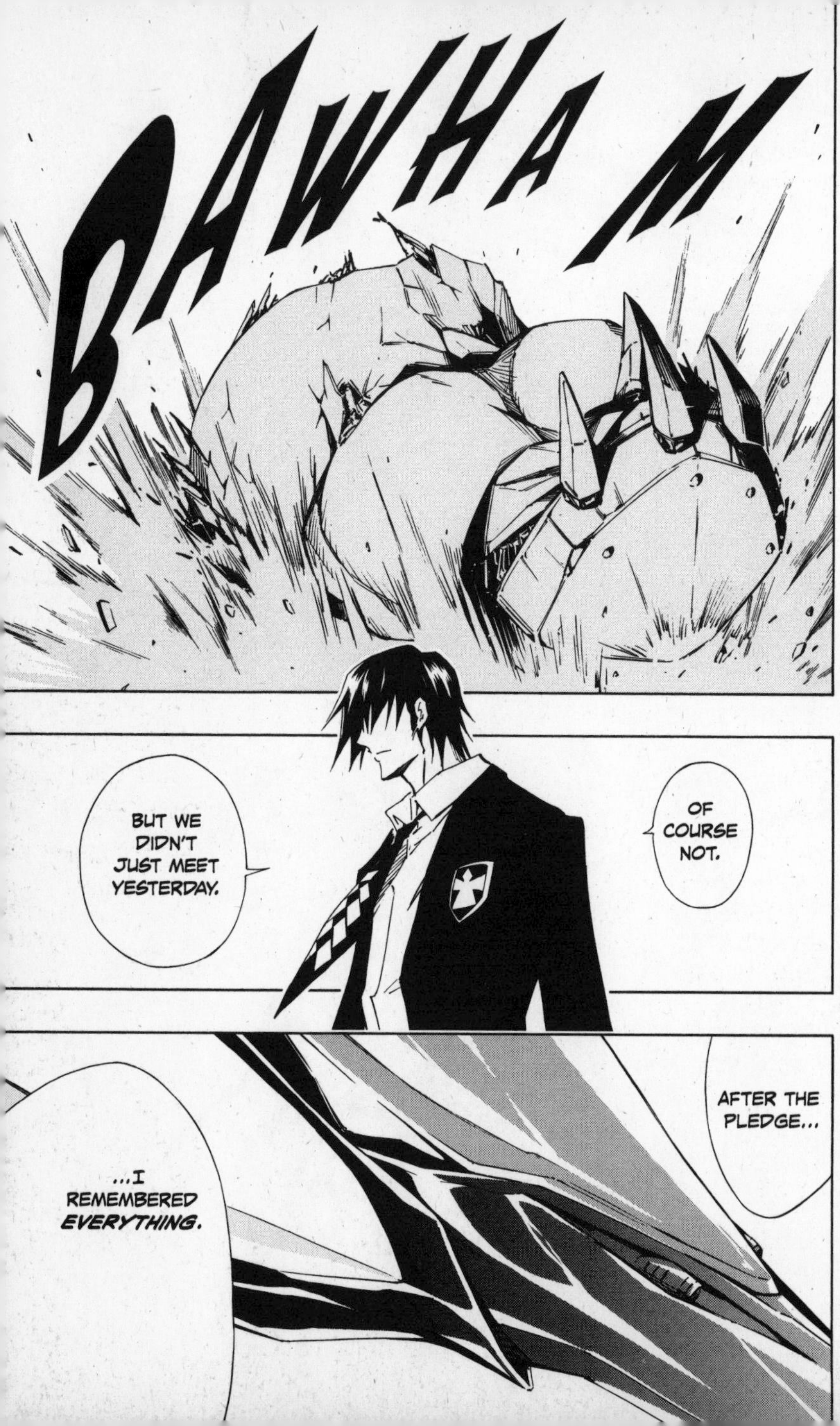
BAWHAM
OF COURSE NOT.
BUT WE DIDN'T JUST MEET YESTERDAY.
AFTER THE PLEDGE...
...I REMEMBERED *EVERYTHING*.

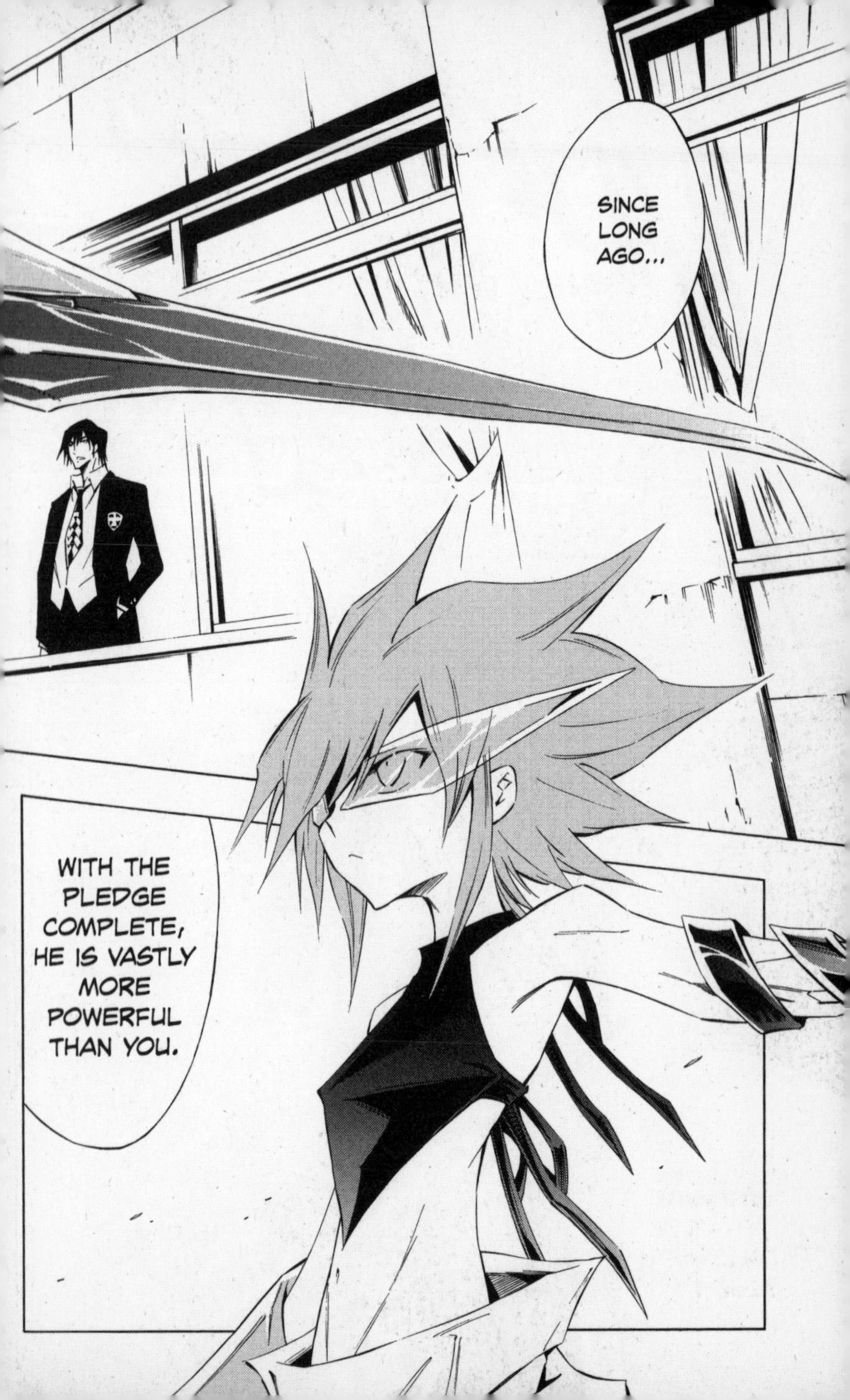
SINCE LONG AGO...
WITH THE PLEDGE COMPLETE, HE IS VASTLY MORE POWERFUL THAN YOU.

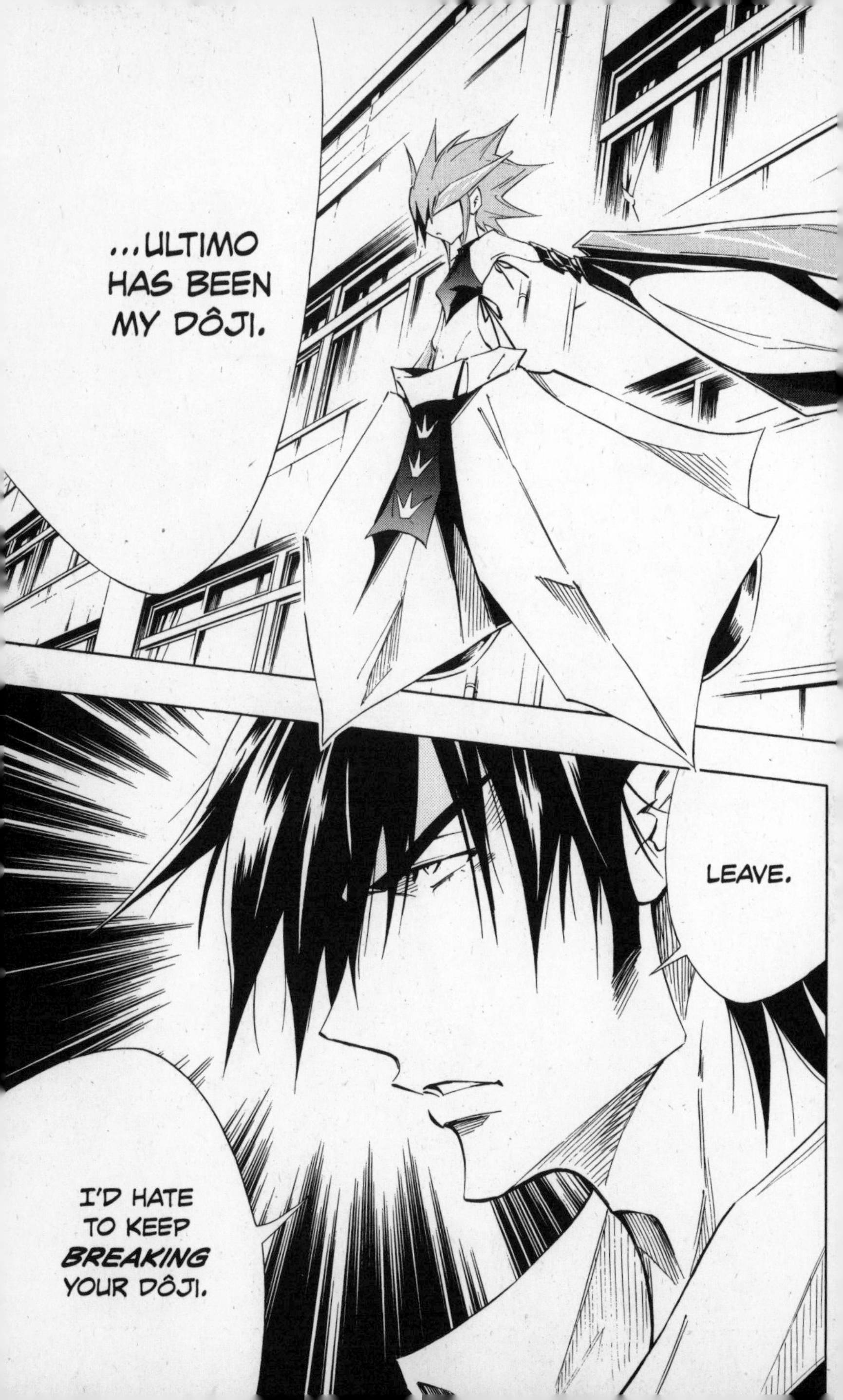
...ULTIMO HAS BEEN MY DÔJI.
LEAVE.
I'D HATE TO KEEP BREAKING YOUR DÔJI.

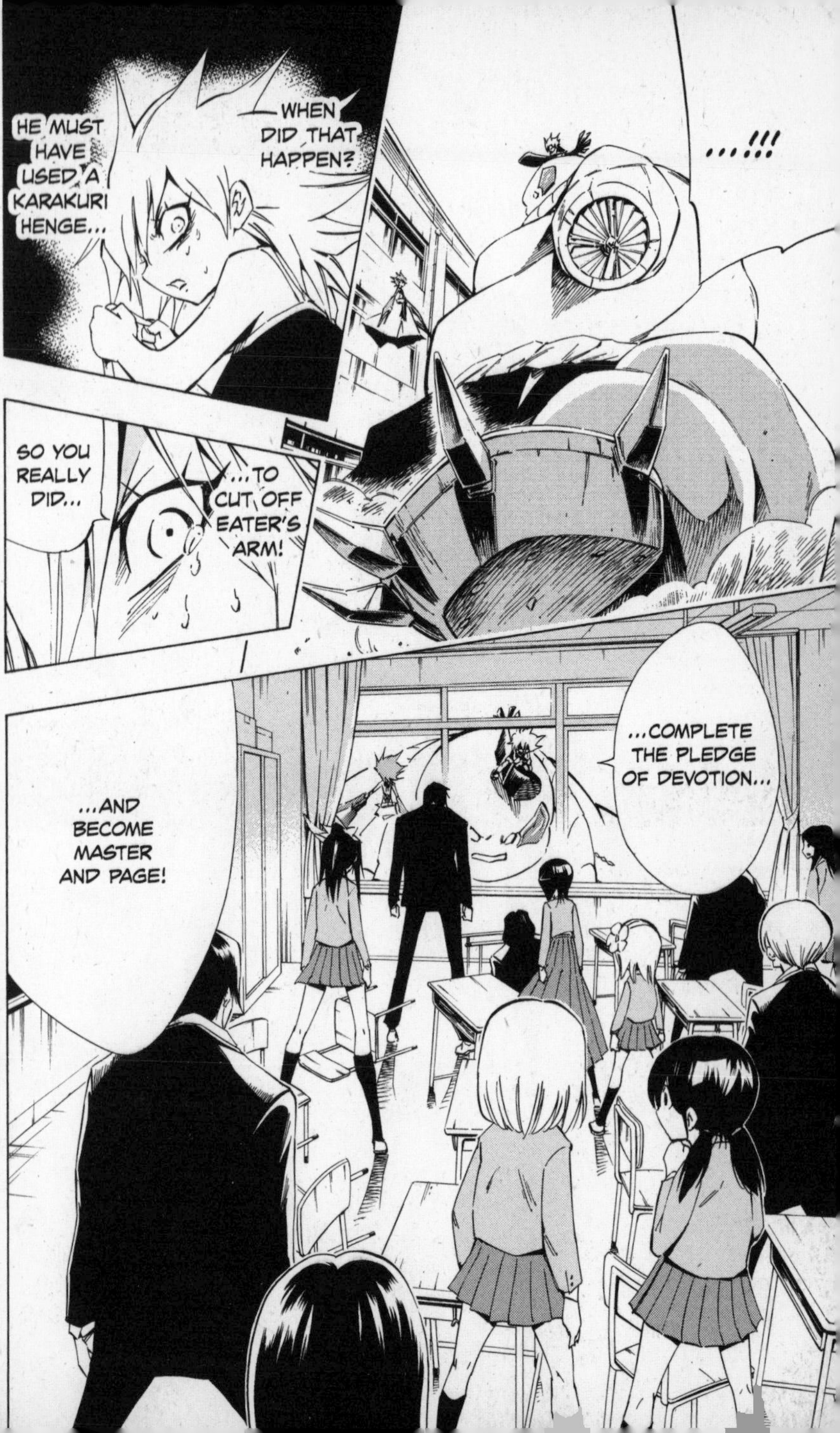
...!!!
WHEN DID THAT HAPPEN?
HE MUST HAVE USED A KARAKURI HENGE...
SO YOU REALLY DID...
...TO CUT OFF EATER'S ARM!
...COMPLETE THE PLEDGE OF DEVOTION...
...AND BECOME MASTER AND PAGE!

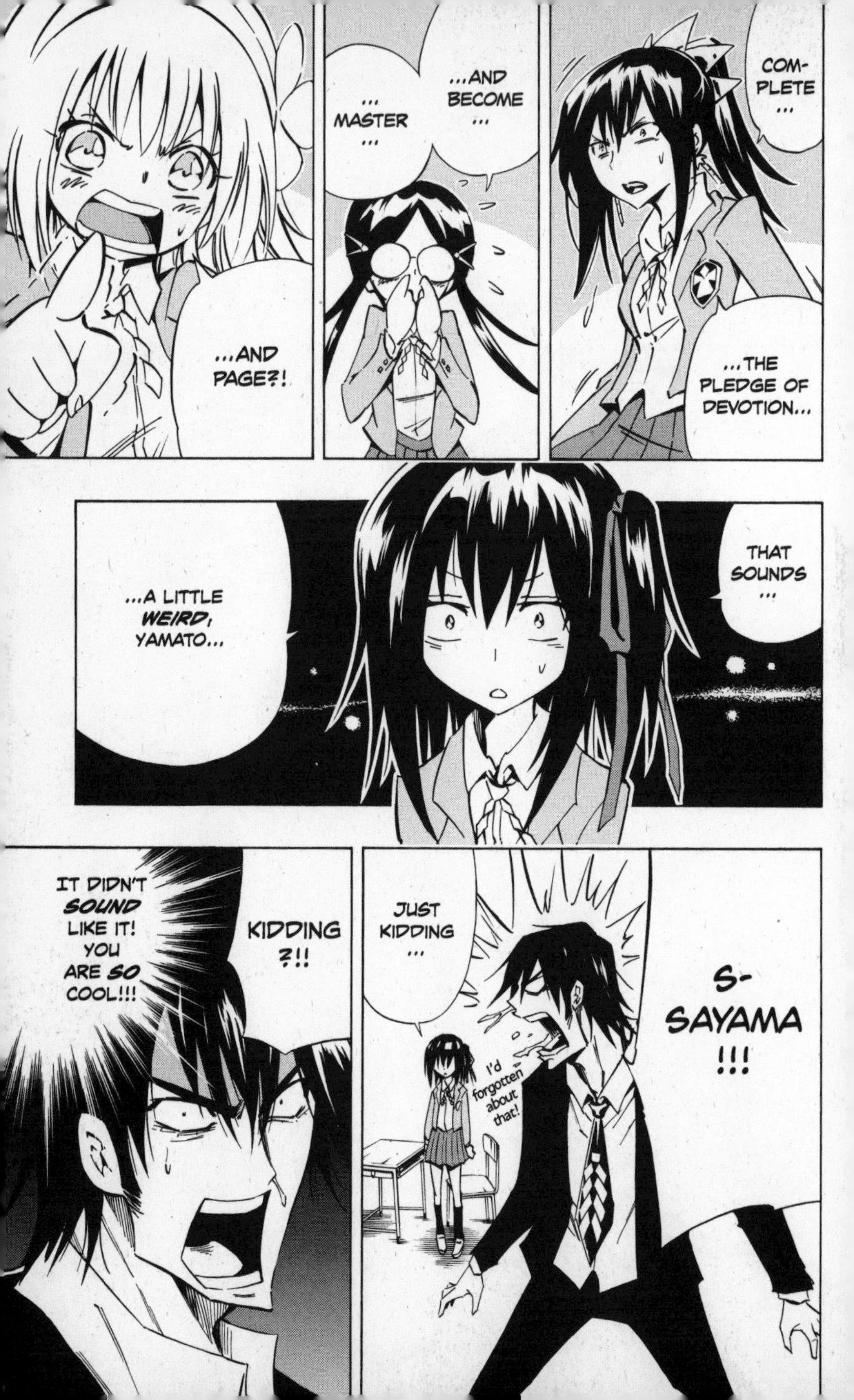
COM-PLETE...
...THE PLEDGE OF DEVOTION...
...AND BECOME...
...MASTER...
...AND PAGE?!
THAT SOUNDS...
...A LITTLE WEIRD, YAMATO...
S-SAYAMA!!!
I'd forgotten about that!
JUST KIDDING...
KIDDING?!!
IT DIDN'T SOUND LIKE IT! YOU ARE SO COOL!!!

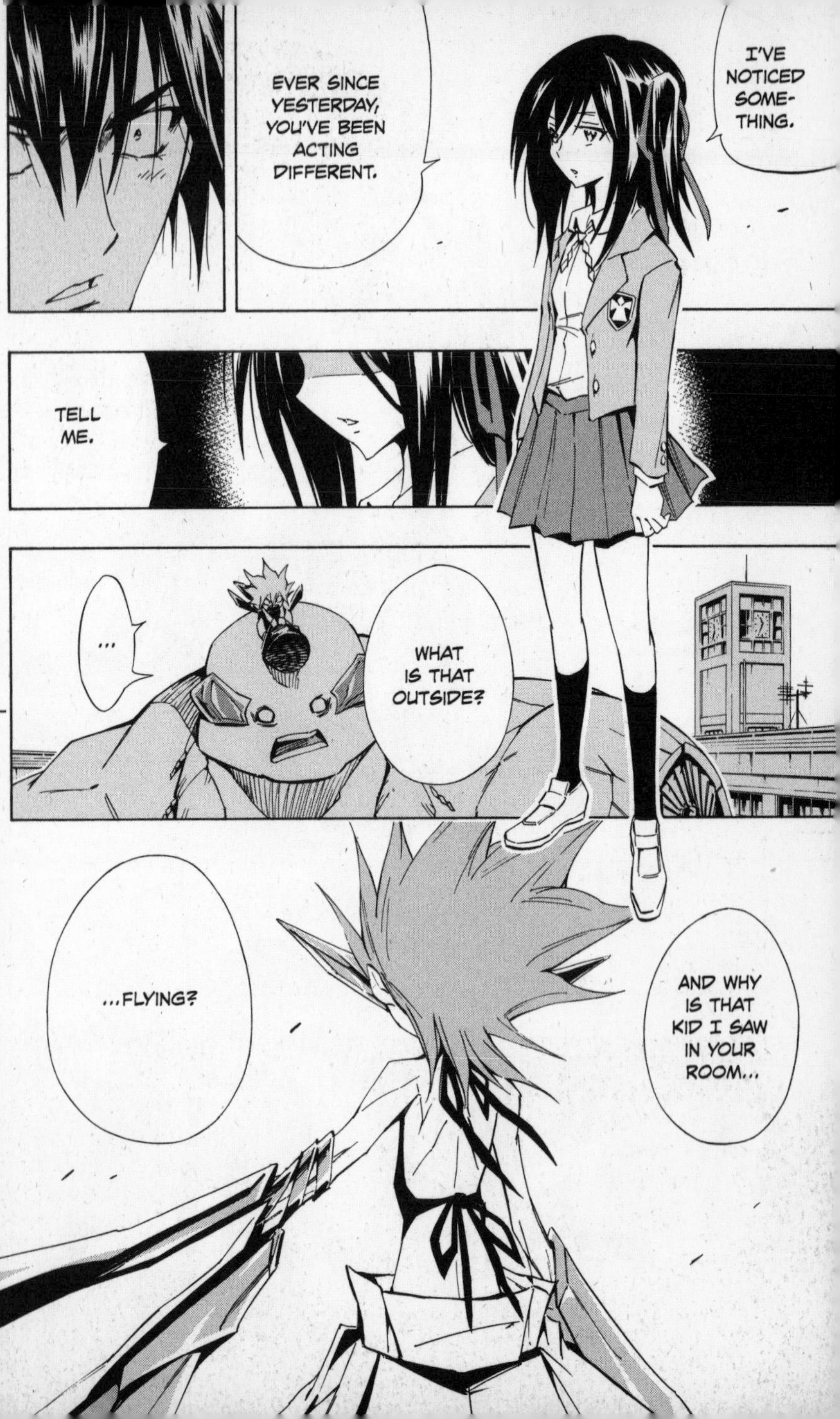
I'VE NOTICED SOME-THING.
EVER SINCE YESTERDAY, YOU'VE BEEN ACTING DIFFERENT.
TELL ME.
WHAT IS THAT OUTSIDE?
...
AND WHY IS THAT KID I SAW IN YOUR ROOM...
...FLYING?

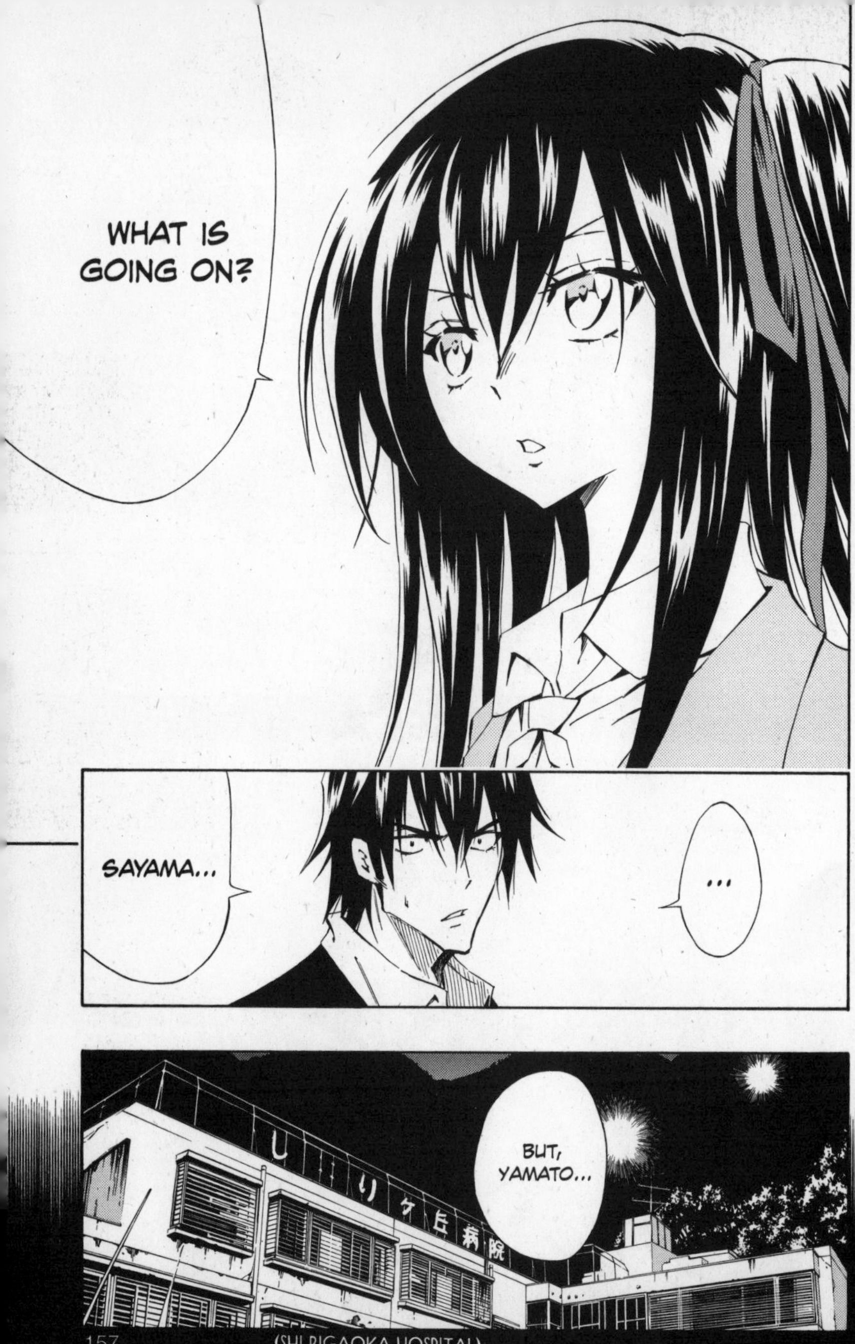
WHAT IS GOING ON?
...
SAYAMA...
BUT, YAMATO...

(SHI RIGAOKA HOSPITAL)

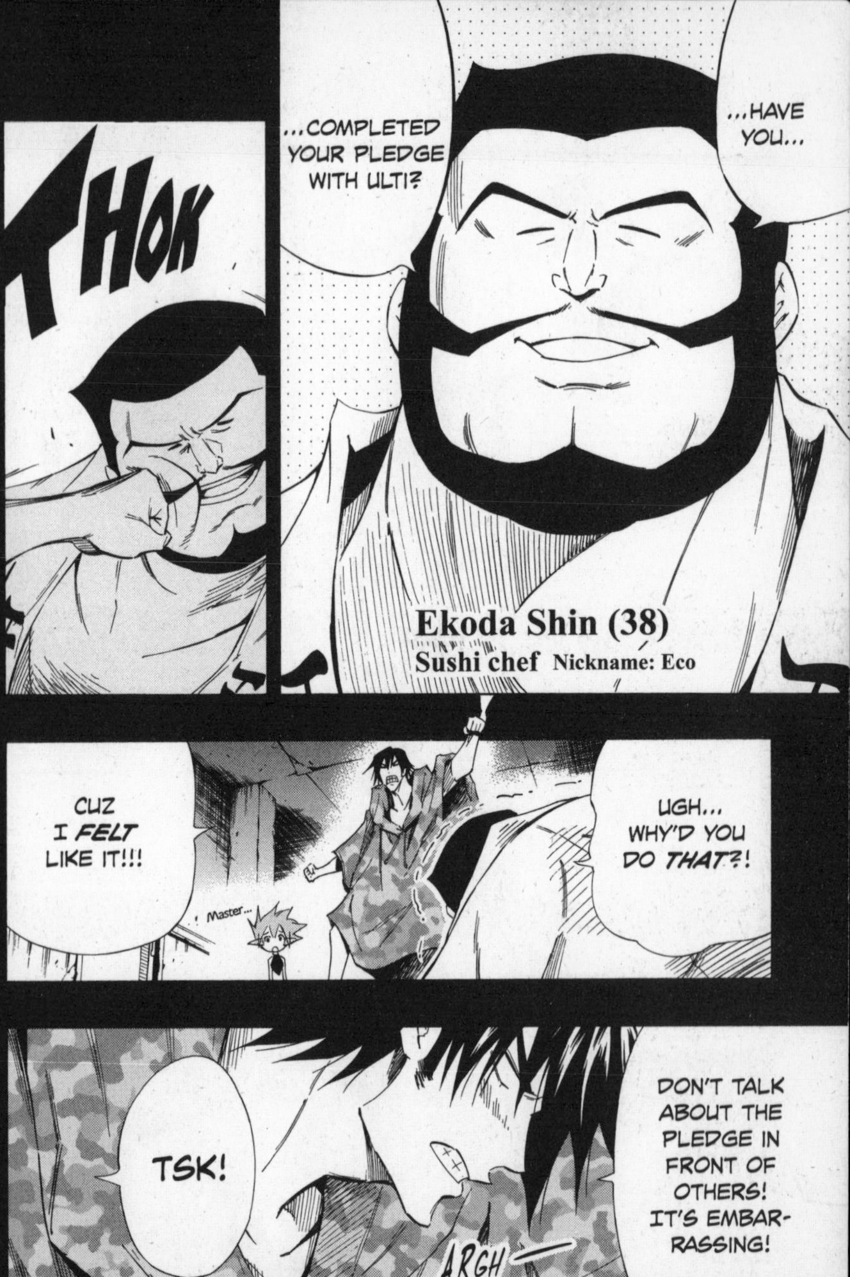
...HAVE YOU...
...COMPLETED YOUR PLEDGE WITH ULTI?
Ekoda Shin (38)
Sushi chef Nickname: Eco
HOK
UGH... WHY'D YOU DO *THAT*?!
Master...
CUZ I *FELT* LIKE IT!!!
DON'T TALK ABOUT THE PLEDGE IN FRONT OF OTHERS! IT'S EMBAR-RASSING!
ARGH—
TSK!

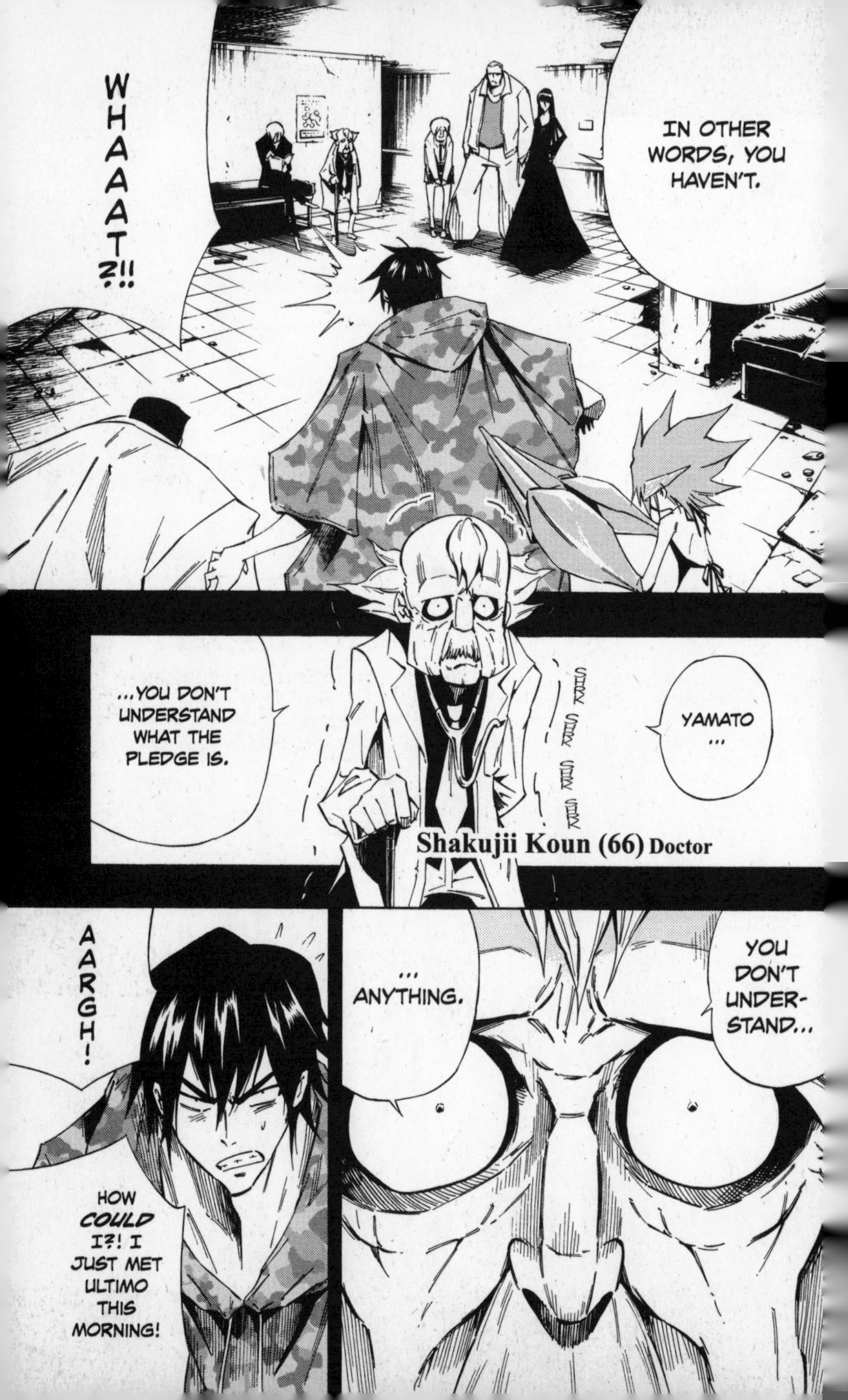
IN OTHER WORDS, YOU HAVEN'T.
WHAAAAT?!!
YAMATO ...
SHRK SHRK SHRK SHRK
...YOU DON'T UNDERSTAND WHAT THE PLEDGE IS.
Shakujii Koun (66) Doctor
YOU DON'T UNDER-STAND...
... ANYTHING.
AARGH!
HOW COULD I?! I JUST MET ULTIMO THIS MORNING!

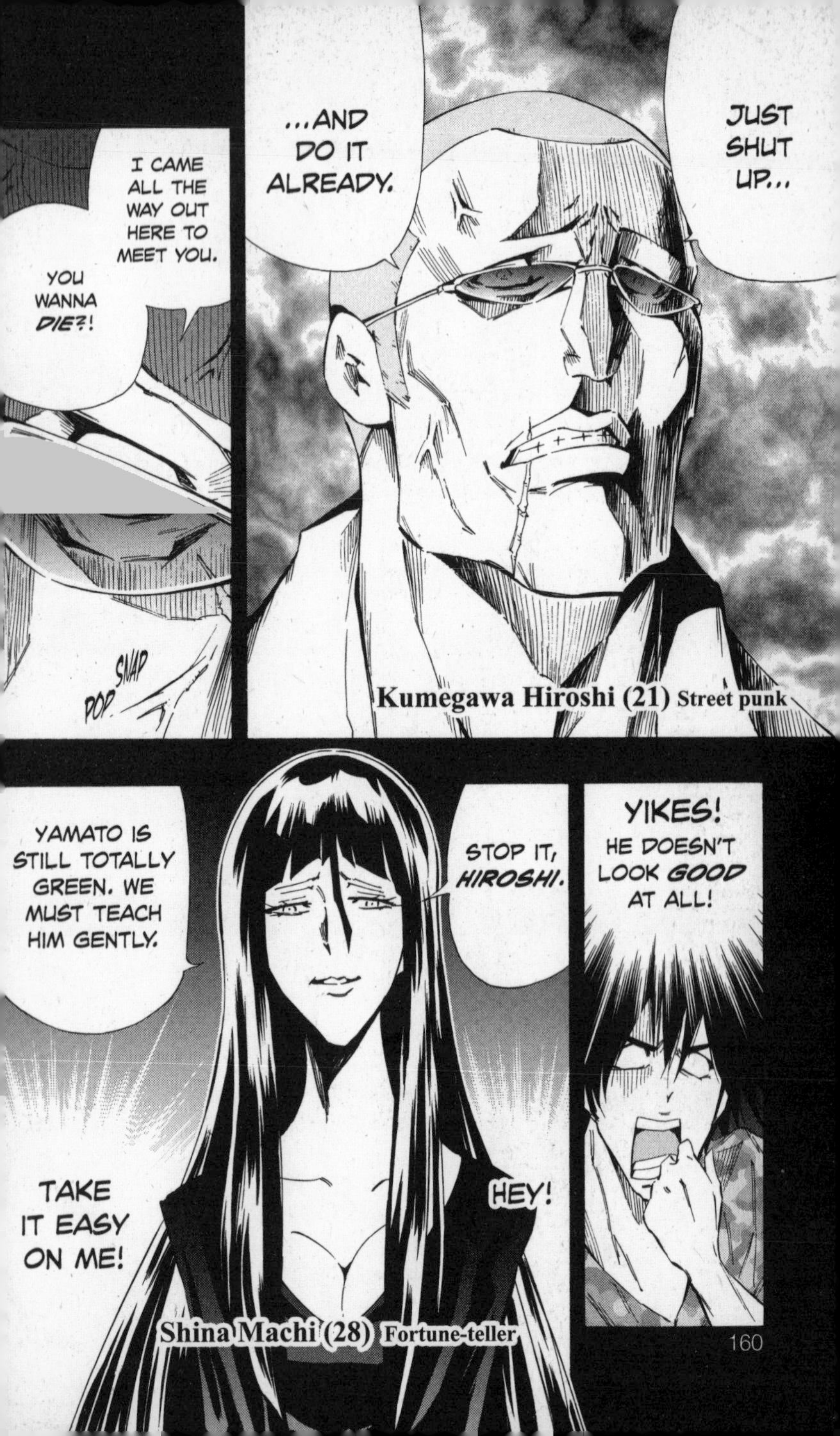
JUST SHUT UP...
...AND DO IT ALREADY.
Kumegawa Hiroshi (21) Street punk
I CAME ALL THE WAY OUT HERE TO MEET YOU.
YOU WANNA DIE?!
SNAP
POP
YIKES! HE DOESN'T LOOK GOOD AT ALL!
STOP IT, HIROSHI.
YAMATO IS STILL TOTALLY GREEN. WE MUST TEACH HIM GENTLY.
HEY!
TAKE IT EASY ON ME!
Shina Machi (28) Fortune-teller

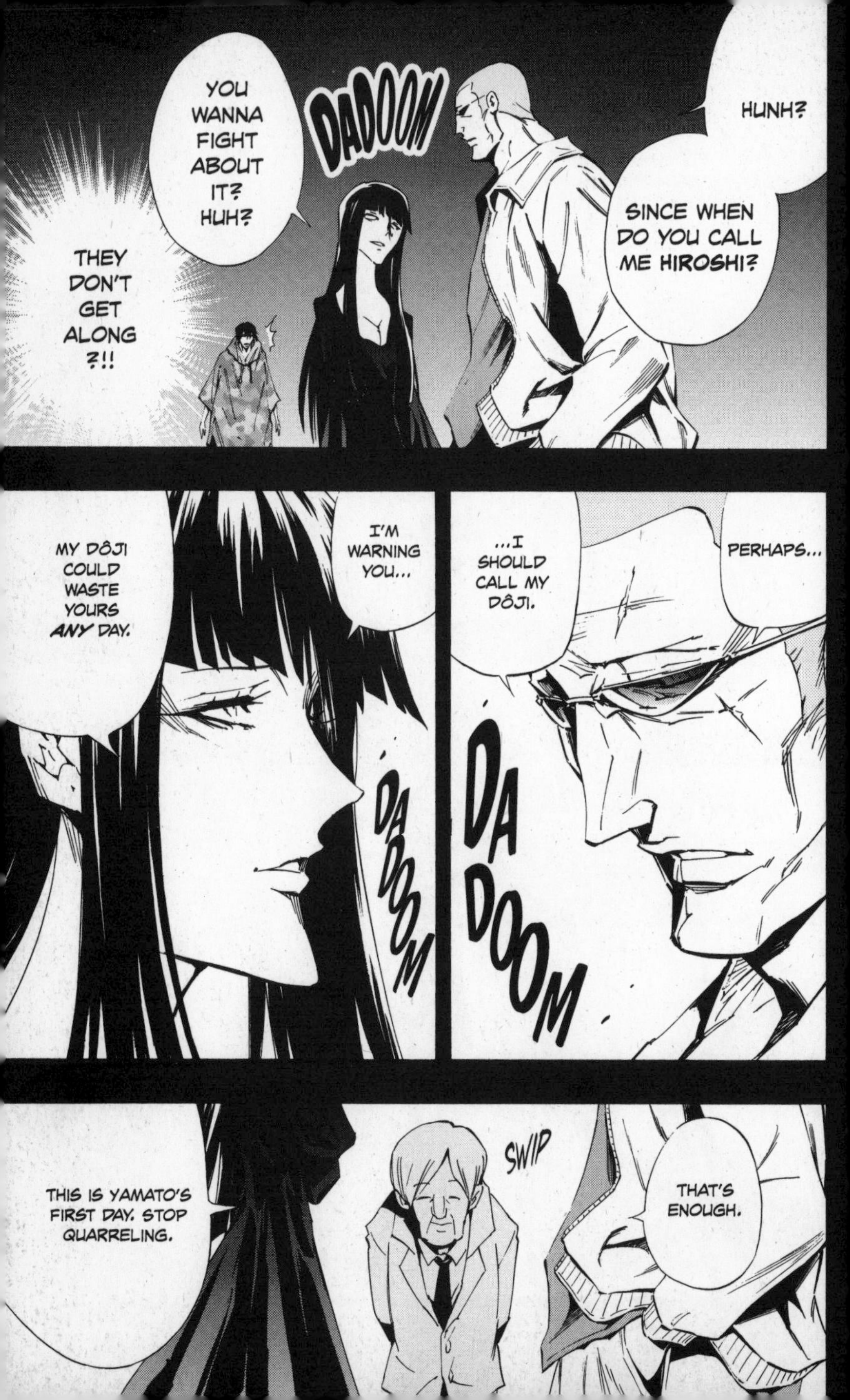
HUNH?
SINCE WHEN DO YOU CALL ME HIROSHI?
DADOOM
YOU WANNA FIGHT ABOUT IT? HUH?
THEY DON'T GET ALONG ?!!
PERHAPS...
...I SHOULD CALL MY DÔJI.
DA DOOM
I'M WARNING YOU...
MY DÔJI COULD WASTE YOURS *ANY* DAY.
DADOOM
SWIP
THAT'S ENOUGH.
THIS IS YAMATO'S FIRST DAY. STOP QUARRELING.

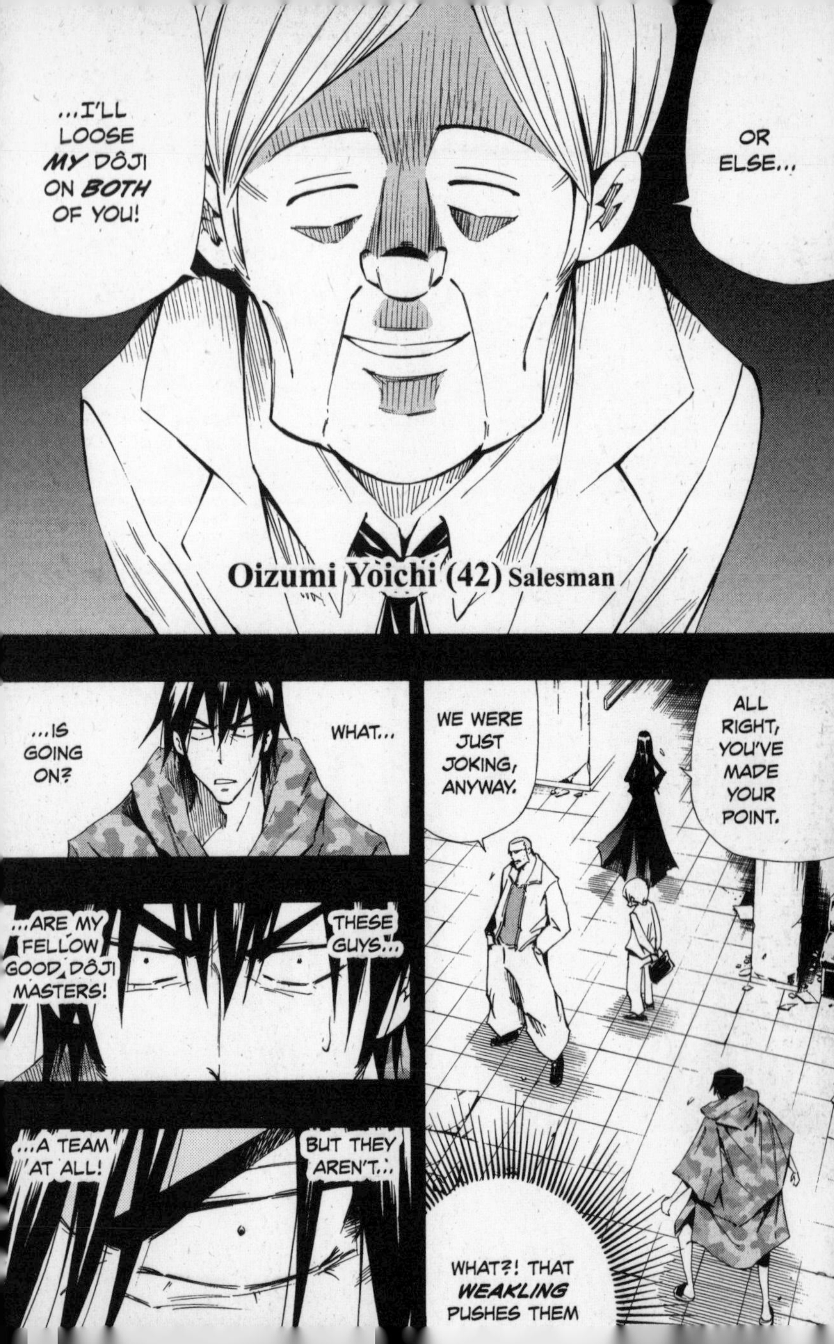
OR ELSE...
...I'LL LOOSE *MY* DÔJI ON *BOTH* OF YOU!
Oizumi Yoichi (42) Salesman
ALL RIGHT, YOU'VE MADE YOUR POINT.
WE WERE JUST JOKING, ANYWAY.
WHAT?! THAT *WEAKLING* PUSHES THEM
WHAT...
...IS GOING ON?
THESE GUYS...
...ARE MY FELLOW GOOD DÔJI MASTERS!
BUT THEY AREN'T...
...A TEAM AT ALL!

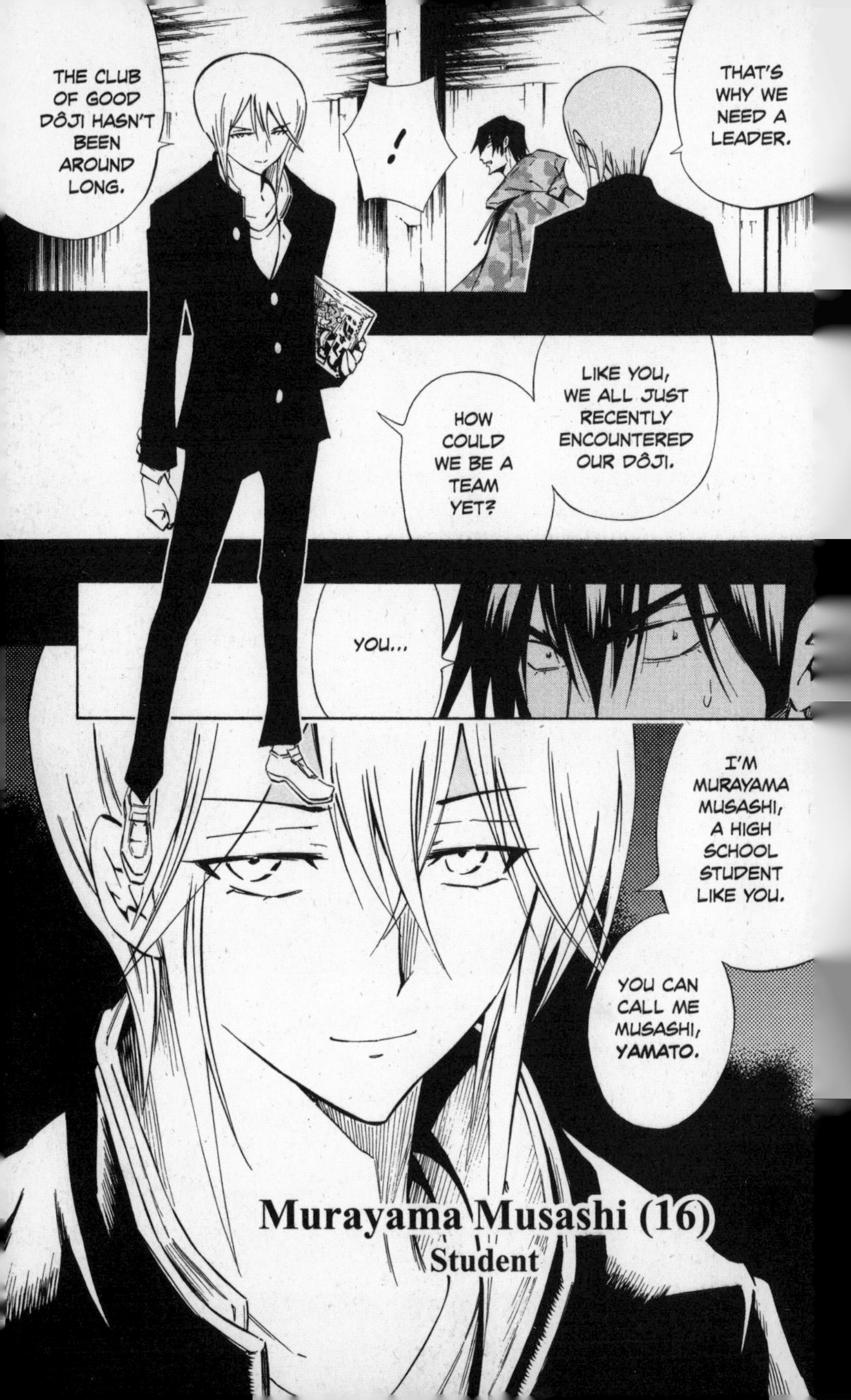

THAT'S WHY WE NEED A LEADER.
!
THE CLUB OF GOOD DÔJI HASN'T BEEN AROUND LONG.
LIKE YOU, WE ALL JUST RECENTLY ENCOUNTERED OUR DÔJI.
HOW COULD WE BE A TEAM YET?
YOU...
I'M MURAYAMA MUSASHI, A HIGH SCHOOL STUDENT LIKE YOU.
YOU CAN CALL ME MUSASHI, YAMATO.
Murayama Musashi (16)
Student

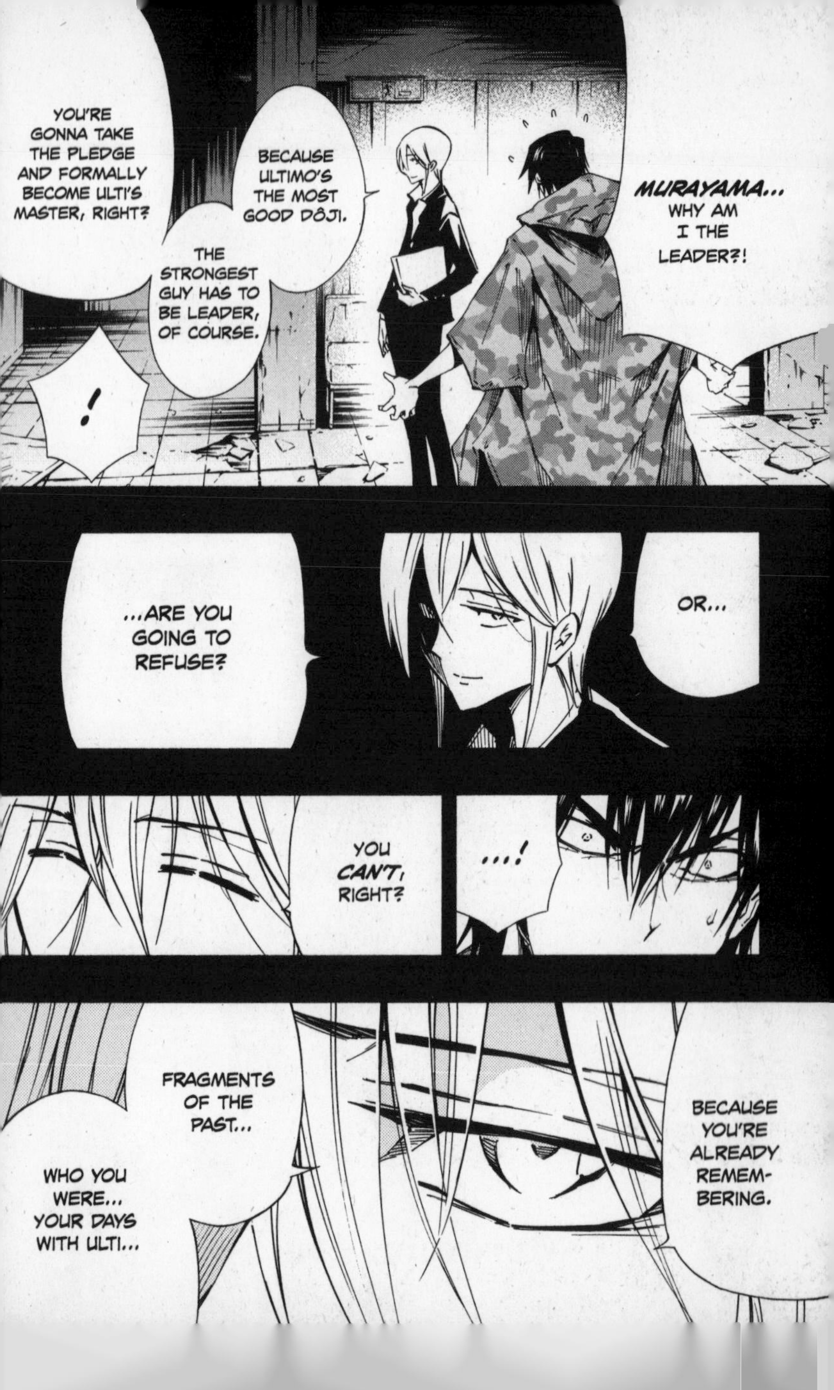
MURAYAMA... WHY AM I THE LEADER?!
BECAUSE ULTIMO'S THE MOST GOOD DÔJI.
THE STRONGEST GUY HAS TO BE LEADER, OF COURSE.
YOU'RE GONNA TAKE THE PLEDGE AND FORMALLY BECOME ULTI'S MASTER, RIGHT?
!
OR...
...ARE YOU GOING TO REFUSE?
...!
YOU CAN'T, RIGHT?
BECAUSE YOU'RE ALREADY REMEMBERING.
FRAGMENTS OF THE PAST...
WHO YOU WERE... YOUR DAYS WITH ULTI...

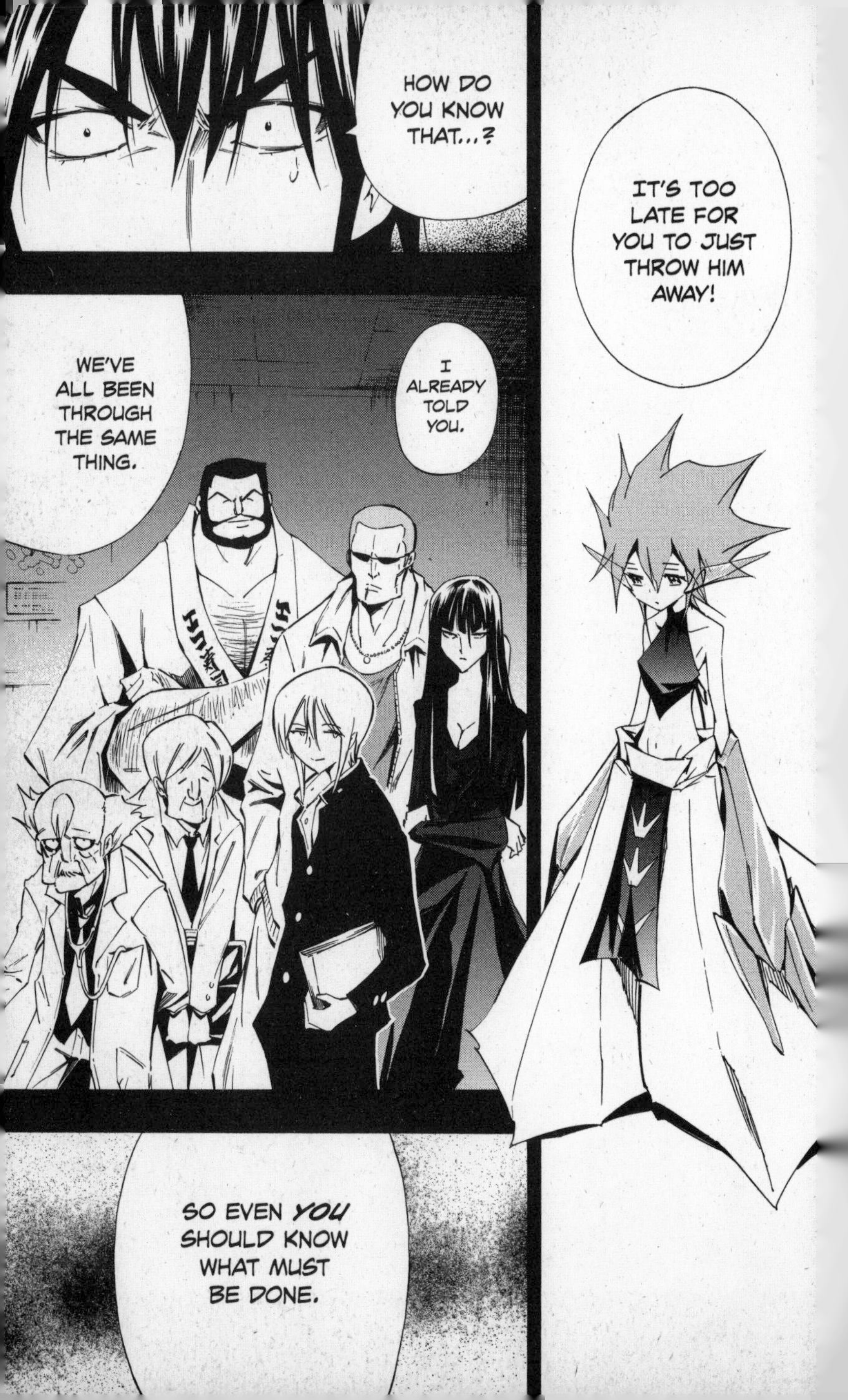
IT'S TOO LATE FOR YOU TO JUST THROW HIM AWAY!
HOW DO YOU KNOW THAT...?
I ALREADY TOLD YOU.
WE'VE ALL BEEN THROUGH THE SAME THING.
SO EVEN *YOU* SHOULD KNOW WHAT MUST BE DONE.

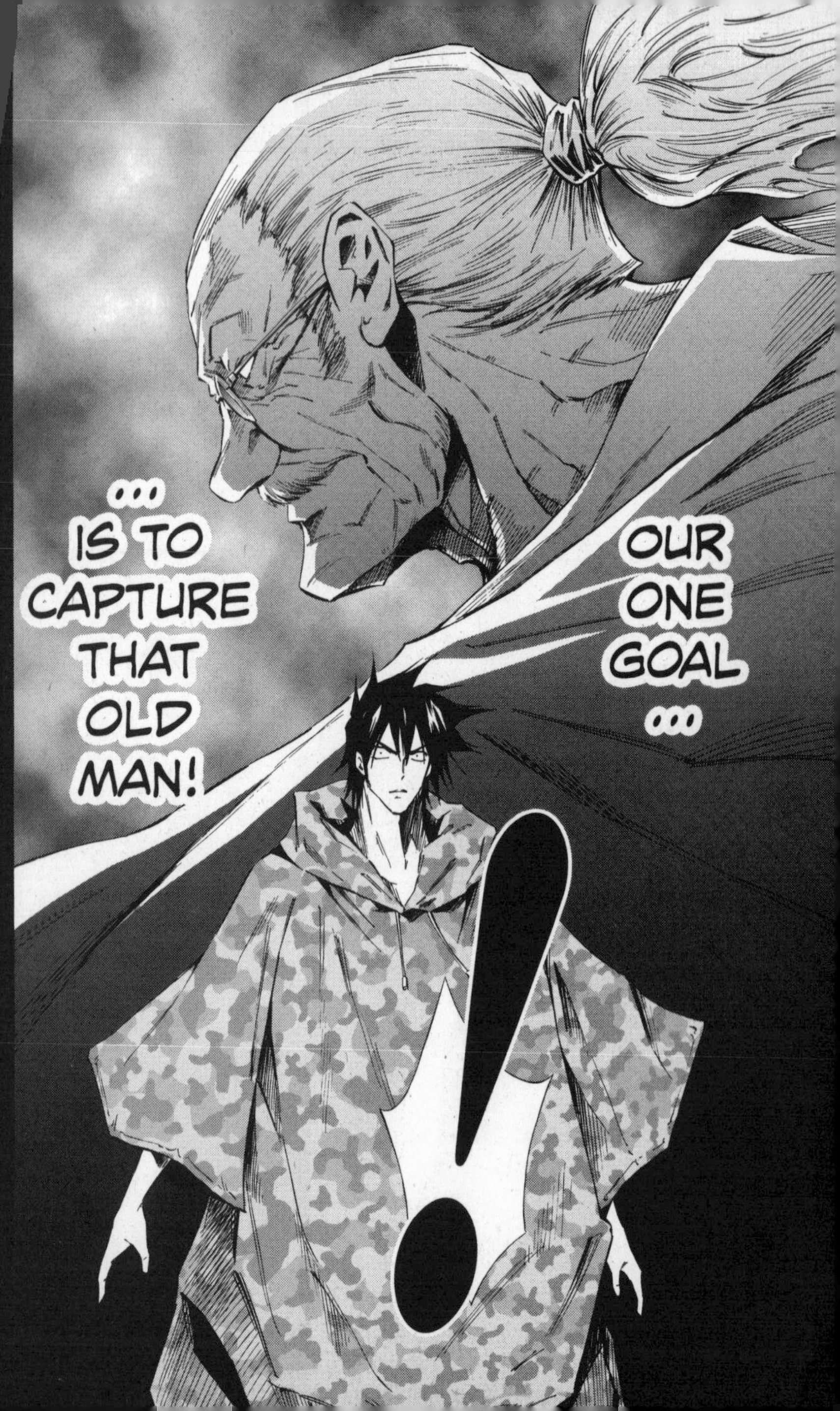
OUR ONE GOAL ...
... IS TO CAPTURE THAT OLD MAN!

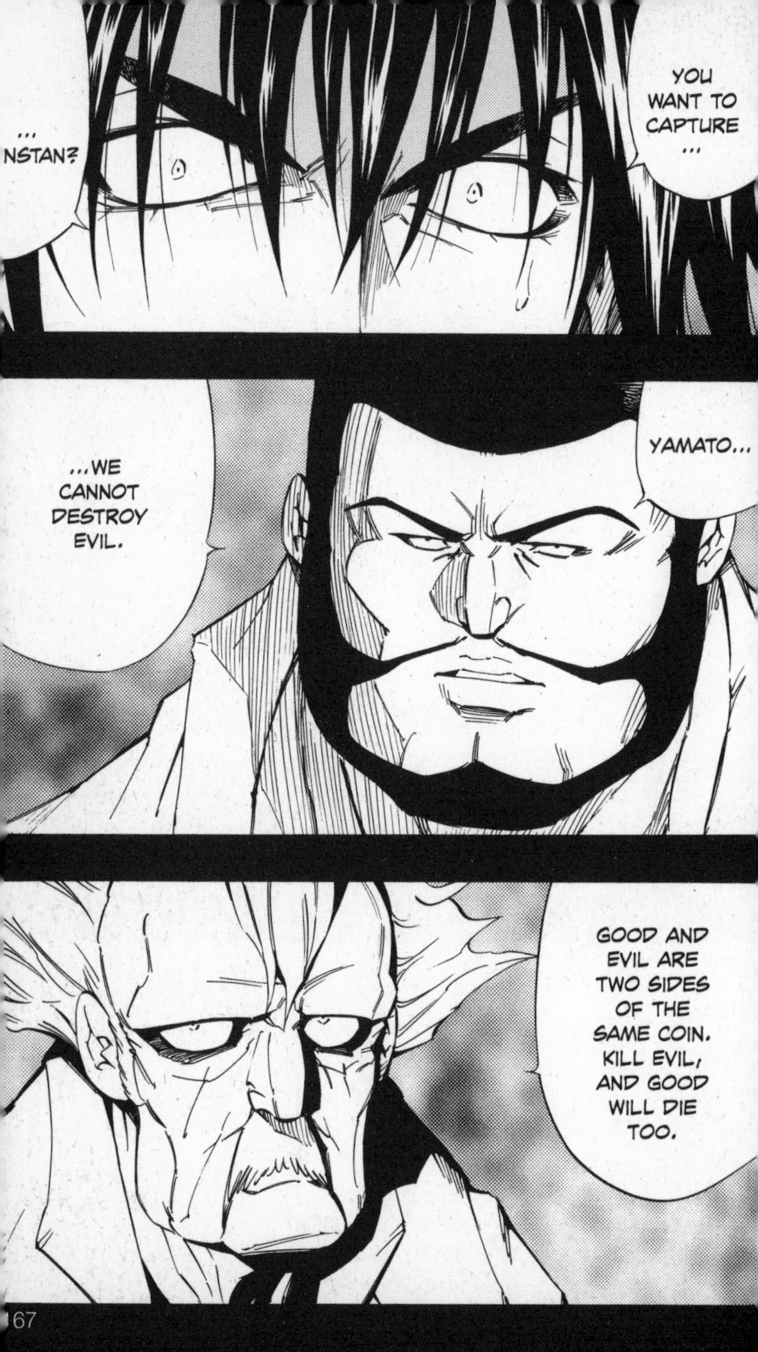
YOU WANT TO CAPTURE ...
... NSTAN?
YAMATO...
...WE CANNOT DESTROY EVIL.
GOOD AND EVIL ARE TWO SIDES OF THE SAME COIN. KILL EVIL, AND GOOD WILL DIE TOO.

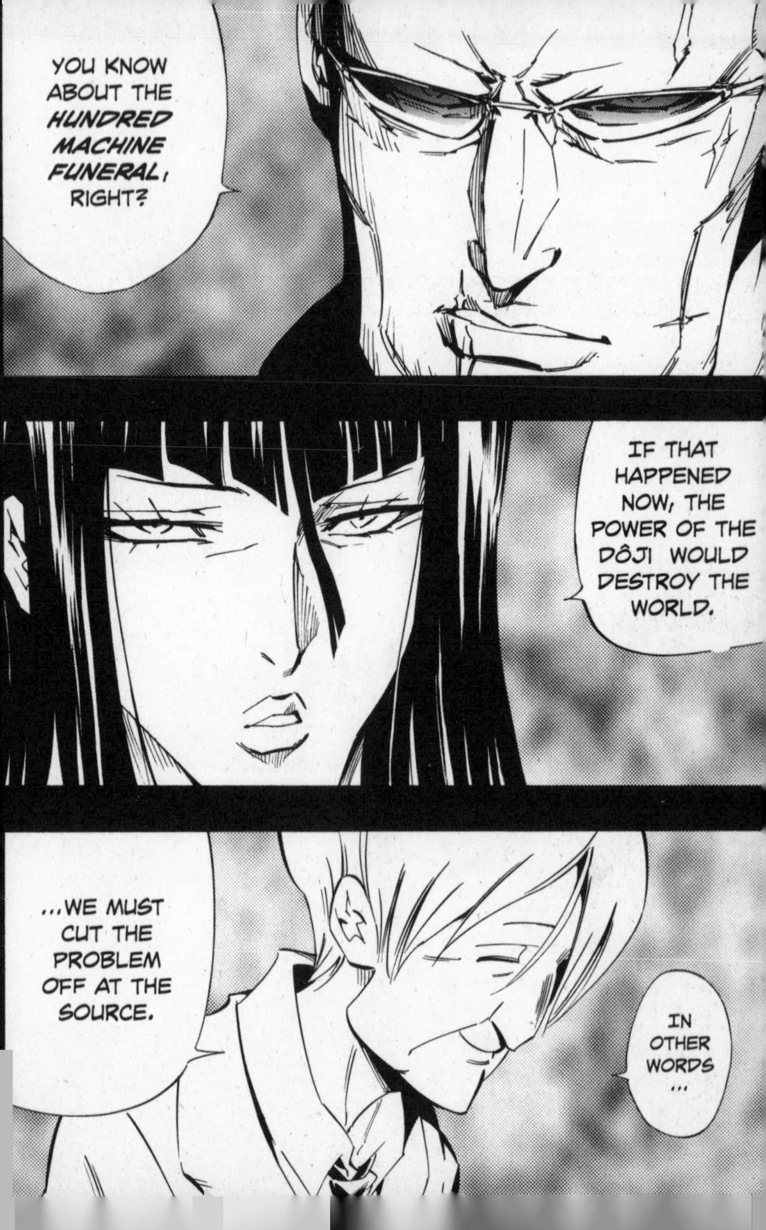
YOU KNOW ABOUT THE *HUNDRED MACHINE FUNERAL*, RIGHT?
IF THAT HAPPENED NOW, THE POWER OF THE DÔJI WOULD DESTROY THE WORLD.
IN OTHER WORDS ...
...WE MUST CUT THE PROBLEM OFF AT THE SOURCE.

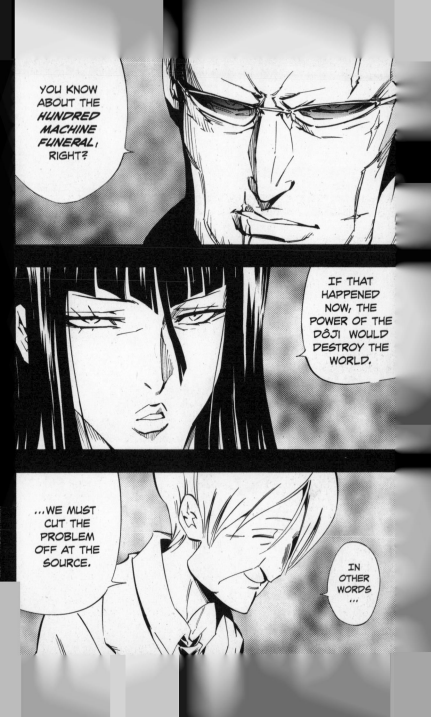

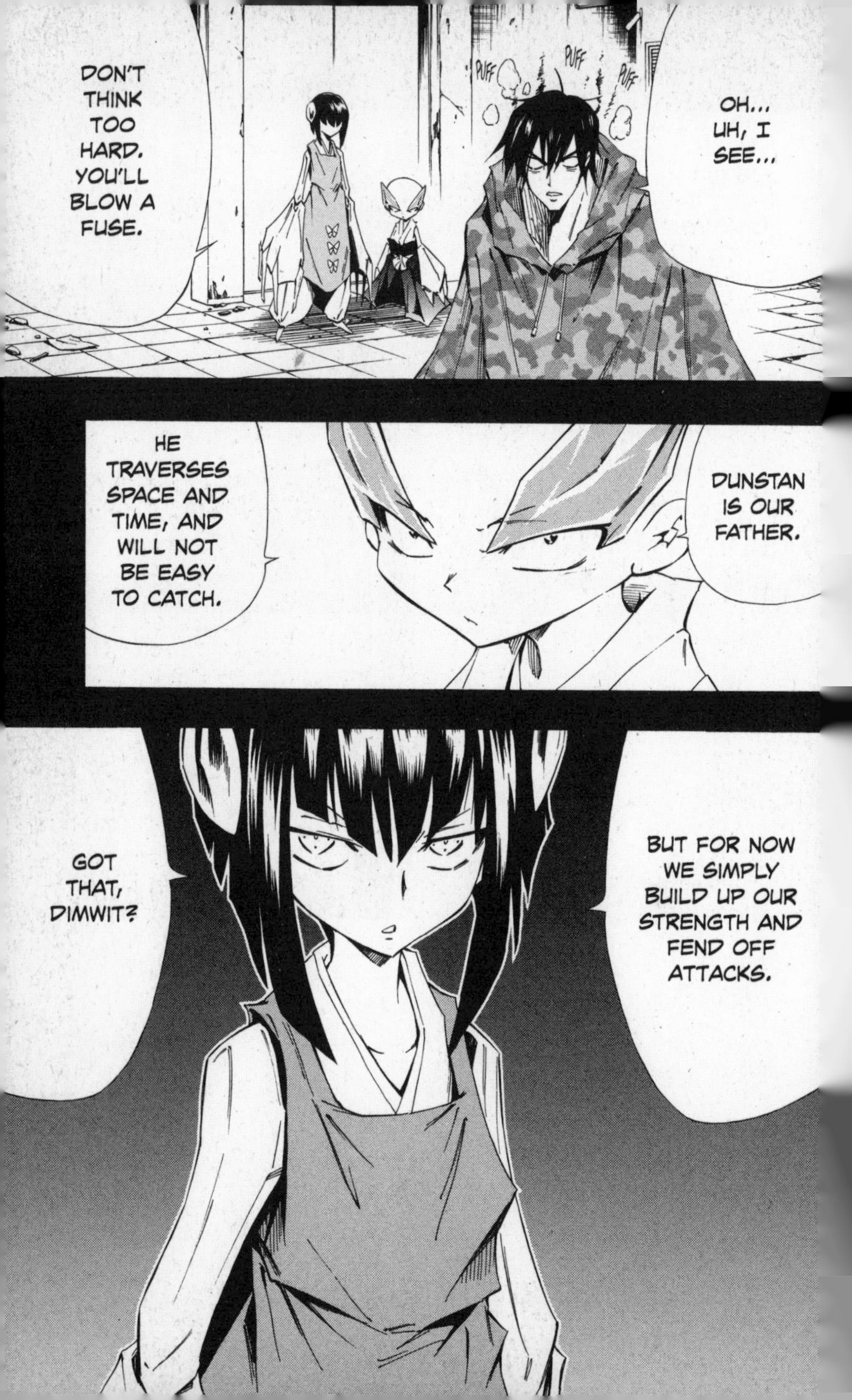
PUFF
PUFF
PUFF
OH... UH, I SEE...
DON'T THINK TOO HARD. YOU'LL BLOW A FUSE.
DUNSTAN IS OUR FATHER.
HE TRAVERSES SPACE AND TIME, AND WILL NOT BE EASY TO CATCH.
BUT FOR NOW WE SIMPLY BUILD UP OUR STRENGTH AND FEND OFF ATTACKS.
GOT THAT, DIMWIT?

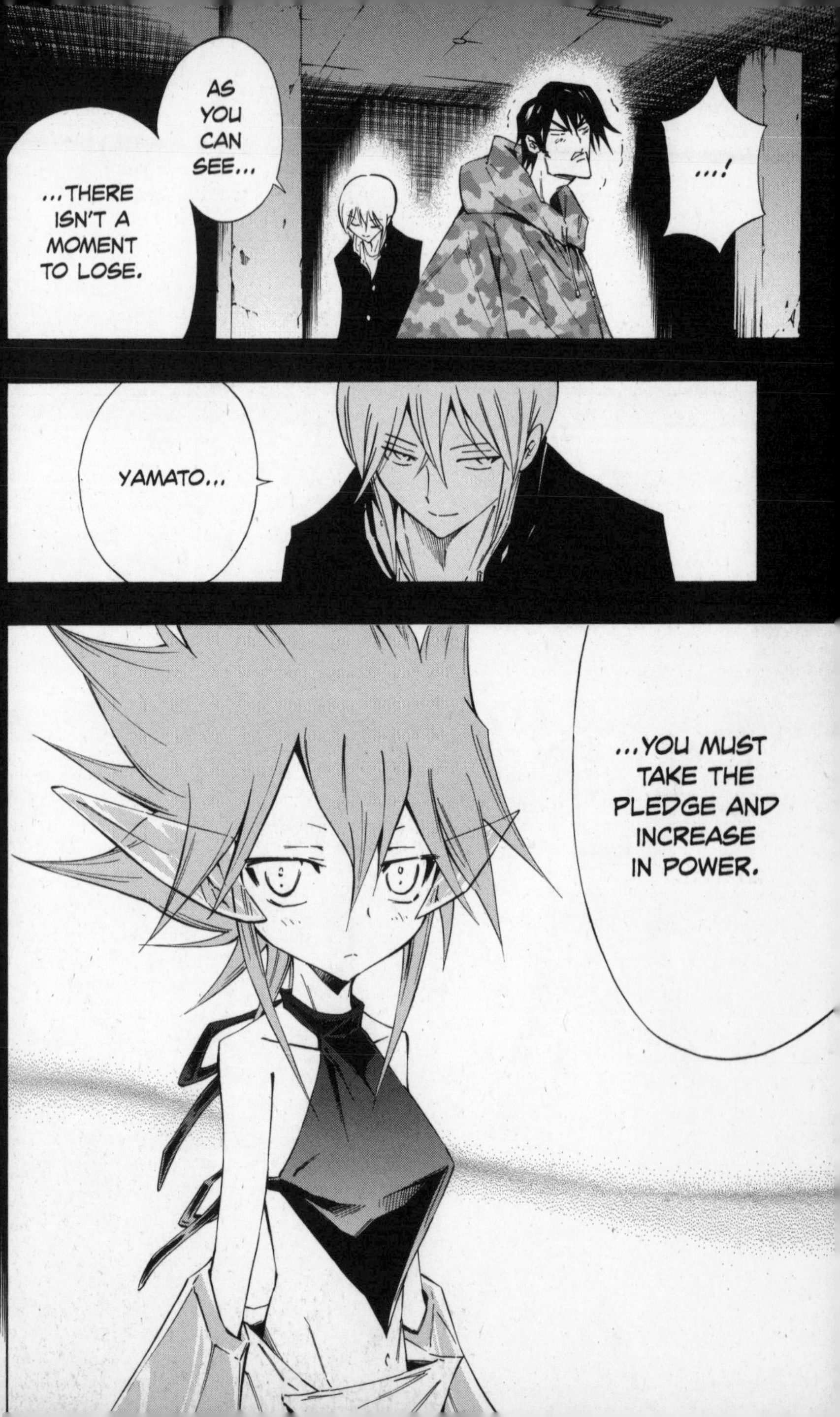
...!
AS YOU CAN SEE...
...THERE ISN'T A MOMENT TO LOSE.
YAMATO...
...YOU MUST TAKE THE PLEDGE AND INCREASE IN POWER.

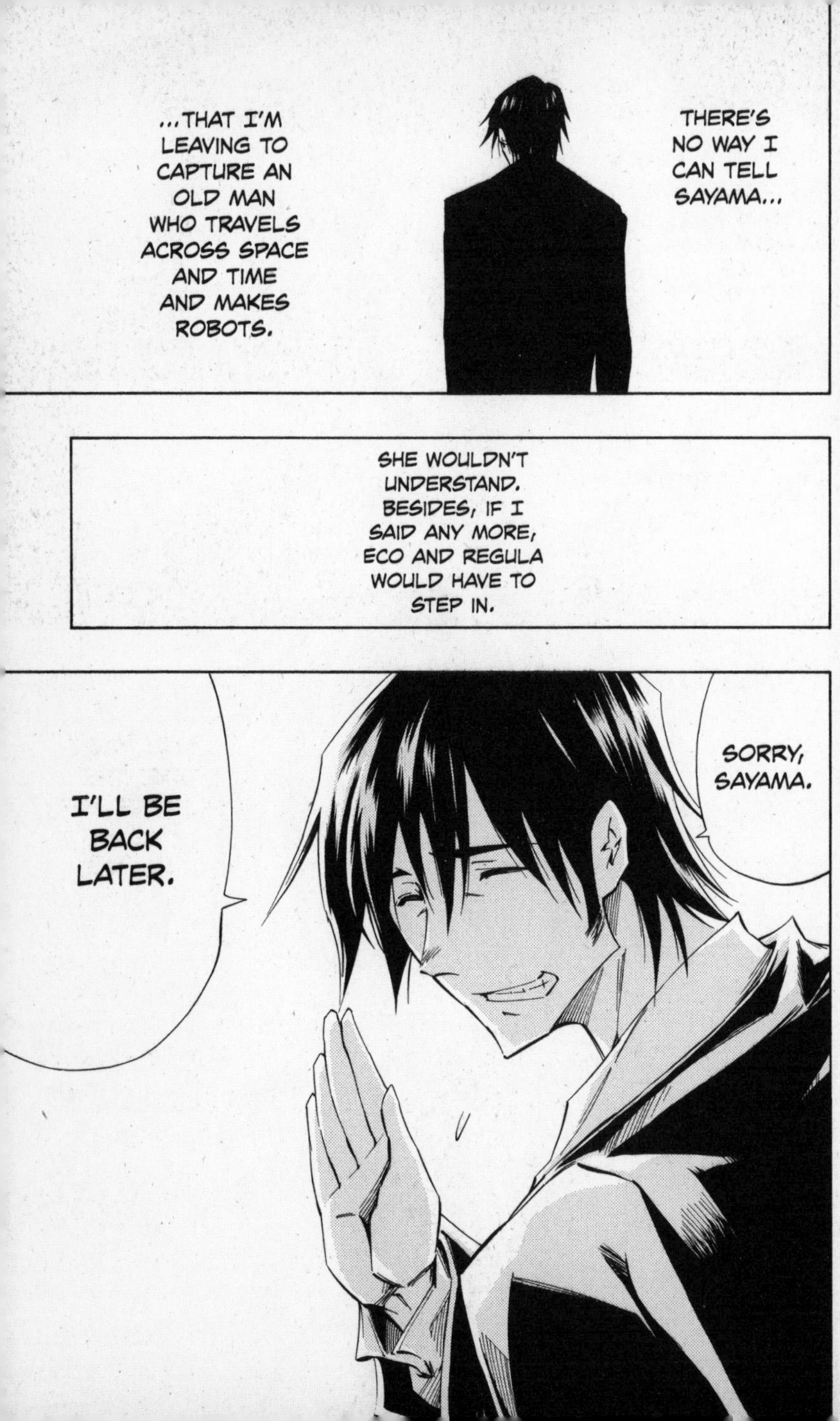
THERE'S NO WAY I CAN TELL SAYAMA...
...THAT I'M LEAVING TO CAPTURE AN OLD MAN WHO TRAVELS ACROSS SPACE AND TIME AND MAKES ROBOTS.
SHE WOULDN'T UNDERSTAND. BESIDES, IF I SAID ANY MORE, ECO AND REGULA WOULD HAVE TO STEP IN.
SORRY, SAYAMA.
I'LL BE BACK LATER.

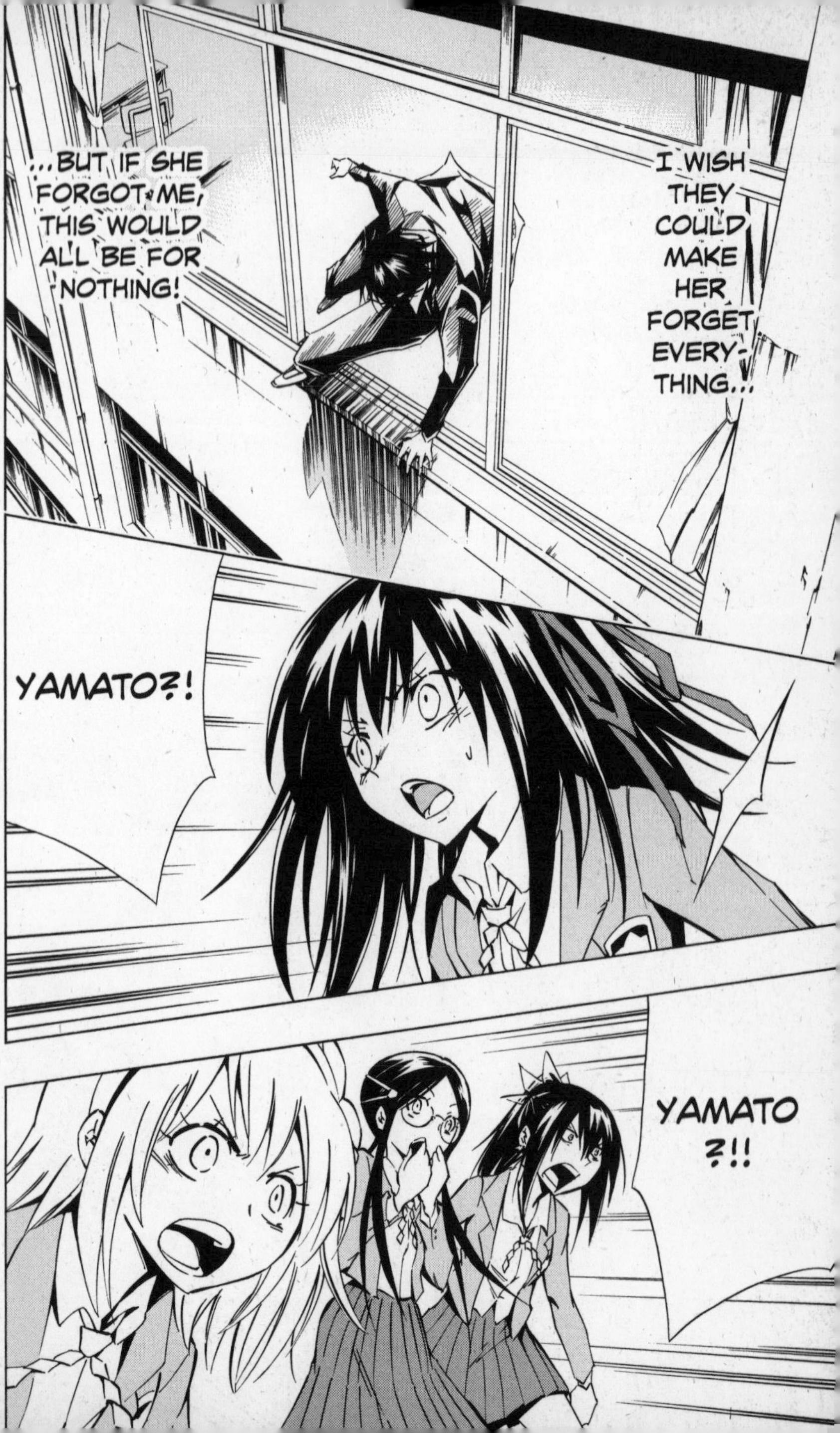
I WISH THEY COULD MAKE HER FORGET EVERY-THING...
...BUT IF SHE FORGOT ME, THIS WOULD ALL BE FOR NOTHING!
YAMATO?!
YAMATO?!!

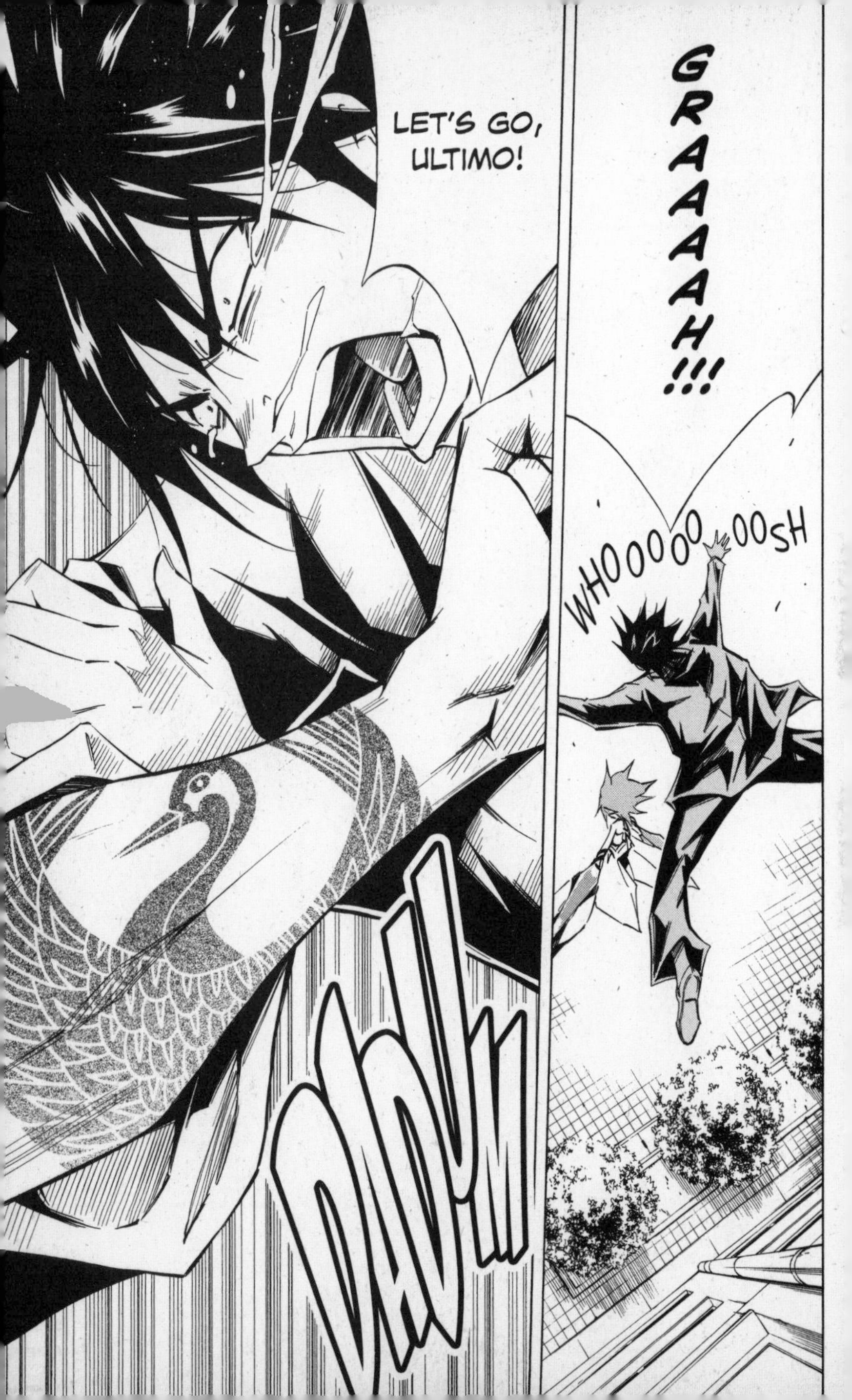
GRAAAAAH!!!
WHOOOOO OOSH
LET'S GO, ULTIMO!

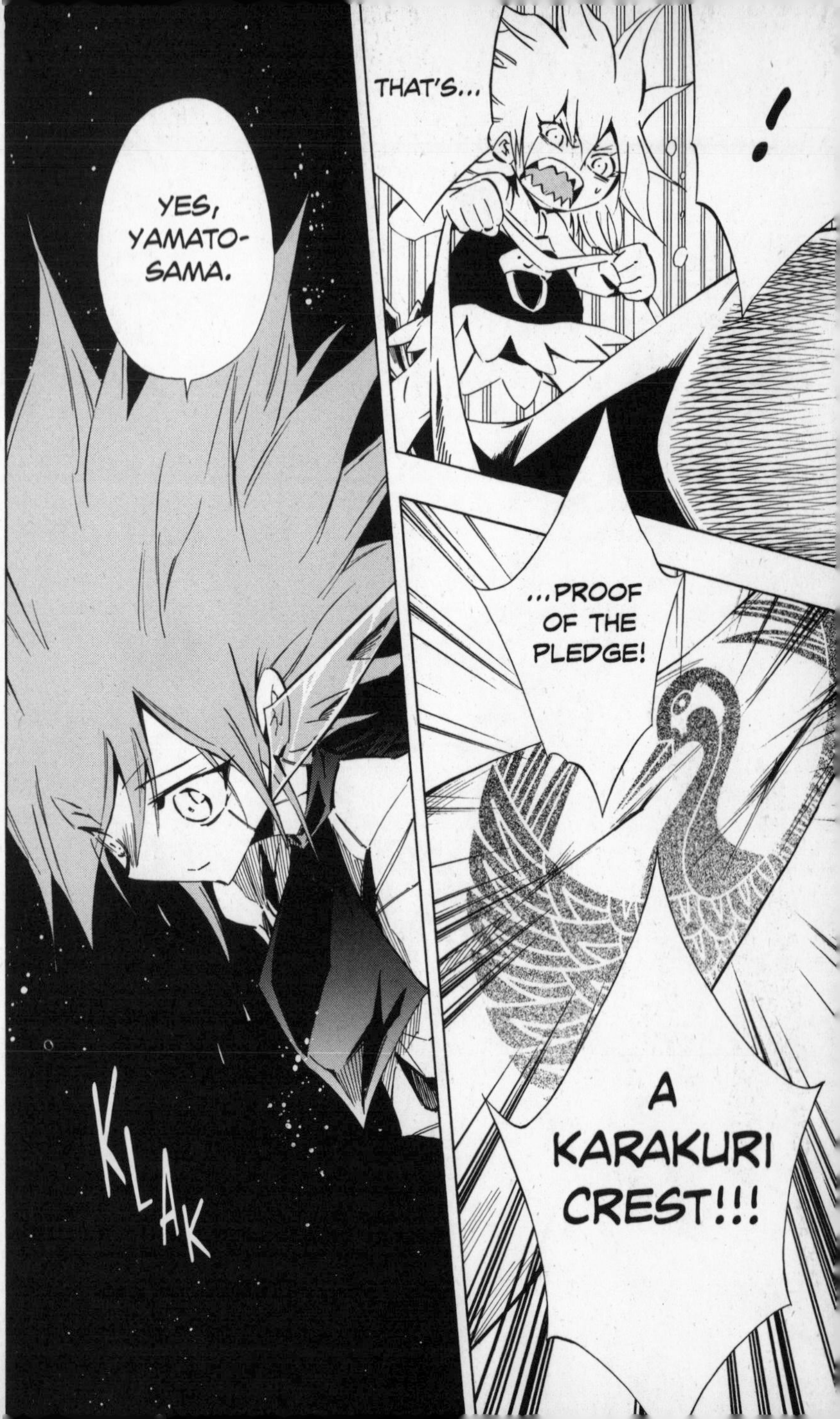
THAT'S...
!
...PROOF OF THE PLEDGE!
A KARAKURI CREST!!!
YES, YAMATO-SAMA.
KLAK

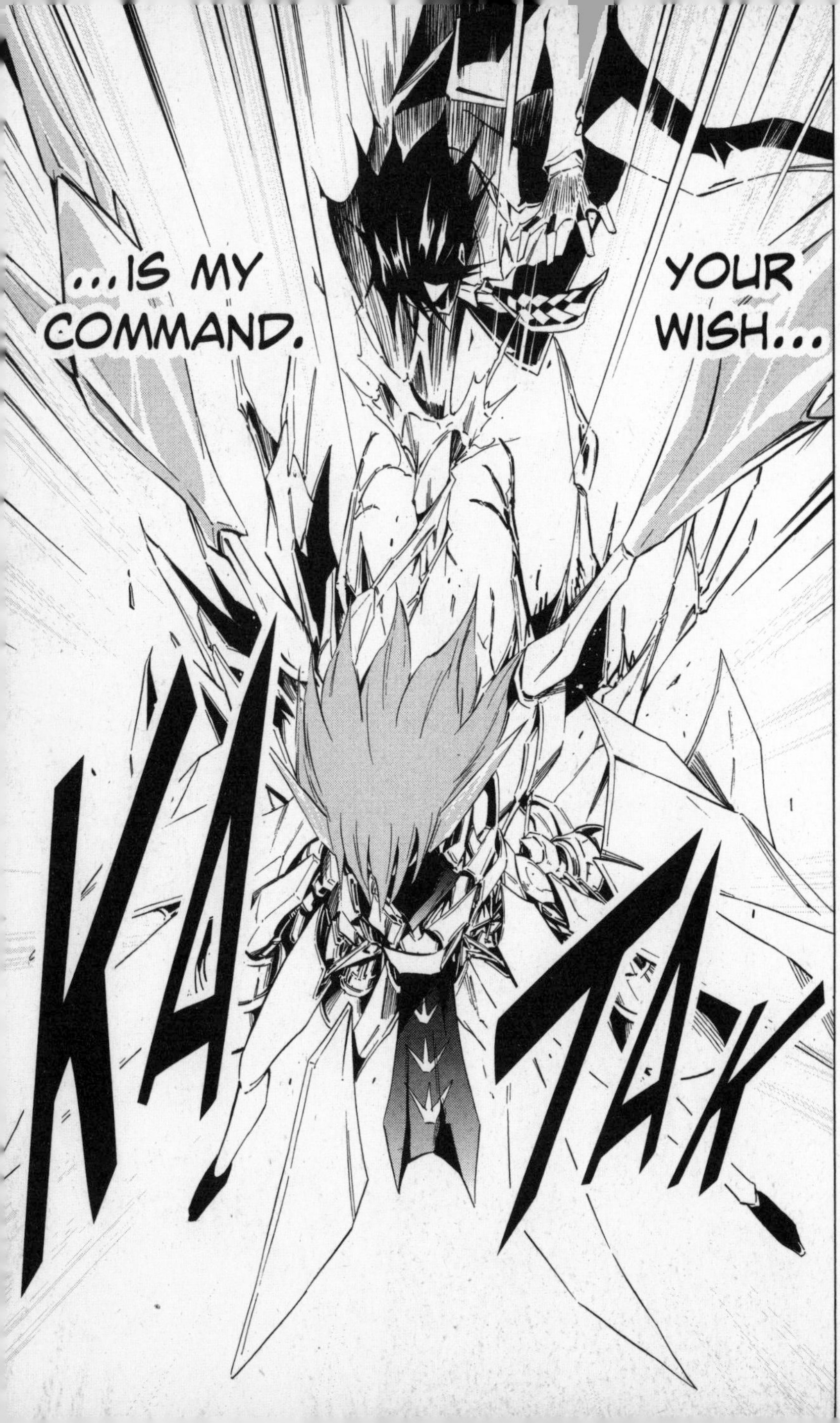
YOUR WISH...
...IS MY COMMAND.
KA-TAK

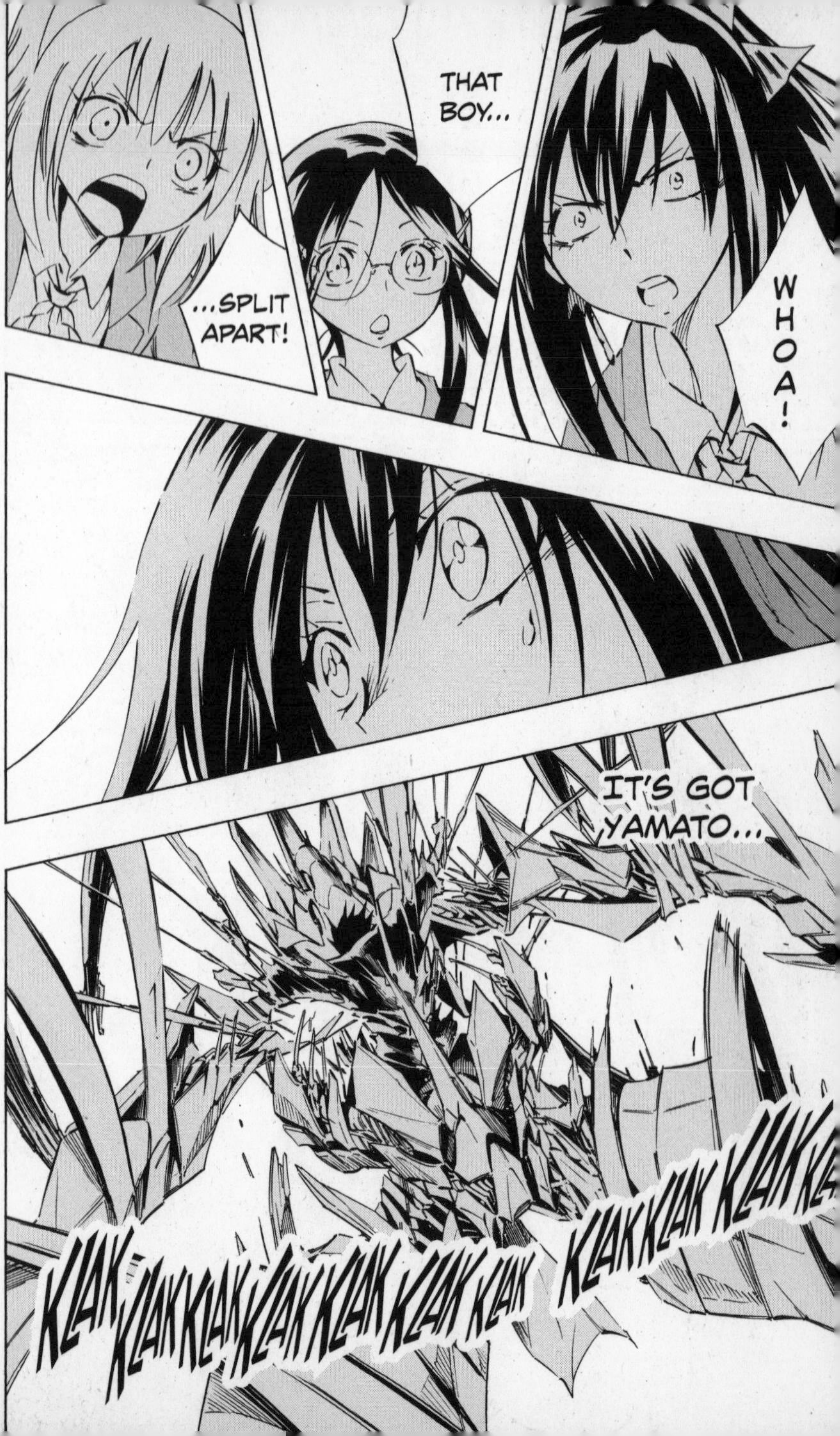
WHOA!
THAT BOY...
...SPLIT APART!
IT'S GOT YAMATO...
KLAK KLAK KLAK KLAK
KLAK KLAK KLAK KLAK KLAK KLAK KLAK KLAK

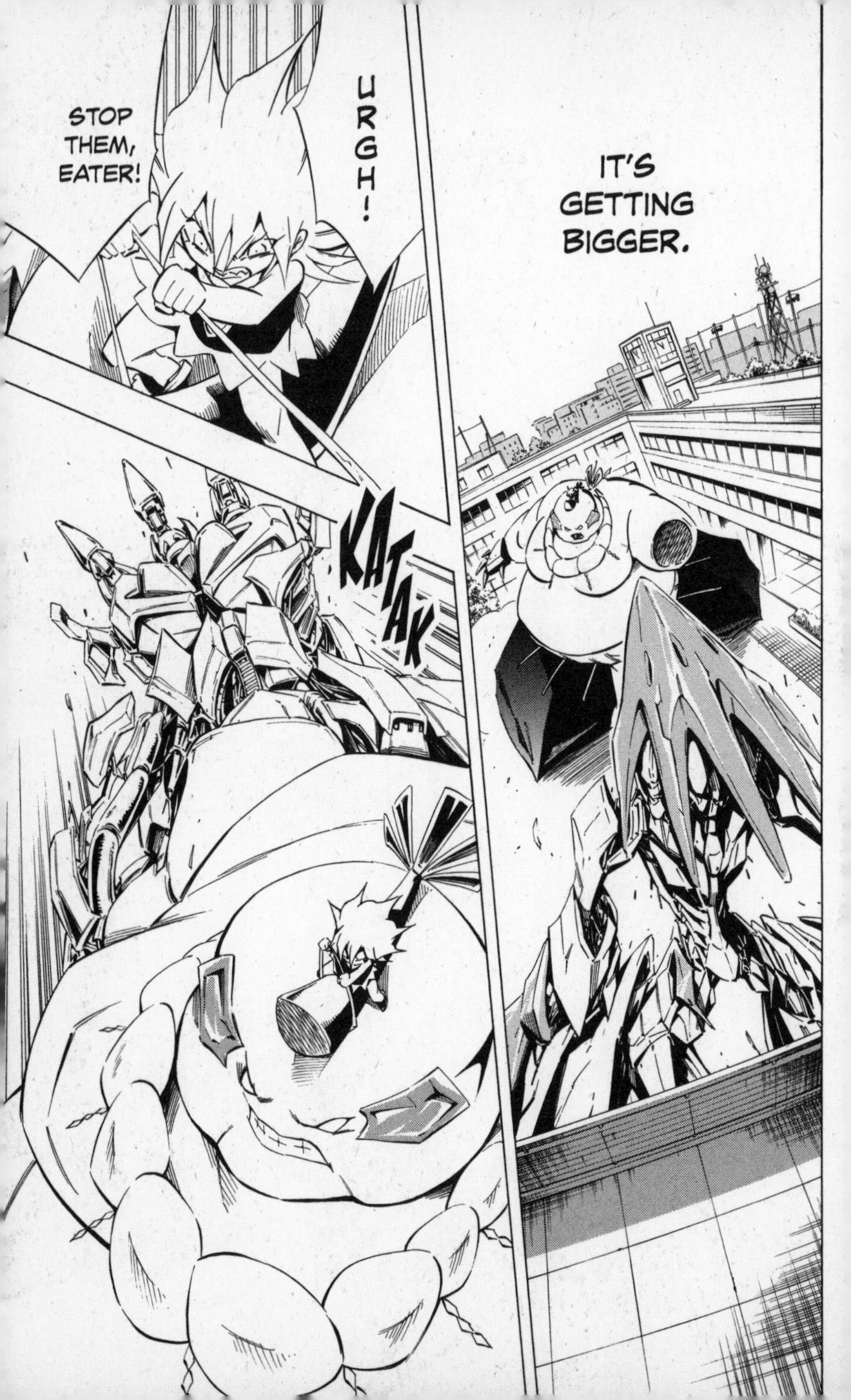
IT'S GETTING BIGGER.
URGH!
STOP THEM, EATER!
KATAK

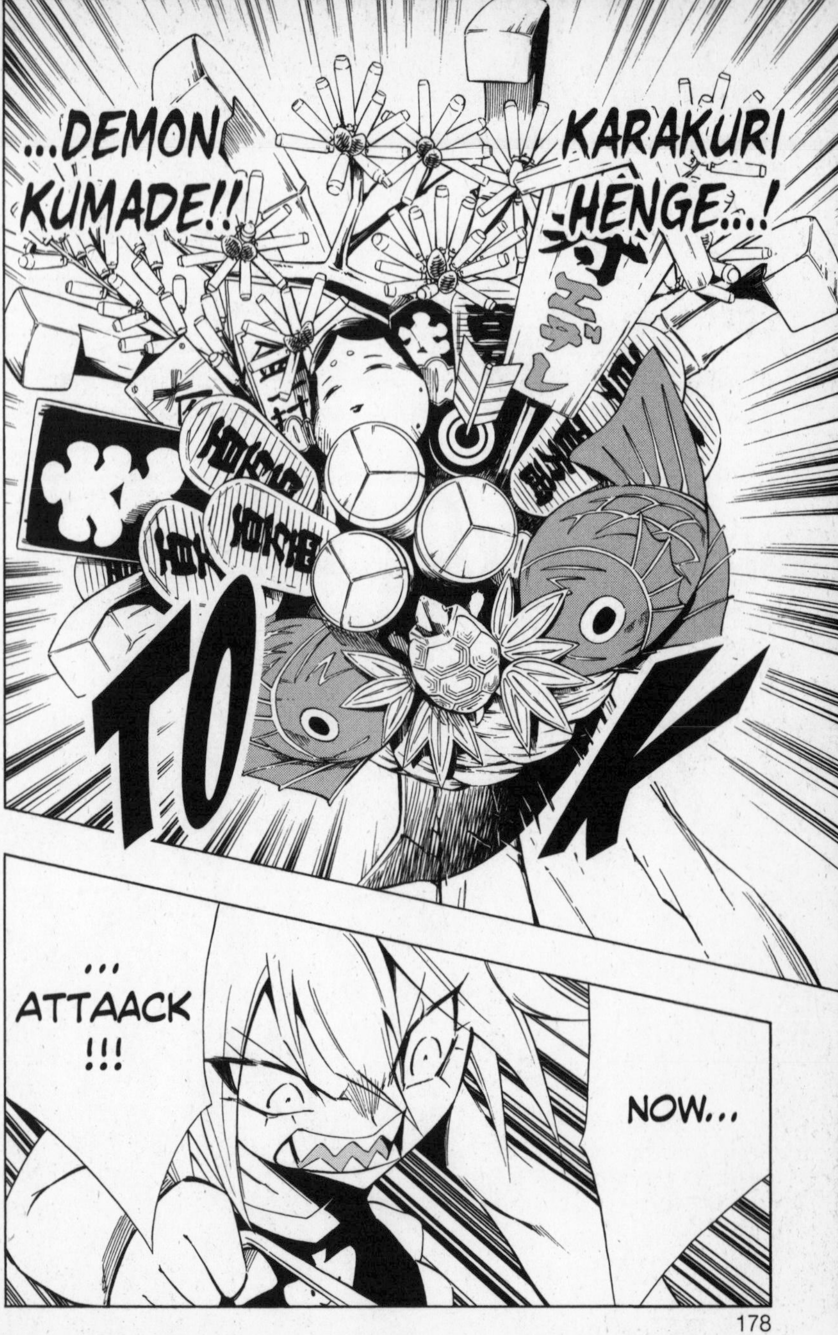
KARAKURI HENGE...!
...DEMON KUMADE!!
TOK
NOW...
...ATTAACK!!!

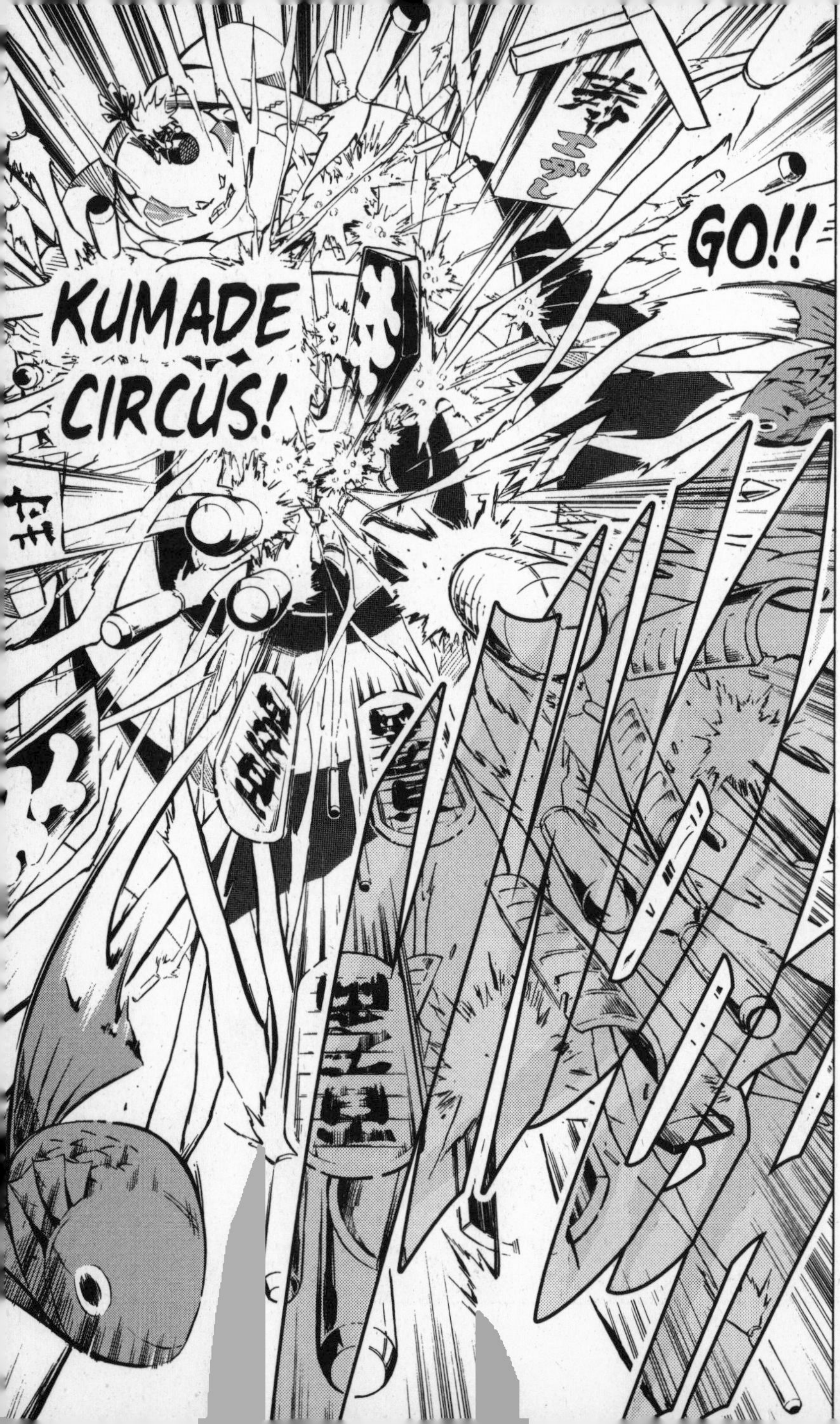
GO!!
KUMADE CIRCUS!

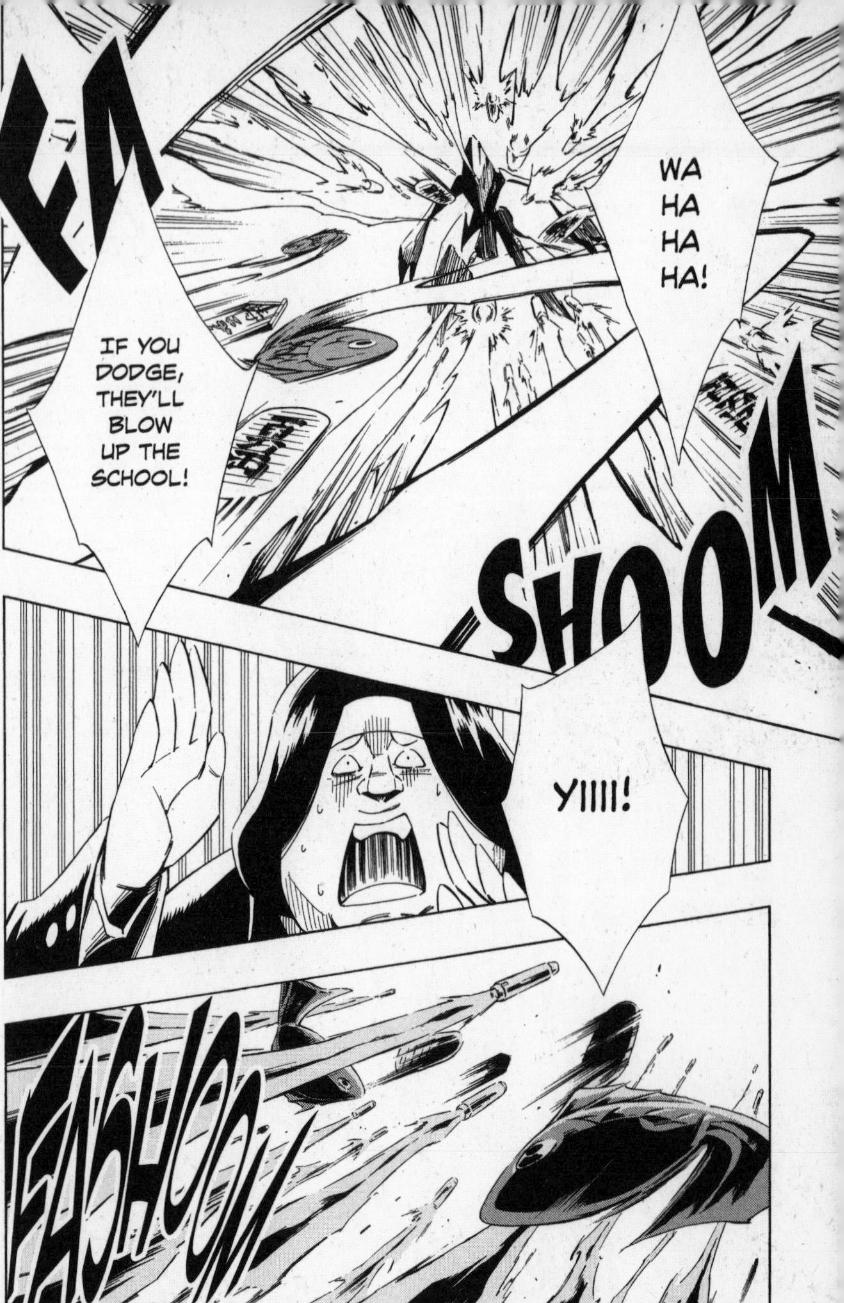
WA HA HA HA!
FA
IF YOU DODGE, THEY'LL BLOW UP THE SCHOOL!
SHOOM
YIIII!
FASHOOM

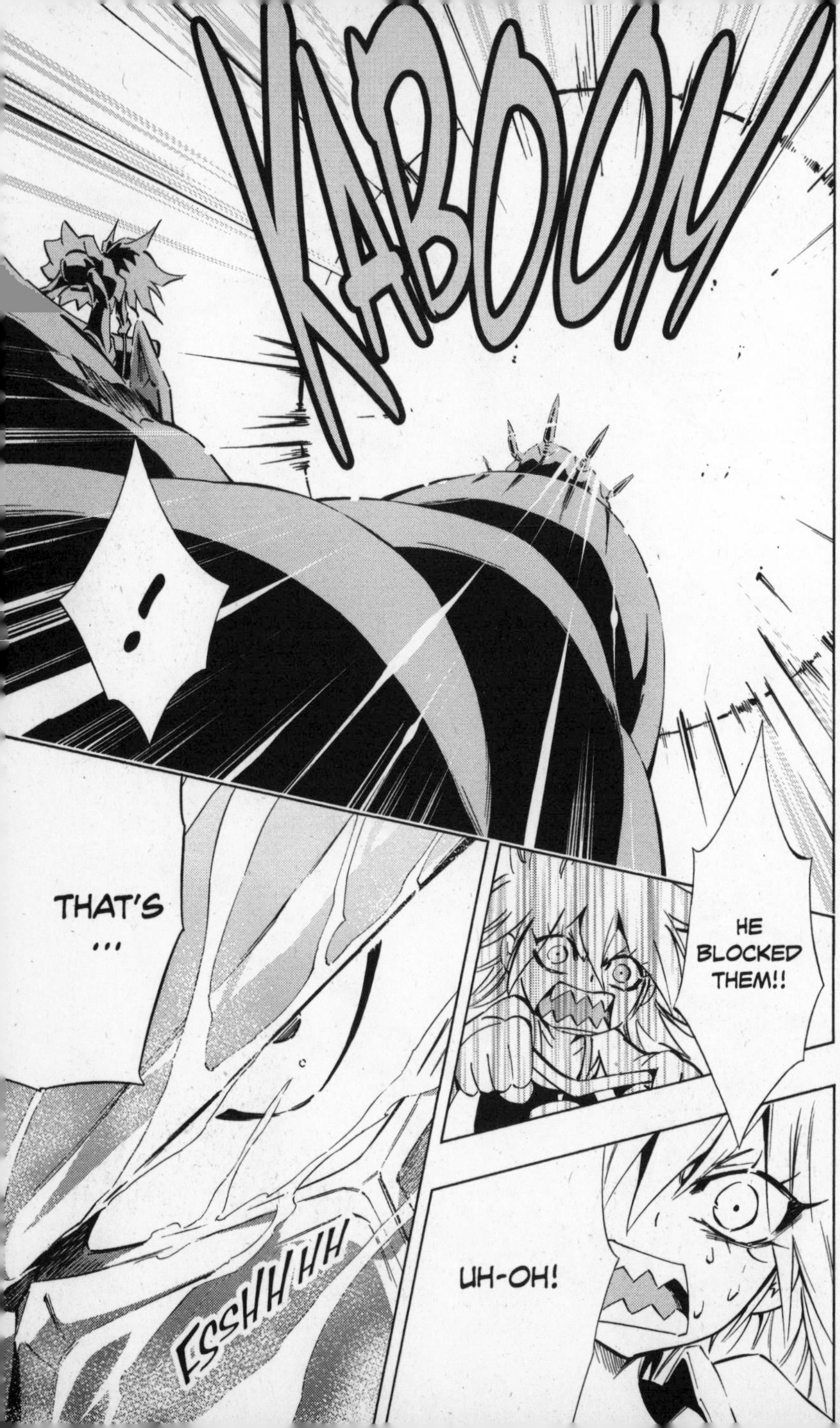
KABOOM
!
HE BLOCKED THEM!!
THAT'S...
UH-OH!
FSSHHHHH

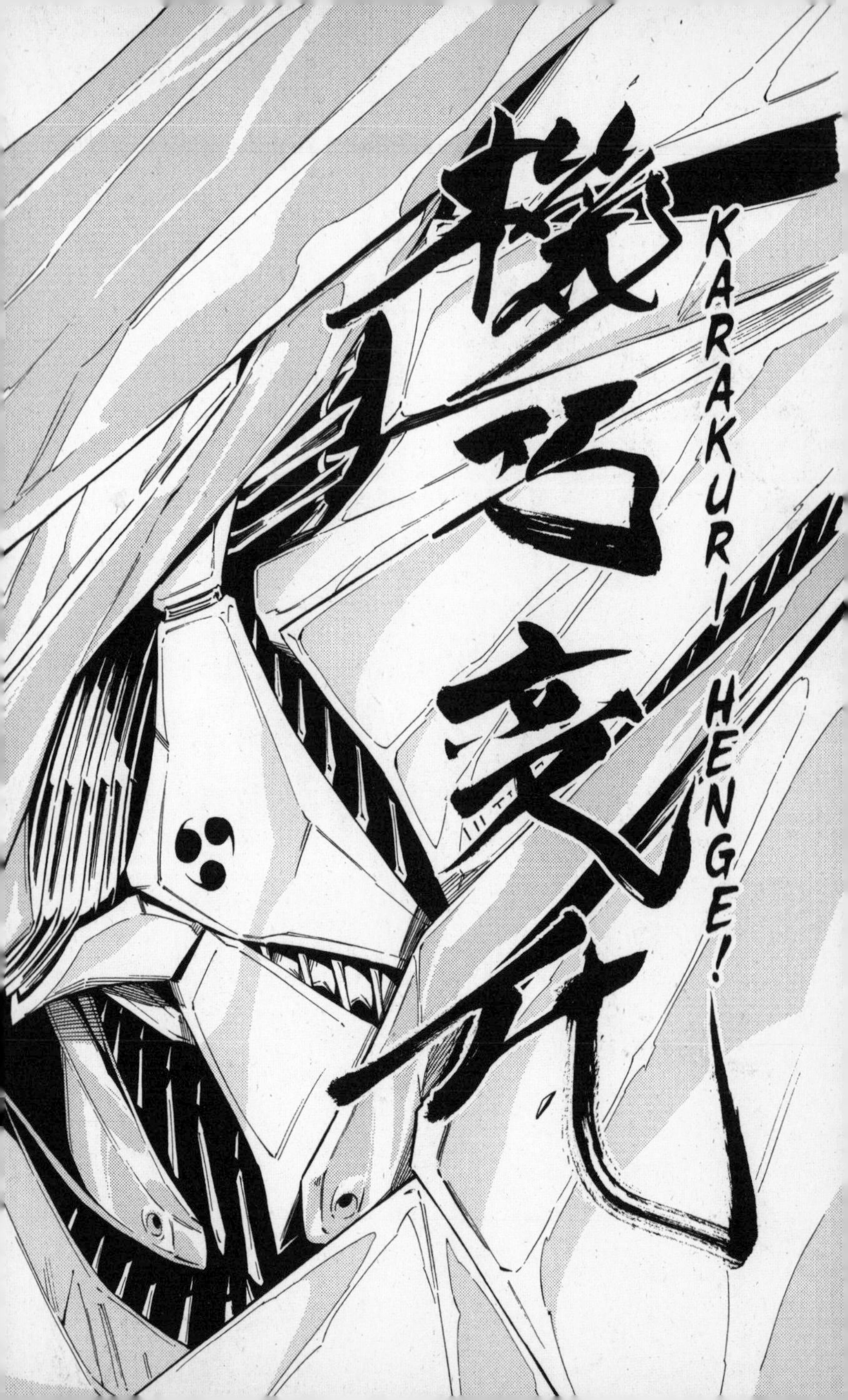
機巧変化
KARAKURI HENGE!

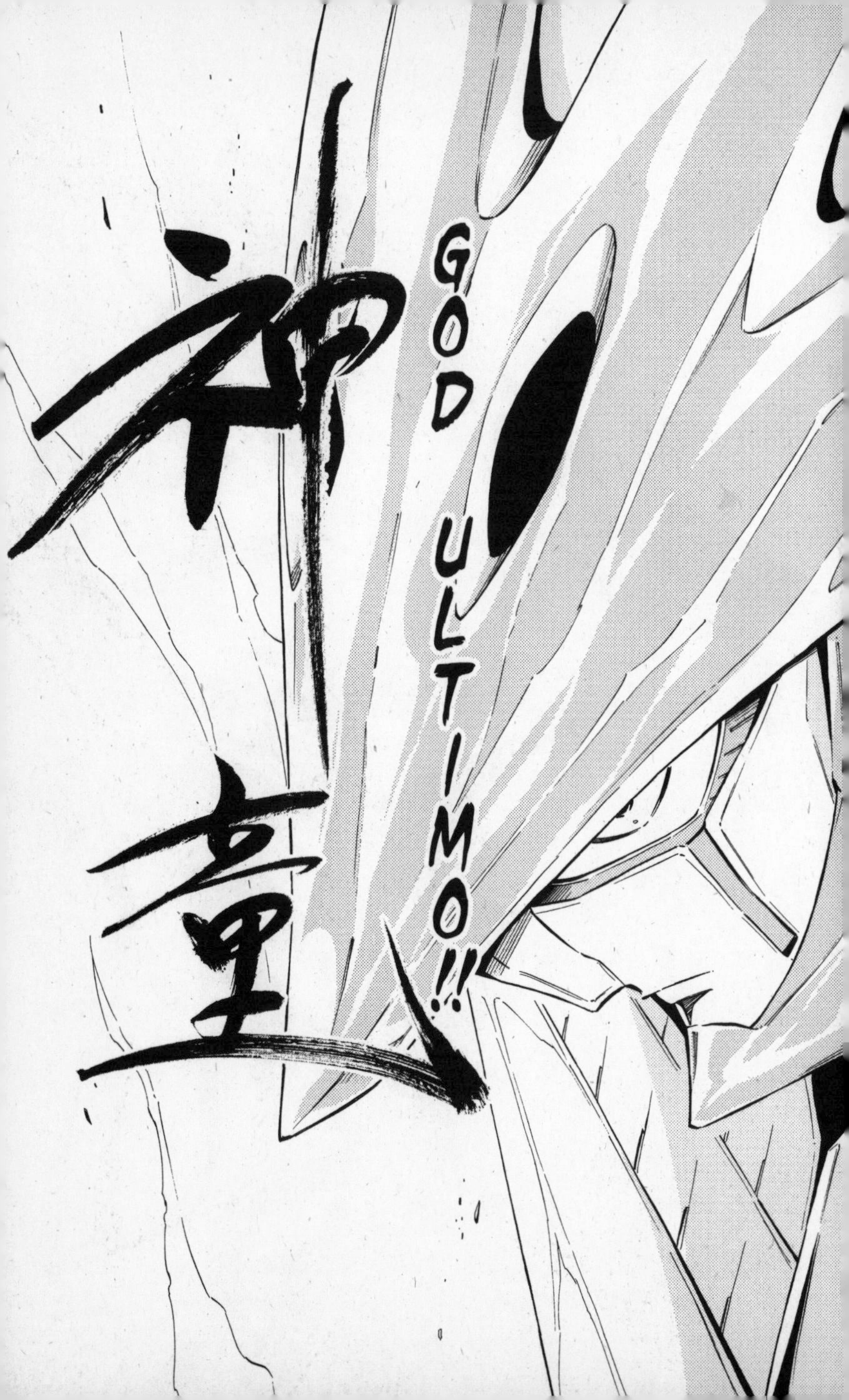
神童
GOD ULTIMO!!

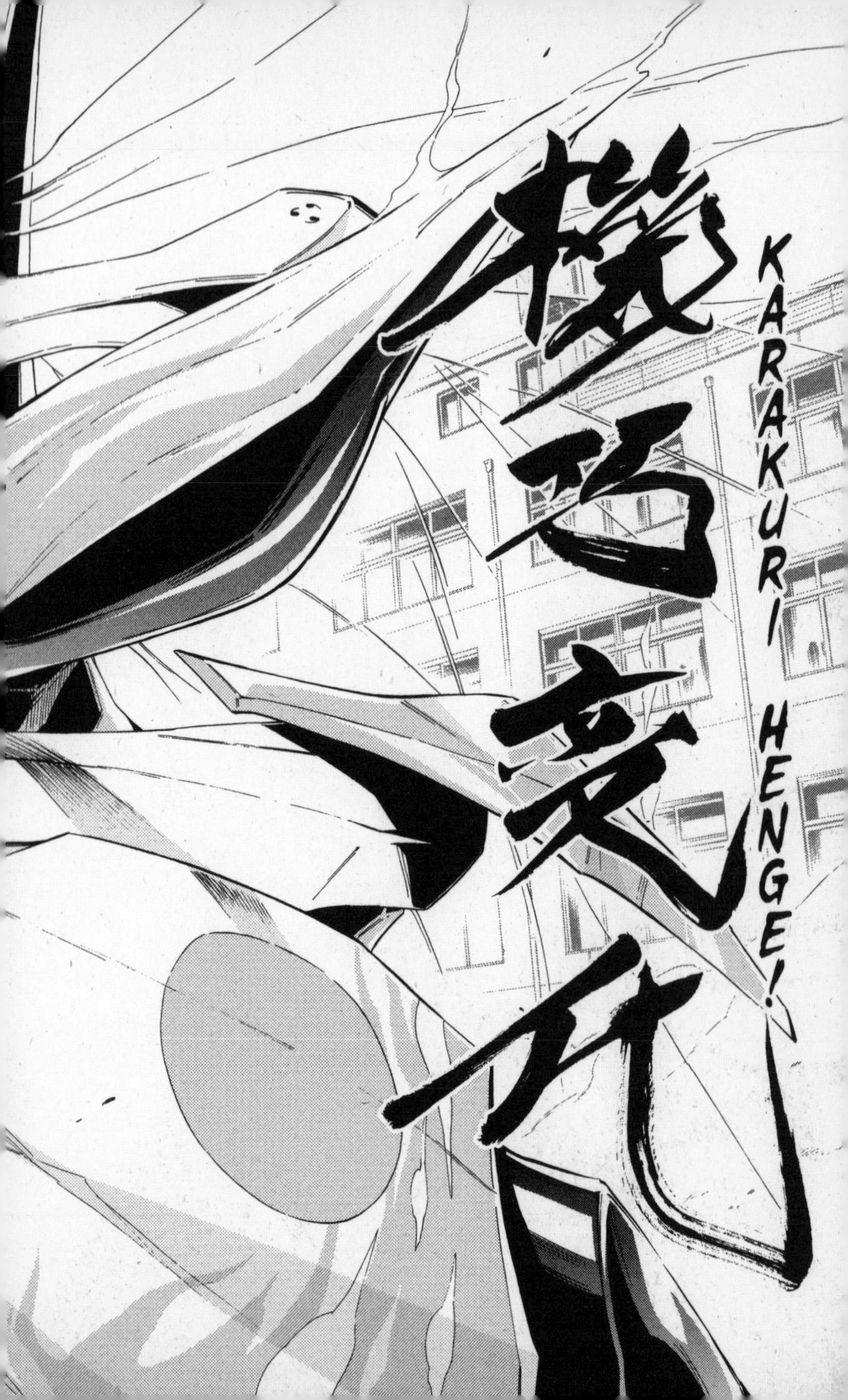
機巧変化
KARAKURI HENGE!

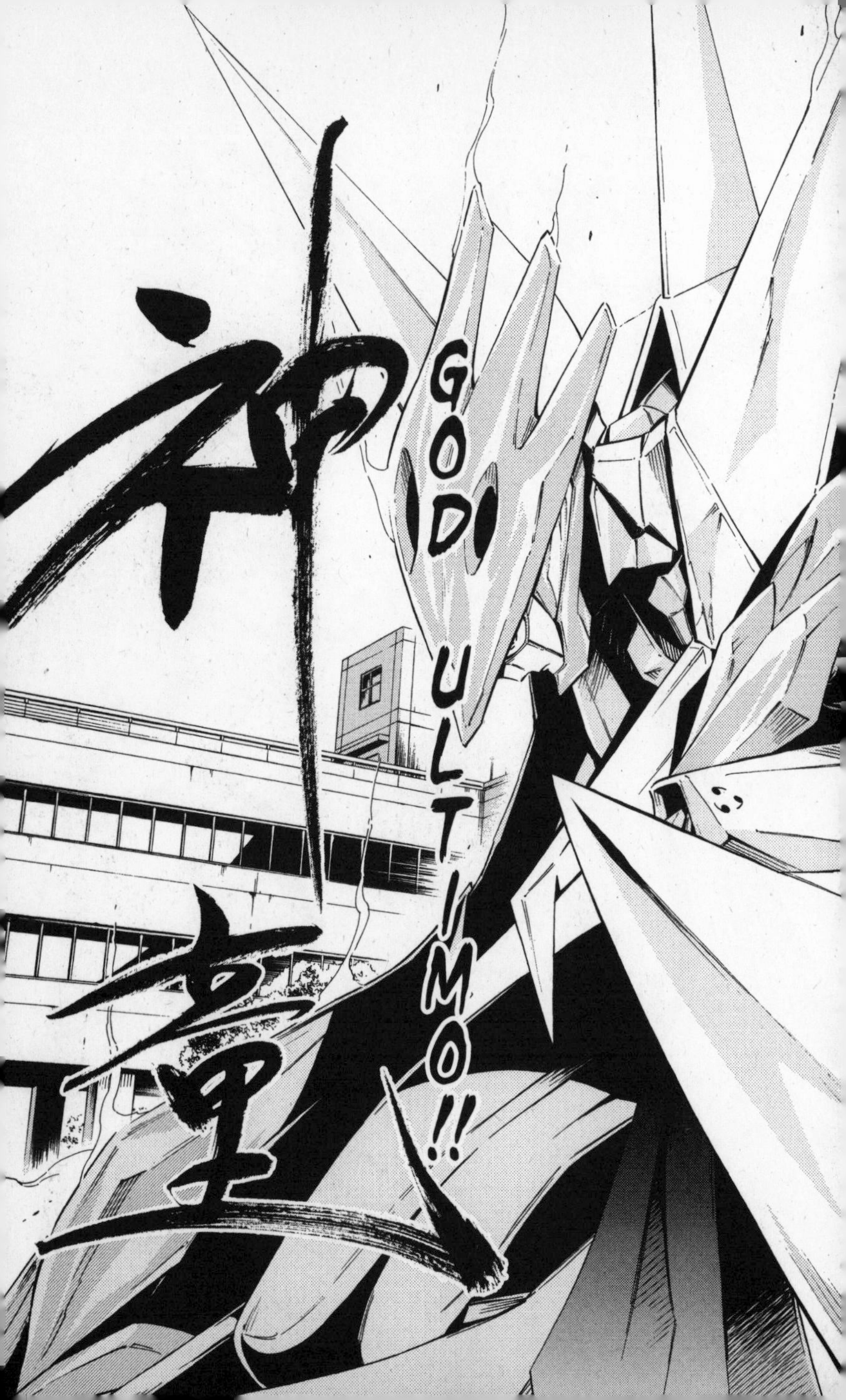
GOD ULTIMO!!

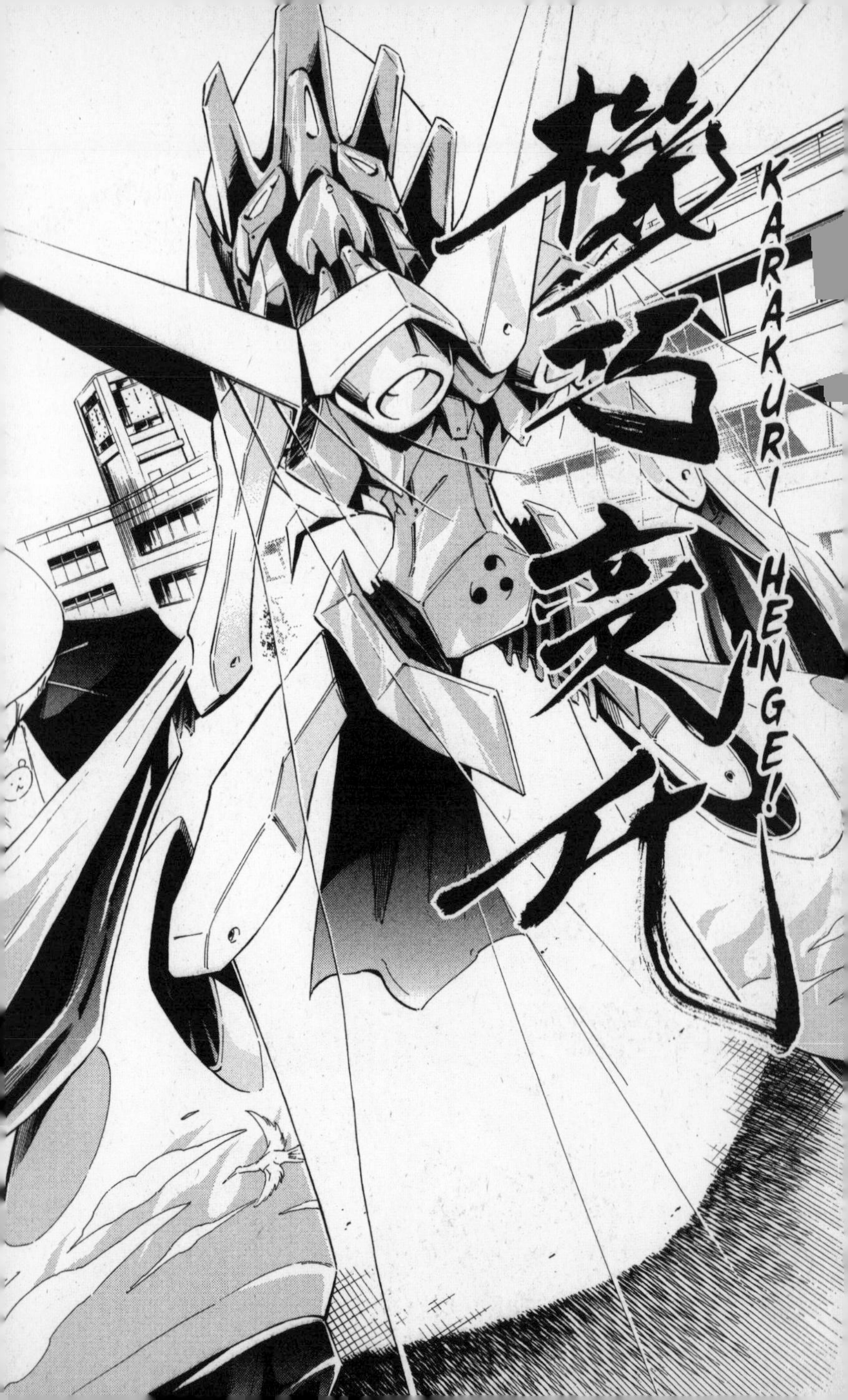
機巧変化
KARAKURI HENGE!

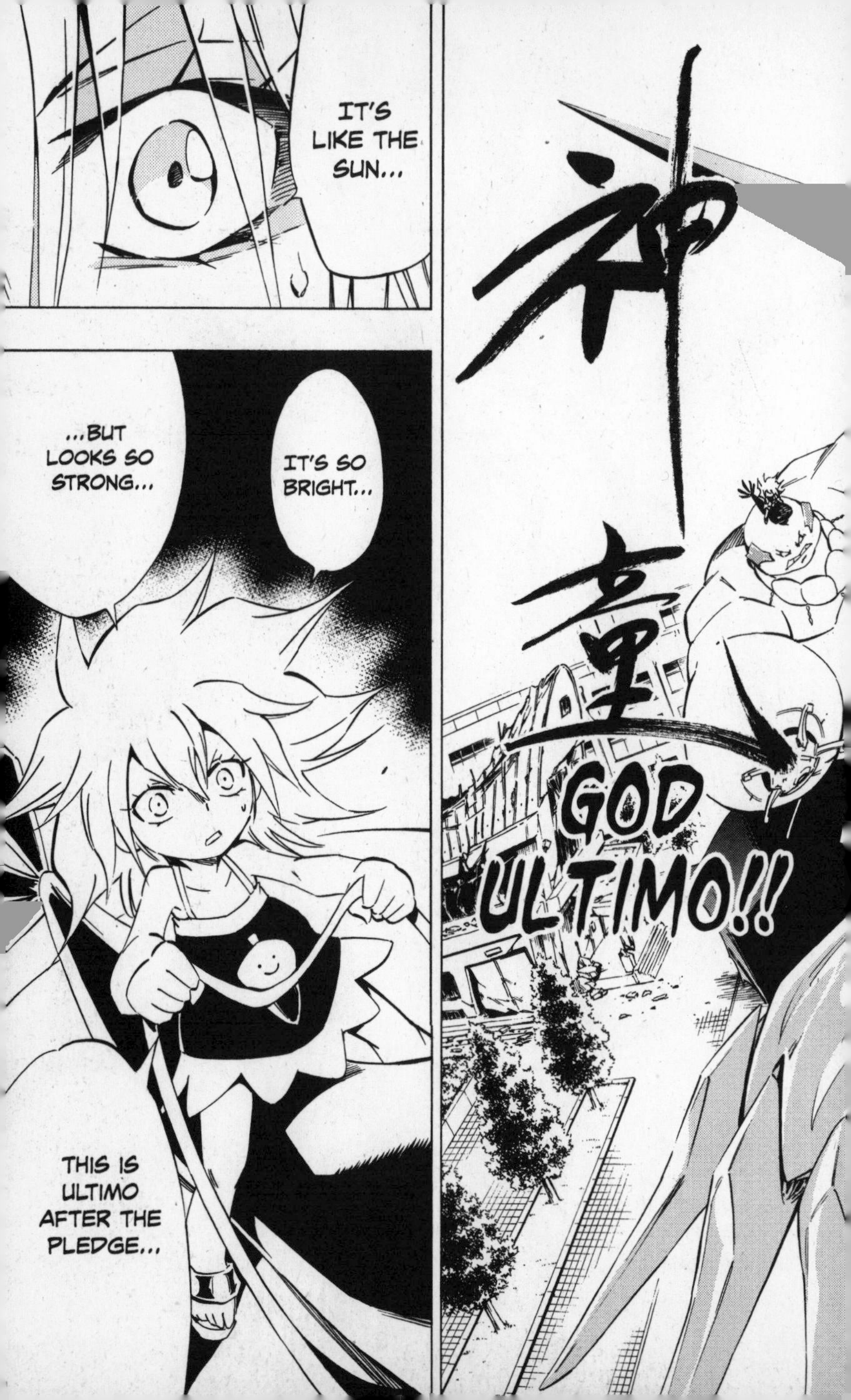
神童
GOD ULTIMO!!
IT'S LIKE THE SUN...
IT'S SO BRIGHT...
...BUT LOOKS SO STRONG...
THIS IS ULTIMO AFTER THE PLEDGE...

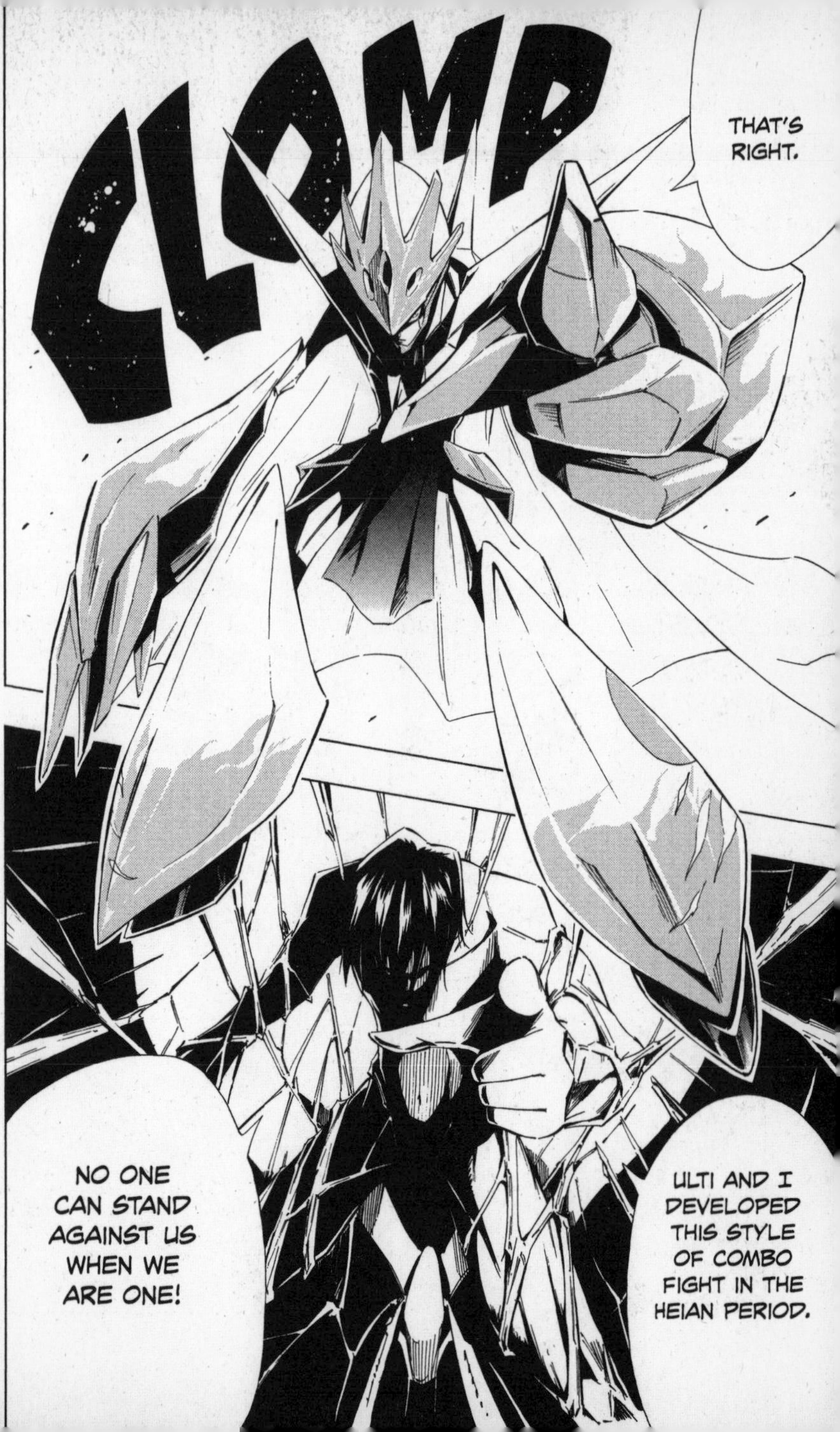
THAT'S RIGHT.
CLOMP
ULTI AND I DEVELOPED THIS STYLE OF COMBO FIGHT IN THE HEIAN PERIOD.
NO ONE CAN STAND AGAINST US WHEN WE ARE ONE!

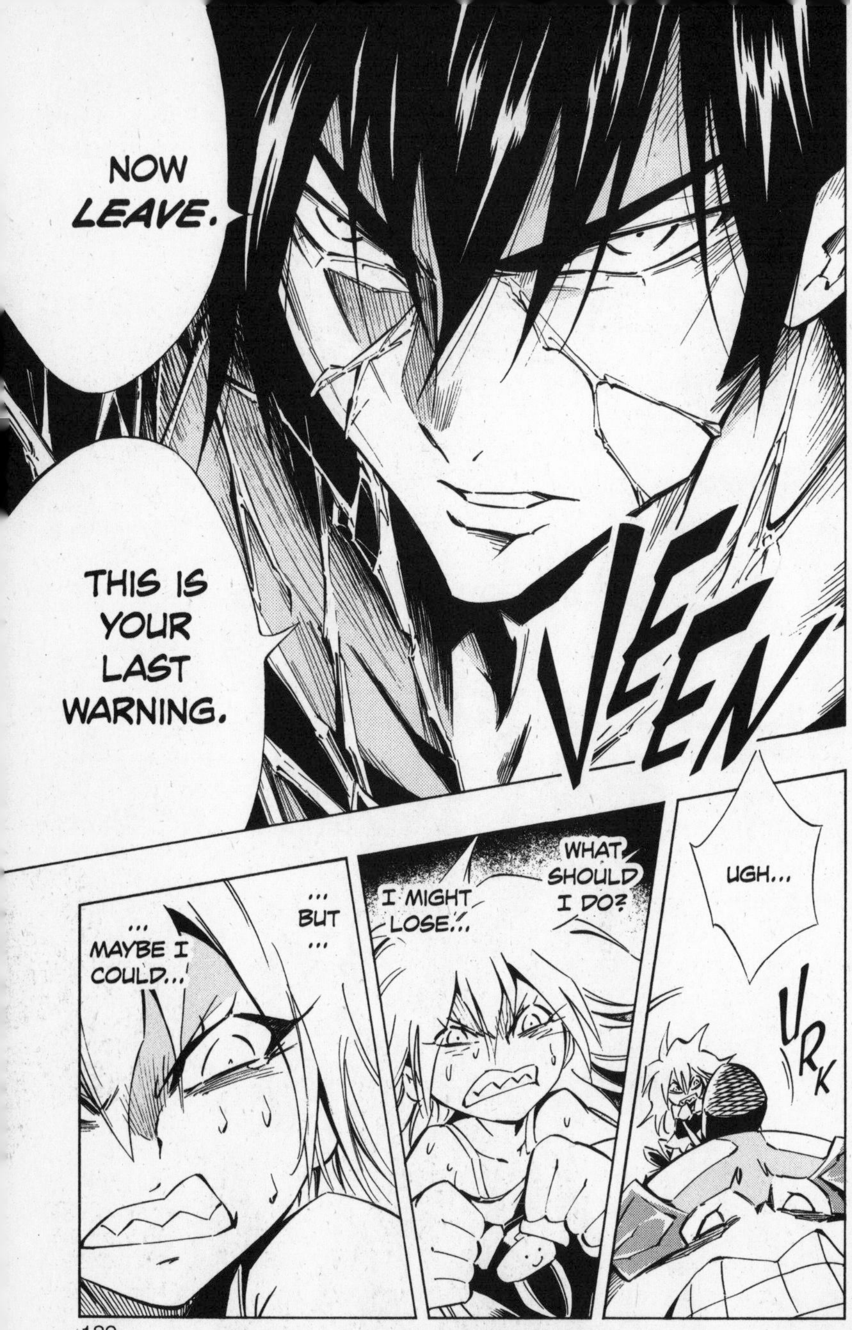
NOW LEAVE.
THIS IS YOUR LAST WARNING.
VEEN
UGH...
URK
WHAT SHOULD I DO?
I MIGHT LOSE...
... BUT ...
... MAYBE I COULD...

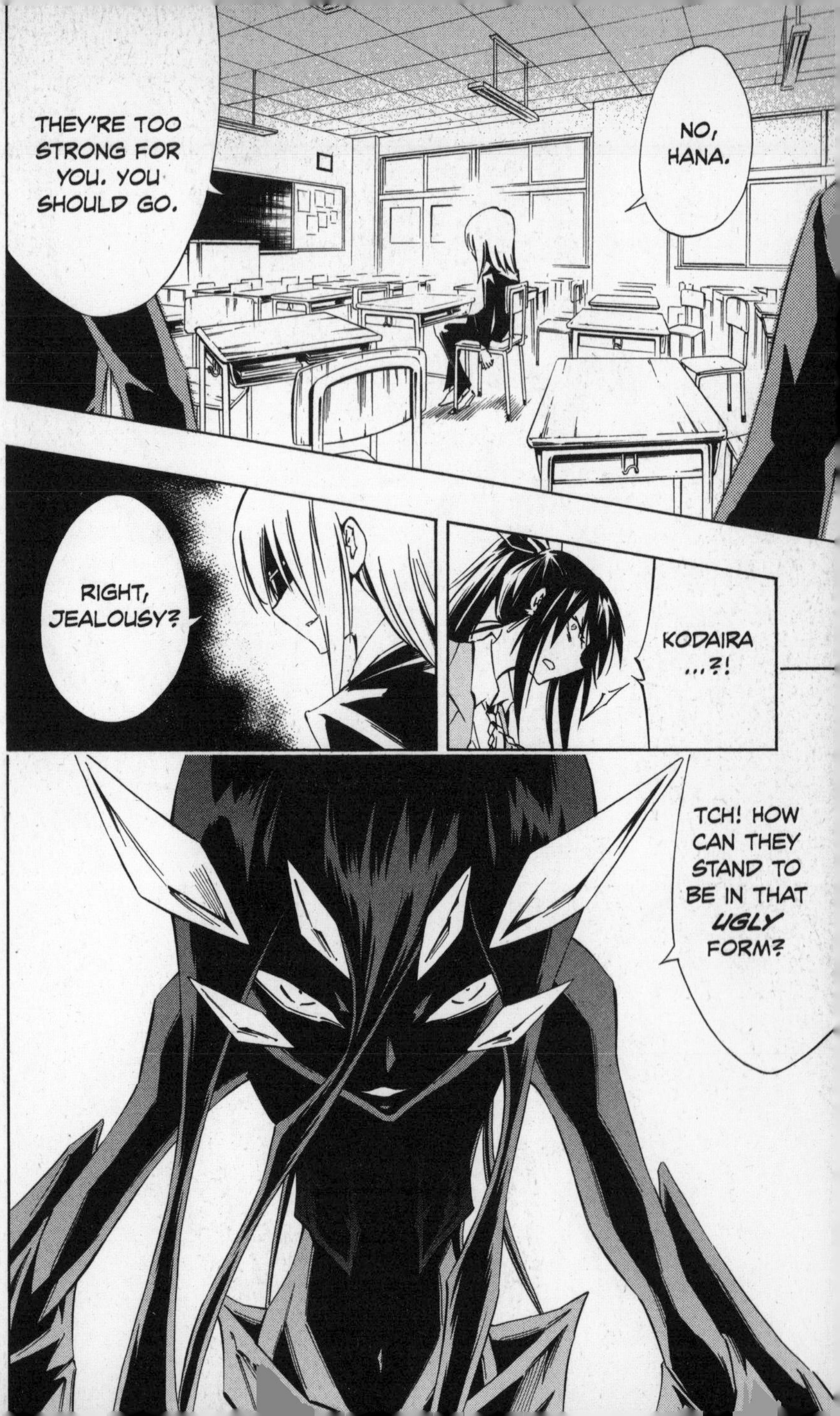
THEY'RE TOO STRONG FOR YOU. YOU SHOULD GO.
NO, HANA.
KODAIRA ...?!
RIGHT, JEALOUSY?
TCH! HOW CAN THEY STAND TO BE IN THAT *UGLY* FORM?

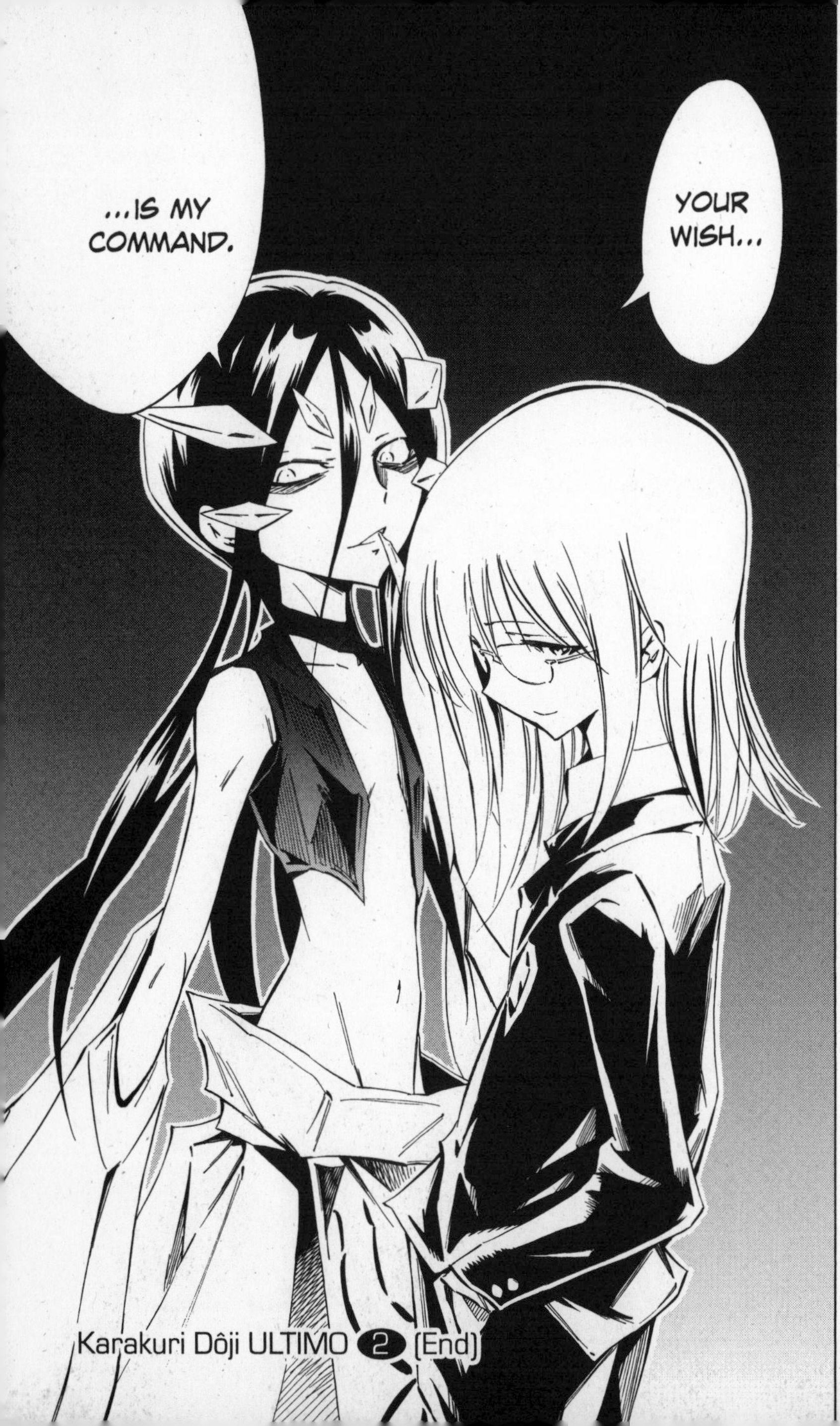
YOUR WISH...
...IS MY COMMAND.
Karakuri Dôji ULTIMO 2 (End)

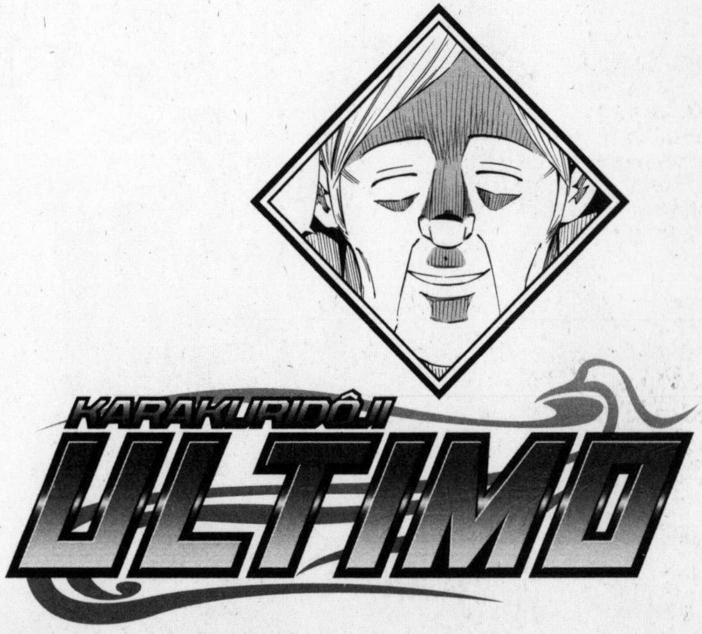

KARAKURIDÔJI
ULTIMO

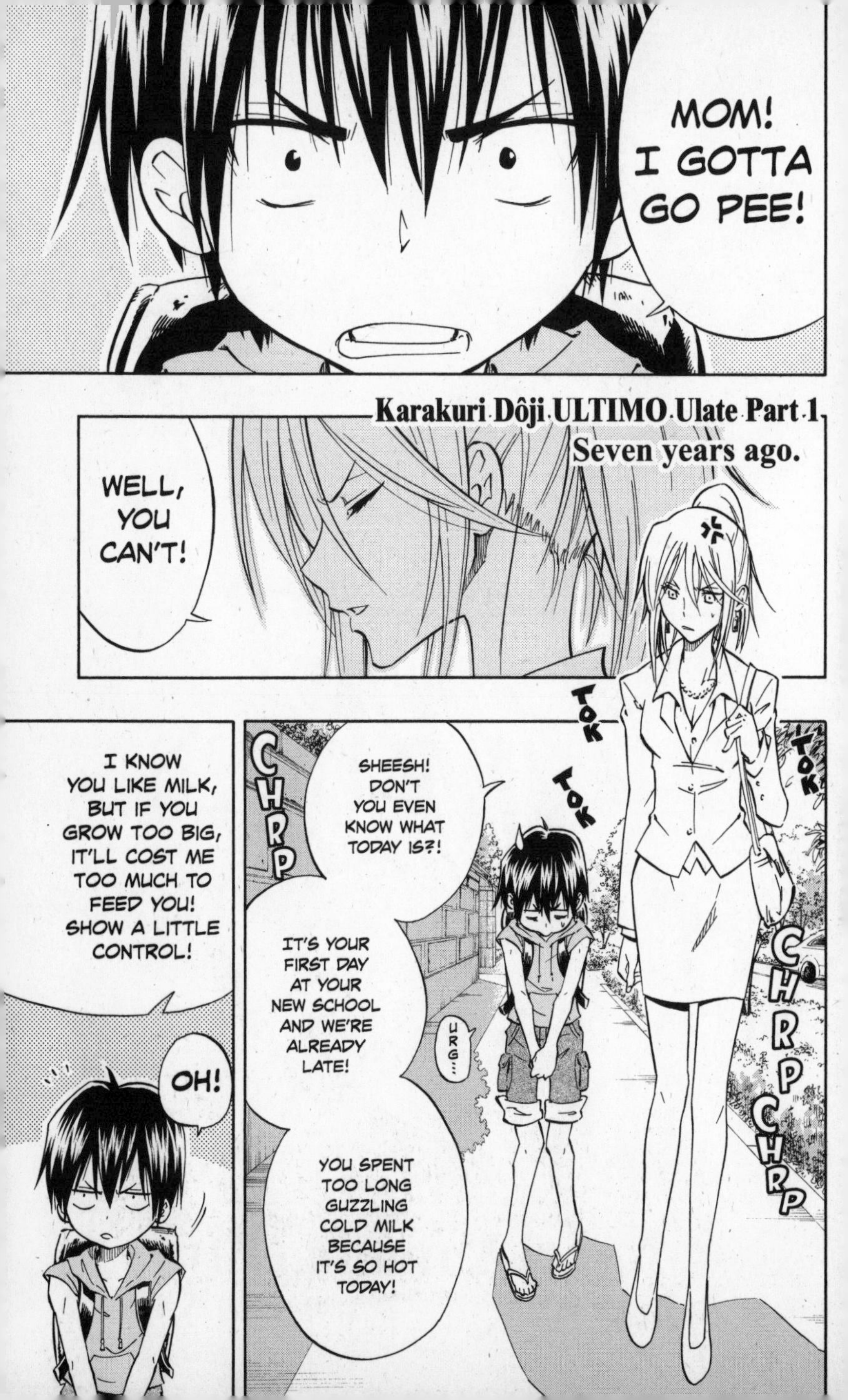
MOM! I GOTTA GO PEE!
Karakuri Dôji ULTIMO Ulate Part 1
Seven years ago.
WELL, YOU CAN'T!
TOK
TOK
TOK
CHRP
SHEESH! DON'T YOU EVEN KNOW WHAT TODAY IS?!
IT'S YOUR FIRST DAY AT YOUR NEW SCHOOL AND WE'RE ALREADY LATE!
URG...
CHRP CHRP CHRP
YOU SPENT TOO LONG GUZZLING COLD MILK BECAUSE IT'S SO HOT TODAY!
I KNOW YOU LIKE MILK, BUT IF YOU GROW TOO BIG, IT'LL COST ME TOO MUCH TO FEED YOU! SHOW A LITTLE CONTROL!
OH!

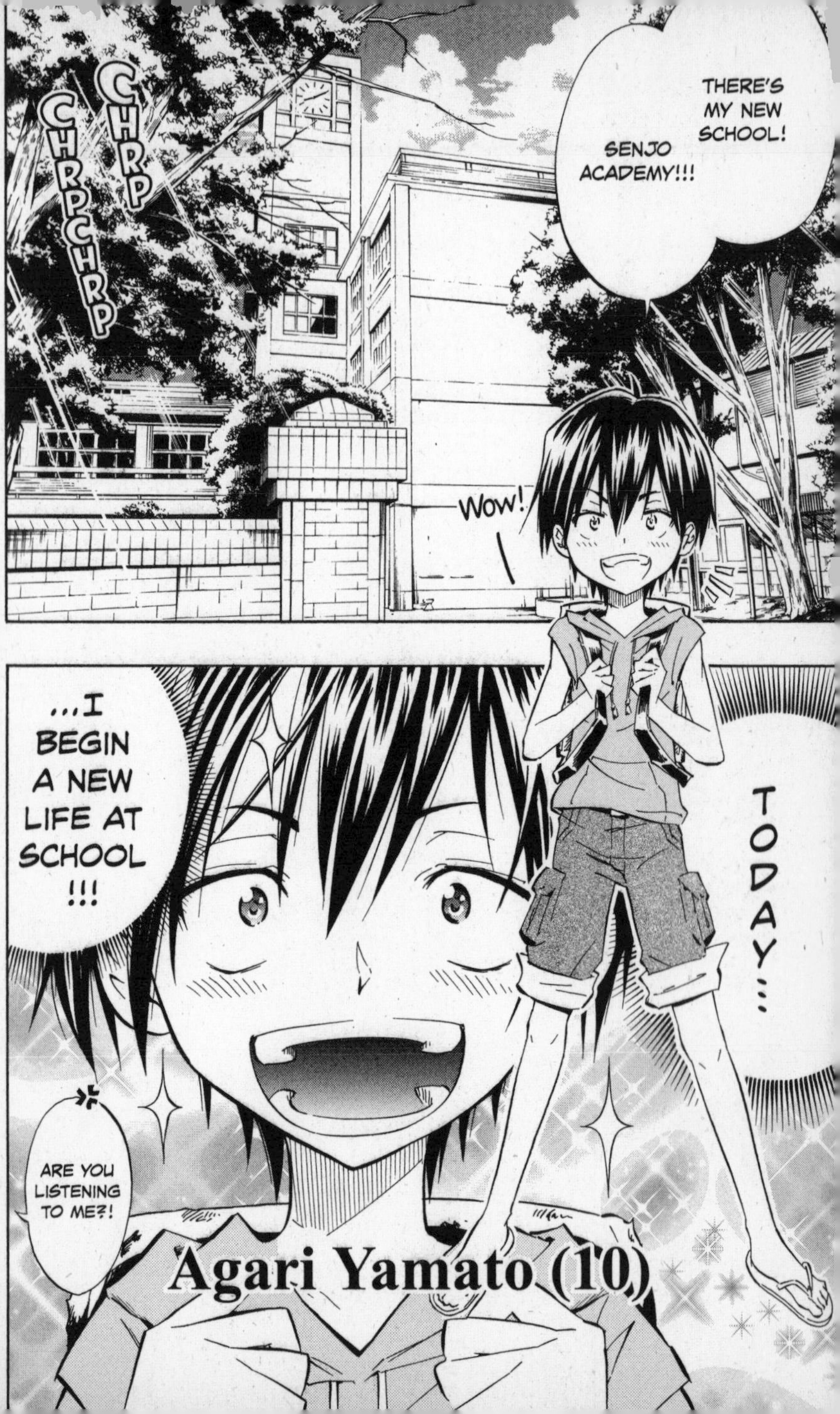
THERE'S MY NEW SCHOOL!
SENJO ACADEMY!!!
WOW!
CHRP CHRP
CHRPCHRPCHRP
TODAY...
...I BEGIN A NEW LIFE AT SCHOOL!!!
ARE YOU LISTENING TO ME?!
Agari Yamato (10)

ULTIMO ULATE

PART 1

BRIGHT-EYED FIFTH GRADERS!

original
story **STAN LEE**
HIROYUKI TAKEI

art &
story **JK**

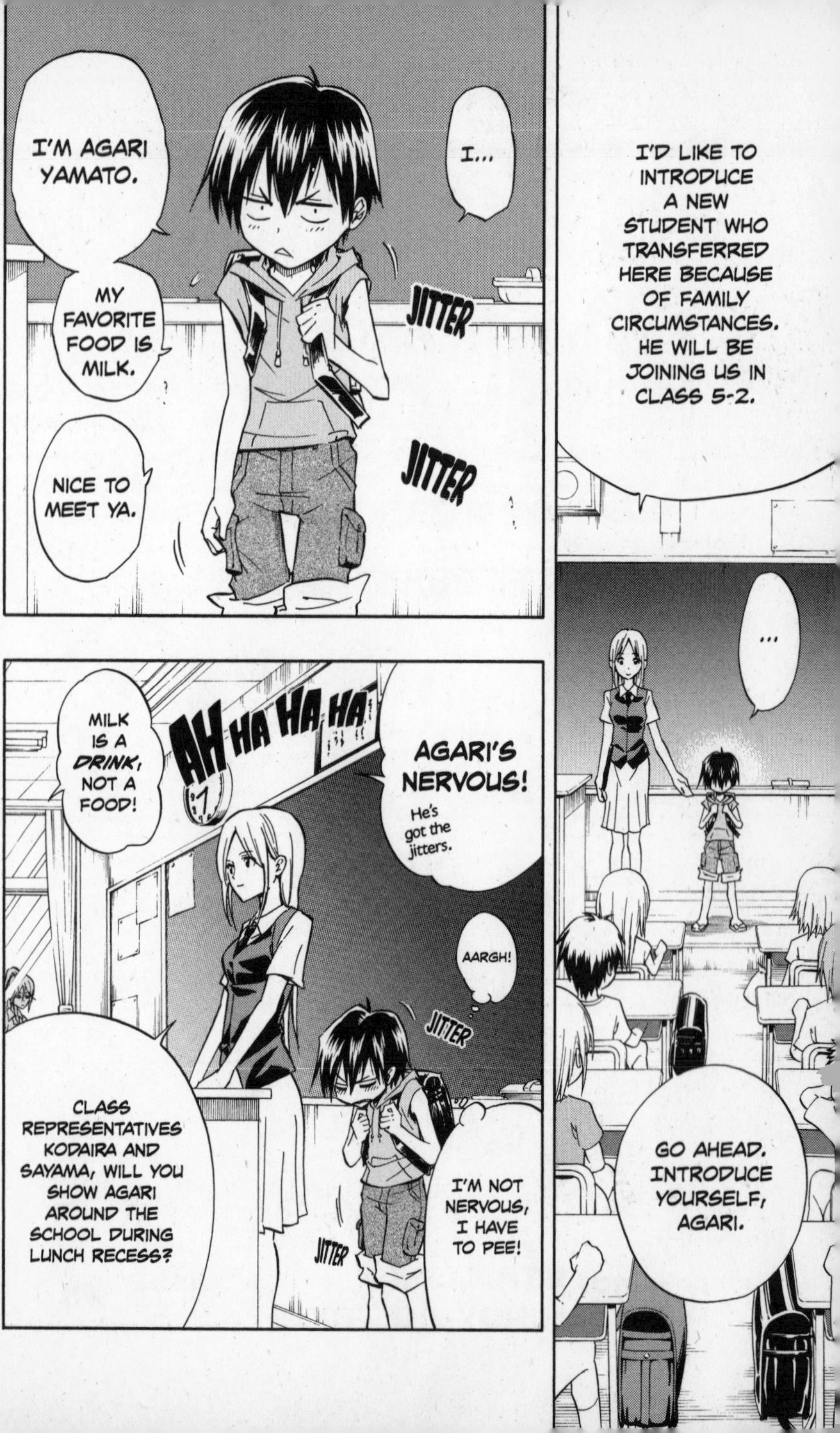
I'D LIKE TO INTRODUCE A NEW STUDENT WHO TRANSFERRED HERE BECAUSE OF FAMILY CIRCUMSTANCES. HE WILL BE JOINING US IN CLASS 5-2.
...
GO AHEAD. INTRODUCE YOURSELF, AGARI.
I...
I'M AGARI YAMATO.
JITTER
MY FAVORITE FOOD IS MILK.
JITTER
NICE TO MEET YA.
AGARI'S NERVOUS!
He's got the jitters.
AH HA HA HA
MILK IS A *DRINK*, NOT A FOOD!
AARGH!
JITTER
I'M NOT NERVOUS, I HAVE TO PEE!
JITTER
CLASS REPRESENTATIVES KODAIRA AND SAYAMA, WILL YOU SHOW AGARI AROUND THE SCHOOL DURING LUNCH RECESS?

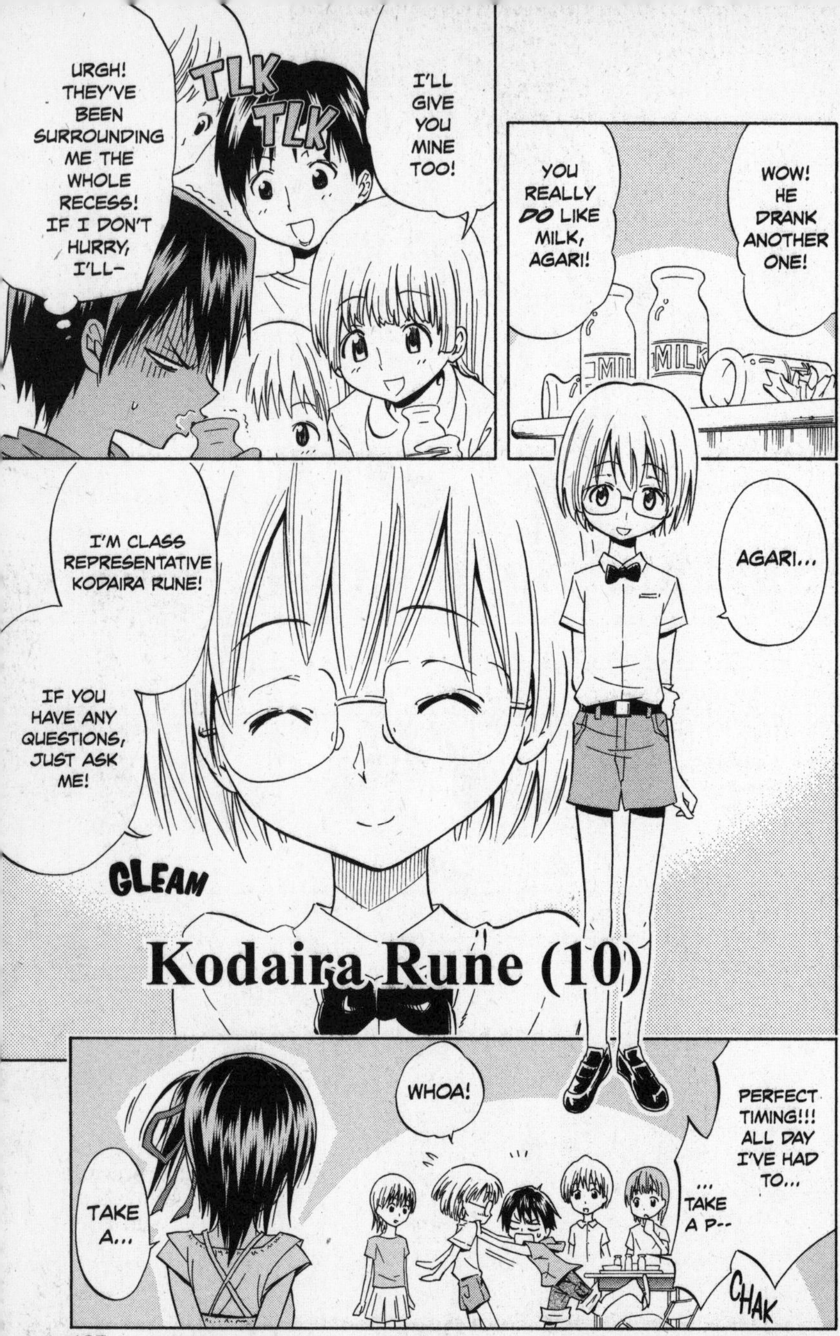
WOW! HE DRANK ANOTHER ONE!
YOU REALLY DO LIKE MILK, AGARI!
I'LL GIVE YOU MINE TOO!
TLK TLK
URGH! THEY'VE BEEN SURROUNDING ME THE WHOLE RECESS! IF I DON'T HURRY, I'LL–
AGARI...
I'M CLASS REPRESENTATIVE KODAIRA RUNE!
IF YOU HAVE ANY QUESTIONS, JUST ASK ME!
GLEAM
Kodaira Rune (10)
PERFECT TIMING!!! ALL DAY I'VE HAD TO...
... TAKE A P--
CHAK
WHOA!
TAKE A...

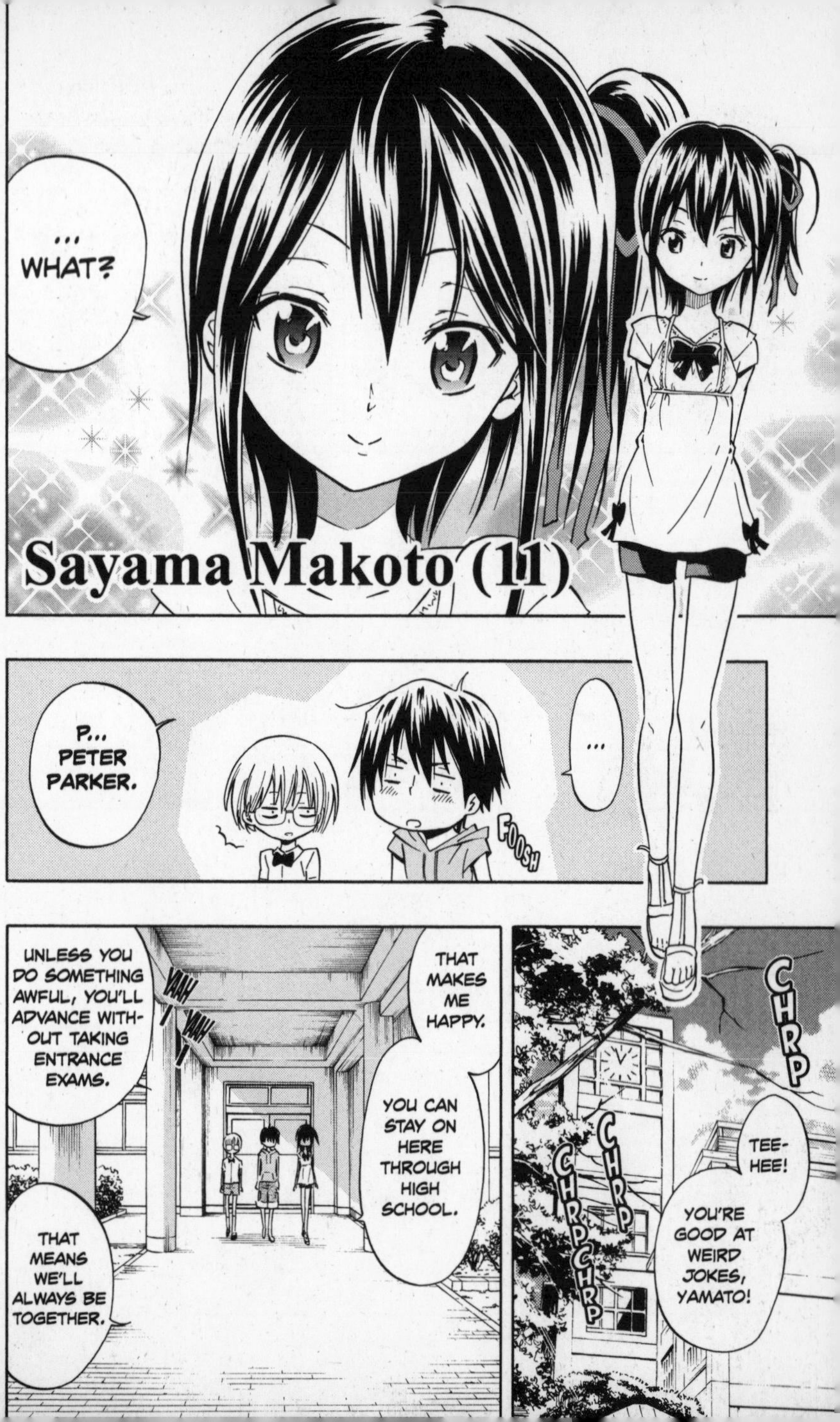

... WHAT?
Sayama Makoto (11)
...
P... PETER PARKER.
FOOSH
CHRP
TEE-HEE!
YOU'RE GOOD AT WEIRD JOKES, YAMATO!
CHRP
CHRPCHRP
THAT MAKES ME HAPPY.
YOU CAN STAY ON HERE THROUGH HIGH SCHOOL.
UNLESS YOU DO SOMETHING AWFUL, YOU'LL ADVANCE WITH-OUT TAKING ENTRANCE EXAMS.
YAAH
YAAH
THAT MEANS WE'LL ALWAYS BE TOGETHER.

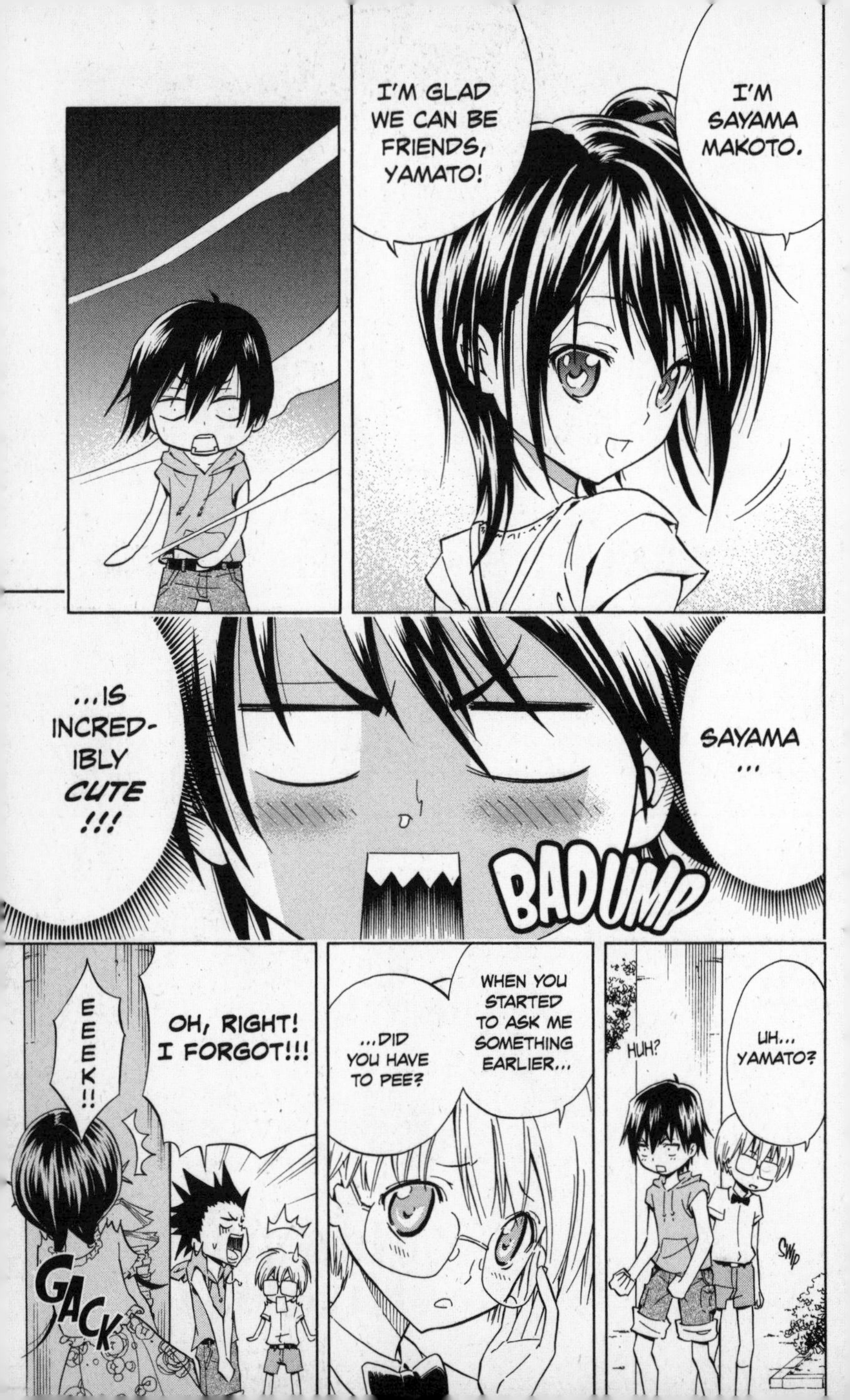
I'M SAYAMA MAKOTO.
I'M GLAD WE CAN BE FRIENDS, YAMATO!
SAYAMA ...
...IS INCREDIBLY CUTE!!!
BADUMP
UH... YAMATO?
HUH?
WHEN YOU STARTED TO ASK ME SOMETHING EARLIER...
...DID YOU HAVE TO PEE?
OH, RIGHT! I FORGOT!!!
EEEK!!
GACK

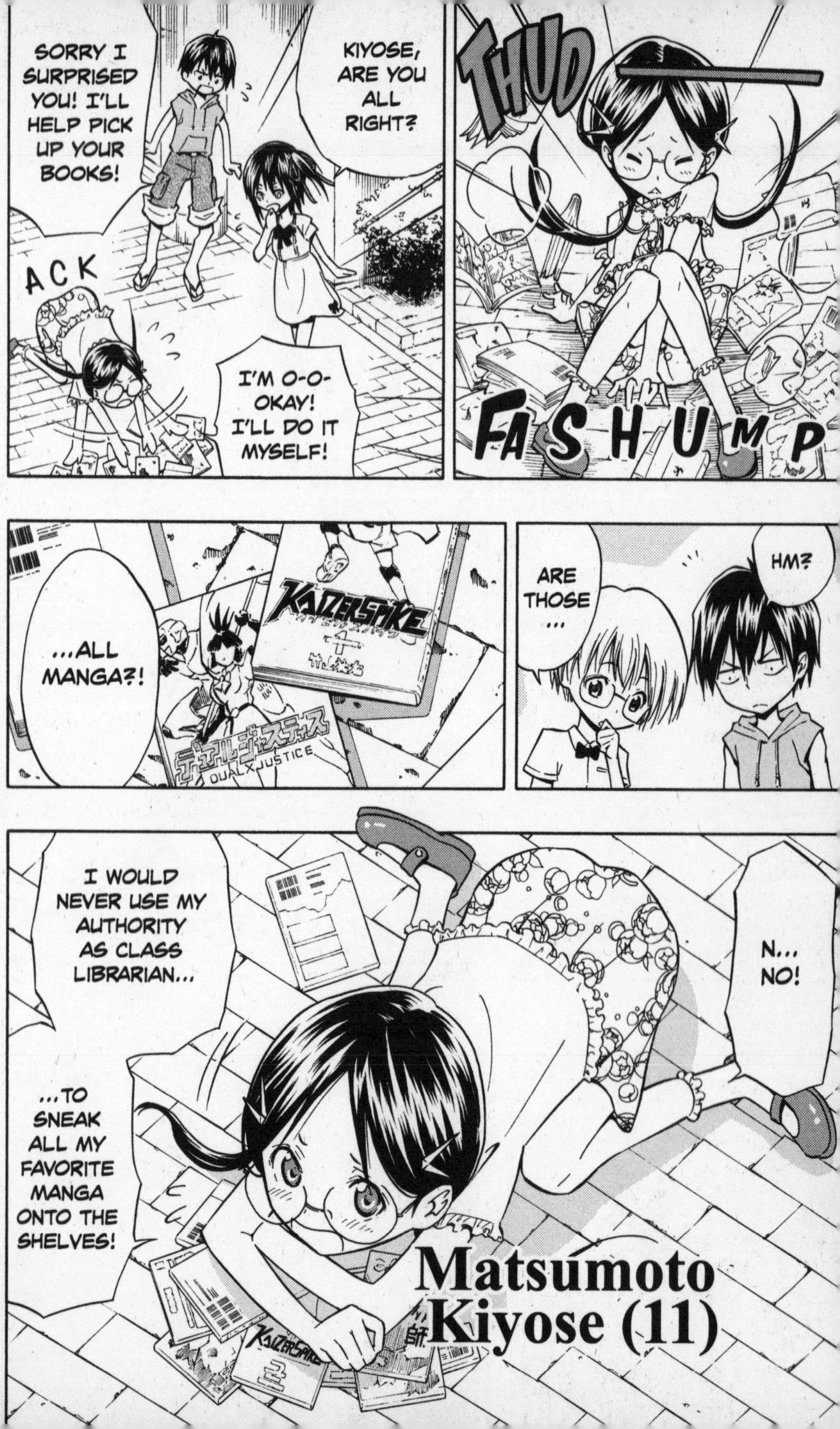
THUD
FASHUMP
KIYOSE, ARE YOU ALL RIGHT?
SORRY I SURPRISED YOU! I'LL HELP PICK UP YOUR BOOKS!
ACK
I'M O-O-OKAY! I'LL DO IT MYSELF!
HM?
ARE THOSE ...
...ALL MANGA?!
KAIZERSPIKE
DUALXJUSTICE
N... NO!
I WOULD NEVER USE MY AUTHORITY AS CLASS LIBRARIAN...
...TO SNEAK ALL MY FAVORITE MANGA ONTO THE SHELVES!
KAIZERSPIKE
Matsumoto Kiyose (11)

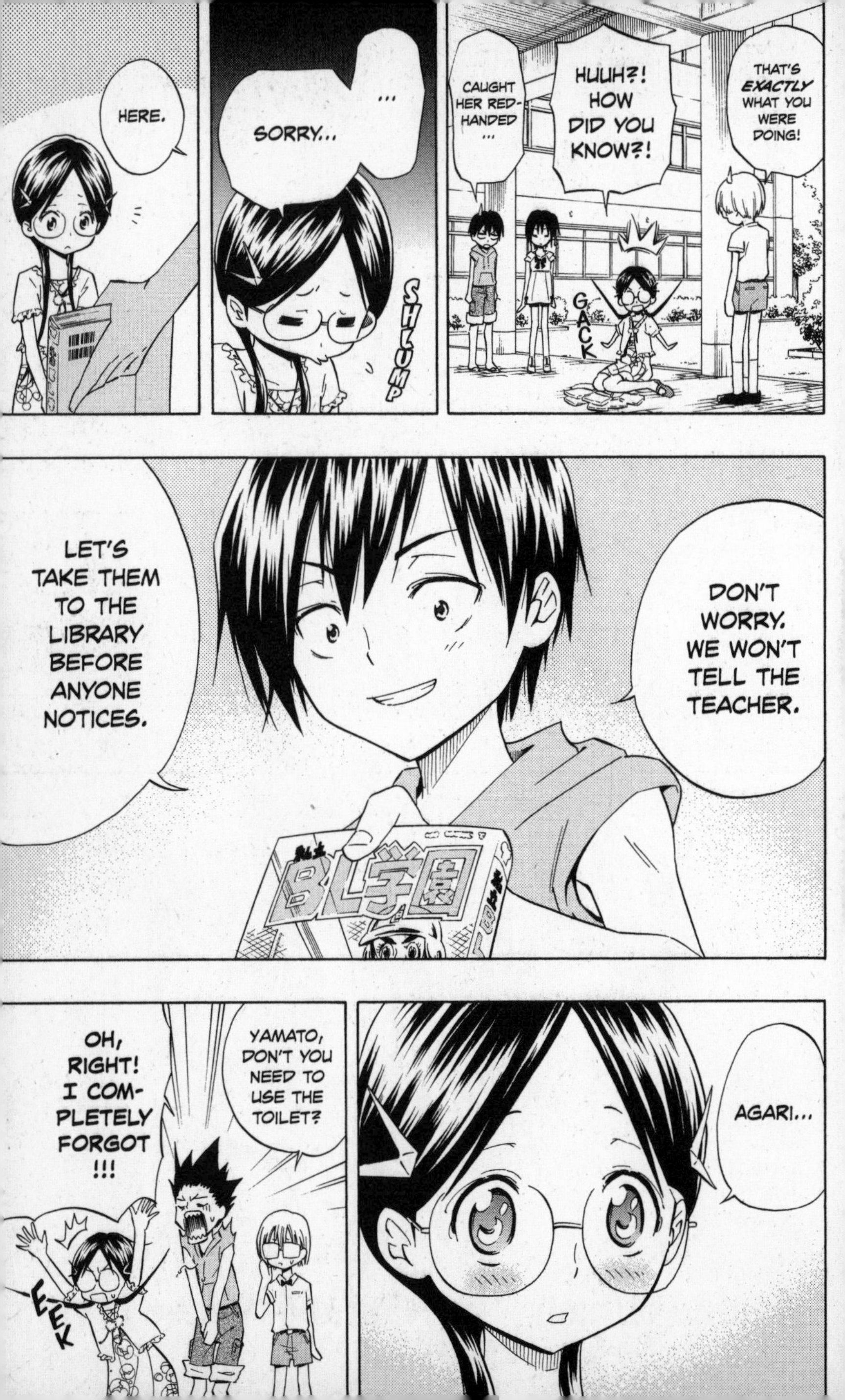
THAT'S *EXACTLY* WHAT YOU WERE DOING!
HUUH?! HOW DID YOU KNOW?!
CAUGHT HER RED-HANDED ...
GACK
...
SORRY...
SHLUMP
HERE.
DON'T WORRY. WE WON'T TELL THE TEACHER.
LET'S TAKE THEM TO THE LIBRARY BEFORE ANYONE NOTICES.
AGARI...
YAMATO, DON'T YOU NEED TO USE THE TOILET?
OH, RIGHT! I COM-PLETELY FORGOT !!!
EEK

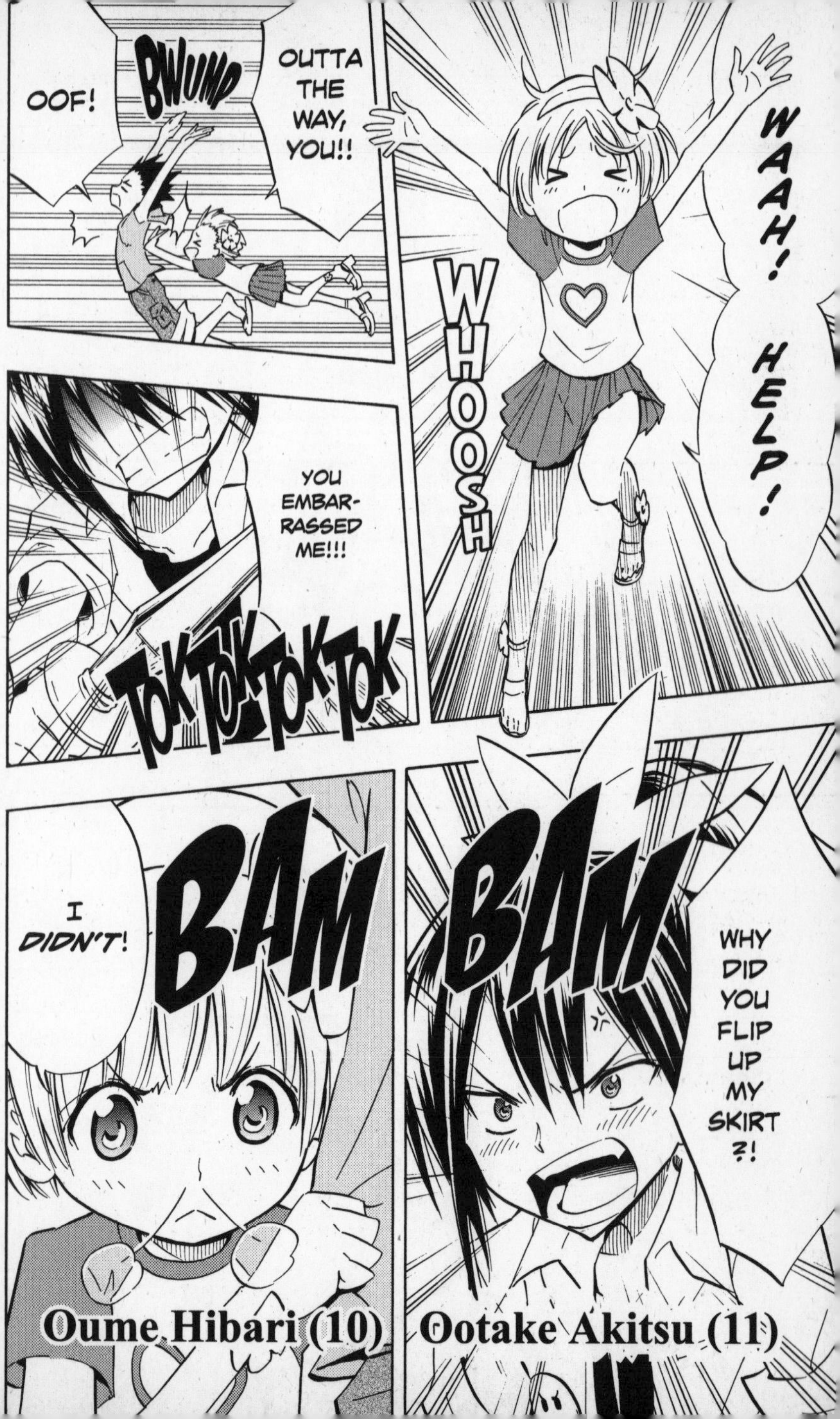
WAAH! HELP!
WHOOSH
OUTTA THE WAY, YOU!!
BWUMP
OOF!
YOU EMBARRASSED ME!!!
TOKTOKTOKTOK
WHY DID YOU FLIP UP MY SKIRT?!
BAM
Ootake Akitsu (11)
BAM
I DIDN'T!
Oume Hibari (10)

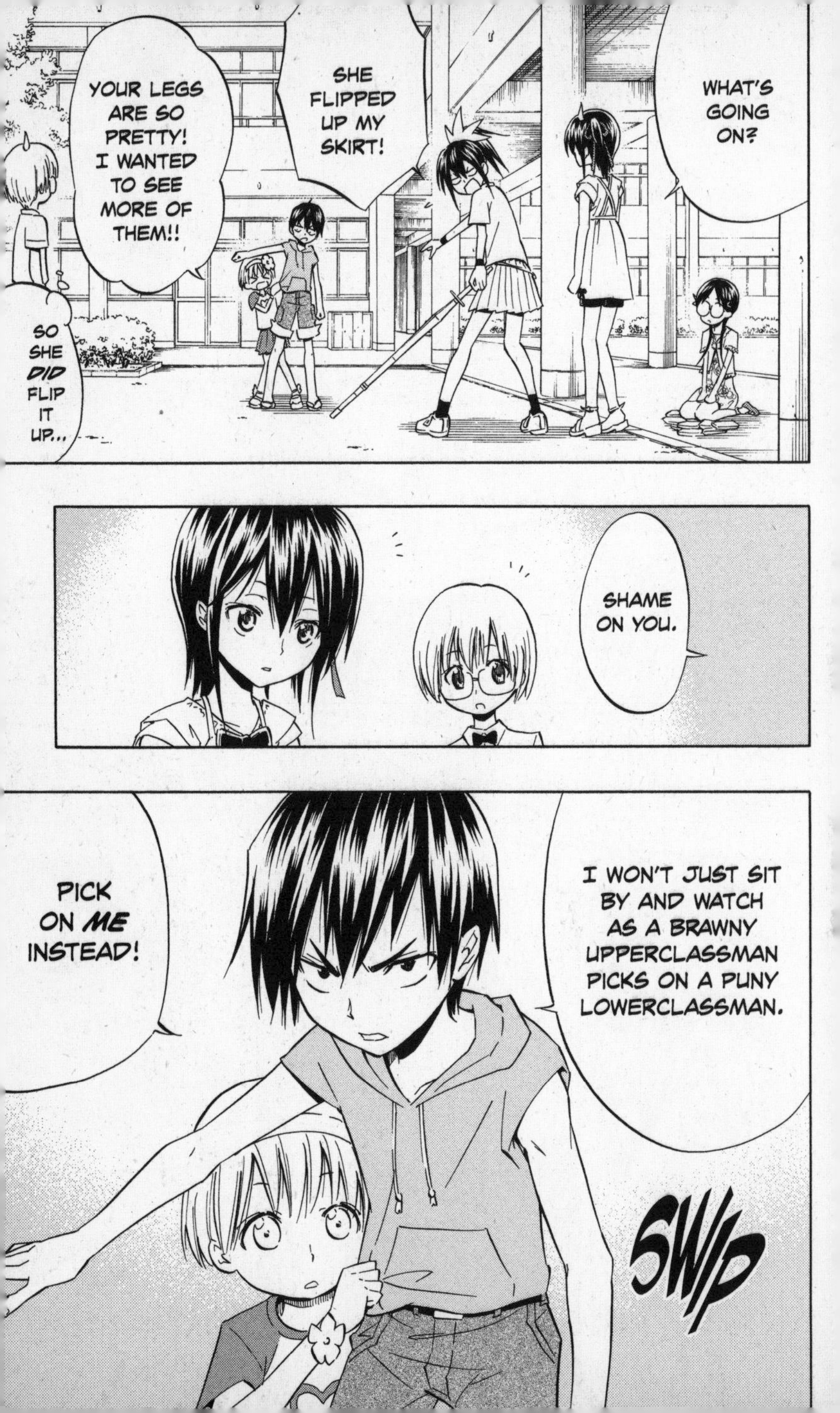
WHAT'S GOING ON?
SHE FLIPPED UP MY SKIRT!
YOUR LEGS ARE SO PRETTY! I WANTED TO SEE MORE OF THEM!!
SO SHE *DID* FLIP IT UP...
SHAME ON YOU.
I WON'T JUST SIT BY AND WATCH AS A BRAWNY UPPERCLASSMAN PICKS ON A PUNY LOWERCLASSMAN.
SWIP
PICK ON *ME* INSTEAD!

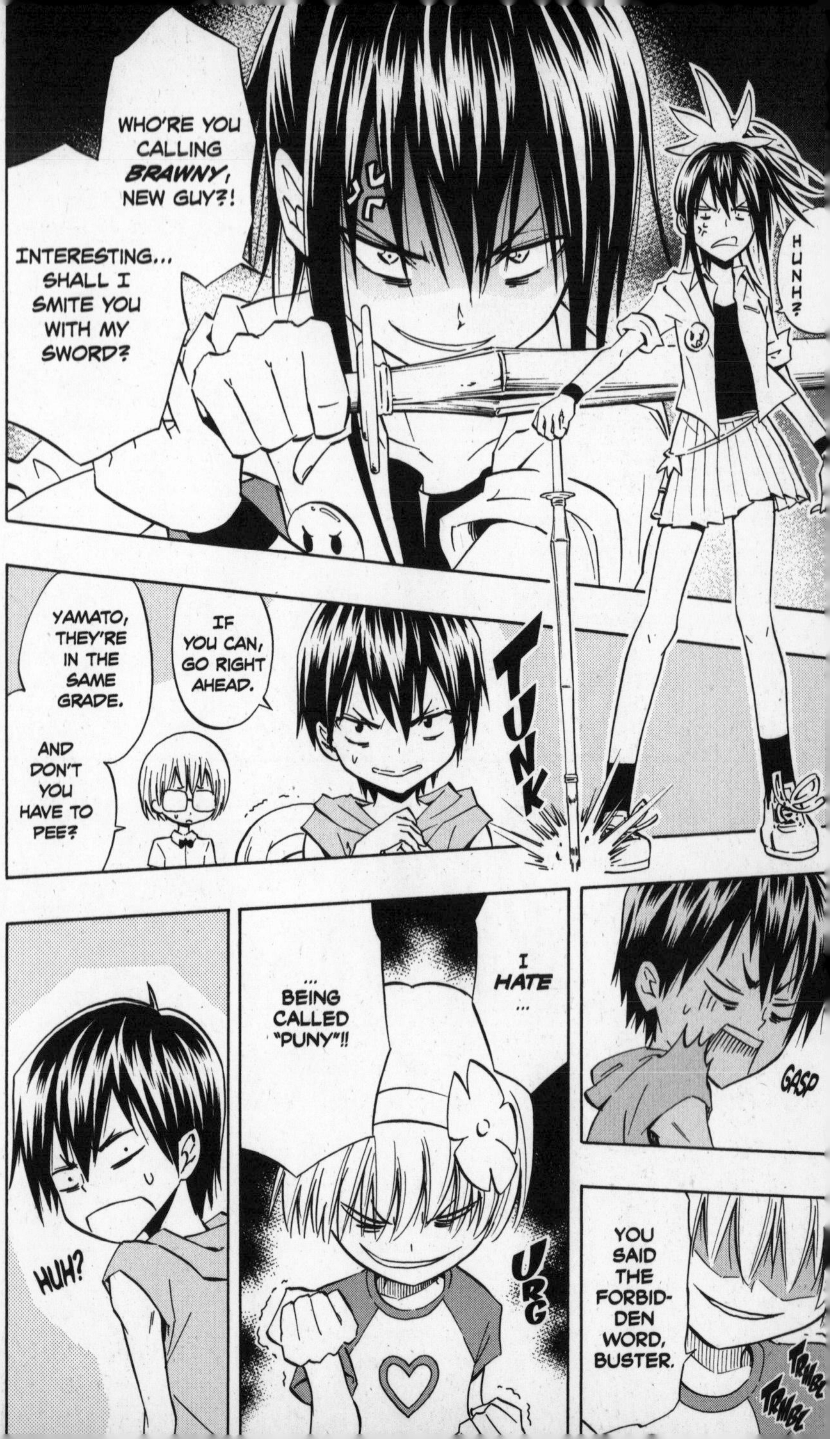
HUNH?
WHO'RE YOU CALLING BRAWNY, NEW GUY?!
INTERESTING... SHALL I SMITE YOU WITH MY SWORD?
TUNK
IF YOU CAN, GO RIGHT AHEAD.
YAMATO, THEY'RE IN THE SAME GRADE.
AND DON'T YOU HAVE TO PEE?
GASP
YOU SAID THE FORBIDDEN WORD, BUSTER.
TRMBL TRMBL
I HATE...
...BEING CALLED "PUNY"!!
URG
HUH?

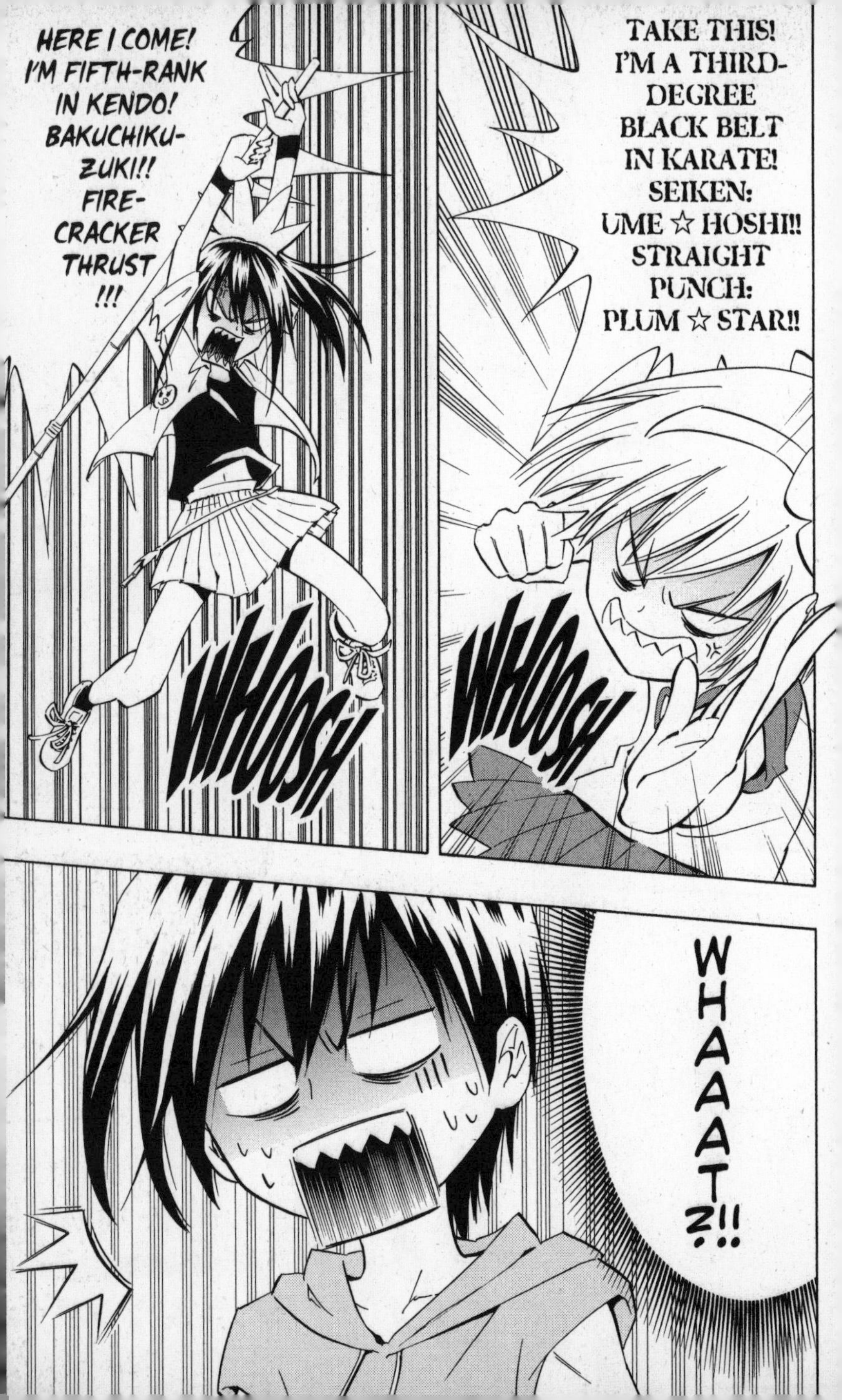
TAKE THIS! I'M A THIRD-DEGREE BLACK BELT IN KARATE! SEIKEN: UME ☆ HOSHI!! STRAIGHT PUNCH: PLUM ☆ STAR!!
WHOOSH
HERE I COME! I'M FIFTH-RANK IN KENDO! BAKUCHIKU-ZUKI!! FIRE-CRACKER THRUST!!!
WHOOSH
WHAAAAT?!!

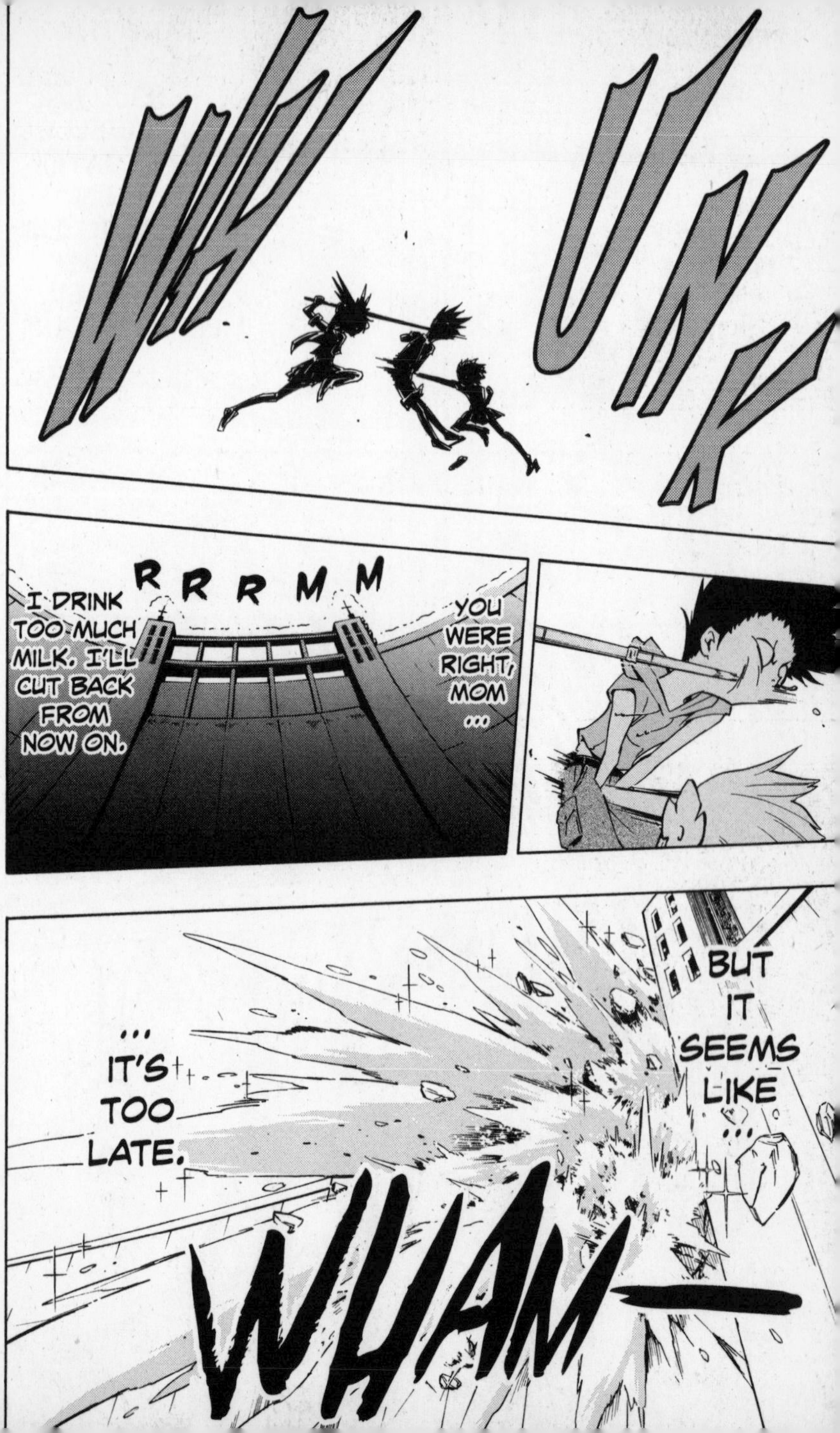
WHUNK
RRRMM
YOU WERE RIGHT, MOM...
I DRINK TOO MUCH MILK. I'LL CUT BACK FROM NOW ON.
BUT IT SEEMS LIKE...
...IT'S TOO LATE.
WHAM

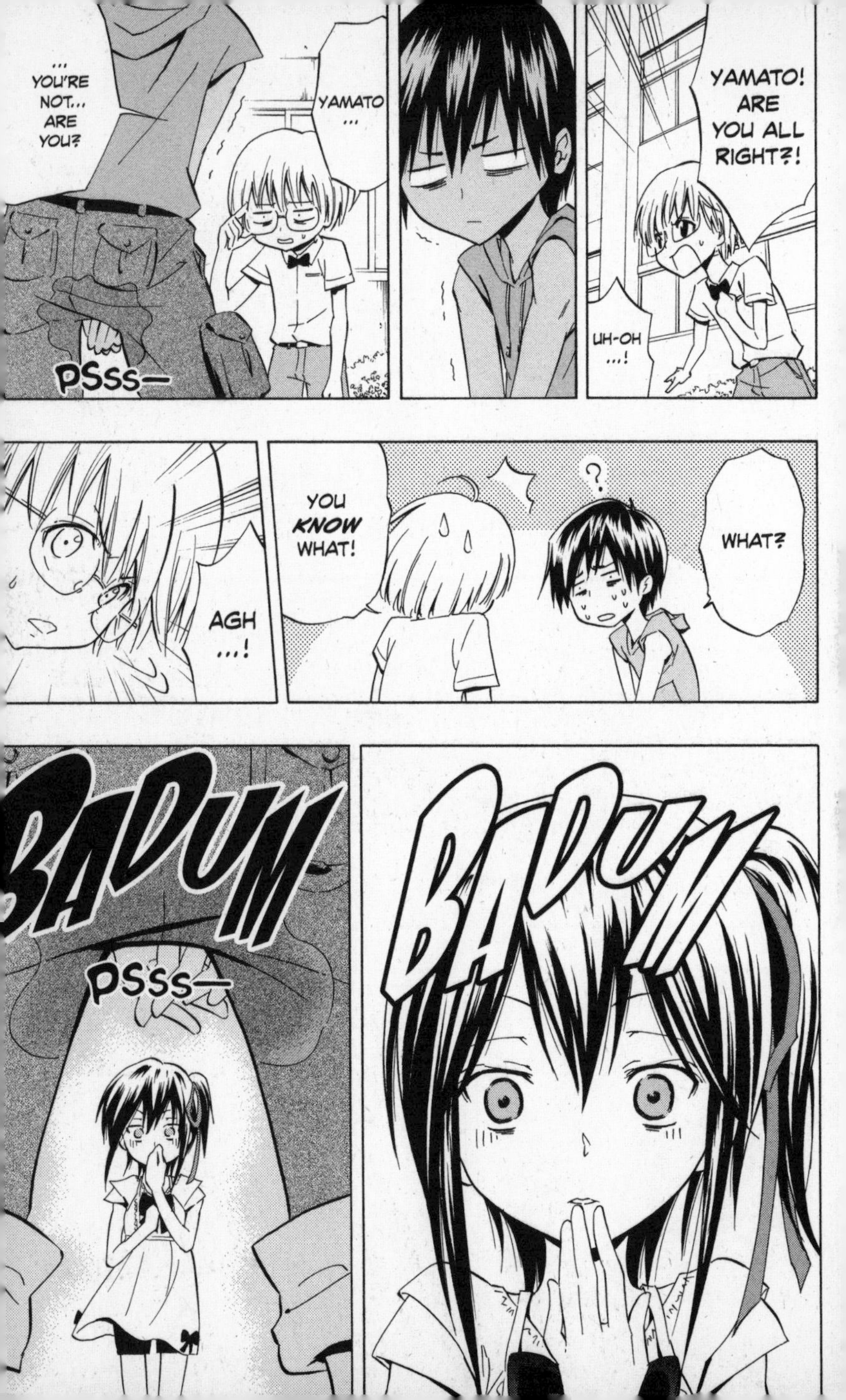
YAMATO! ARE YOU ALL RIGHT?!
UH-OH ...!
YAMATO ...
... YOU'RE NOT... ARE YOU?
PSSS—
WHAT?
YOU *KNOW* WHAT!
AGH ...!
BADUM
BADUM
PSSS—

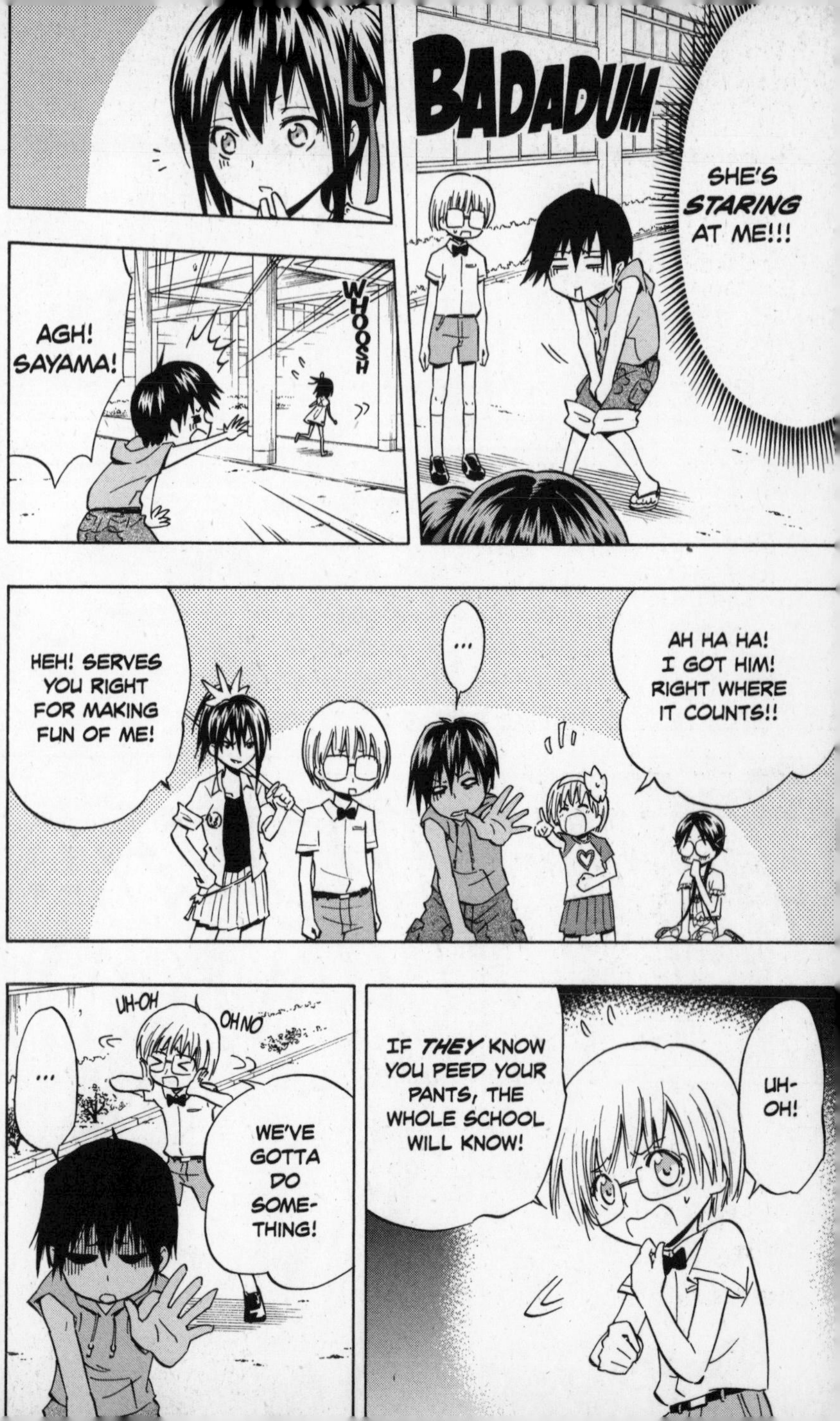
BADADUM
SHE'S STARING AT ME!!!
WHOOSH
AGH! SAYAMA!
AH HA HA! I GOT HIM! RIGHT WHERE IT COUNTS!!
...
HEH! SERVES YOU RIGHT FOR MAKING FUN OF ME!
UH-OH!
IF THEY KNOW YOU PEED YOUR PANTS, THE WHOLE SCHOOL WILL KNOW!
WE'VE GOTTA DO SOME-THING!
OH NO
UH-OH
...

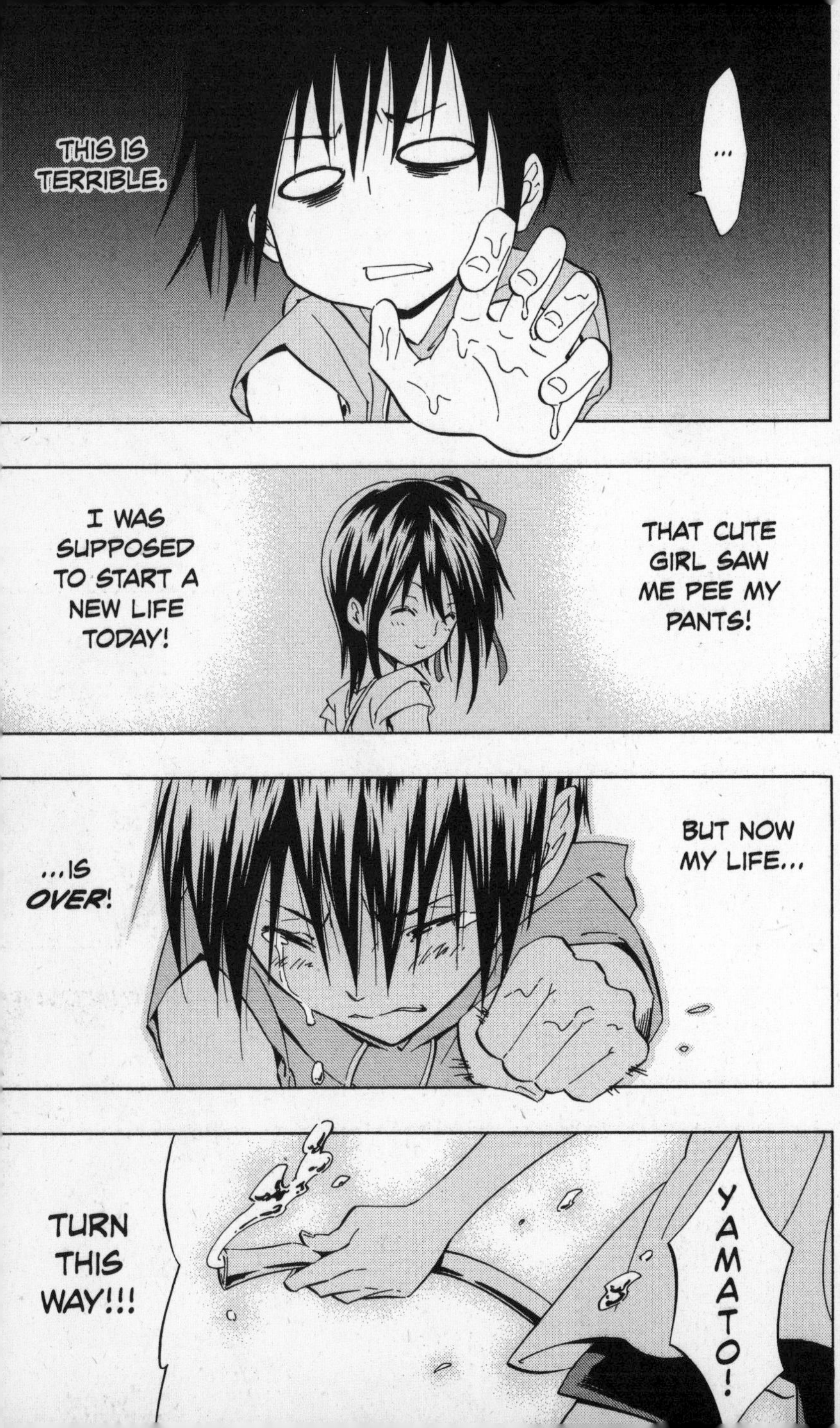
...
THIS IS TERRIBLE.
THAT CUTE GIRL SAW ME PEE MY PANTS!
I WAS SUPPOSED TO START A NEW LIFE TODAY!
BUT NOW MY LIFE...
...IS *OVER*!
YAMATO!
TURN THIS WAY!!!

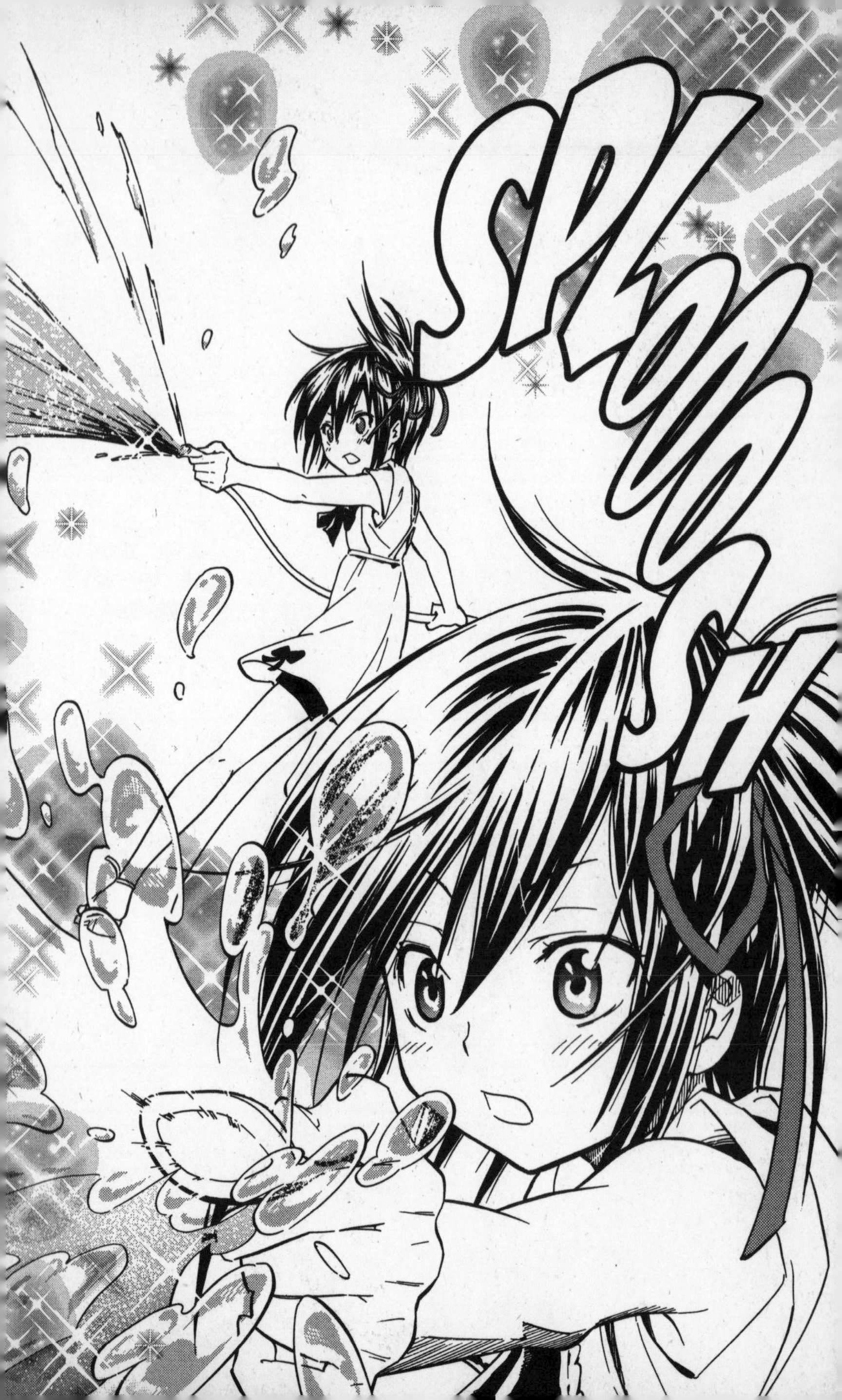
SPLOOOSH

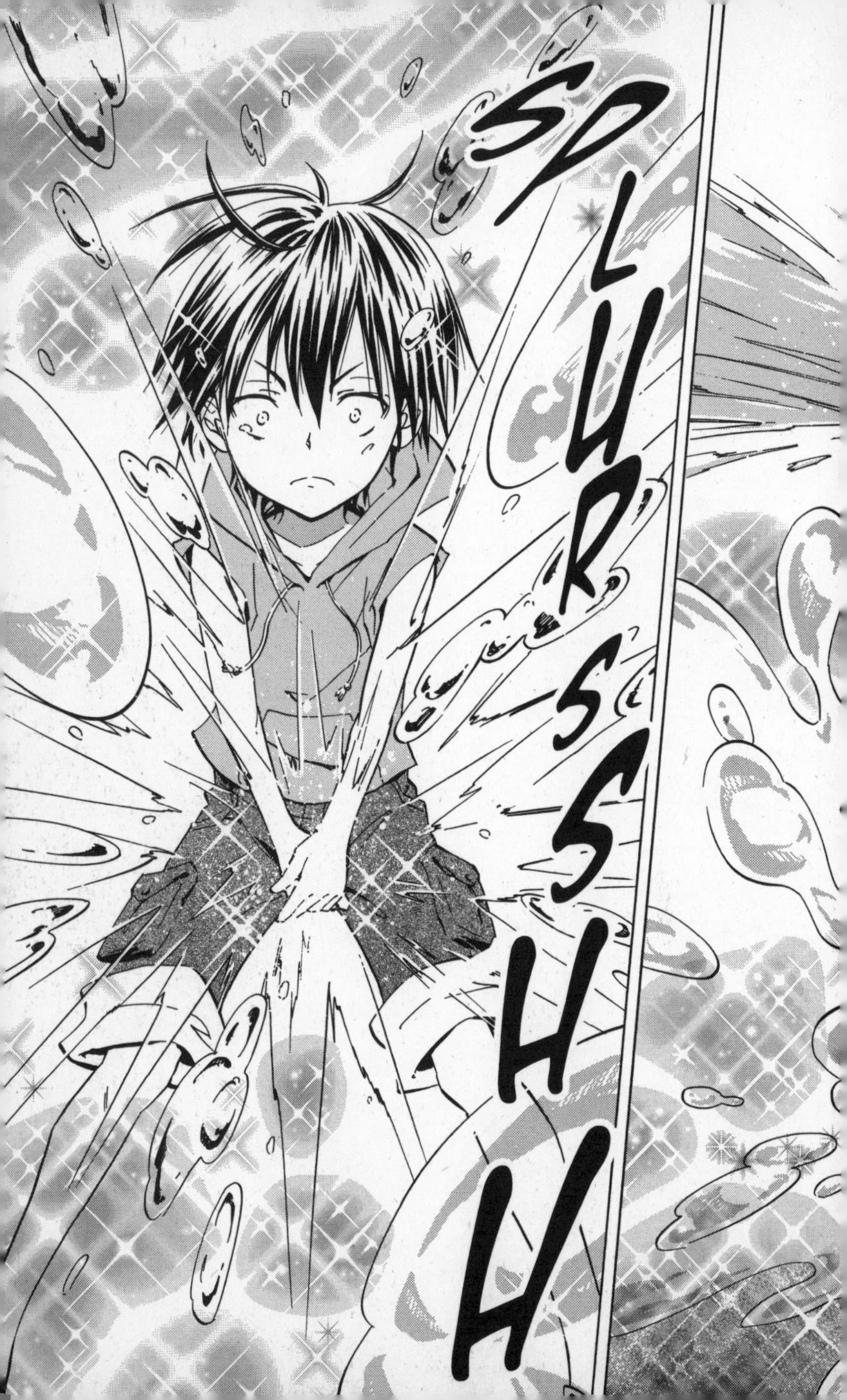
SPLURSSHHH

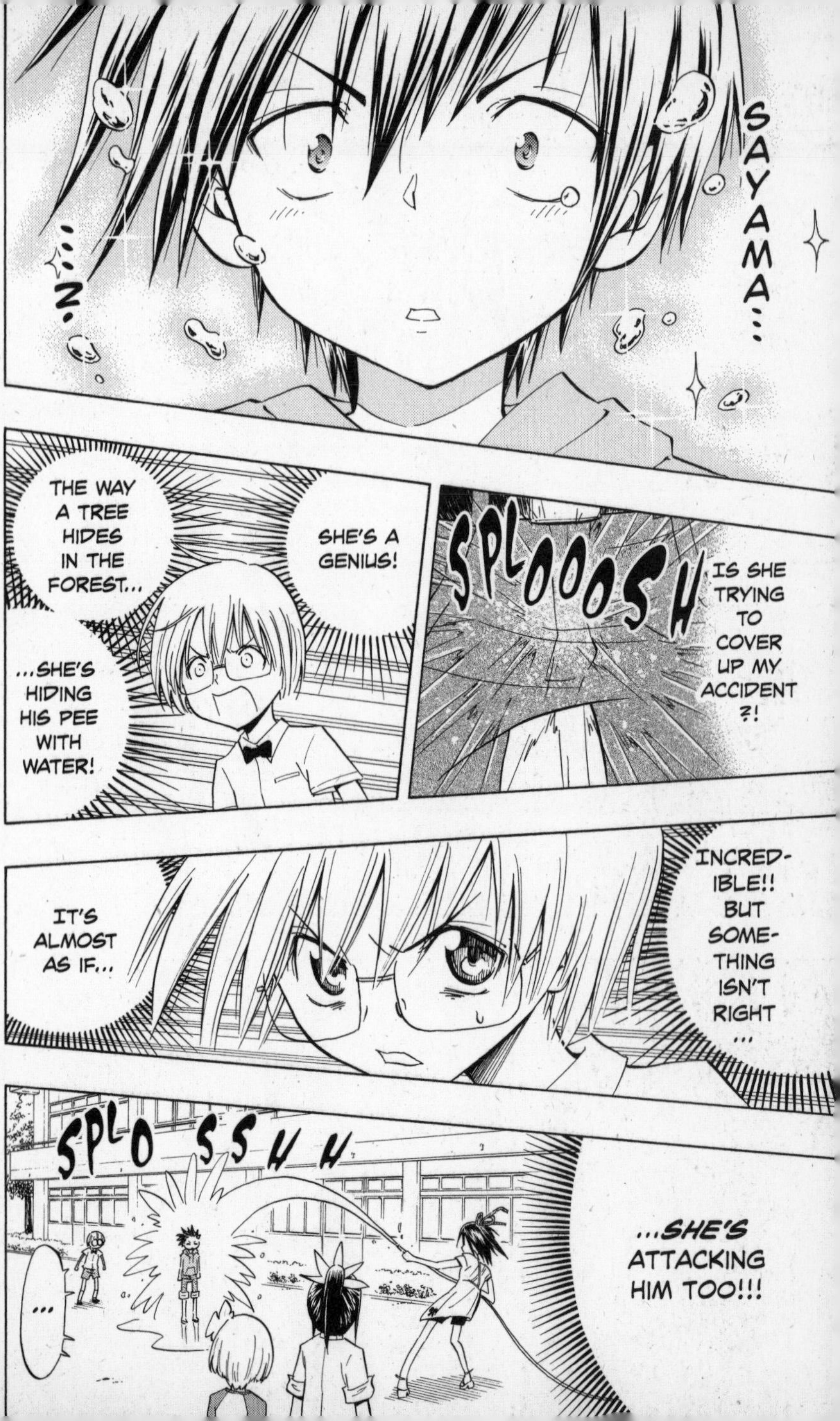

SAYAMA...
...N...
SPLOOOSH
IS SHE TRYING TO COVER UP MY ACCIDENT?!
SHE'S A GENIUS!
THE WAY A TREE HIDES IN THE FOREST...
...SHE'S HIDING HIS PEE WITH WATER!
INCREDIBLE!! BUT SOMETHING ISN'T RIGHT...
IT'S ALMOST AS IF...
...SHE'S ATTACKING HIM TOO!!!
SPLOSSHH
...

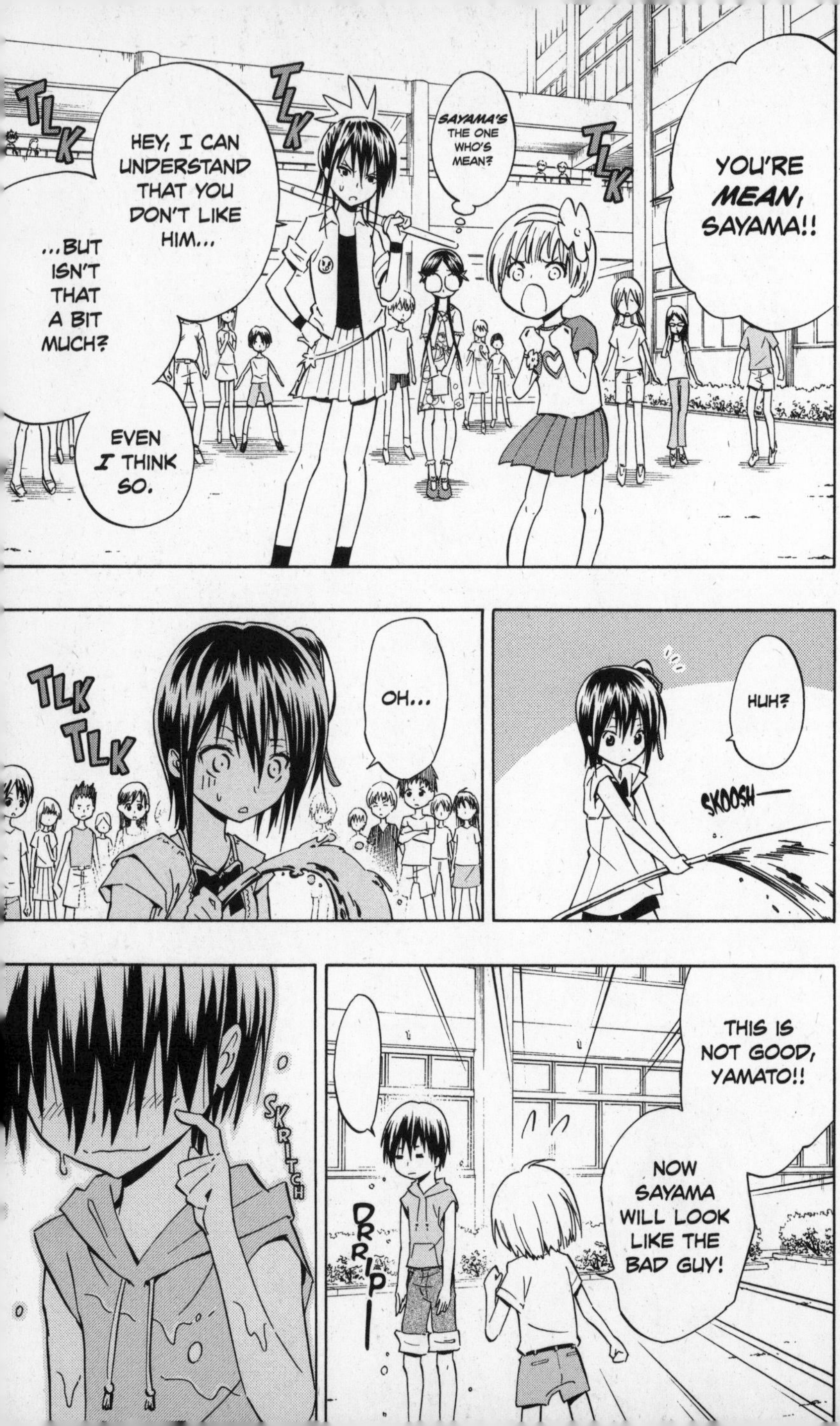

YOU'RE *MEAN*, SAYAMA!!
TLK
SAYAMA'S THE ONE WHO'S MEAN?
TLK
TLK
HEY, I CAN UNDERSTAND THAT YOU DON'T LIKE HIM...
...BUT ISN'T THAT A BIT MUCH?
EVEN *I* THINK SO.
HUH?
SKOOSH—
OH...
TLK TLK
THIS IS NOT GOOD, YAMATO!!
NOW SAYAMA WILL LOOK LIKE THE BAD GUY!
DRRIP
SKRITCH

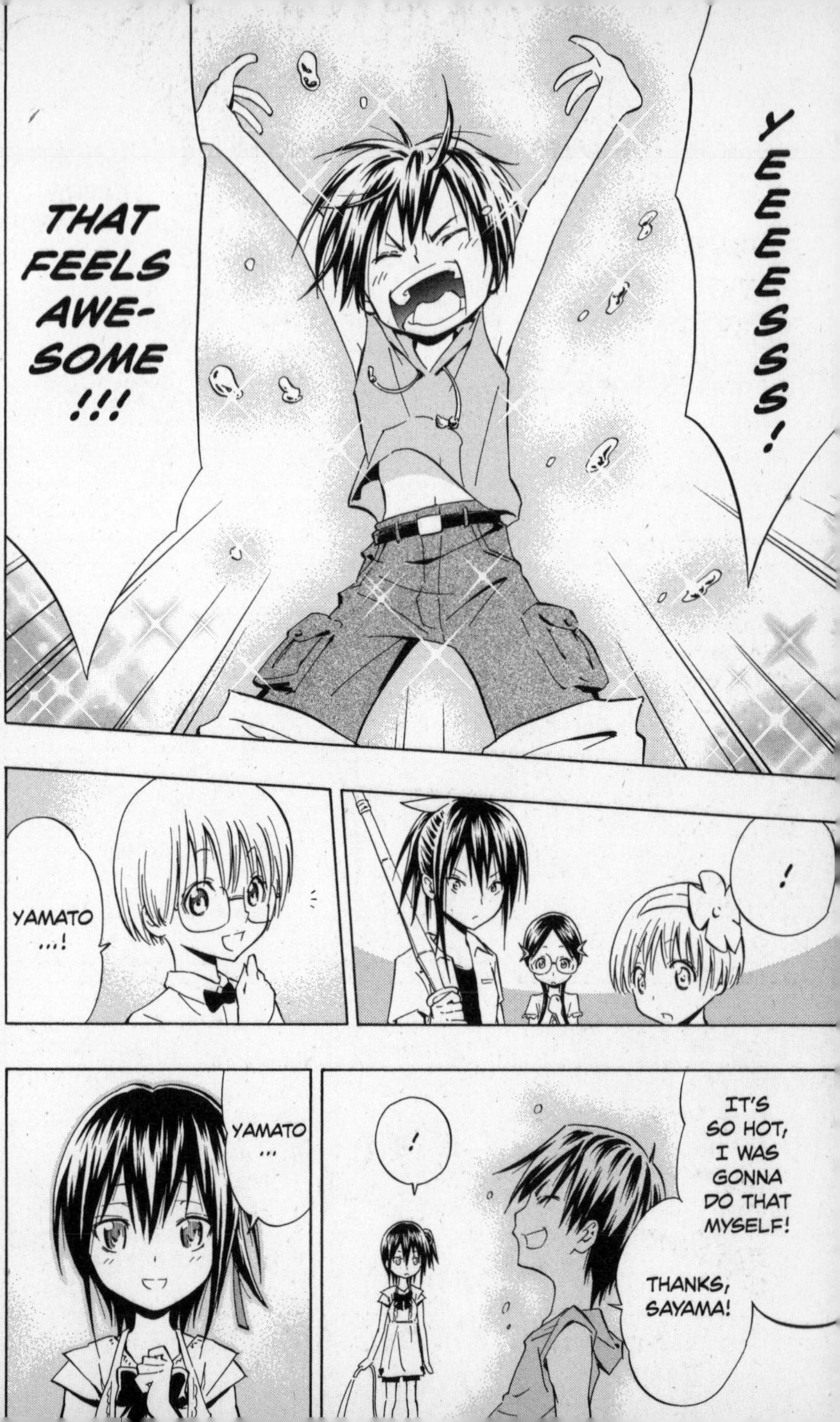
YEEEESSSS!
THAT FEELS AWE- SOME!!!
!
YAMATO ...!
IT'S SO HOT, I WAS GONNA DO THAT MYSELF!
THANKS, SAYAMA!
!
YAMATO ...

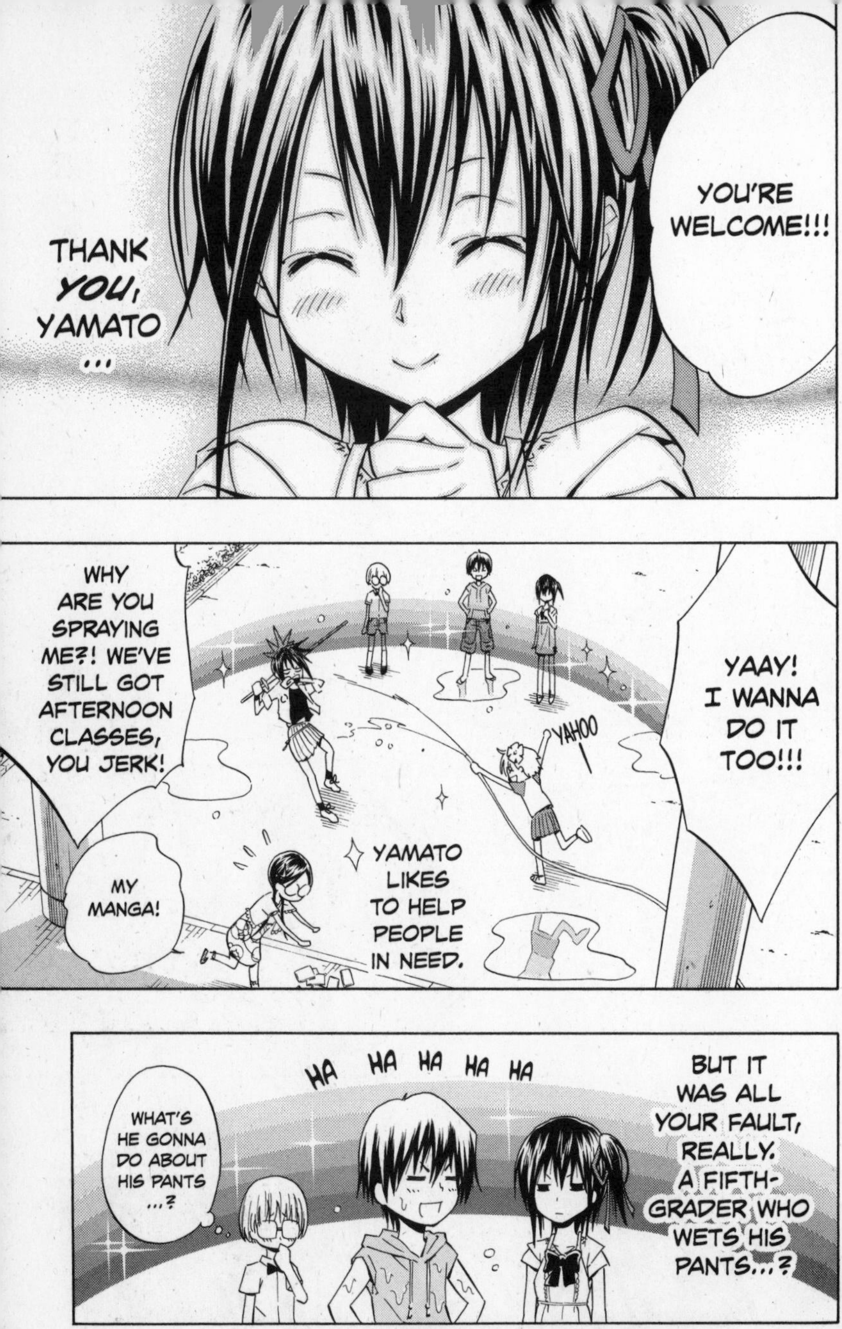
YOU'RE WELCOME!!!
THANK YOU, YAMATO...
YAAY! I WANNA DO IT TOO!!!
YAHOO
WHY ARE YOU SPRAYING ME?! WE'VE STILL GOT AFTERNOON CLASSES, YOU JERK!
YAMATO LIKES TO HELP PEOPLE IN NEED.
MY MANGA!
BUT IT WAS ALL YOUR FAULT, REALLY. A FIFTH-GRADER WHO WETS HIS PANTS...?
HA HA HA HA HA
WHAT'S HE GONNA DO ABOUT HIS PANTS...?

 Karakuri Dôji ULTIMO ULATE (End)

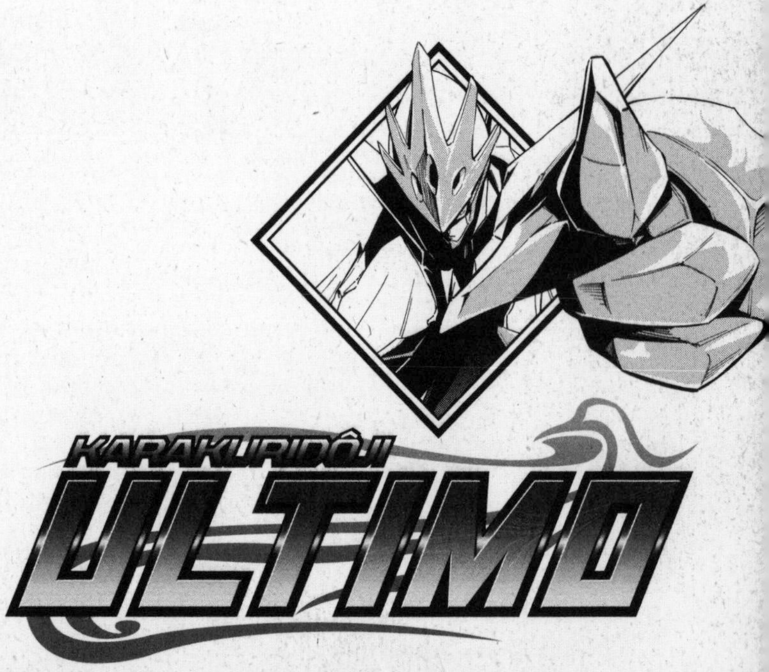

KARAKURIDÔJI
ULTIMO

ULTIMO
Volume 2

Original Concept: Stan Lee
Story and Art by: Hiroyuki Takei

SHONEN JUMP Manga Edition

This graphic novel contains material
that was originally published in English
in SHONEN JUMP #83–85
Artwork in the magazine may have been
slightly altered from that presented here.

Translation | John Werry
Series Touch-up Art & Lettering | James Gaubatz
Design | Fawn Lau
Series Editor | Joel Enos
Graphic Novel Editor | Jann Jones

VP, Production | Alvin Lu
VP, Sales & Product Marketing | Gonzalo Ferreyra
VP, Creative | Linda Espinosa
Publisher | Hyoe Narita

KARAKURI DOJI ULTIMO © 2008 by Stan Lee—POW!
Entertainment/Dream Ranch, Hiroyuki Takei
All rights reserved. First published in Japan in 2009 by
SHUEISHA Inc., Tokyo. English translation rights arranged
by SHUEISHA Inc.

The stories, characters and incidents mentioned in this
publication are entirely fictional.

No portion of this book may be reproduced or transmitted in
any form or by any means without written permission from
the copyright holders.

Printed in the U.S.A.

Published by VIZ Media, LLC
P.O. Box 77010
San Francisco, CA 94107

10 9 8 7 6 5 4 3 2 1
First printing, July 2010

RATED
PARENTAL ADVISORY
ULTIMO is rated T for Teen and
is recommended for ages 13 and
up. This volume contains fantasy
violence.
T
FOR
TEEN
ratings.viz.com

VIZ
MEDIA
www.viz.com

SHONEN
JUMP
www.shonenjump.com

STAN LEE

As a kid, Stanley Martin Lieber spent a lot of time dreaming up wild adventures. By the time he got to high school, he was putting his imagination to work writing stories at Timely, a publishing company that went on to become the legendary Marvel Comics. Starting with the *Fantastic Four*, Lee and his partner Jack Kirby created just about every superhero you can think of, including *Spider-Man*, the *X-Men*, the *Hulk*, *Iron Man*, *Daredevil* and *Thor*. Along the way, he wrote under many pen names, but the one that stuck was Stan Lee.

HIROYUKI TAKEI

Unconventional author/artist Hiroyuki Takei began his career by winning the Osamu Tezuka Cultural Prize (named after the famous artist of the same name). After working as an assistant to famed artist Nobuhiro Watsuki, Takei debuted in *Weekly Shonen Jump* in 1997 with *Butsu Zone*, an action series based on Buddhist mythology. His multicultural adventure manga *Shaman King*, which debuted in 1998, became a hit and was adapted into an anime TV series. His new series *Ultimo* (*Karakuri Dôji Ultimo*) is currently being serialized in the U.S. in SHONEN JUMP. Takei lists Osamu Tezuka, American comics and robot anime among his many influences.

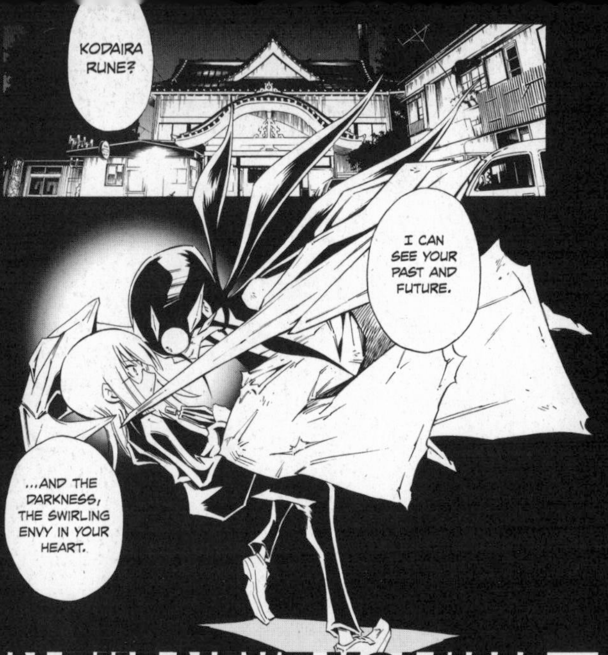
KODAIRA RUNE?
I CAN SEE YOUR PAST AND FUTURE.
...AND THE DARKNESS, THE SWIRLING ENVY IN YOUR HEART.

IN THE NEXT VOLUME...

...WORLD ANNIHILATION

Yamato's best friend Rune is now a dôji master to the envious trickster Jealousy. But why is Rune using Jealousy to attack Yamato and Ultimo? The answer lies deep in the past and will shock everyone–even Rune! Plus, meet Murayama, a warrior with a prophecy that could spell some serious trouble for the entire world.

AVAILABLE DECEMBER 2010!

Read it first in SHONEN JUMP magazine!

$7.95

SHAMAN KING

Manga on sale now!

Yoh Asakura sees ghosts. Does he have what it takes to become... the Shaman King?!

SHONEN JUMP MANGA

SHAMAN KING © 1998 by Hiroyuki Takei/SHUEISHA Inc.

On sale at:
www.shonenjump.com
Also available at your local bookstore and comic store.

www.viz.com

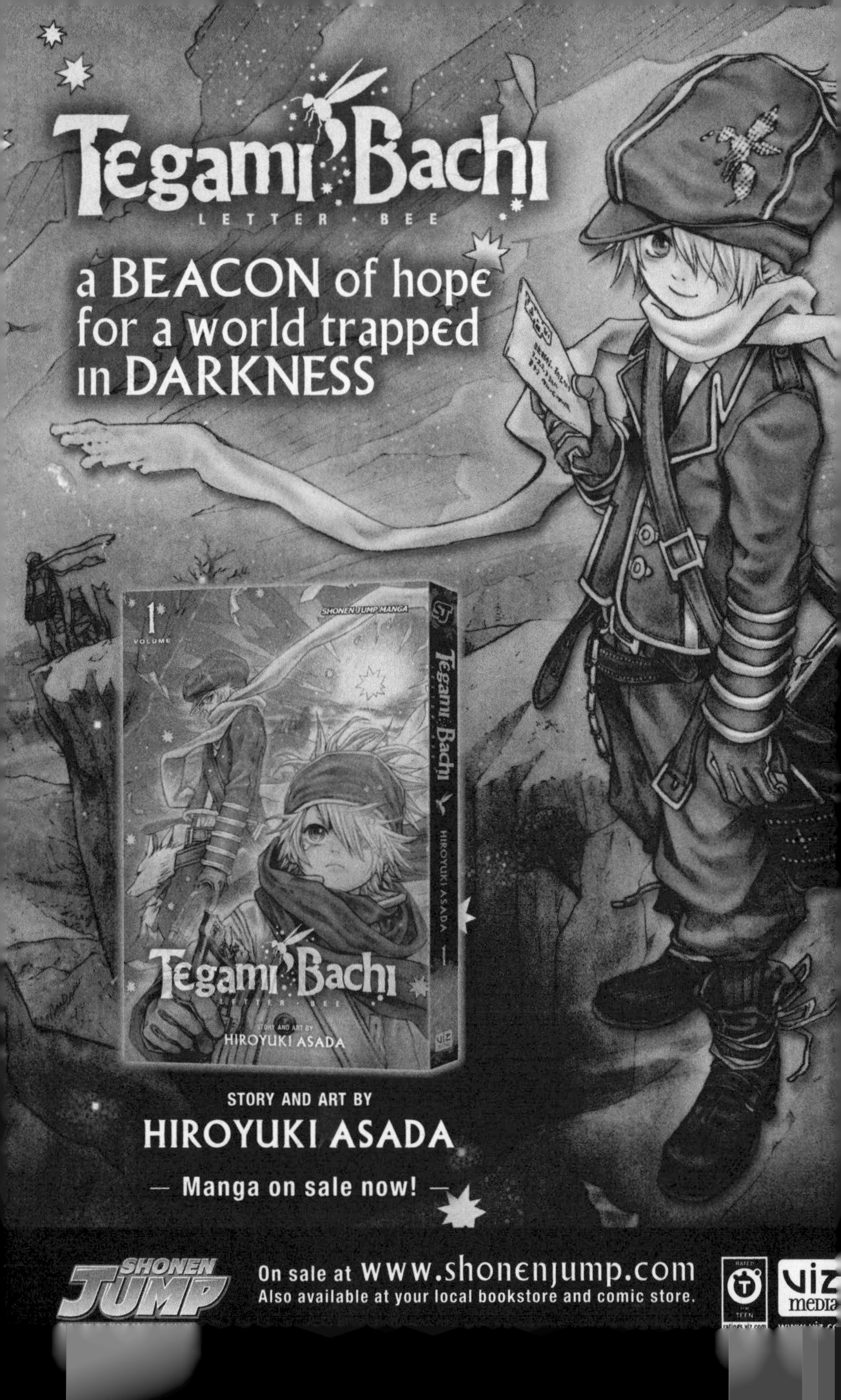

Tegami Bachi
LETTER • BEE
a BEACON of hope for a world trapped in DARKNESS
SHONEN JUMP MANGA
1 VOLUME
Tegami Bachi
LETTER BEE
STORY AND ART BY
HIROYUKI ASADA
Tegami Bachi
HIROYUKI ASADA
STORY AND ART BY
HIROYUKI ASADA
— Manga on sale now! —
SHONEN JUMP
On sale at www.shonenjump.com
Also available at your local bookstore and comic store.
viz media

Perspective

3 volumes
in
ONE!!

Get BIG

RATED
A
ALL AGES
ratings.viz.com

RATED
T
TEEN
ratings.viz.com

viz
MEDIA
www.viz.com

Change Your

From Akira Toriyama, the creator of *Dr. Slump*, *COWA!*, and *SandLand*

Relive Goku's quest with the new VIZBIG Editions of *Dragon Ball* and *Dragon Ball* Z! Each features:

- Three volumes in one
- Exclusive cover designs
- Color manga pages
- Larger trim size
- Color artwork
- Bonus content

And more!

* *

On sale at:
www.shonenjump.com
Also available at your local bookstore and comic store

DRAGON BALL © 1984 by BIRD STUDIO/SHUEISHA Inc.

★ VIZBIG
EDITION

SHONEN JUMP

THE WORLD'S MOST POPULAR MANGA

STORY AND ART BY
TITE KUBO

STORY AND ART BY
EIICHIRO ODA

STORY AND ART BY
HIROYUKI ASADA

JUMP INTO THE ACTION BY TELLING US WHAT YOU LOVE (AND WHAT YOU DON'T)

LET YOUR VOICE BE HEARD!

SHONENJUMP.VIZ.COM/MANGASURVEY

HELP US MAKE MORE OF THE WORLD'S MOST POPULAR MANGA!

EACH © 2001 by Tite Kubo/SHUEISHA Inc.
E PIECE © 1997 by Eiichiro Oda/SHUEISHA Inc.
GAMIBACHI © 2006 by Hiroyuki Asada/SHUEISHA Inc.

SHONEN JUMP

THE WORLD'S MOST POPULAR MANGA

350+ pages of the coolest manga available in the U.S., PLUS anime news, and info on video & card games, toys AND more!

50% OFF the cover price!
That's like getting 6 issues

FREE!

12 HUGE issues for ONLY $29⁹⁵*

3 EASY WAYS TO SUBCRIBE
1 Send in a subscription order form
2 Log on to: www.shonenjump.com
3 Call 1-800-541-7919

ratings.viz.com   www.viz.co

* Canada price: $41.95 USD, including GST, HST, and QST. US/CAN orders only. Allow 6-8 weeks for delive

ONE PIECE © 1997 by Eiichiro Oda/SHUEISHA Inc. BLEACH © 2001 by Tite Kubo/SHUEISHA Inc.
NARUTO © 1999 by Masashi Kishimoto/SHUEISHA Inc.

SAVE 50% OFF
THE COVER PRICE!

IT'S LIKE GETTING 6 ISSUES

FREE!

OVER 350+ PAGES PER ISSUE

This monthly magazine contains 7 of the coolest manga available in the U.S., PLUS anime news, and info about video & card games, toys AND more!

❏ **I want 12 HUGE issues of SHONEN JUMP for only $29.95*!**

NAME

ADDRESS

CITY/STATE/ZIP

EMAIL ADDRESS   **DATE OF BIRTH**

❏ YES, send me via email information, advertising, offers, and promotions related to VIZ Media, SHONEN JUMP, and/or their business partners.

❏ **CHECK ENCLOSED** (payable to SHONEN JUMP)   ❏ **BILL ME LATER**

CREDIT CARD: ❏ Visa   ❏ Mastercard

ACCOUNT NUMBER   **EXP. DATE**

SIGNATURE

CLIP&MAIL TO:
SHONEN JUMP Subscriptions Service Dept.
P.O. Box 515
Mount Morris, IL 61054-0515

P9GNC1

* Canada price: $41.95 USD, including GST, HST, and QST. US/CAN orders only. Allow 6-8 weeks for delivery.
ONE PIECE © 1997 by Eiichiro Oda/SHUEISHA Inc. BLEACH © 2001 by Tite Kubo/SHUEISHA Inc.
NARUTO © 1999 by Masashi Kishimoto/SHUEISHA Inc.

ratings.viz.com   www.viz.com